also by america's test kitchen

The Outdoor Cook

The Healthy Back Kitchen

Gatherings

Everyday Bread

The Complete Guide to Healthy Drinks

Boards

Foolproof Preserving and Canning

The Complete Modern Pantry

Fresh Pasta at Home

The Complete Small Plates Cookbook

Desserts Illustrated

Vegan Cooking for Two

Modern Bistro

More Mediterranean

The Complete Plant-Based Cookbook

Cooking with Plant-Based Meat

The Savory Baker

The New Cooking School Cookbook:
    Advanced Fundamentals

The New Cooking School Cookbook:
    Fundamentals

The Complete Autumn and Winter Cookbook

One-Hour Comfort

The Everyday Athlete Cookbook

Cook for Your Gut Health

Foolproof Fish

Five-Ingredient Dinners

The Ultimate Meal-Prep Cookbook

The Complete Salad Cookbook

The Chicken Bible

The Side Dish Bible

Meat Illustrated

Vegetables Illustrated

Bread Illustrated

Cooking for One

How Can It Be Gluten-Free Cookbook Collection

Bowls

Easy Everyday Keto

Everything Chocolate

The Perfect Cookie

The Perfect Pie

The Perfect Cake

How to Cocktail

Spiced

The Ultimate Burger

The New Essentials Cookbook

Dinner Illustrated

America's Test Kitchen Menu Cookbook

Cook's Illustrated Revolutionary Recipes

Tasting Italy: A Culinary Journey

Cooking at Home with Bridget and Julia

The Complete Mediterranean Cookbook

The Complete Vegetarian Cookbook

The Complete Cooking for Two Cookbook

The Complete Diabetes Cookbook

The Complete Slow Cooker

The Complete One Pot

The Complete Summer Cookbook

The Complete Make-Ahead Cookbook

Just Add Sauce

How to Braise Everything

How to Roast Everything

Nutritious Delicious

What Good Cooks Know

Cook's Science

The Science of Good Cooking

Master of the Grill

Kitchen Smarts

Kitchen Hacks

100 Techniques

100 Recipes

The New Family Cookbook

The Cook's Illustrated Baking Book

The Cook's Illustrated Cookbook

The America's Test Kitchen Family Baking Book

America's Test Kitchen Twentieth Anniversary
    TV Show Cookbook

The Best of America's Test Kitchen
    (2007–2023 Editions)

The Complete America's Test Kitchen TV Show
    Cookbook 2001–2024

Healthy and Delicious Instant Pot

Mediterranean Instant Pot

Cook It in Your Dutch Oven

Vegan for Everybody

Sous Vide for Everybody

Air Fryer Perfection

Healthy Air Fryer

Toaster Oven Perfection

Multicooker Perfection

Food Processor Perfection

Pressure Cooker Perfection

Instant Pot Ace Blender Cookbook

Naturally Sweet

Paleo Perfected

The Best Mexican Recipes

Slow Cooker Revolution Volume 2:
    The Easy-Prep Edition

Slow Cooker Revolution

The America's Test Kitchen D.I.Y. Cookbook

COOK'S COUNTRY TITLES

Big Flavors from Italian America

One-Pan Wonders

Cook It in Cast Iron

Cook's Country Eats Local

The Complete Cook's Country TV Show Cookbook

FOR A FULL LISTING OF ALL OUR BOOKS:

CooksIllustrated.com

AmericasTestKitchen.com

praise for america's test kitchen titles

Kitchen Gear

The Ultimate Owner's Manual

Boost your equipment IQ with **500+** expert tips

Optimize your kitchen with **400+** recommended tools

WITH LISA McMANUS AND HANNAH CROWLEY

AMERICA'S TEST KITCHEN

Library of Congress Cataloging in Publication Data has been applied for.

ISBN 978-1-954210-69-1

AMERICA'S TEST KITCHEN
21 Drydock Avenue, Boston, MA 02210

Printed in Canada
10 9 8 7 6 5 4 3 2 1

Distributed by Penguin Random House Publisher Services
Tel: 800.733.3000

FRONT COVER
PHOTOGRAPHY: Steve Klise
ILLUSTRATION: Molly Gillespie
EQUIPMENT: Steven Raichlen Ultimate Suede Grilling Gloves (page 383)

DEDICATION
To our team, past and present, for relentlessly pursuing the truth and having fun along the way. To our families, for their love and support. And to our editor, Sara, and designer, Molly, for doing a bang-up job.

-LISA AND HANNAH

EDITORIAL DIRECTOR, BOOKS: Adam Kowit

EXECUTIVE FOOD EDITOR: Dan Zuccarello

DEPUTY FOOD EDITORS: Leah Colins and Stephanie Pixley

EXECUTIVE MANAGING EDITOR: Debra Hudak

PROJECT EDITOR: Sara Zatopek

SENIOR EDITOR: Sacha Madadian

CONTRIBUTING EDITOR: Cheryl Redmond

TEST COOKS: Olivia Counter, Hannah Fenton, Hisham Hassan, Laila Ibrahim, José Maldonado, and David Yu

DESIGN DIRECTOR: Lindsey Timko Chandler

BOOK DESIGNER AND ASSOCIATE ART DIRECTOR: Molly Gillespie

ART DIRECTOR, REVIEWS: Marissa Angelone

PHOTOGRAPHY DIRECTOR: Julie Bozzo Cote

SENIOR PHOTOGRAPHY PRODUCER: Meredith Mulcahy

SENIOR STAFF PHOTOGRAPHERS: Steve Klise and Daniel J. van Ackere

STAFF PHOTOGRAPHER: Kevin White

ADDITIONAL PHOTOGRAPHY: Joseph Keller and Carl Tremblay

ILLUSTRATIONS BY: Katie Barranger, Molly Gillespie, Erin Griffiths, Jay Layman, and Toby Leigh

FOOD STYLING: Joy Howard, Sheila Jarnes, Catrine Kelty, Chantal Lambeth, Gina McCreadie, Kendra McNight, Ashley Moore, Christie Morrison, Marie Piraino, Elle Simone Scott, Kendra Smith, and Sally Staub

PROJECT MANAGER, PUBLISHING OPERATIONS: Katie Kimmerer

SENIOR PRINT PRODUCTION SPECIALIST: Lauren Robbins

PRODUCTION AND IMAGING COORDINATOR: Amanda Yong

PRODUCTION AND IMAGING SPECIALISTS: Tricia Neumyer and Dennis Noble

COPY EDITOR: Elizabeth Wray Emery

PROOFREADER: Kelly Gauthier

INDEXER: Elizabeth Parson

CHIEF CREATIVE OFFICER: Jack Bishop

EXECUTIVE EDITORIAL DIRECTORS: Julia Collin Davison and Bridget Lancaster

contents

welcome to america's test kitchen

This book has been tested, written, and edited by the folks at America's Test Kitchen, where curious cooks become confident cooks. Located in Boston's Seaport District in the historic Innovation and Design Building, it features 15,000 square feet of kitchen space including multiple photography and video studios. It is the home of *Cook's Illustrated* magazine and *Cook's Country* magazine and is the workday destination for more than 60 test cooks, editors, and cookware specialists. Our mission is to empower and inspire confidence, community, and creativity in the kitchen.

We start the process of testing a recipe with a complete lack of preconceptions, which means that we accept no claim, no technique, and no recipe at face value. We simply assemble as many variations as possible, test a half-dozen of the most promising, and taste the results blind. We then construct our own recipe and continue to test it, varying ingredients, techniques, and cooking times until we reach a consensus. As we like to say in the test kitchen, "We make the mistakes so you don't have to." The result, we hope, is the best version of a particular recipe, but we realize that only you can be the final judge of our success (or failure). We use the same rigorous approach when we test equipment and taste ingredients.

All of this would not be possible without a belief that good cooking, much like good music, is based on a foundation of objective technique. Some people like spicy foods and others don't, but there is a right way to sauté, there is a best way to cook a pot roast, and there are measurable scientific principles involved in producing perfectly beaten, stable egg whites. Our ultimate goal is to investigate the fundamental principles of cooking to give you the techniques, tools, and ingredients you need to become a better cook. It is as simple as that.

To see what goes on behind the scenes at America's Test Kitchen, check out our social media channels for kitchen snapshots, exclusive content, video tips, and much more. You can watch us work (in our actual test kitchen) by tuning in to *America's Test Kitchen* or *Cook's Country* on public television or on our websites. Listen to *Proof*, *Mystery Recipe*, and *The Walk-In* (AmericasTestKitchen.com/podcasts) to hear engaging, complex stories about people and food. Want to hone your cooking skills or finally learn how to bake—with an America's Test Kitchen test cook? Enroll in one of our online cooking classes.

However you choose to visit us, we welcome you into our kitchen, where you can stand by our side as we test our way to the best recipes in America.

[f] facebook.com/AmericasTestKitchen

[Instagram] instagram.com/TestKitchen

[YouTube] youtube.com/AmericasTestKitchen

[TikTok] tiktok.com/@TestKitchen

[Twitter] twitter.com/TestKitchen

[Pinterest] pinterest.com/TestKitchen

AmericasTestKitchen.com
CooksIllustrated.com
CooksCountry.com
OnlineCookingSchool.com

JOIN OUR COMMUNITY OF RECIPE TESTERS

Our recipe testers provide valuable feedback on recipes under development by ensuring that they are foolproof in home kitchens. Help the America's Test Kitchen book team investigate the how and why behind successful recipes from your home kitchen.

gear up

introduction

Hi—Lisa McManus and Hannah Crowley here. We're the executive editors of America's Test Kitchen Reviews and lifelong kitchen gear geeks, and we have an important message to share: When it comes to successful, enjoyable home cooking, starting with the right kitchen equipment is every bit as important as following a good recipe.

Why? Well, think about all the ways that your equipment can make or break your experience in the kitchen. A skillet that heats unevenly might leave you with nothing to show for your efforts but a scorched mess. An ice cream maker that turns out soupy frozen desserts might have you swearing off homemade ice cream forever. An unnecessarily complicated design that's hard to clean might relegate an otherwise useful tool to a spot of dishonor at the back of your least accessible cabinet. Not to mention all the money wasted on these ineffective pieces. On the other hand, tools that work as they're intended make your life easier and your time in the kitchen more rewarding. A sharp vegetable peeler breezes through tough squash skin; a good coffee maker extracts the perfect balance of flavors from coffee beans; an absorbent dish towel makes cleaning up after yourself just that much less tedious.

In short, the equipment you use matters. That's why we work so hard to steer you toward products that will work for you. When we review a product, we don't stop at simply telling you what to buy; we tell you exactly why the winners won and the losers lost. We spend our days debating the finer points of spatula handling and sponge design. We weigh and measure gear, investigate materials, and interview experts to help us explain why we got good or bad results in the kitchen. We come up with creative ways to simulate months or even years of real-world use so that we can be sure the products we recommend will work just as well for you in your kitchen as they did for us in the test kitchen. And once a product earns our coveted ATK Recommended seal of approval, we continue to use and monitor it to make sure it remains the best.

When you bring a piece of equipment into your kitchen, we want you to be able to use it to the fullest. That means we explain which tasks each piece is best at handling, and when you should opt for a specialized tool over something more everyday—or vice versa. (Should you make tonight's dinner in a stainless-steel pan, or nonstick, or cast-iron? Do you really need pie weights?) It means we teach you how to care for your tools. (Oil your cutting boards! Don't bang utensils against the sides of enameled pans!) It means we lay out all the whats and whys of your equipment (what does "all-clad" mean, and why does it matter?) in plain language so you come away with a better understanding of how it works.

That's what this book is all about: practical tips, real-talk advice, and a liberal sprinkle of just-for-fun trivia. Learn what all the best cake pans have in common, how to use a salad spinner the right way, and how to efficiently pack a cooler. Question your preconceived notions: Do you really need to scrub a darkened baking sheet until it sparkles? And benefit from the unconventional wisdom we've gained through decades of hands-on research: Find out why Hannah isn't a fan of nonstick pans, why Lisa swears that using a wood-fired stove made her a better cook, and why both of us think you should go ahead and buy a knife sharpener already. We'll also provide you with recipes that will help you learn foundational techniques and use your tools in new and exciting ways.

Understanding your tools opens up a whole world of cooking possibilities. So come on: Let's geek out about gear together and become more confident, adventurous, capable cooks.

Lisa   Hannah

5 Questions
with Lisa and Hannah

Lisa and Hannah are equipment nerds extraordinaire, the hosts of the YouTube series *Gear Heads*, and the executive editors of America's Test Kitchen Reviews. We asked them what it's really like to be professional equipment reviewers, which kitchen hacks they swear by, and why they're so passionate about what they do.

What Did You Do Before You Joined America's Test Kitchen?

Lisa: I studied journalism and worked as a magazine editor and writer and on newspapers as a news reporter, columnist and editor, overnight desk copy editor, features editor, and food editor. I'm not a trained chef, though I've worked in catering and as waitstaff. As a home cook I think I have certain advantages in this job, since I have no preconceptions or specialized kitchen training that might actually get in the way of me questioning everything. As a reporter, I know how to find experts and dig out the science behind what is happening in our kitchen tests, and then communicate the results to our readers and viewers.

Hannah: Like Lisa I came from the world of journalism. I was a reporter at a newspaper for a few years when they launched a food section. The experienced reporters were more interested in court cases than food, so I got to take my fill of the food assignments—and I've been writing about food ever since. Before working in newspapers I was a server in restaurants, taught skiing to ambivalent toddlers, and worked on a farm where I found out I am very allergic to raspberry branches. I have worked alongside chefs for years and learned a ton but, like Lisa, I am ultimately a home cook. I started cooking when I was 12 and my mom made it one of my chores to cook dinner for the family once a week. Though I complained at the time, those dinners sparked a lifelong passion.

What Is It You Enjoy So Much About Reviewing Kitchen Equipment?

Lisa: I was probably born to do this. I am always in the kitchen, always thinking about food, and I love to cook and eat. I am also a huge cheapskate and prone to buyer's remorse: I hate spending money on things that are disappointing and don't work, and I also don't want to own too much stuff, so I really think about every purchase I make and will research it to an extreme.

Hannah: I love researching, reporting, and writing. I'm also very thrifty and hate waste so I find it very satisfying to help folks spend their money wisely on products that work well and last. I also enjoy topics where I have the opportunity to do deep journalistic dives. I like finding and interviewing experts and doing the strange things that come with this job, such as carting a bag of knives on the train through Boston to MIT to use their half-million-dollar microscope.

What's Been Your Favorite Thing to Review?

Lisa: I really liked testing slow cookers. I bought a complete extra set and took them apart with an engineer from MIT to figure out exactly how they worked and what made the good ones more successful. It was incredibly satisfying to understand their inner workings. Another favorite: gallon-size freezer storage bags. To test their durability, I filled them with tomato sauce and pushed them off the counter onto a tarp-lined floor. There were some massive saucy explosions—and even better, a few bags never burst, but landed like little red pillows, intact!

Hannah: Oyster knives and seafood scissors were pretty fun. I got to learn how to shuck oysters like a pro by going to restaurants and watching expert shuckers pop shells open, practically just by looking at them. Plus, the oysters were delicious, and you make a lot of friends in the kitchen when you have a pile of oysters (and lobster and crab legs in the case of the seafood scissors testing) on your station.

What About Your Least Favorite?

Lisa: I don't really have "least favorite" reviews, but I do dislike the monotony of our fried-egg test for nonstick pans, where we heat each skillet to a precise temperature, fry an egg with no fat, and repeat until we've fried at least 50 eggs, one at a time, or until an egg sticks, indicating that the pan's nonstick coating has failed. You cook 50 eggs in a row—and there are 11 more pans to go. (I've never secretly prayed for a pan to fail like I do with that test.) You have to pay attention, too, or you'll mess it up.

Hannah: Probably blenders. Any goodwill I earned while testing oyster knives was quickly lost when I was running blenders nonstop for weeks next to cooks trying to develop recipes. I ended up yelling "Fire in the hole!" before starting up a blender so I didn't constantly make my poor colleagues jump out of their skins.

What's Your Least Favorite Kitchen Chore? (And How Do You Make It More Bearable?)

Lisa: My least favorite kitchen chore has to be cleaning up after cooking a meal. I've become extremely good at cleaning as I go so I can sit down to dinner with an already-clean kitchen. If something has to fry for 2 minutes, I set a timer and start cleaning—loading dishwasher-safe items in the dishwasher, hand-washing the rest and chucking it in the drying rack, wiping down counters, putting away spices—until the timer rings. (This habit also keeps me from poking at food when it needs to cook in peace.)

Hannah: Dishes seem to spontaneously multiply in my house. When our team reviewed dish soap, I picked up a great tip: Soaking dishes in warm, soapy water for just 5 to 10 minutes makes them a whole lot easier to get clean. The soap's surfactants—tadpole-shaped chemicals with water-loving heads and oil-loving tails—are working whether you're actively washing the dishes or not, and it only takes a few minutes for them to free dishes of their grime. It's like having a million tiny dishwashers give you a head start—so while I still have dishes to do, they go by a lot faster.

It Takes a Team

Researching, writing, editing, and rigorously fact checking each review we publish is no small feat; it truly takes a team. These are the inquisitive, discerning, meticulous people who make it all happen.

Kate Shannon

One of Kate's proudest professional accomplishments is finding a life-changing kitchen sponge (really) and proving once and for all that it's a bad idea to leave a soggy sponge in the bottom of your sink. Prior to joining America's Test Kitchen, she attended Boston University's culinary program and worked as both a line cook and a cheesemonger.

Miye Bromberg

Miye's areas of expertise include booze, blades, and bread. If it's absurd or dangerous, she's probably tested it too. A native of New York, she now lives in Kentucky, where she spends her free time watching movies, mapping local taco trucks, and traveling long distances to eat dosas.

Carolyn Grillo

Carolyn studied French patisserie at Le Cordon Bleu in Paris and worked as a baker before joining America's Test Kitchen. Her culinary background helps her evaluate bakeware and write about ingredients. Carolyn is also responsible for editing *The Well-Equipped Cook*, a weekly newsletter about kitchen equipment.

Chase Brightwell

Chase left a career in infectious disease research to answer fascinating food questions full-time. He loves combining culinary passion with analytical methods to evaluate equipment from air fryers to gooseneck kettles. He lives in Maine with his husband and black lab and has never met a biscuit he didn't like.

Sawyer Phillips

Sawyer learned to bake in her family's bakery and has been interested in food ever since. After graduating from Emerson College with a degree in journalism, she worked at NBC as a researcher. Her favorite part of her job is learning and writing about African-American foodways.

Valerie Sizhe Li

Valerie is inspired by how things are made—be it a kitchen gadget or a small-batch condiment. Having visited more than 50 countries, she finds food to be the universal language that builds bridges and connects people. Her work has appeared in *USA Today*, *Eater*, *Punch*, and other publications.

Sarah Sandler

Before joining America's Test Kitchen, Sarah was an intern for *Saveur* and Chef Daniel Boulud, and spent a summer baking at Levain Bakery. She is deeply passionate about anchovies, she bakes sourdough bread weekly, and she carries a travel-size tin of Maldon salt with her wherever she goes.

Paul Adams

After working as a restaurant cook, a food journalist, and a science reporter and editor, Paul almost inevitably became the science research editor at America's Test Kitchen, where he specializes in fielding random questions and making things from scratch.

How and Why
We Test

Equipping your kitchen requires an investment of time and money. But how can you tell the real deals from the trendy pretenders? That's what we aim to help with, and it's why we take our reviews so seriously.

It takes us an average of 160 hours to produce each story we publish. We write only about products we've tested ourselves, and we don't accept advertising. We purchase all of our own products at retail prices and never accept any free or "loaner" products from manufacturers. We conduct hours of online research surveying the market before we decide which brands and product models to include in a testing lineup. We look for products that are widely available so we know you'll be able to find them. We consider prestige brands as well as upstart newcomers, but we never test products in the prototype stage, as what eventually makes it to market might be quite different from the initial model.

When it's time to start testing, our process only gets more rigorous. We never cut corners: If finding the best blender in every price bracket means spending $10,000 in total on different models, then that's what we do. (We typically purchase at least two of each product we test. That way if the first one doesn't work we can go back and test the second to make sure our results are solid.) We test products for durability,

repeatedly running them through the dishwasher, whacking them against a concrete ledge, or heating them up and plunging them into a bucket of ice water to simulate thermal shock. We don't like torturing equipment; we just want to make sure that the pieces we recommend will last. We have testers of different sizes, skill levels, and dominant hands try out products and give feedback. We also call on experts—scientists, professors, industry specialists, and our own science research editor—to help us understand our test results.

A product that passes all of our tests and earns the ATK Recommended seal of approval is one we think is truly worthwhile. We would never recommend something to you that we wouldn't use ourselves: We stock our winners in the test kitchen, where our team and our 60-plus colleagues use them regularly to monitor their performance and durability.

We're exhaustive but practical, scientific but approachable. And we always put function first. We've been doing this for more than 25 years—and we are never done learning.

The Four Tenets of Our Gear Testing Philosophy

1 · It Must Serve the User

A "good" tool isn't necessarily the one with the most bells and whistles—it's the one that works for you. Maybe you're left-handed, or you're low on space, or you need a skillet that's induction-compatible. We highlight both the strengths and weaknesses of each piece we test so you can find the tool that best fits your needs—even if that model isn't our overall favorite.

2 · Original Research Over Brand Marketing

We buy all the equipment we test and never accept freebies or advertising. Whether we're reviewing wooden spoons or the trendy gadget of the moment, you can be sure that our opinions are our own.

3 · Functionality Over Aesthetics

A pretty pan quickly loses its appeal if it doesn't cook evenly or if it's impossible to get clean. That's why we prioritize function, ease of use, durability, and value far above aesthetics.

4 · Longevity Over Disposability

Whether we're talking pricey high-end blenders or humble spatulas, we look for pieces that will continue to perform for a long time to come—not end up in a landfill in a few months' time.

What Happens to All That Gear After the Review?

We hold on to all the gear we test for at least a year. This gives us time to photograph it, film it, and do any follow-up testing deemed necessary. But once that year is up, it's time to clear out the old stuff to make room for the new. So, what, do we just throw it away? Nope! We organize our annual equipment giveaway.

What's the equipment giveaway, you ask?

It's our colleagues' very favorite day at the office. It's an all-day bonanza, a chance to make off with armfuls of free kitchen gear—everything from big-ticket items such as Instant Pots and flat-top grills to basics like spatulas and vegetable peelers. It's glorious.

Planning the giveaway begins months in advance and involves coordinating with multiple other teams to ensure that everything goes off without a hitch. In the weeks before the giveaway, we contact local nonprofits to see what they need for their kitchens and cooking programs, giving them first pick of the equipment we've accumulated over the past year. Then, a few days before the big day, we start moving everything out of storage, sorting it, and setting up, a process that takes the whole team at least two full working days.

It's a lot of work, that's for sure. But it's a win-win-win: We get to empty out our storage space, our coworkers get free stuff, and nothing is wasted.

The Smart Way to
Equip Your Kitchen

Stocking a kitchen from scratch is an intimidating prospect, but it doesn't have to be hard. Here are the most important things to consider as you get started.

Choose Multifunctional Pieces

The more things you can do with a single piece of equipment, the fewer pieces you'll need. You can make most basic to moderately-complicated recipes with just a handful of common kitchen tools (see page 11).

Invest in Tools That Will Last

Investing in good-quality equipment doesn't have to mean spending hundreds on the absolute top-of-the-line models. But it does mean spending a little more in the short-term to save money in the long-term: A moderately priced, good-quality pan that you have to buy only once will cost less in several years' time than an inexpensive but shoddily made pan that warps and needs to be replaced after a few months. Do some research before you buy (we can help with that!) so you can be sure your money is well spent.

Buy Items You'll Actually Use

No two collections of kitchen equipment should look exactly the same, because no two people like to cook in exactly the same way. Before you buy any new gear, think about what and how you enjoy cooking. If you loathe washing dishes, you'll want to prioritize ease of cleanup—no gadgets with nooks and crannies or appliances with fiddly pieces you have to clean individually. If you rarely bake, do you really need a Bundt pan? And if you don't know how you like to cook, you probably need just a little more experience to figure it out, so stick to the basics for now. You can always add more to your collection later.

Don't Try to Buy Everything at Once

Who has the budget for that, anyway? Completely stocking a kitchen can be expensive, but if you do it over time, buying a few pieces here and a few pieces there as your skills progress, you're less likely to feel the pinch in your wallet.

Outfit Yourself Like a Test Cook

These items are so useful that our test cooks like to keep them at hand (or foot) at all times.

Apron (page 343): Keeps clothes clean and provides convenient pockets for holding small tools (including some of the other items on this list).

Kitchen Clogs (page 344): You spend a lot of time on your feet in the kitchen. Good shoes provide support and cushioning to keep your feet happy. They also protect your feet from falling blades (yikes).

Dish Towel (page 401): A must-have for drying your hands between washes and mopping up small spills.

Digital Timer (page 374): Helps you track your recipe's progress even when you step away from the kitchen.

Instant-Read Thermometer (page 373): With one of these in your pocket you're only a second away from determining your food's doneness.

The Gear-Buying Timeline

When You're Just Starting Out

Build yourself a capsule kitchen (see page 11). These fundamental tools will allow you to cook a huge variety of recipes, from one-pan weeknight dinners to simpledesserts to fresh-baked bread.

Once You Have the Basics

It's time to add a few more tools to your capsule kitchen. For now, stick with relatively mundane pieces that will expand your cooking possibilities or make the kitchen tasks you do all the time easier. For example, you might want to add a paring knife for precise slicing, a manual citrus juicer for adding tart spritzes to your meals, or a 13 by 9-inch baking pan for making easy sheet cakes.

Now That You Know What You Like

Now that you have a feel for the cooking tasks you really enjoy and those you prefer to avoid, lean into your preferences. Are you endlessly fascinated by the process of brewing the perfect cup of coffee? Treat yourself to a precision coffee scale, a pour-over coffee maker, or even an espresso machine. (For more ideas, check out "Customize Your Collection.")

Once You're Well Established

You've finally become one of those cooks who has almost everything. We recommend buying the highest-quality equipment you can from the get-go, but if you're still holding on to any less-than-great tools from when you were just getting started, now is the time to upgrade.

Customize Your Collection

When choosing the next piece to add to your kitchen equipment collection, first ask yourself, "What do I want to be able to do in the kitchen?"

I want to...

Optimize my kitchen: To save on counter space, consider replacing countertop appliances with mini versions that can be stored in a drawer, such as an immersion blender (page 133) and single-serve coffee maker (page 185) in place of a full-size blender and coffee maker. And save space with smart storage solutions, like a compact spice rack (page 317), magnetic knife strip (page 314), and utensil crock (page 317).

Cook just enough for one or two: Quarter sheet pans (page 120) fit inside many toaster ovens (page 120), so you can cook a meal for two without turning on your actual oven. An 8- or 10-inch skillet (page 45) is just big enough to cook for-two-size portions. And if you do wind up with leftovers, you can't go wrong with a set of sturdy, stackable food storage containers (page 326).

Expand my baking repertoire: Bake professional-quality breads with a baking stone or steel (page 268) for better browning, a baking peel for transferring loaves (and pizzas) to the oven (page 269), and a lame (page 250) for scoring the dough and creating intricate patterns.

Dominate the backyard cookout: Assuming you already have a grill, get yourself a good pair of grill tongs (page 159), a grill brush (page 159), and a chimney starter (page 160) for quickly lighting coals without the need for lighter fluid. Or invest in an outdoor pizza oven (pages 266–267) or a nice cooler (pages 170–171) for keeping drinks frosty.

Eat (and actually enjoy) more vegetables: Prepping vegetables gives you the perfect excuse to play with some fun specialized knives: Try a bird's beak paring knife (page 73) or a nakiri—a Japanese vegetable cleaver (page 73)—on for size. A good vegetable peeler (page 84) makes quick work of removing tough rinds, and a mandoline (page 88) or food processor (pages 133–134) will help you slice piles of produce in minutes. Finding yourself with more kitchen scraps than usual? A compost bin (page 354) will turn those vegetable peels into useful plant food.

Feed a crowd: Two words: Slow cooker (page 129). With this underrated appliance you can set a big batch of food to cook and forget about it until it's time to serve. A rimmed baking sheet (pages 58, 219–223) can be used to make huge slab pies and sheet cakes. If you love to cook outdoors, a flat-top grill (page 168) will let you whip up piles of burgers, vegetables, eggs, and more in record time.

The Capsule Kitchen

In fashion, a capsule wardrobe is a collection of classic pieces that can be mixed and matched to create a large number of unique outfits using just a few clothes. Why not apply the same concept to kitchen gear?

The tools in our capsule kitchen allow you to cook the widest variety of recipes possible using the least amount of gear. If you have limited space or are just starting out, stock your kitchen with these basics to provide a solid foundation for your future cooking endeavors.

real talk with lisa & hannah
OUR TOP CAPSULE KITCHEN ADD-ONS

 LM The first items I'd add to my capsule kitchen would be rimmed baking sheets in a few sizes, from half- to quarter- to eighth-sheet pans, plus a grid-style cooling rack that fits neatly inside the largest sheet pan. This combo becomes a baking and roasting pan, a broiling pan, a place to hold fried foods before and after cooking, and much more.

 HC I'd have to add a good serrated bread knife, a deft little paring knife, an additional smaller cutting board, and two saucepans: both a larger 4-quart version and a smaller 1- to 2-quart one. And while it may seem like a luxury to many, for me, a pizza steel is totally essential.

Chef's Knife

This is the most versatile knife in our kitchen, used for every-thing from mincing herbs to chopping vegetables to doing basic butchery (think breaking down a chicken or filleting a fish).

Cutting Board

A cutting board provides a stable surface for all your prep work, keeps your counter clean, and helps prevent your knife from dulling too quickly. Boards made of either wood or plastic are fine—the choice depends on what you prefer.

Measuring Spoons and Measuring Cups

Accurately measuring ingredients is important in all cooking. Measuring spoons let you measure small amounts; we prefer sets that come with a ⅛-teaspoon measure (not all do). And even in a pared-down capsule kitchen, you should have a set of dry measuring cups as well as a liquid measuring cup.

Mixing Bowl

A mixing bowl is used for everything from whisking together a vinaigrette to melting butter to stirring together cake batter.

Fish Spatula

Despite the specificity of its name, the thin metal edge and subtle curve of a fish spatula actually make it the best all-purpose spatula for flipping food.

Silicone Spatula

A silicone spatula is your best friend for all things mixing, stirring, and scrap-ing. Its flexible, slightly rounded head is built for getting right into corners.

Tongs

Tongs let you securely grab hot foods with ease. We use them to turn and transfer large roasts, toss and portion pasta, and manipulate fiddly pieces such as dumplings or vegetables.

Instant-Read Thermometer

 An instant-read therm-ometer tells you when your food is done, when oil is hot enough for frying, when meat has reached its ideal doneness, when pie fillings are set, and more.

Cast-Iron Skillet

 Skillets come in a variety of different materials, all of which have their own prop-erties (see pages 32–45 for more). A cast-iron skillet is a versatile choice for everything from searing a steak to shallow-frying to oven-roasting to baking. A seasoned cast-iron skillet is also naturally nonstick.

Dutch Oven

 Dutch ovens do it all. You can use them for boiling, braising, searing, frying, and baking. Use one to boil pasta, make corn on the cob, cook up a batch of soup, develop fond, make a one-pot dinner for the whole family, and bake bread. You can even turn one into a makeshift steamer or panini press.

Hannah's
Gift Guide

Buy the right piece of kitchen equipment for the right person, and you have a present that's both thoughtful and practical. These are some of Lisa and Hannah's go-to tools for gifting under a variety of circumstances. Flip to the pages listed in parentheses for more information about our favorite models.

for a wedding

These luxurious yet hard-working pieces will get the newlyweds off to an auspicious start.

Dutch oven (page 364)

Heavy-duty cutting board (page 370)

Stand mixer (page 381)

for eco-conscious cooks

Help the environmentally conscious cook in your life reduce their footprint with these tools for cutting down on kitchen waste.

Silicone food covers (page 400)

Reusable food wraps (page 400)

Countertop compost bin (page 404)

stocking stuffers

These cute yet practical little items are the perfect size for stuffing into stockings.

Rasp-style grater (page 372)

Mini whisk (page 374)

Instant-read thermometer (page 373)

for the office holiday party

You don't know who exactly is going to end up with your gift, and you probably have a $20 limit. These gifts hit the sweet spot between silly, inexpensive, and useful—and may just send that *one* coworker a playful message about keeping the office microwave clean.

Jar spatula (page 374)

Silicone microwave lid (page 378)

Angry Mama microwave cleaner (page 359)

Lisa's
Gift Guide

for a housewarming

It's the little things that make someone feel at home.

Salt box (page 318)

***Good* dish towels (page 401)**

Magnetic knife strip (page 399)

for new empty-nesters

They've likely got free time on their hands for the first time in a while—so why not set up your empty-nester friends with some treat yourself–style gear?

Pour-over coffee maker (page 385)

Cocktail shaker (page 388)

Sous vide immersion circulator (page 379)

for college-bound students

Send your new college student off to school with the essentials (a good mug for transporting coffee from class to class is definitely an essential).

Travel mug (page 384)

Personal blender (page 380)

12-inch nonstick skillet (page 363)

big-ticket gifts for people you like a lot

These pricey pieces will really make your lucky giftee feel special.

Manual pasta machine (page 393)

Portable outdoor pizza oven (page 394)

Robot vacuum (page 404)

for cooks who have (almost) everything

The key to buying for someone who has everything? Get them the *good* version—or maybe a guide to making the most of what they already have. (Wink wink.)

Metal spatula (page 374)

***Good* serrated bread knife (page 368)**

This book!

Are You a
Gear Head?

Think you know everything there is to know about the equipment in your kitchen? Take this quiz to put your kitchen gear smarts to the test. Consider taking it twice—once before and once after reading this book—and comparing your results to see how much you've learned.

1. According to the Specialty Coffee Association, the water used to brew coffee should ideally be within what temperature range?

A. 185 to 190 degrees Fahrenheit

B. 194 to 205 degrees Fahrenheit

C. 210 to 212 degrees Fahrenheit

D. 220 to 229 degrees Fahrenheit

2. When discussing a knife's affordance, what are we talking about?

A. How much the knife costs

B. The angle of the blade

C. How smoothly the knife glides through food

D. How many different ways you can comfortably grip the handle

3. Which of the following is NOT an advantage of an edge-grain cutting board over an end-grain cutting board?

A. It requires less oil to maintain

B. It is naturally more resistant to bacterial growth

C. It absorbs less moisture

D. It has fewer glued joints that can fail over time

4. Which of these is NOT a real type of spatula?

A. Forkula

B. Spoonula

C. Offset

D. Jar

5. Pans made of which of the following metals are compatible with induction stovetops?

A. Ferromagnetic stainless steel

B. Cast iron

C. Carbon steel

D. All of the above

6. Is it ever OK to put something that contains metal in the microwave?

A. No, it's never OK

B. It's OK as long as the metal part is made of a nonreactive metal such as tin

C. It's OK as long as the metal part is intentionally designed for the micro-wave, with no sharp corners

D. It's OK as long as the metal part is 100% pure, with no contaminants

7. Which of the following should you NOT do when using an outdoor fryer?

A. Fry on a clear day with no rain, wind, or snow

B. Fry under a tree or overhang such as a roof, awning, or porch

C. Leave at least two feet between the propane tank and the burner

D. Turn the propane burner off before adding or removing food

8. Which of the following methods can you use to determine approximately how much propane is left in a propane tank?

A. Pour hot water down the side of the tank and then use your hand to feel the temperature of the tank in different spots

B. Weigh the tank and then divide its weight by 15

C. Strike the tank with a mallet and listen to the sound it makes

D. Keep track of how many hours you've used the tank since filling it and subtract that number from 20

study guide

Want to brush up on the questions you got wrong? You could read this entire book cover to cover— we highly encourage it!— or you could look up the explanations on the following pages.

1. Page 184

2. Page 74

3. Page 82

4. Page 97

5. Page 22

6. Page 116

7. Page 167

8. Page 151

9. Page 43

10. Pages 83, 101, 250, and 282

11. Page 193

12. Pages 268–269

13. Page 318

14. Page 346

15. Page 352

9. What should you do if you notice your nonstick skillet getting a little less nonstick?

A. Spray it with nonstick cooking spray

B. Give it a good wash with soap and the scrubbing side of a sponge, then let it soak in the sink overnight

C. Heat it for 30 seconds, rub a thin layer of vegetable oil over its surface, and then wipe it clean

D. Replace it immediately

10. Which of the following kitchen gear substitutions is NOT recommended?

A. Kitchen tongs for a jar lifter

B. Sharp paring knife for a bread lame

C. Rubber band for a jar opener

D. Cutting board set in a rimmed baking sheet for a carving board

11. Which of the following foods is best juiced at low speed?

A. Strawberries

B. Carrots

C. Spinach

D. Sweet Potatoes

12. Which of the following should you do to maintain your baking stone or steel?

A. Scrape off burnt-on food using a spatula or stiff brush

B. Remove it from the oven when not in use

C. Wash it with soap and water after each use

D. Soak it in a 50% bleach solution to remove stains

13. Which of the following spices contains compounds capable of dissolving certain plastics?

A. Fennel seeds

B. Juniper berries

C. Ground white peppercorns

D. Ground cloves

14. According to public health experts, how often should you replace your kitchen sponge?

A. Every week

B. Every 1 to 2 weeks

C. Every 2 to 3 weeks

D. Every month

15. Which of the following things should you never clean with vinegar?

A. Natural stone countertops

B. The inside of a microwave

C. Plastic cutting boards

D. Fruits and vegetables

answer key

9. C 10. A 11. A 12. A 13. D 14. B 15. A
1. B 2. D 3. B 4. A 5. D 6. C 7. B 8. A

turn up
the heat

RECIPES

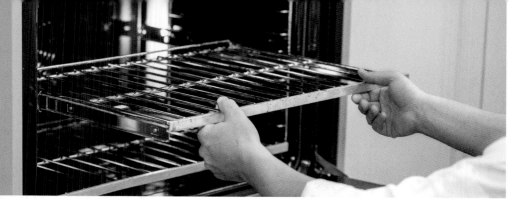

OVEN MODE

BAKE

TEMPERATURE

400

Don't Try This at Home

A skillet is no good if it warps the first—or the fiftieth—time you use it, or if its handle jiggles loose after an accidental fall. We make it a point to evaluate the durability of just about everything we review, but we can't exactly use every piece of equipment daily for years before passing down a verdict. That's where our abuse tests come in.

Take the infamous 50-egg test, for example. We use this test, a cookware industry standard, to assess nonstick pans. At the beginning of testing we cook eggs sunny side–up in a dry nonstick skillet one after another until they begin to stick or until we've made 50 eggs—whichever comes first. Then we do it all over again with the next pan, and the next, and the next. And then, at the very end of our testing process, we do the same test once again to see how each skillet's nonstick coating has held up over time. It's a tedious task at the best of times, but

as they say, you can't suss out the best nonstick skillets without breaking a few hundred eggs. (OK, maybe we're the only ones who say that.)

And our abuse testing doesn't end there. Most cooks will probably fry at least a few eggs over their non-stick skillet's lifespan, but will they intentionally plunge their piping-hot pans into ice-cold water, or smash them repeatedly against a concrete block? We sincerely hope not. We do these tests not because they reflect real-world use, and not because we take pleasure in smashing up perfectly good pans, but because they're extreme enough to simulate years' worth of wear and tear in a matter of days or even seconds. A skillet that can survive being bashed against concrete multiple times with only minor dents to show for it is the kind of solidly constructed workhorse we want in our kitchens—and in yours.

Master Your Stove

You may read reviews before picking the perfect air fryer and you might agonize over the ideal Dutch oven, but have you given as much thought to your stove? If you simply inherited one when you moved into your current home, then chances are you haven't thought much about it at all—and yet it's one of the most important appliances in your kitchen. Here's what you need to know.

head to head

STOVES

GAS STOVES	ELECTRIC STOVES	INDUCTION STOVES
Work by using a natural gas flame to heat cookware situated above on a grate	Work by heating up electric coils that then transfer heat to the pan	Work by creating a magnetic field that directly heats up induction-compatible cookware
Respond quickly to changes in temperature settings	May feature a smooth glass stovetop or raised metal coils	Respond quickly to changes in temperature settings
Less fuel efficient: lose lots of heat to surrounding air	Respond more slowly to changes in temperature settings	More fuel efficient: lose less heat to surrounding air
May contribute to indoor air pollution		More expensive to repair
		Not compatible with all cookware

Are Gas Stoves Bad for the Environment?

Natural gas stoves have an undeniable allure, conjuring images of chefs in white coats tossing heavily laden skillets over a blue flame. They're powerful and agile, but sadly, their advantages do come at a cost. Namely, some studies have indicated that gas stoves contribute to indoor air pollution and may also be worse for the environment at large than initially thought. Even when not in use, they can leak methane and other pollutants.

If you're concerned about the environment and your home's air quality, you may want to reconsider installing a new gas stove in your home. And if you currently have a gas stove, be sure to build in a good ventilation system.

How Do Induction Burners Work?

Unlike stoves that rely on gas flames or electric coils to heat pans, induction burners and stoves work by generating heat directly within the pans themselves. Under sleek ceramic-glass surfaces, induction stoves and portable induction burners contain coils of copper wire. Electricity passes through these coils, creating a magnetic field that induces (hence the name "induction") an electric current in the metal of the pan, causing atomic-scale friction—which makes the pan hot. (Note that not all pans will conduct a current; see page 22 for more information about induction-compatible pans.)

Lisa Says . . .

Ever find yourself in need of an extra burner? Try a portable one (see page 291). They're useful for lots of situations: Think holidays, power outages, traveling in an RV, or car camping. I like to use mine with my wok for searingly powerful stir-frying, or to make a hot pot dinner at the table, where my whole family dips foods in the bubbling broth. If I'm going to do a lot of deep frying, I like to take the burner and the whole project outdoors to keep my kitchen clean.

real talk with lisa

A WOOD-BURNING STOVE MADE ME A BETTER COOK

I once had the chance to cook on a 19th-century cast-iron wood stove. I loved the experience of cooking like our ancestors, which forced me to rely on my senses instead of using high-tech thermometers and temperature gauges or just following recipe instructions. Having no choice but to pay all my attention to the food itself helped me learn better how to identify doneness cues and to trust my own cooking instincts. My takeaway: Always trust your own eyes and ears and nose to tell you how your cooking is coming along—and you won't go wrong.

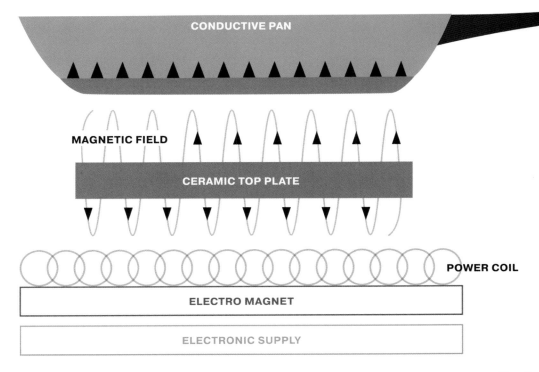

Is Induction the Future of Cooking?

You may associate induction stoves with eco-friendliness. But it should be noted that, at least until more of our electricity is generated through renewable sources such as solar and wind, induction cooking isn't really more eco-friendly than other cooking methods since the electricity it takes to power the induction burners is generated primarily by burning fossil fuels.

We can't say for sure whether induction is the future of cooking. But we can tell you the pros and cons that come with it so you can decide whether induction is the future of your cooking.

I'm Considering an Induction Stove— Will I Need to Replace All My Pans?

Induction burners generate heat using magnetism, so to be induction compatible, a pan needs to contain ferromagnetic metal such as ferromagnetic stainless steel, cast iron, or carbon steel. It's important to take this into consideration when thinking about switching to induction; you may need to invest in a few new pans and part with others.

induction stove pros and cons

PROS	CONS
Fast Induction stoves heat compatible pans remarkably quickly	**Not all pans are compatible** Pans must contain ferromagnetic metal to heat via induction
Powerful While individual stoves vary, some induction stovetops have extrapowerful burners that rival professional gas ranges	**Can become overloaded** Cooking with multiple pans at high temperatures can cause the stove to shut down
Responsive The electromagnetic current reacts instantly when you change the temperature setting	**Power issues** Vulnerable to voltage spikes and power outages
Safer The glass top of an induction stove gets warm from being under a hot pan, but it never gets as searingly hot as a glass-topped electric-coil stove	**Breakable** Glass top can be damaged by dropping or dragging heavy pans
Steady heat Induction stoves excel at holding steady temperatures	**Expensive to repair** Many stoves need to be serviced within five years
Fuel efficient Less heat is lost to the surrounding air because induction cooking heats only the pan, not the burner	**Warped pans won't work** Pans won't heat up where they don't make contact with the induction surface
Easy to clean No grates or electric-coil burners to clean around, and the surface doesn't get as hot, so there's less burnt-on food	**Noisy** Some induction burners and stoves emit a high-pitched whine as they cook

test it yourself

IS IT INDUCTION COMPATIBLE?

If you have or are thinking of getting an induction stove, you'll need to know whether your cookware is induction compatible. The easiest way to find out? Use a magnet. If the magnet sticks to the bottom of a pan, that pan will work with an induction stovetop. If the magnet doesn't stick, you'll need to pair the pan with an induction interface disk if you want to use it on an induction burner.

worth it

INDUCTION INTERFACE DISK

Placed between your induction burner and your non–induction compatible pan, these thin disks of induction-compatible metal heat up and then transfer that heat to your pan. While not as efficient as induction-compatible pans, they're great if you want to keep using an heirloom pan or aren't yet ready to overhaul your cookware collection.

Master Your Oven

Like the stove, your oven is an essential yet often underrated part of your kitchen. Now's the time to take a peek inside its inner workings.

How Does Preheating Work?

The obvious subtext to this question is: Do I really need to preheat my oven?

Short answer: Yes. You really do.

We know it can be a pain. We know it can be easy to forget. But the reason you need to preheat your oven is directly related to how ovens work at a fundamental level. Ovens cook by moving hot air over and around your food, and it takes time to heat up that air.

Ovens are constantly cycling on and off in order to reach and then maintain the set temperature. In an effort to heat up faster, they may initially overshoot the set temperature by up to 50 degrees; to counteract this, they then shut off for a short period to allow the temperature to come back down— until it gets too low, at which point the oven cycles on again and the process repeats. After the first dramatic cycle of heating and cooling, ovens even out at a relatively consistent temperature. This is the point at which your oven will alert you that it's preheated and you can start cooking.

The takeaway: Those initial temperature swings won't be kind to your food if you jump the gun by adding your food before your oven is fully preheated. The few minutes it takes to preheat are worth it.

Why Do Some Recipes Get So Specific About Oven Rack Position?

The inside of your oven is hot. Food plus heat equals cooked food. So surely it doesn't really matter where you place your oven racks, right?

Wrong. The position of the oven rack has a huge impact on how food gets cooked because of the way heat circulates throughout an oven. Here's the lowdown on when to use each position.

Top rack: Once your oven preheats, it will be consistently hotter at the top because of simple physics: Heat rises. Use this position for any dish that needs a gloriously brown top.

Middle rack: The middle of your oven provides the most even circulation of heat, meaning you'll get the most even cooking or baking here. Use it for things such as cookies, cake, and roast chicken.

Bottom rack: Since it's closest to the heat source, the bottom rack is ideal for getting great color on the bottom of your food. Use it for roasted vegetables or to make sheet-pan pizza with a deliciously crispy crust.

What's the Point of Rotating and Switching Baking Sheets?

Just as ovens aren't uniformly hot from top to bottom, their temperature can also vary from front to back. Ovens lose heat from the front when the door is opened, and can also slowly leak heat through the seal around the door. That's why many recipes call for rotating baking sheets (or other cooking vessels) and switching them between racks midway through cooking. Moving the sheets means food is less likely to sit squarely in a hot or cool zone for the entire duration of cooking and more likely to end up evenly cooked. (For more information on exactly when you should rotate baking sheets, check out page 219.)

Do I Have to Clean My Oven?

Drips and splatters add up to a grimy oven over time. If it gets bad enough, you're at risk of smoking out your kitchen or even starting a grease fire. So yes, you do need to clean your oven.

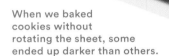

When we baked cookies without rotating the sheet, some ended up darker than others.

So How Do I Get My Oven Clean?

Like most cleaning tasks, the easiest way to clean your oven is to address little messes as they occur. If you see splatters after you cook, use a damp cloth or sponge to lightly scrub them away once the oven has cooled down.

If your oven needs a deeper clean, first make sure there's plenty of ventilation. Wear rubber gloves and old clothes and cover the floor around your oven to protect yourself and your floor from strong oven-cleaning products.

If you have a self-cleaning oven, simply run the self-cleaning cycle following your oven manufacturer's instructions. Self-cleaning cycles work by making the oven extremely hot—upward of 800 degrees in some cases. This reduces any residue to ash, which you need to wipe out afterward with a damp cloth. Some ovens also have steam-cleaning cycles, which run about 400 degrees, for lighter cleaning. Again, you'll need to wipe out loosened residue afterward.

If you don't have a self-cleaning oven, use an oven-cleaning product. These come in aerosol spray, gel, and liquid forms, and are used to dissolve baked-on foods from your oven. Most require a few hours to sit on the oven's interior surfaces and loosen residue. Some work best if the oven is slightly warm. Turn it on to warm (175 to 200 degrees Fahrenheit) for 15 minutes and then shut it off before you spray. Follow all instructions on the cleaning product's label very carefully for the best results.

Hannah Says . . .

I once flubbed sliding a pizza into the oven, dumping half the toppings onto the bottom. I still ate it (even ugly pizza tastes good), but the problem came when I used my oven next. During preheating it started billowing smoke. Nothing like some flaming cheese to convince you of the importance of cleaning your oven.

What's a Convection Oven?
Is It Anything Like a Regular Oven?

A convection oven is essentially a conventional oven equipped with a fan. By constantly moving hot air around the food, a convection oven is able to cook food faster, more evenly, and with more efficient browning. This is great for roasting meat and vegetables, driving off moisture in foods such as granola, and baking items that benefit from strong browning such as pizza and pies. It's best to avoid the convection setting when making fragile baked goods that need time to rise and set like cookies, cakes, and soufflés; cooking anything that shouldn't be browned (think: angel food cake); or toasting very lightweight pieces that you don't want blown around the oven, such as bread crumbs or shredded coconut.

Fun fact: an air fryer, despite its name, is simply a miniature convection oven, so if you want to experience what convection cooking can do before investing in a large-scale version, try an air fryer on for size. (See page 122 for more about air fryers.)

Lisa Says . . .

The first time you use the convection setting for a recipe that wasn't written for a convection oven, set the oven 25 degrees below the called-for temperature. (But first, double check your manual: Some ovens automatically drop the temperature by 25 degrees when the convection setting is turned on.) If the lower temperature causes the food to spread too much or brown too slowly, try cooking at the recipe's called-for temperature next time.

Hannah Says . . .

Were you taught that you should always keep the oven door ajar while broiling? You may have been told that because many ovens temporarily shut off the broiler if the temperature gets too high. Leaving the door open a crack keeps the oven's temperature lower, so the broiler stays on. Still, it's best to check your manual to see what the manufacturer recommends for using your broiler safely. If the manual says to close the door, then you should shut it!

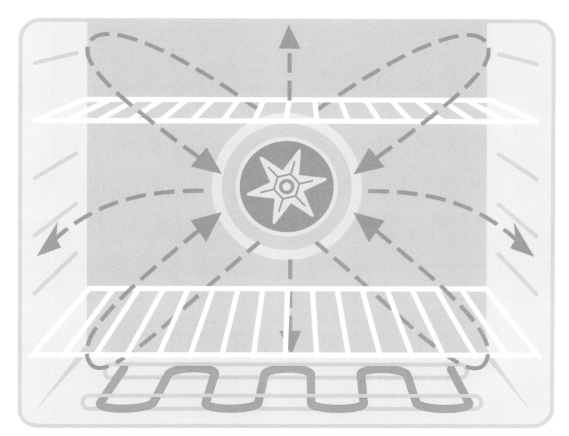

In convection ovens, circulating air distributes heat more quickly and evenly.

6 **Ways** to Hack Your Stove and Oven

Every stove and oven is different, and even the pros are sometimes foiled by their idiosyncrasies. Learn how to identify and adapt to the quirks of your own stove and oven so you can keep your cool as you sear, bake, and broil your way to delicious food.

1 USE A FLAME TAMER

Gas stoves are highly responsive, but we still sometimes find that even the very lowest setting—the lowest we can go without extinguishing the flame—is still too hot to cook certain temperamental foods, such as polenta, without scorching them. That's where a flame tamer comes in handy. A flame tamer is nothing more than a ring of material that elevates your pan so it's slightly further away from the heat source. You can buy one or make your own; this really isn't high-tech equipment we're talking about here. To make one, just shape a sheet of heavy-duty aluminum foil into a 1-inch-thick ring that fits on your burner, making sure that the ring is of even thickness.

2 QUICKLY ADJUST THE HEAT ON AN ELECTRIC STOVE

If you have an electric stove, you know that quick heat adjustments aren't really in the cards—the heating element takes a few minutes to heat up or cool down each time you adjust the heat setting.

The solution to your sluggish electric stove woes? Use two burners. When you know you need to go quickly from low to high heat (or vice versa), start heating a second burner a few minutes ahead of time. That way the heating element is already at the correct temperature by the time you need it. And if you ever find that your food is boiling out of control, just move the pan entirely off the hot burner and onto one that isn't in use until things calm down a little.

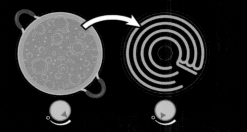 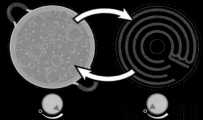

3 USE THE RIGHT-SIZE BURNER FOR YOUR PAN

Does it really matter if you use the larger or smaller burner? Yes! You should always try to match the burner size as closely as you can to the size of your pan. Using a small pan on a bigger burner is just inefficient, as a lot of the heat the burner produces is going to escape into the air rather than be conducted through the pan to your food. In a pinch, you can use a larger pan on the smaller burner, but be sure to give it more time to preheat and know that even then your food may cook unevenly.

4

TAKE YOUR OVEN'S TEMPERATURE

Thermometers are essential tools for checking if your food is ready (see page 92). But did you know that you should also be taking the temperature of your oven? Some ovens can be as much as 50 degrees off the desired temperature. An oven thermometer hangs inside your oven and lets you know what's actually going on in there. Once you know, you can either set your oven temperature a few degrees higher or lower to compensate or call in a professional to recalibrate it.

Note: Some variation in oven temperature is expected (see page 23 for more on how ovens heat). It's normal for a single temperature reading to be around 10 degrees too high or too low, depending on whether your oven is currently cycling on or off. But if several readings all show that your oven is too hot or too cool by 25 degrees or more, that's a problem.

5

ADD THERMAL BALLAST

To hold your oven's temperature steadier, you can add something called "thermal ballast." Thermal ballast is anything that absorbs and slowly releases heat, and you may already have the perfect tool for the job in your kitchen—a pizza stone or steel. Not only is it OK to leave these heavy pieces in your oven most of the time, but doing so can actually be beneficial. Just a few notes: First, don't place pans directly on the steel or stone unless you want extra heat and browning applied to the bottom of your food (think pizza). Remove the steel or stone before baking delicate items such as cookies or cakes, as it can disrupt the oven's heat-circulation pattern. Finally, don't place the steel or stone on the oven floor; many ovens have vents there that must not be blocked for safety reasons.

6

FIND YOUR BROILER'S HOT SPOTS

Most broilers heat up the center and back of the oven, leaving the sides and front relatively cool. To find out what your broiler's heating pattern is, make a "map" with toasted pieces of white bread. Once you know where your broiler's hotter and cooler spots are, you can use that information to position and, if necessary, switch food partway through cooking for more even browning.

1 Position oven rack 4 inches from broiler element and heat broiler. Line entire surface of large rimmed baking sheet with single layer of white bread slices.

2 Place bread in oven under heated broiler. Cook until all slices have started to brown (some pieces may turn black; if bread starts to smoke, remove baking sheet immediately).

3 Remove baking sheet from oven, being careful to make note of its orientation. Take photo of your broiler map and keep it near your oven.

Skillets 101

Understanding this most basic and essential of kitchen workhorses will help you use yours to the fullest. It's time for a skillet crash course.

Why Would I Ever Need More Than One Skillet?

When you start to learn about skillets, you quickly discover that there are more types of them out there than you ever realized. Do you really need a cast-iron skillet? What's so great about copper or carbon-steel skillets? Do you need a 12-inch and a 10-inch and an 8-inch? Why can't there just be one?

Here's the thing. Whether you can get by with just one skillet or whether you need multiple in different sizes and materials largely comes down to how you like to cook. Skillets made of different materials have their own strengths and weaknesses; read pages 32–45 for a deep dive into the most common types of skillets you'll find on the market. Smaller skillets are great for small families and cooking tasks, while a full-size 12-inch skillet is great for building an entire dinner in one pan and for making sure the food isn't crowded when you want good browning. Some skillets are really good at a certain task, such as ensuring that delicate foods slide right off of their surface in one unblemished piece. Others have specific strengths, like quick and even heating or getting superhot and delivering a world-class sear, but are also pretty good at other common cooking tasks, making them a viable choice for a single-skillet cookware collection.

If you want to cover all your bases, we recommend stocking a stainless-steel skillet, a cast-iron skillet, and a nonstick skillet, but this isn't gospel. Some cooks swear that a carbon-steel skillet is the only one they need, and others prefer to switch between a large variety of skillets depending on the task at hand. Ultimately, it's up to you, and the more you learn, the better equipped you'll be to decide for yourself what's essential in your own kitchen.

Skillet, Frying Pan, Sauté Pan . . . What's the Difference?

What's in a name? Are these all different kinds of pans?

In a word, no. Regional differences can account for some of these name variants; what you might call a frying pan, we call a skillet, but we're both referring to the same tool.

One exception: While some skillet manufacturers mislabel their products as sauté pans, real sauté pans have straight, tall sides that make them immediately recognizable (see page 60 for more about sauté pans).

My Skillet Didn't Come with a Lid. What Do I Do?

It still baffles us that so many skillets are sold without a matching lid. Lids come in handy for steaming, containing splatters, and keeping food warm while the rest of the meal comes together, so not having one on hand can put a big wrench in your dinner operations. Luckily, you can buy lids separately. It doesn't have to be fancy; just get one that's made to fit a 12-inch skillet (or a 10- or 8-inch skillet if that's what you have).

real talk with lisa & hannah

LM

MY DESERT-ISLAND SKILLET: STAINLESS STEEL

If I were going to be stranded on a desert island with just *one* skillet, I'd be so torn. But I'd have to go with a fully clad stainless-steel pan with an aluminum core. It's never going to wear out, like a nonstick pan, or rust, like cast iron or carbon steel (to be expected when you're on the salty beach of a desert island). It's easy to maintain (I could use sand to scrub the surface from time to time) and it won't react with anything acidic, such as tangy pineapple juice. It's roomy and it heats evenly—helpful for cooking over the irregular heat of a campfire. I could also use its shiny surface to signal passing ships and planes, so I will be rescued. (But only after enjoying a nice, long beach vacation with plenty of great food.)

HC

MY DESERT-ISLAND SKILLET: CARBON STEEL

Lisa took this question very literally! She's wisely considering how she'd season the pan, and she's right—carbon steel or cast iron will rust in the salty, sandy, oil-less environment of our fabled desert island. But if I had only one skillet to use for the rest of my life, my pick, hands down, would be carbon-steel. It sears beautifully but is lighter than cast iron, something I appreciate because your girl here loves a tossy-toss. I also love that carbon steel can go on the stove or grill, or in the oven. With some minor maintenance you get a naturally non-stick cooking surface—no plastic coatings for me, thank you very much. Hopefully Lisa and I are stranded together. We can cook in her pan and use mine to defend ourselves against the wild boars until we get back to proper seasoning conditions.

anatomy of

A GOOD SKILLET

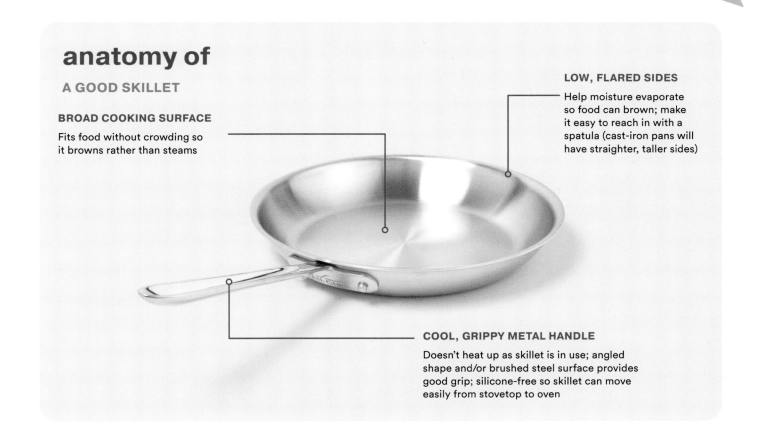

BROAD COOKING SURFACE
Fits food without crowding so it browns rather than steams

LOW, FLARED SIDES
Help moisture evaporate so food can brown; make it easy to reach in with a spatula (cast-iron pans will have straighter, taller sides)

COOL, GRIPPY METAL HANDLE
Doesn't heat up as skillet is in use; angled shape and/or brushed steel surface provides good grip; silicone-free so skillet can move easily from stovetop to oven

the right skillet for the job

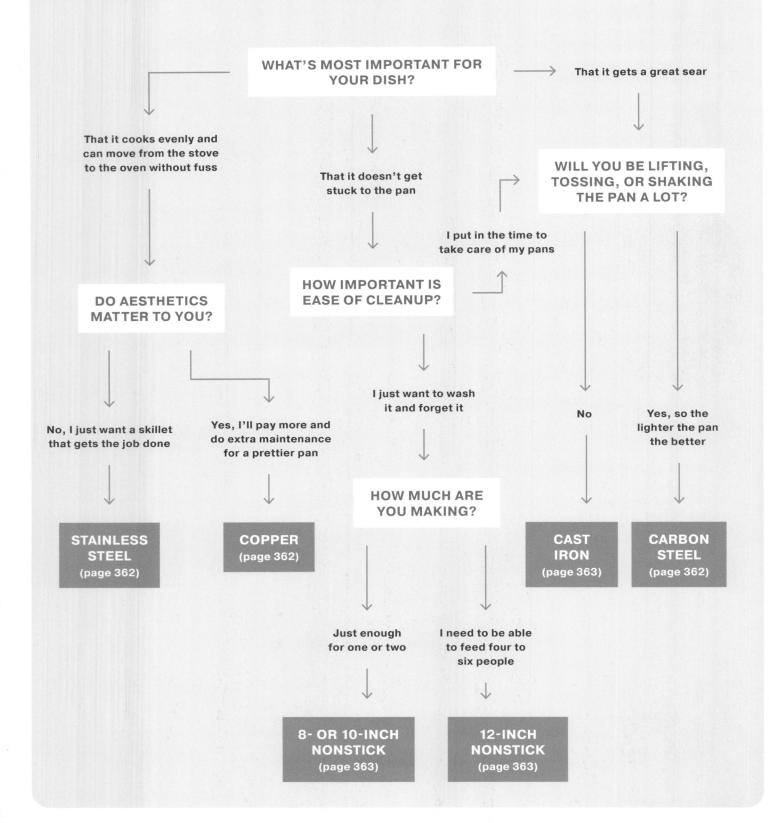

WHAT'S MOST IMPORTANT FOR YOUR DISH?

That it gets a great sear

That it cooks evenly and can move from the stove to the oven without fuss

That it doesn't get stuck to the pan

WILL YOU BE LIFTING, TOSSING, OR SHAKING THE PAN A LOT?

I put in the time to take care of my pans

DO AESTHETICS MATTER TO YOU?

HOW IMPORTANT IS EASE OF CLEANUP?

I just want to wash it and forget it

No, I just want a skillet that gets the job done

Yes, I'll pay more and do extra maintenance for a prettier pan

No

Yes, so the lighter the pan the better

HOW MUCH ARE YOU MAKING?

STAINLESS STEEL
(page 362)

COPPER
(page 362)

CAST IRON
(page 363)

CARBON STEEL
(page 362)

Just enough for one or two

I need to be able to feed four to six people

8- OR 10-INCH NONSTICK
(page 363)

12-INCH NONSTICK
(page 363)

CAST
IRON

COPPER

12-INCH
NONSTICK

8- OR
10-INCH
NONSTICK

STAINLESS
STEEL

CARBON
STEEL

Stainless Steel and Copper

Stainless-steel pans are the unflashy workhorses of the skillet world; copper pans are their bright and dazzling cousins. Regardless of their differences in appearance and trendiness, both types of skillet excel at cooking evenly and responding quickly to changes in heat, making them the go-to choices for many everyday cooking tasks.

head to head

STAINLESS-STEEL AND COPPER SKILLETS

FULLY CLAD STAINLESS-STEEL SKILLETS	COPPER SKILLETS
Typically less expensive	Typically more expensive
Made by sandwiching a layer of highly conductive metal (usually aluminum) between layers of durable, nonreactive stainless steel	Made by sandwiching a highly conductive copper core between layers of nonreactive metal such as stainless steel, or by lining the interior of a solid copper pan with nonreactive stainless steel or tin
Aluminum conducts heat relatively quickly compared to most metals, but 1.5 times more slowly than copper	Copper conducts heat 1.5 times faster than aluminum
	Exposed copper will tarnish if not polished regularly
	Tin-lined pans are easily damaged at temperatures above approximately 450 degrees Fahrenheit

Hannah Says . . .

Copper is second only to silver when it comes to responsiveness. But copper pans can cost a pretty penny, and honestly, their extra agility just doesn't make that much difference to the quality of your cooking. My advice? Copper is cool if you have the dough, but a good quality stainless-steel skillet is almost as responsive and requires less care.

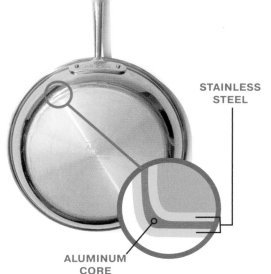

STAINLESS STEEL

ALUMINUM CORE

What Does "Fully Clad" Mean? What About "Ply"?

In fully clad pans, the entire body of the pan—rather than just the bottom—is composed of three or more layers of different metals bonded together. In the case of stainless-steel pans, aluminum is typically sandwiched between layers of stainless steel to give you the best of both metals: aluminum's relatively speedy heat conduction modulated by slower-transmitting, heat-retaining steel for a pan that heats evenly and holds on to that heat. It's these layers that are known as "ply." We prefer pans with three layers (referred to as "tri-ply") over those with more layers. We've found that pans with more layers are heavier and, depending on the material of the additional metal, can heat more slowly. And stay away from disk-bottom pans, which have a layer of more conductive metal only on the bottom. These are prone to heating unevenly and scorching food near the edges.

Why Does My Food Always Stick?

Some sticking is actually desirable when you're cooking with stainless steel or copper. It's part of the process of creating fond, the superflavorful browned bits that form on the bottom and sides of a pan when you sear proteins or vegetables; we often use fond to create pan sauces, or scrape it back into the dish to add flavor. If you're cooking especially delicate foods such as eggs or fish, opt for nonstick or well-seasoned cast iron or carbon steel. Otherwise, accept that a little bit of sticking is a normal part of the process, although you can minimize it by fully preheating the pan and using plenty of fat.

If you preheat your pan and cook with fat and your food is still sticking more than you want, you may need just a little patience. When meat is first added to a pan, sulfur atoms in the protein react with metal atoms in the pan, forming a strong chemical bond that fuses the meat to the pan. Once the meat has formed a brown, crispy crust, the links between the protein and metal will loosen, allowing the protein to release much more cleanly than if you force it before it's ready.

Some sticking is normal in a stainless-steel skillet.

Once food has browned, it should release fairly easily.

real talk with lisa

YOU GET WHAT YOU PAY FOR

As one of the hardest-working pans in the kitchen, a skillet is an important investment. Sure, you can buy the cheapest possible skillet at a discount store, but I guarantee that you will be struggling while you use it, disappointed in your cooking results, and shocked at how quickly it will wear out. It will soon be on its way to the landfill, while you're shelling out for yet another pan. It's a matter of science: The shape, weight, balance, materials, and overall construction of a well-designed skillet all work together to make it cook beautifully, feel comfortable and efficient, and last longer. Bottom line: You deserve a great skillet. Don't skimp.

PAN-SEARED CHICKEN BREASTS WITH BROWNED BUTTER SAUCE

serves 4

The high conductivity of a stainless steel or copper skillet means the pan cools quickly once removed from the heat, so the butter is less likely to burn. If you can't tell the color of the butter through the foam in step 4, quickly spoon some onto a white plate.

4	(6- to 8-ounce) boneless, skinless chicken breasts, trimmed
1¼	teaspoons table salt, divided
½	teaspoon pepper
¼	cup all-purpose flour
2	tablespoons extra-virgin olive oil
6	tablespoons unsalted butter, cut into 6 pieces
2	tablespoons capers, rinsed
2	tablespoons lemon juice
3	tablespoons minced fresh chives, divided

1 Sandwich chicken between 2 sheets of plastic wrap on cutting board. Using meat pounder, gently pound thickest part of each breast to ¾-inch thickness to match thin part of breast. Pat chicken dry with paper towels and sprinkle with 1 teaspoon salt and pepper.

2 Place flour in shallow dish. Dredge chicken in flour to coat both sides, shake off excess, and transfer to plate. Heat oil in 12-inch skillet over medium heat until just smoking. Add chicken, smooth side down. Cover and cook until light golden brown on first side, about 8 minutes.

3 Flip chicken and continue to cook, uncovered, until chicken registers 160 degrees, about 4 minutes longer. Using metal spatula, loosen chicken if stuck to skillet and transfer to cutting board. Tent with aluminum foil and let rest for 10 minutes.

4 Meanwhile, melt butter in now-empty skillet over medium heat. Add capers and cook, swirling skillet and scraping skillet bottom occasionally with wooden spoon, until milk solids in butter are color of milk chocolate and have toasty aroma, 3 to 5 minutes (it's OK if skillet bottom is very browned and bits don't release when scraped).

5 Immediately remove skillet from heat and stir in lemon juice, scraping up browned bits. Stir in 2 tablespoons chives and remaining ¼ teaspoon salt.

6 Slice chicken and transfer to serving platter. Spoon sauce over chicken and sprinkle with remaining 1 tablespoon chives. Serve.

Why Are Copper Pans Lined with a Different Metal?

Copper is a highly reactive metal, meaning that it will leach into foods high in water or acidity when in direct contact with them. Copper is poisonous when ingested in high quantities, so for safety's sake manufacturers coat copper pans with a nonreactive metal such as stainless steel or tin.

What's the Difference Between a Lined Copper Skillet and a Copper-Core Skillet?

Lined copper skillets have a very thin layer of nonreactive metal lining their cooking surface, leaving the skillet's copper exterior exposed. In the old days, tin was the only metal used to line copper pans. These days, tin has largely been supplanted by stainless steel, which is less responsive to heat but much more durable. It also offers a benefit: As the steel slows copper's quick vertical transfer of heat (up from the burner to the food), it forces heat to travel sideways through the copper. This spreads the heat rapidly across the entire cooking surface, making the pan cook more evenly and reducing hot spots.

Copper core skillets, as their name suggests, feature copper cores sandwiched between layers of stainless steel and/or aluminum. We've found that these pans cook remarkably evenly, are easy to maintain, and are lighter than pans made primarily from copper; for sheer cooking performance, they're probably the best choice. The downside? With less exposed copper, they aren't as beautiful.

Tin-lined pans are super-responsive but, because heat passes through them so quickly, they cook less evenly.

Stainless steel–lined pans are less responsive but, because the steel helps spread the heat throughout the pan, they cook more evenly.

How Can I Keep My Copper Pan Looking Its Best?

It can be a little shocking how fast copper's appearance changes when you cook with it. Right away, the shiny, golden-red surface gets blotchy and streaky and the rich color fades to yellow; with use and time, copper will turn the deep brown of an old penny—or even green. This patina is harmless, and many people actually prefer this look.

But if you do want to restore your cookware to its original coppery glow, it's easy enough to do. A good store-bought copper polish will have your pan looking shiny and new in no time. (It's also possible to shine up a pan by buffing it with a homemade mixture of lemon juice or vinegar and salt, but this method is a much bigger pain— it takes longer and makes a mess. Our advice: Take the easy route and use a store-bought polish.)

Cast Iron and Carbon Steel

When you want a skillet that can get hot—really, really hot—and deliver a first-rate sear, cast iron and carbon steel are the way to go. Once you get to know how these skillets work, it's easy to see why they're the go-to for many professional chefs and home cooks alike.

What Do You Mean, Cast Iron and Carbon Steel Do the Same Job?

Grouping cast-iron and carbon-steel pans into the same category may seem surprising. On the surface, these two types of pans couldn't seem more different. Cast iron is heavy and rustic and conjures images of cowboys cooking steaks and cornbread over an open fire. Carbon steel is sleeker and more refined, bringing to mind restaurant chefs in white coats.

But when you look at function, it all starts to make sense. Both cast iron and carbon steel excel at searing. Carbon steel is super-responsive, heating and cooling quickly; thick cast iron heats more slowly but holds on to that heat for a long time. Both pans also require seasoning, and with proper seasoning develop a naturally nonstick surface that ensures your food releases cleanly every time.

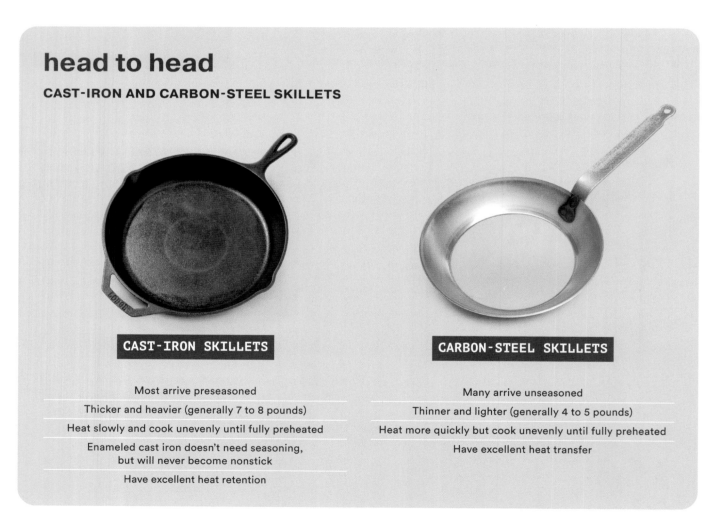

head to head

CAST-IRON AND CARBON-STEEL SKILLETS

CAST-IRON SKILLETS

Most arrive preseasoned

Thicker and heavier (generally 7 to 8 pounds)

Heat slowly and cook unevenly until fully preheated

Enameled cast iron doesn't need seasoning, but will never become nonstick

Have excellent heat retention

CARBON-STEEL SKILLETS

Many arrive unseasoned

Thinner and lighter (generally 4 to 5 pounds)

Heat more quickly but cook unevenly until fully preheated

Have excellent heat transfer

Why Do Professional Chefs Swear by Carbon-Steel Skillets?

A carbon-steel skillet can do everything a stainless-steel, cast-iron, and nonstick pan can do—and in some cases, can do it even better.

Carbon steel is an alloy made of about 1 percent carbon and 99 percent iron; despite its name, it actually contains a bit less carbon than cast iron. This slightly lower carbon content makes carbon steel less brittle than cast iron, so pans made with it can be thinner and more lightweight. The smooth surface of carbon steel makes it easy to acquire a slick patina of polymerized oil during seasoning.

All of this adds up to a pan that's relatively lightweight and maneuverable, like a stainless-steel skillet; is excellent at searing, like a cast-iron skillet; and that becomes naturally nonstick over time, like cast iron—without the drawbacks of PTFE- or ceramic-coated nonstick skillets (see page 44 for more on these). With all of these advantages, it's little wonder that they're such a staple in professional kitchens.

BUTTER-BASTED RIB STEAK

serves 2

Carbon steel gets superhot, so if you're lucky enough to have one of these pans in your arsenal, it's the perfect choice for a recipe such as this one, where you want to get a great sear on the exterior of a cut of meat before the interior overcooks. Its relative lightness also makes a carbon-steel skillet preferable to cast iron here (though cast iron will work) since you'll need to tilt the skillet until the butter pools on one side so it can be scooped up and used to baste the steak.

1	(1¼-pound) bone-in rib steak or (1-pound) boneless rib-eye steak, 1½ inches thick, trimmed
1	teaspoon pepper
½	teaspoon table salt
1	tablespoon extra-virgin olive oil
3	tablespoons unsalted butter
1	shallot, peeled and quartered through root end
2	garlic cloves, lightly crushed and peeled
5	sprigs fresh thyme

1 Pat steak dry with paper towels and sprinkle with pepper and salt. Heat oil in 12-inch skillet over medium-high heat until just smoking. Place steak in skillet and cook for 30 seconds. Flip steak and continue to cook for 30 seconds. Continue flipping steak every 30 seconds for 3 more minutes.

2 Slide steak to back of skillet, opposite handle, and add butter to front of skillet. Once butter has melted and begun to foam, add shallot, garlic, and thyme sprigs. Holding skillet handle, tilt skillet so butter pools near base of handle. Use metal spoon to continuously spoon butter and aromatics over steak, concentrating on areas where crust is less browned. Baste steak, flipping it every 30 seconds, until steak registers 120 to 125 degrees (for medium-rare), 1 to 2 minutes.

3 Remove skillet from heat and transfer steak to cutting board; tent with aluminum foil and let rest for 10 minutes. Discard aromatics from pan and transfer butter mixture to small bowl. Cut meat from bone (if bone-in), slice steak thin against grain, and serve with butter mixture.

Can I Supplement the Iron in My Diet by Cooking in Cast Iron?

Unfortunately for those looking for an easy way to increase their iron intake, not really. When we tested the amount of iron present in tomato sauces that had been simmered in seasoned and unseasoned cast-iron pans, only the sauces cooked in unseasoned cast iron contained an appreciable amount of added iron. Sauces cooked in seasoned pans contained only a few more milligrams of iron than tomato sauce that was cooked in a stainless-steel pot. Because you wouldn't use an unseasoned pan for cooking (and would be left with unpleasantly metallic-tasting food and a damaged pan if you did so), we don't think you should count on cast-iron cooking to supplement your iron intake.

Hannah Says . . .

Lightweight cast-iron pans are a little easier to maneuver than thicker and heavier traditional cast iron, but that comes with a big tradeoff: Lightweight pans aren't very good at holding on to heat. In my opinion, that defeats the whole purpose of cooking with cast iron. If you want a lighter, more agile pan, opt instead for stainless steel or carbon steel.

SOUTHERN-STYLE CORNBREAD

serves 8

Cast iron is coveted for its ability to hold on to heat. Here, preheating a cast-iron skillet before pouring in the batter results in cornbread with crispy, well-browned edges. You will need a 10-inch cast-iron pan for this recipe. You can use any type of fine- or medium-ground cornmeal here; do not use coarse-ground cornmeal.

2¼	cups (11¼ ounces) stone-ground yellow cornmeal
1½	cups sour cream
½	cup whole milk
¼	cup vegetable oil
5	tablespoons unsalted butter
2	tablespoons sugar
1	teaspoon baking powder
1	teaspoon baking soda
¾	teaspoon table salt
2	large eggs

1 Adjust oven rack to middle position and heat oven to 450 degrees. Toast cornmeal in 10-inch cast-iron skillet over medium heat, stirring frequently, until fragrant, about 3 minutes. Transfer cornmeal to large bowl, whisk in sour cream and milk, and set aside.

2 Wipe skillet clean with paper towels. Add oil to now-empty skillet, place skillet in oven, and heat until oil is shimmering, about 10 minutes. Using potholders, remove skillet from oven, carefully add butter, and gently swirl to incorporate. Being careful of hot skillet handle, pour all but 1 tablespoon oil-butter mixture into cornmeal mixture and whisk to incorporate. Whisk sugar, baking powder, baking soda, and salt into cornmeal mixture until combined, then whisk in eggs.

3 Quickly scrape batter into skillet with remaining fat and smooth top. Transfer skillet to oven and bake until top begins to crack and sides are golden brown, 12 to 15 minutes, rotating skillet halfway through baking. Using potholders, transfer skillet to wire rack and let cornbread cool for at least 15 minutes before serving.

Do I Need to Season My Cast-Iron Skillet?

Seasoning involves heating a thin layer of oil until it bonds with the pan in a process known as polymerization. Over time, these thin layers of polymerized oil build up to create a naturally nonstick, durable surface that keeps moisture away from the metal's surface so it can't rust.

These days almost all cast-iron skillets come preseasoned, and unless you have a skillet with significant damage, you'll almost never need to season one from scratch. Just make sure to dry your cast-iron skillet completely after each use, spread a very thin layer of oil over its entire surface, and heat it until the surface looks dry.

What About My Carbon-Steel Skillet?

In contrast to cast-iron skillets, carbon-steel skillets often arrive unseasoned. Because carbon steel pans have such a smooth surface, it takes just a single application of oil for a new pan to be slick enough for cooking, but be aware that a new carbon-steel pan may look brown, blotchy, and streaky for months before it builds up a solid patina. Follow these steps to create that first layer of seasoning. Repeat these steps once if your food sticks the first time you try to cook in the pan.

1 Remove pan's wax or grease coating using very hot water, dish soap, and vigorous scrubbing with bristle brush. Dry pan, then put it over low heat to finish drying. Add ⅓ cup oil, ⅔ cup salt, and peels from two potatoes. (You can substitute one sliced onion for peels.)

2 Cook over medium heat, occasionally moving peels around pan and up sides to rim, 8 to 10 minutes. (If using onion, cook for 15 minutes or until onion turns very dark brown and almost burnt.)

3 Discard contents, allow pan to cool, and rinse thoroughly. Dry pan and return it to medium heat to finish drying.

Can My Rusty Old Cast-Iron or Carbon-Steel Pan Be Salvaged?

Unless that rusty pan has a large crack or hole running straight through it, it can be salvaged. You may think this means stripping and reseasoning it from scratch, but in fact, the vast majority of the time even a moderately rusty pan can be fixed without stripping it. No need to risk your oven (many manufacturers will void your oven's warranty if you use the self-cleaning cycle to strip a cast-iron pan) or resort to harsh chemicals—all you need is a little elbow grease.

First, give the pan a hearty scrub with steel wool to remove any crusty bits of old burnt-on food and scrape away the worst of the rust. Once the pan's surface is fairly smooth again, give it a rinse and dry it thoroughly. From there, simply spread a superthin layer of oil all over the pan, heat it on the stove until the oil bakes on, and repeat a few times until the pan looks black and glossy once more. Voilà! Good as new.

FREQUENTLY ASKED QUESTIONS: SEASONING EDITION

Q: What's the best type of oil to use?

A: You can use any type of cooking oil or fat you prefer, but we recommend using a plant-based oil such as vegetable or canola. The more unsaturated the oil, the more readily it will oxidize and polymerize.

Q: Is it OK to clean my cast-iron pan with soap?

A: It's fine to use a little soap, but you really don't have to. Rinse the pan with steamy hot tap water and scrub with a stiff-bristled brush and the mess will dissolve away. Then all you need to do is wipe the pan dry, rub a very thin layer of oil all over it, heat it, and let that oil bond to the surface.

Q: Is it ever OK to cook acidic foods in cast iron?

A: If you have an enameled cast-iron skillet, you can cook all the highly acidic foods you like with impunity. If you have a traditional cast-iron skillet, you can cook acidic foods, but you'll want to use a little more care. First, make sure your pan is well seasoned; seasoning keeps the acid from interacting with the iron—to a point. We found we could simmer tomato sauce in a cast-iron skillet for up to 30 minutes before detecting a metallic flavor. Second, don't let acidic foods sit in the skillet for too long after they finish cooking; quickly transfer any leftovers to a storage container and clean your pan promptly.

real talk with lisa

YOUR PANS ARE MADE OF TOUGH STUFF

I once discovered three carbon-steel half-sheet pans that had been left outside on the ground by my back porch for years. (An old housemate had planned to throw them out but never actually did it.) I realized what they were, brought them in, and scrubbed and heated and oiled them right on the stove, moving them around over the burner. I've been using them for the past four or five years—they're now gorgeously seasoned and good as new. So if a thin sheet of carbon steel wasn't destroyed by rusting in a New England backyard, a thick cast-iron pan isn't going to be easily taken out of the game, either.

Nonstick

Seventy percent of the skillets sold in the US are nonstick; chances are there's one somewhere in your kitchen. Here's what you should know to use it efficiently and safely.

Should I Spring for a Premium Nonstick Skillet?

Price is very important to us when evaluating nonstick skillets. Nonstick coating technology has come a long way in recent years; whereas nonstick skillets used to have a life expectancy of only about two to three years, these days a good skillet could last up to five to seven years if treated right. That's a big improvement, but to us a nonstick skillet still just isn't worth investing in the way a cast-iron, carbon-steel, or stainless-steel skillet is. When you buy one of these other pans, it's the start of a lifelong relationship; nonstick, by comparison, is a temporary fling.

Our recommendation? Don't bother spending hundreds on a nonstick pan. It won't last longer than a pan that costs a fraction as much, and you're setting yourself up for regret when, a few years down the line, it's time to move on.

Lisa Says . . .

Silicone handles are comfy, but most aren't ovensafe above 400 degrees or so. That's why I prefer plain metal handles: Well-designed ones stay cool on the stovetop and provide a secure grip, and I can transfer my skillet from stovetop to oven worry-free.

PAN-FRIED SOLE

serves 4

Nonstick skillets excel at cooking delicate foods such as these flaky fish fillets. Try to purchase fillets that are of similar size. If using smaller fillets (3 ounces each), serve two fillets per person and reduce the cooking time on the second side to about 1 minute. You will need to cook smaller fillets in three or four batches and wipe out the skillet with paper towels after the second and third batches to prevent any browned bits from scorching.

4	(6- to 8-ounce) skinless sole fillets, split lengthwise down natural seam
½	teaspoon table salt
¼	teaspoon pepper
½	cup all-purpose flour
2	tablespoons vegetable oil, divided
2	tablespoons unsalted butter, cut into 2 pieces, divided
	Lemon wedges

1 Adjust oven rack to middle position and heat oven to 200 degrees. Pat sole dry with paper towels and sprinkle with salt and pepper. Spread flour in shallow dish. Dredge sole in flour, shaking off excess, and transfer to large plate.

2 Heat 1 tablespoon oil in 12-inch nonstick skillet over medium-high heat until shimmering. Add 1 tablespoon butter and swirl until melted. Add thick halves of fillets to skillet and cook until golden on first side, about 3 minutes. Using 2 spatulas, flip fillets and cook until second sides are golden and fish flakes apart when gently prodded with paring knife, about 2 minutes. Transfer to ovensafe platter and keep warm in oven. Wipe skillet clean with paper towels and repeat with remaining 1 tablespoon oil, remaining 1 tablespoon butter, and thin halves of fillets. Serve with lemon wedges.

How Can I Make My Nonstick Skillet Last Longer?

Over years of testing and daily use of nonstick cookware, we've learned a few things about how (not) to treat it for optimal performance.

DON'T: Use metal utensils, including spatulas, whisks, and slotted spoons, in the skillet. These will scratch the non-stick coating. Instead, choose wooden spoons or silicone-coated utensils.

DON'T: Cut food directly in the skillet.

DON'T: Put it in the dishwasher (see page 47).

DON'T: Preheat the skillet empty or put it under the broiler. (See "Are Nonstick Coatings Safe?" for more on why very high temperatures should be avoided.)

DON'T: Stack it with other pans. If you must stack it, use a soft cloth, paper plate, or paper towels as a buffer between the nonstick pan and others.

DON'T: Put the hot skillet under cold water. The sudden temperature change can cause the metal to warp.

Following these guidelines can help prevent your pan from meeting an early demise, but keep in mind that no matter how gently you treat nonstick cookware, it won't last forever. Once you notice big scratches, flaking coating, or food sticking on a regular basis, it's time to replace.

What Do You Mean, I Should Season My Nonstick Skillet?

You can extend the life of a nonstick skillet that's starting to become a little less nonstick by seasoning it. Unlike seasoning cast iron or carbon steel, here the oil doesn't get hot enough to polymerize into a natural nonstick barrier. Instead, the oil fills in microscopic holes and cracks in the skillet's surface, which can quickly improve the performance of a skillet that's become slightly sticky over time. Here's how.

See Lisa and Hannah in action as they test the limits of nonstick skillets.

1 Place clean, dry skillet over medium heat for about 30 seconds. (This is just long enough to warm the skillet without it getting hot enough to lead to off-gassing.)

2 Apply small amount of canola or vegetable oil to skillet and use folded paper towel or cloth to rub oil across entire surface of skillet. Turn off heat, let skillet cool, then wipe out any excess oil.

Are Nonstick Coatings Safe?

Talk about a controversial question.

Here's what you should know. Traditional nonstick coatings are made by spraying anywhere from one to five layers of a nonstick coating over a metal (usually aluminum) base. Traditional nonstick coatings contain a compound called polytetrafluoroethylene (PTFE), which makes them strong, flexible, and slick. These coatings gradually degrade and become less nonstick with use, and are easily scratched by metal tools or abrasive cleaners. But the real concern is the "off-gassing" that can occur when PTFE coatings are heated above 500 degrees Fahrenheit; at these temperatures, the coatings begin to break down and release fumes that, in high enough concentrations, can be harmful.

How concerning is this, really? Well, it is good to take some precautions when using nonstick cookware. For one, don't heat empty nonstick pans; always add some oil first, since cooking oil will begin to smoke before the pan reaches a dangerous temperature. Avoid turning to nonstick pans when using high-heat cooking methods. You should also follow your pan's manufacturer's instructions regarding using your pan in the oven. Carefully following these steps will mitigate the dangers of PTFE nonstick coatings.

If you're still concerned, you might consider opting for an alternative to traditional nonstick pans, such as ceramic nonstick. Cast-iron and carbon-steel pans (see pages 36–40) are also good alternatives, since they become naturally nonstick with use.

Can My Nonstick Skillet Go in the Oven?

Because the coatings of nonstick skillets make them less ovensafe than stainless-steel or cast-iron skillets, we call for putting them in the oven only occasionally. We never broil food in a nonstick skillet; a properly functioning broiler will quickly heat cookware to more than 500 degrees, which can damage the nonstick coating and potentially cause PTFE-based coatings to emit unsafe fumes. The silicone handles of some nonstick skillets can be problematic, too. Most of those handles aren't ovensafe at temperatures greater than 400 degrees.

Lisa Says . . .

Using nonstick cooking spray on your nonstick pan won't make your pan more nonstick. It will actually do the opposite, by clinging to and gunking up its surface. A little bit of oil should be all you need to get food to slide right off your nonstick skillet. If that isn't working, it may be time to replace it.

real talk with hannah

WHY MY NONSTICK PAN IS GATHERING DUST

I have at least one skillet of every style in my kitchen. Which one gathers the most dust? Nonstick. I don't like the idea of cooking on plastic and worrying about off-gassing with PTFE-coated pans, and most ceramic pans are just so fallible. I bought a 10-inch ceramic pan to try, and the first time I used it I wasn't paying attention and cooked over high heat. Just like that, the nonstick ceramic surface was ruined. What's the point of a nonstick pan that's lost its nonstick ability? I prefer pans made of cast iron and carbon steel. Yes, you have to dry and oil them after washing, but you don't have to baby them while cooking.

head to head

NONSTICK SKILLETS

PTFE-COATED NONSTICK SKILLETS	CERAMIC-COATED NONSTICK SKILLETS
PTFE is an insulator, so pans heat slightly slower	Ceramic conducts heat, so pans heat more quickly
PTFE coating is more flexible and less likely to be damaged during everyday use	Ceramic coating is more brittle and likely to develop microscopic cracks during everyday use
Degrade and release fumes at temperatures above 500 degrees Fahrenheit	Do not off-gas at high temperatures
Food is less likely to stick	Food is more likely to stick

OMELET WITH CHEDDAR AND CHIVES

makes 1 omelet

An 8-inch nonstick skillet is the ideal vessel for cooking a single, perfectly formed rolled omelet.

3	large eggs
	Pinch table salt
1	ounce extra-sharp cheddar cheese, shredded (¼ cup)
1½	teaspoons unsalted butter
1½	teaspoons chopped fresh chives

1 Beat eggs and salt in bowl until few streaks of white remain.

2 Sprinkle cheese in even layer on small plate. Microwave at 50 percent power until cheese is just melted, 30 to 60 seconds. Set aside.

3 Melt butter in 8-inch nonstick skillet over medium heat, swirling skillet to distribute butter across skillet bottom. When butter sizzles evenly across skillet bottom, add eggs. Cook, stirring constantly with rubber spatula and breaking up large curds, until eggs are mass of small to medium curds surrounded by small amount of liquid egg. Immediately remove skillet from heat.

4 Working quickly, scrape eggs from sides of skillet, then smooth into even layer. Using fork, fold cheese into 2-inch-wide strip and transfer to center of eggs perpendicular to handle. Cover for 1 minute. Remove lid and run spatula underneath perimeter of eggs to loosen omelet. Gently ease spatula under eggs and slide omelet toward edge of skillet opposite handle until edge of omelet is even with lip of skillet. Using spatula, fold egg on handle side of skillet over filling. With your nondominant hand, grasp handle with underhand grip and hold skillet at 45-degree angle over top half of plate. Slowly tilt skillet toward yourself while using spatula to gently roll omelet onto plate. Sprinkle chives over omelet and serve.

worth it

8-INCH NONSTICK SKILLET

For some jobs, grabbing a petite 8-inch skillet is just easier than pulling out a full-size version. Make it a nonstick 8-inch skillet, and you have the ultimate egg-frying, flipping, omelet-ing vessel—lightweight, maneuverable, and easy to clean. They also excel at cooking scaled-down recipes and for toasting nuts, bread crumbs, spices, and more.

5 Tips for Handling Your Skillets Like a Pro

Chances are, you've made at least one common skillet-cooking mistake before. Maybe you've spilled half the contents of your fully loaded skillet onto the stovetop with an overly ambitious stir or toss, or maybe you've experienced the heartbreak of removing a perfectly good nonstick skillet from the dishwasher to find its nonstick coating compromised. No more. Learn what the pros know (and avoid future mishaps) with these tips.

1 SKILLET TOSS LIKE A BOSS

When executed correctly, a skillet toss—the flick of the wrist that sends food arcing up from the pan and then landing neatly back into the same pan—not only makes you look cool, but also quickly redistributes food across the pan. This helps it heat more evenly, and the agitation can also help emulsify sauces.

Before you try it yourself, you'll want to make sure you're using a lightweight skillet with sloped edges. You'll also want to practice a few times off the heat. We recommend using something light, like marshmallows or chunks of bread, to practice with until you get the hang of the motion. Start with gentle, small tosses so it's easier to catch the food; you can toss with more height once you get the hang of the motion.

1 Shake pan gently to ensure no food is stuck. Tilt skillet down and push forward to slide food to front of skillet.

2 Flick your wrist to send food into air, then immediately pull skillet back to gently catch food.

Lisa Says . . .

You can go your whole life cooking beautifully without ever once doing a skillet toss. It's a shortcut that comes in handy for busy restaurant cooks, but people don't really need to do this at home. You can modify the idea by giving your pan a good shake to redistribute food in the skillet even if you never lift it off the heat. If you want to learn how, that's fine. It is kinda cool, but you don't have to master it. Seriously.

2 (ALMOST) ALWAYS PREHEAT YOUR SKILLET

Preheating your skillet for at least a few minutes makes for more even cooking. When food meets an already-hot surface, it quickly begins to sear and form tasty fond, and it's also much less likely to stick (see page 33 to learn why). In contrast, adding food to a cold skillet makes it much more likely to steam and become soggy as the pan slowly comes up to temperature. That's why we recommend that you (almost) always preheat your skillet. Just add a little bit of oil and set it over medium or medium-high heat; when the oil begins to shimmer or just starts to smoke, you know your pan is hot and ready to go.

One exception: Skip the preheating if a recipe calls for using the cold-start technique, which involves adding protein to a cold pan and allowing its fat to render slowly as the pan heats.

3 WASH BY HAND

Straight talk: Don't put your good cookware in the dishwasher. Why? The high heat and harsh detergents used in a dishwasher cycle can corrode metal and dry out the surface of your pans—even stainless-steel ones. Dish detergent will also break down the seasoning on your cast-iron and carbon-steel pans and, if your dishwasher doesn't get them completely dry, this will lead to rusty patches that you'll need to scrub away and reseason. (See page 40 for how to properly clean cast iron and carbon steel.) And nonstick coatings (both PTFE-based and ceramic) are delicate; even if the manufacturer of your skillet claims that it's dishwasher safe, you may find that its nonstick ability is dramatically reduced after a trip through the dishwasher.

We know no one loves washing dishes by hand, but when it comes to the longevity and performance of your skillets, it really is worth it to roll up your sleeves and do it yourself.

4 MAKE A DISCOLORED STAINLESS-STEEL SKILLET SHINE

You may find your previously spotless stainless-steel skillet coated with a layer of sticky, discolored residue that ordinary dish soap seems powerless to touch after cooking over high heat with lots of oil. This is actually desirable when it happens to cast iron or carbon steel (see page 39 for more about this process, known as seasoning) but not when it happens to your good stainless-steel skillet.

The good news is, it's fixable. All you need is some Bar Keepers Friend, a product that contains surfactant, oxalic acid, and mineral abrasive to break down and physically scrape away grease. With a little effort your pan will be spotless again in no time.

5 GENTLY LIFT UP BURNT-ON MESSES

To get burnt-on food off of your pans, just fill the pan with water and set it to a simmer. Soon, the hot water will rehydrate the burnt food and most of it will begin to lift right off. Any remaining residue should come off with a few passes of a soft sponge.

An Unparalleled Pot

A Dutch oven is many cooks' desert island pot—the one cooking vessel they couldn't do without. Considering all the things this mighty and versatile vessel can do, that comes as no surprise to us.

Do I Need to Spend Hundreds on a Dutch Oven?

In our experience, there are two good reasons why you want to spend more. First, pricier models are less likely to chip or get damaged over time. Treat them right, and you may never have to buy another Dutch oven again. And second, they're often lighter-weight than less expensive models, making them easier to maneuver and wash. That said, you can absolutely find a good Dutch oven for hundreds of dollars less than you'd spend on one from a premium brand.

How Do I Keep My Dutch Oven Looking Pristine?

We like to say that a Dutch oven is a tool, not a piece of art—the minor stains and dings it acquires over time are a testament to all the good things you've made in it. But if you have a Dutch oven with a light-colored interior, it is worth giving it a thorough cleaning now and then to prevent darkening that can make it harder to monitor your food's browning. To remove stains, just let a solution of 1 part bleach to 3 parts water sit in the pot (in a well ventilated area away from pets and children) overnight, then pour it out and rinse very well.

If you've got a stubborn burnt-on mess to contend with, fill the pot with water and bring it to a simmer. The stuck-on food will begin to lift right off. After dumping out the water and letting the pot cool, you can swipe up any remaining residue with a sponge.

And finally, to keep an enameled Dutch oven looking its best, treat the coating with a certain amount of care to avoid chipping. As tempting as it is to whack utensils against the rim of the pot to dislodge food, don't do it. This is one of the easiest ways to chip the enamel.

What If a Standard Dutch Oven Is Too Heavy for Me?

Most Dutch ovens are made from enameled cast iron, and as such they're heavy. Luckily, lightweight versions made from stainless steel can do nearly everything their heavier siblings can do. The exception: They don't retain heat as well, so they aren't as good for tasks such as baking bread.

Most of the same criteria that make for a good cast-iron Dutch oven also apply to lightweight versions: You want one that holds 6 to 7 quarts of food; has low, straight sides and a broad, light-colored cooking surface; and has large, looped handles. And since we're talking about lightweight Dutch ovens, after all, they should ideally weigh only 6.5 pounds or less—far lighter than cast iron.

We half-submerged a stained Dutch oven in a bleach solution overnight to demonstrate how effectively the solution removes stains.

anatomy of

A GOOD DUTCH OVEN

LIGHT-COLORED INTERIOR

Makes it easier to monitor browning

LOW, STRAIGHT SIDES

Offer better visibility and allow sauces to reduce more quickly

BROAD COOKING SURFACE

Allows you to cook more food at once without overcrowding

CAST-IRON CONSTRUCTION

Is durable and has excellent heat retention

LARGE, LOOPED HANDLES

Are easy to grip, even while wearing oven mitts

FREQUENTLY ASKED QUESTIONS: DUTCH OVEN EDITION

Q: What size should I get?

A: If you have room for only one Dutch oven in your kitchen (and let's be real, how many of us actually have the room and/or budget for more?), a large 6- to 7-quart Dutch oven is the most versatile size you can buy. That said, smaller Dutch ovens are lighter and more maneuverable, which can be a big plus. A medium 5-quart pot may be a good option if you need something a little lighter and rarely deep-fry or cook for a crowd. Three-quart pots are great for smaller jobs such as cooking grains or making meals for one or two people.

Q: Does my Dutch oven have to be enameled?

A: Most cast-iron Dutch ovens are covered in a layer of enamel, a type of glass, but you can find models that are uncoated. While you don't have to worry about chipping the enamel with uncoated cast-iron pots, they do require extra care, since you'll need to dry and oil them immediately after use as you would a cast-iron skillet. Their dark interiors make it harder to monitor your food's browning and the formation of fond, but uncoated pots resist staining and, because they conduct heat well, they're great for producing browned, crusty bread.

Q: Can I use metal utensils with an enameled cast-iron Dutch oven?

A: You can, but you should be gentle to avoid chipping the enamel. Don't whack your utensils against the rim of the pot to dislodge food, don't scrape metal utensils against the bottom of the pot using repetitive motions, and don't use sharp knives to cut food directly in the pot.

Q: Is chipped enamel dangerous?

A: The enamel on your Dutch oven is basically a layer of glass coating the raw cast iron beneath. While chipped enamel can certainly be a bummer (especially considering how pricey some of these pots are), it's still safe to use your pot. Just make sure there are no loose pieces of chipped enamel in the pot before you use it and, if it's a large chip, take care to dry the exposed cast iron well to avoid rust.

Q: Can I use my Dutch oven on a glass stovetop?

A: These pots tend to be pretty heavy, so you'll need to be careful when moving them around on delicate surfaces such as a glass stovetop. Don't slam your Dutch oven down or drag it across the glass; instead, pick it up and set it down gently to move it on and off the burner.

Can I Use My Dutch Oven for Deep Frying?

A Dutch oven is a great choice for deep frying, especially in large batches. It's big enough to hold lots of oil and food, and its straight sides contain most splatters while providing good visibility. Here are our top tips for using yours to turn out great fried food.

1 Make sure to fill the pot no more than halfway with oil to avoid splattering once food is added. Follow the guidelines in individual recipes for how high the oil level in the pot should be.

2 Use a clip-on or remote probe thermometer to gauge how hot the oil is; this type of thermometer stays out of your way while it gives you a constant reading of the temperature (see page 93 for more information).

3 Add food to the hot oil in batches so it's easier to manage. (Also, even in a Dutch oven, overcrowding the pot will make the temperature drop too much and will result in soggy—rather than crispy—fried food.)

4 Prepare a landing spot for the food as it comes out of the pot. A wire rack set in a baking sheet contains crumbs and drips while keeping food crispy.

5 Have tongs, a spider skimmer, or a slotted spoon (see page 95) handy to remove food from the oil and make sure to drain the food over the pot before transferring it to the wire rack.

6 Unless you're frying fish or the oil has started to smoke, you can reuse the cooking oil up to three times; let it cool and then strain it through a fine-mesh strainer lined with a coffee filter. Store it in an airtight container in the freezer. (See page 354 for information on disposing of cooking oil.)

Why Is a Light Interior So Important?

Dutch ovens with light interiors provide better visibility than ones with dark interiors. When searing foods, you need to monitor how dark the fond is getting so it doesn't burn, and that's harder to do against a dark backdrop. And when you're using a thermometer for frying, a light interior makes it easier to ensure that the tip of the probe isn't touching the pot, which can cause it to give a false reading.

real talk with hannah

YOUR DUTCH OVEN CAN DO IT ALL

My Dutch oven is the busiest pot in my kitchen. It's so stained from use I can't even take cute food pictures in it until I clean it up a bit. I cook a lot of rigatoni (my favorite pasta) in it. (My husband loves spaghetti, it's a point of contention.) I drain the pasta and build a sauce right in the Dutch oven before combining everything, because as far as I'm concerned, the fewer dishes, the better. I also love to roast a whole chicken on top of potatoes and shallots for an incredible one-pot main-and-side combo. And as a huge fan of deep-fried food, I use my Dutch oven for deep frying all the time; it's big enough to hold plenty of oil and its straight sides keep splatters contained. And I love baking crusty loaves of bread and homey fruit desserts; the Dutch oven holds enough to make apple pandowdy for a crowd.

real talk with hannah

PRAISE THE BRAISE(R)

I didn't know what a braiser was until I was gifted one years ago for my wedding. Now this pan, which is like a cross between a skillet and a Dutch oven, is one of my favorite cooking and serving vessels. As its name suggests, it's great for braising, but braised recipes are only a small fraction of what I use my braiser for. Shakshuka, sautéed greens, roast chicken, paella, and a giant blueberry crumble are just a few of the things I've made recently in mine. They're great for anything that doesn't have a ton of liquid (deeper pots are better for that). Bonus: It's so pretty that it can go right from the stove to the table, making it one of my favorite serving vessels to break out for parties.

Lisa Says . . .

The phenolic knobs found on some older Dutch ovens are ovensafe only to 390 degrees (check the owner's manual). So if you plan to put the covered pot in the oven at higher temps, you may need to buy a replacement knob made of metal. You can also simply remove it and cover the pot with foil before putting the lid on to get a good seal.

Is an Oval Dutch Oven Good for Anything?

We prefer round Dutch ovens because their shape better conforms to that of a standard stove burner, so they heat more evenly. That's not to say you can't cook with an oval Dutch oven; simply preheat it for longer before you begin cooking to allow more time for heat to conduct across the pot's entire surface. One thing oval Dutch ovens excel at? Baking rustic bâtard-shaped (oblong) loaves of bread. A round Dutch oven is better for making boule-shaped (round) loaves like in the recipe at right.

SPICY OLIVE BREAD

makes 1 loaf

Using a Dutch oven in conjunction with your regular oven, you can bake amazing loaves of artisan-style bread with open crumbs and crackly, caramelized crusts. The Dutch oven traps heat and steam, acting like a miniature bread oven. Almost any variety of brined or oil-cured olive works in this recipe. Use a round Dutch oven here.

¾	cup pitted olives, rinsed, patted dry, and chopped coarse
2	garlic cloves, minced
3	cups (16½ ounces) bread flour
2	teaspoons instant or rapid-rise yeast
2	teaspoons table salt
2	teaspoons red pepper flakes
1⅓	cups (10⅔ ounces) water, room temperature
2	tablespoons sugar
1	tablespoon extra-virgin olive oil

1 Combine olives and garlic in bowl. Whisk flour, yeast, salt, and pepper flakes together in bowl of stand mixer. Whisk water, sugar, and oil in 2-cup liquid measuring cup until sugar has dissolved. Using dough hook on low speed, slowly add water mixture to flour mixture and mix until cohesive dough starts to form and no dry flour remains, about 2 minutes, scraping down bowl as needed.

2 Increase speed to medium-low and knead until dough is smooth and elastic and clears sides of bowl, about 8 minutes. Reduce speed to low; slowly add olive mixture, ¼ cup at a time; and mix until mostly incorporated, about 1 minute. Transfer dough and any loose olives to lightly floured counter and knead by hand to form smooth, round ball, about 30 seconds. Place dough, seam side down, in lightly greased large bowl or container, cover tightly with plastic wrap, and let rise until nearly doubled in size, 1½ to 2 hours.

3 Lay 18 by 12-inch sheet of parchment paper on counter and lightly spray with vegetable oil spray. Transfer dough to lightly floured counter. Using your lightly floured hands, press and stretch dough into 10-inch round, deflating any gas pockets larger than 1 inch. Working around circumference of dough, fold edges toward center until ball forms. Flip dough ball seam side down and, using your cupped hands, drag in small circles on counter until dough feels taut and round and all seams are secured on underside of loaf.

4 Place loaf, seam side down, in center of prepared parchment and cover loosely with greased plastic wrap. Let rise until loaf increases in size by about half and dough springs back minimally when poked gently with your knuckle, 30 minutes to 1 hour.

5 Thirty minutes before baking, adjust oven rack to lower-middle position, place Dutch oven (with lid) on rack, and heat oven to 500 degrees. Holding sharp paring knife or single-edge razor blade at 30-degree angle to loaf, make two 5-inch-long, ½-inch-deep slashes with swift, fluid motion along top of loaf to form cross.

6 Carefully transfer pot to wire rack and uncover. Using parchment as sling, gently lower dough into Dutch oven. Cover pot, tucking any excess parchment into pot, and return to oven. Reduce oven temperature to 425 degrees and bake loaf for 15 minutes. Uncover and continue to bake until loaf is deep golden brown and registers 205 to 210 degrees, about 20 minutes.

7 Using parchment sling, remove loaf from pot and transfer to wire rack; discard parchment. Let cool completely, about 3 hours, before serving.

Through years of daily use in the test kitchen, we've learned that a Dutch oven can do even more than we thought—and we already knew it could do quite a bit. Some of these Dutch oven hacks have made their way into my home cooking. I reach for my heavy Dutch oven when I need to press tofu, press a butterflied chicken, or weigh down sandwiches for paninis. I often use the inverted lid as a rest for greasy utensils or as a makeshift platter for browned pieces of chicken, beef, or pork when I'm cooking in batches. Sometimes I even pop the whole pot into the refrigerator to chill and then use it as a serving vessel for salad or other foods that need to stay cold, since the thick cast-iron walls stay cold much longer than a glass or plastic bowl would.

BEST CHICKEN STEW

serves 6 to 8

In most recipes, fond (flavorful browned bits) forms primarily on the bottom of the pot or skillet as food is seared, but in this recipe, the sides of the Dutch oven provide more than double the amount of surface area for extra fond formation. You can substitute mashed anchovy fillets (rinsed and dried before mashing) for the anchovy paste. Use small red potatoes 1½ inches in diameter.

2	pounds boneless, skinless chicken thighs, halved crosswise and trimmed
½	teaspoon table salt
½	teaspoon pepper
3	slices bacon, chopped
1	pound chicken wings, cut at joint
1	onion, chopped fine
1	celery rib, minced
2	garlic cloves, minced
2	teaspoons anchovy paste
1	teaspoon minced fresh thyme or ¼ teaspoon dried
5	cups chicken broth, divided
1	cup dry white wine, plus extra for seasoning
1	tablespoon soy sauce
3	tablespoons unsalted butter, cut into 3 pieces
⅓	cup all-purpose flour
1	pound small red potatoes, unpeeled, quartered
4	carrots, peeled and cut into ½-inch pieces
2	tablespoons chopped fresh parsley

1 Adjust oven rack to lower-middle position and heat oven to 325 degrees. Arrange chicken thighs on rimmed baking sheet and sprinkle with salt and pepper; cover with plastic wrap and set aside.

2 Cook bacon in Dutch oven over medium-low heat, stirring occasionally, until crispy, 5 to 7 minutes. Using slotted spoon, transfer bacon to bowl. Add chicken wings to fat left in pot, increase heat to medium, and cook until well browned on both sides, 10 to 12 minutes; transfer to bowl with bacon.

3 Add onion, celery, garlic, anchovy paste, and thyme to fat left in pot. Cook, stirring occasionally, until dark fond forms on bottom of pot, 2 to 4 minutes. Increase heat to high. Stir in 1 cup broth, wine, and soy sauce, scraping up any browned bits, and bring to boil. Cook, stirring occasionally, until almost dry and vegetables begin to sizzle again, 12 to 15 minutes.

4 Add butter and stir until melted. Stir in flour and cook for 1 minute. Slowly whisk in remaining 4 cups broth, scraping up any browned bits and smoothing out any lumps. Stir in potatoes, carrots, wings, and bacon and bring to simmer. Transfer pot to oven and cook, uncovered, for 30 minutes, stirring once halfway through cooking.

5 Remove pot from oven. Use wooden spoon to draw gravy up sides of pot and scrape browned bits into stew. Stir in thighs and bring to simmer over high heat. Return pot to oven, uncovered, and cook, stirring occasionally, until chicken and vegetables are tender, about 45 minutes.

6 Remove pot from oven. Discard wings and season stew with up to 2 tablespoons extra wine. Stir in parsley and season with salt and pepper to taste. Serve.

Wok Your World

Cooks have briskly tossed, stirred, and flipped food in this vessel for centuries. But is a wok worth keeping in your kitchen?

Will a Wok Work on My Stove?

Woks have traditionally been used on Chinese stoves with pit-shaped burners. These concave burners cradle the wok and heat the entire outside surface, not just the bottom. The round-bottomed woks that are typically used with this type of burner just aren't well suited for a flat Western-style stove burner; the lack of contact with the heating element makes the woks inefficient at conducting heat from the burner to the food. This issue is even worse when cooking with electric or induction burners, which depend on making direct contact with the pan, than with gas.

Enter the flat-bottomed wok. While not traditional, they're our choice for cooking on a Western stove. The flattened bottom allows this type of wok to have a good amount of direct contact with the heating element, so it gets hot and stays hot even as you load it up with ingredients—and even when using it on an electric or induction burner. When using a wok on an electric or conduction burner, just preheat it for a few extra minutes to give the heat time to conduct up the sides before you begin to cook.

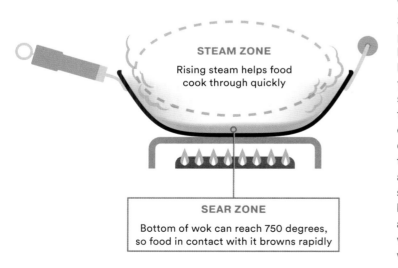

STEAM ZONE

Rising steam helps food cook through quickly

SEAR ZONE

Bottom of wok can reach 750 degrees, so food in contact with it browns rapidly

What Makes Woks So Good For Stir-Frying?

Stir-frying involves using high heat to cook food so rapidly that proteins brown uniformly and vegetables lose their raw edge but retain their vibrant color and fresh crunch. One obvious benefit of cooking in a wok is that its high, sloping walls allow you to move food easily all around the cooking surface without spilling it over the sides, but a wok's tall sides also create two distinct heat zones that work in tandem to cook food efficiently and evenly. The bottom of the wok, which makes direct contact with the heat source, can reach scorching temperatures of up to 750 degrees Fahrenheit, which cooks and browns food rapidly. (This is one reason we think you should never buy a nonstick wok; see page 43 for more on how nonstick coatings react to high heat.) The second zone, a couple inches above the wok's base, is the steam zone, where the moisture escaping from the food is trapped by the wok's walls and works to cook the food through even more quickly. And the vigorous stirring process itself helps food cook through faster by ensuring that all the food's surfaces come into contact with the hot pan.

What Are the Best Woks Made Of?

After testing woks made of cast iron, lightweight cast iron, and carbon steel, we found that we greatly prefer woks made of carbon steel. Carbon-steel woks are lighter and more responsive to heat than cast-iron woks, making it easier to maneuver them and regulate the heat.

We also like woks with long wooden handles that are angled slightly upward because they stay cool and offer better leverage and control.

My Wok Didn't Come with a Lid. Do I Need One?

Dome-shaped wok lids are handy for containing splatters and for steaming in your wok. If yours didn't come with one, you can buy one separately; just look for lids made to fit 14-inch woks (and note that because the lid sits *inside* the wok, a lid designed to fit a 14-inch wok will measure more like 12 inches from rim to rim).

How Should I Season My New Wok?

Our favorite woks are made of carbon steel, which needs a layer of seasoning to protect it from rust. Seasoning a wok works just the same way as seasoning a carbon-steel skillet (see page 39); just be sure to move the oil all the way up to the wok's rim so every bit of its surface gets coated.

What's Wok Hei?

Food cooked in a well-seasoned wok can acquire wok hei, a savory, fragrant essence that is the ultimate reward of a great stir-fry. Its unique flavor and aroma is hard to describe, but "smoky," "allium-like," "grilled," and "metallic" are some of the words we hear most frequently.

Wok cooking experts think wok hei flavor comes down to a few different factors: aroma compounds formed when oil gets very hot, chemical interactions between the food and components of the wok's seasoned steel, and the accelerated Maillard (browning) and caramelization reactions that happen when the heat is turned way up.

Lisa Says . . .

Wok rings are devices designed to support a round-bottomed wok on a flat Western-style stove—but don't bother buying one for your kitchen. These rings offer more stability, but they can't do anything about the lack of contact between a round-bottomed wok and a flat burner. Just get yourself a flat-bottomed wok.

How Should I Clean My Wok?

You've just stir-fried a gorgeous dinner and you're ready to serve—but hold on. It's important to clean your wok while it's still warm. Take a couple extra minutes to clean your wok and you'll be able to relax over your meal.

If your wok is well seasoned and no food is stuck, rinse your still-warm wok under hot tap water inside and out. (If food is stuck to your wok, add a few cups of water and bring it to a boil. This loosens the food so you can scrape it off.) If needed, scrub lightly. Wipe it dry and return the wok to the still-warm burner to dry it thoroughly. Go enjoy your dinner. After dinner, turn the burner to medium to medium-high, add a tiny amount (no more than ½ teaspoon) of vegetable oil, and wipe it around the entire interior of the wok using paper towels until it seems to be gone. (It's not.) Continue heating the wok for a few minutes, wiping away any oil that beads up, and then switch off the burner, leaving your clean, happy wok in place until it's cool.

And if your wok is looking a little rusty? Don't worry. The rust will disappear as soon as you get a layer of oil bonded on. Gently scrub off the rust with steel wool or the scrubby side of a sponge, rinse it well, dry it fully, and then oil the wok as above.

STIR-FRIED CUMIN LAMB

serves 4 to 6

There's no better tool for making stir-fries than a well-seasoned wok; the slick surface means no little pieces will get stuck and burn, and the high sides keep food contained during all that stirring. If lamb shoulder chops are unavailable, you can substitute 1 pound boneless leg of lamb or beef flank steak; trim meat and cut with grain into 2- to 2½-inch-wide strips before freezing and slicing. You can substitute 1 tablespoon of ground cumin for the cumin seeds.

2	(14- to 16-ounce) lamb shoulder chops (blade or round bone), ¾ to 1 inch thick
1	tablespoon water
¼	teaspoon baking soda
4	garlic cloves, minced
1	tablespoon grated fresh ginger
1	tablespoon cumin seeds, ground
2	teaspoons Sichuan chili flakes
1¼	teaspoons Sichuan peppercorns, ground
½	teaspoon sugar
4	teaspoons dark soy sauce
1	tablespoon Shaoxing wine
½	teaspoon cornstarch
¼	teaspoon table salt
5	teaspoons vegetable oil, divided
½	small onion, sliced thin
2	tablespoons coarsely chopped fresh cilantro

1 Cut bones from lamb and trim all visible connective tissue from meat; discard bones. (You should have about 1 pound of lamb after trimming.) Transfer lamb to plate and freeze until firm, about 15 minutes. Slice meat on bias against grain on bias ¼ inch thick. Combine water and baking soda in medium bowl. Add lamb and toss to coat; let sit for 5 minutes.

2 Combine garlic and ginger in small bowl. Combine cumin, chili flakes, peppercorns, and sugar in second small bowl. Add soy sauce, Shaoxing wine, cornstarch, and salt to lamb mixture and toss to coat.

3 Heat empty 14-inch flat-bottomed wok over high heat until just smoking, about 3 minutes. Drizzle 1 teaspoon oil around perimeter of wok and heat until just smoking. Add half of lamb mixture and cook, tossing slowly but constantly, until just cooked through, 1 to 3 minutes; transfer to clean bowl. Repeat with 1 teaspoon oil and remaining lamb mixture; transfer to bowl.

4 Heat remaining 1 tablespoon oil in now-empty wok over medium heat until shimmering. Add garlic mixture and cook, stirring constantly, until fragrant, 15 to 30 seconds. Add onion and cook, tossing slowly but constantly, until onion begins to soften, 1 to 2 minutes. Return lamb to wok and toss to combine. Sprinkle cumin mixture over lamb and toss until onion takes on pale orange color. Transfer to serving platter and sprinkle with cilantro. Serve.

Wok versus nonstick skillet: It's the ultimate stir-fry showdown. Check out our video to see which comes out on top.

What Else Can I Make in My Wok?

Woks are incredibly good for stir-frying, but their utility extends far beyond this one technique. They can be used for small-batch deep frying, although to fry larger amounts, you'll either need to fry in batches or turn to a Dutch oven. They can also be filled partway with water and used to boil, poach, and braise. Coupled with a dome-shaped wok cover, they can even be used to steam food or pop popcorn.

What's a Wok Chuan, and Do I Need One?

Wok chuan is the Cantonese name for the rounded, shovel-like spatulas that are traditionally used for moving and scooping food within a wok. The rounded edge fits nicely into the sides of a traditional round-bottomed wok, and its wide scoop makes it efficient at scooping up a large amount of food in one go. However, wok expert Grace Young notes that wok chuans' rounded shape make them ill-suited for use with the flat-bottomed woks we prefer using on Western-style burners. Instead, we recommend using a flexible multi-purpose spatula such as a fish spatula (see page 97) to move food around a flat-bottomed wok.

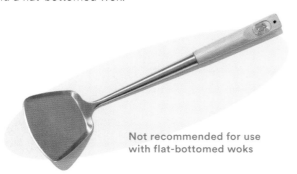

Not recommended for use with flat-bottomed woks

SHRIMP TOAST

serves 6 to 8

Because these finger sandwiches—born of a fusion of Hong Kong and British cuisine—are deep-fried in a wok they require only a couple quarts of oil to become crispy and golden. Any size shrimp can be used in this recipe.

1	pound shrimp, peeled, deveined, and tails removed, divided
1	large egg white
2	teaspoons grated fresh ginger
1	garlic clove, minced
1	teaspoon sugar
½	teaspoon table salt
	Pinch white pepper
6	slices hearty white sandwich bread
2	tablespoons sesame seeds
2	quarts peanut or vegetable oil for frying
2	scallions, sliced thin

1 Finely chop half of shrimp. Cut remaining shrimp into ½-inch pieces. Using wooden spoon or 4 bundled chop-sticks, vigorously stir all of shrimp, egg white, ginger, garlic, sugar, salt, and white pepper in bowl until mixture tightens and becomes very sticky, 2 to 3 minutes.

2 Remove crusts from bread and trim slices to measure roughly 3½ inches square. Spread shrimp mixture evenly over 1 side of each bread slice, then sprinkle with sesame seeds, pressing gently to adhere. (Coated bread can be covered and refrigerated for up to 24 hours.)

3 Set wire rack in rimmed baking sheet and line half of rack with triple layer of paper towels. Add oil to 14-inch flat-bottomed wok until it measures about 1½ inches deep and heat over medium-high heat to 350 degrees. Carefully add 3 slices of bread, shrimp side down, to hot oil and cook until edges of bread are golden brown, about 3 minutes. Adjust burner, if necessary, to maintain oil temperature between 325 and 350 degrees. Using tongs, flip toasts and continue to cook until bread is uniformly golden brown, 30 to 45 seconds.

4 Using spider skimmer or slotted spoon, transfer toasts, shrimp side up, to paper towel–lined side of prepared rack and let drain for 1 minute, then move to unlined side of rack. Return oil to 350 degrees and repeat with remaining toasts. (Before cooking second batch of toast, line rack with fresh layer of paper towels.) Let toasts cool for 5 minutes. Halve toasts diagonally and transfer to serving platter. Sprinkle with scallions and serve.

Good Sheet

Rimmed baking sheets are so versatile that we think at least one or two of them deserve a place in every kitchen. We use them to roast meats and vegetables, toast seeds and nuts, cool food, and bake all kinds of treats (see pages 219–223 for more on how we use them for baking).

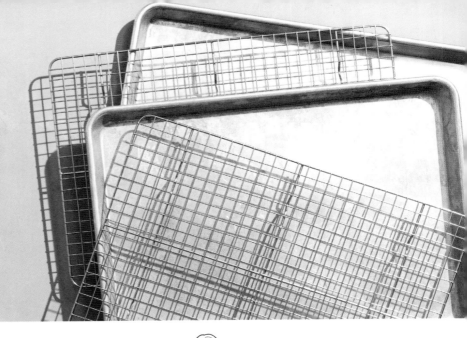

What's the Difference Between a Rimmed Baking Sheet and a Cookie Sheet?

Rimmed baking sheets, also called sheet pans, come in handy for so many different kitchen tasks that it's hard to name them all. We use them to bake cookies, roast vegetables and proteins, and toast nuts and seeds—we even occasionally use one as a makeshift pizza peel or baking stone (see page 251).

But is there a difference between a rimmed baking sheet and a cookie sheet? And are cookie sheets better for—ahem—cookies? Yes and maybe. The main difference between the two is that a cookie sheet lacks the low sides of a rimmed baking sheet, which can have a slight impact on how airflow passes over food. (See page 219 for more about cookie sheets.)

Why Do My Sheet Pans Always Warp in the Oven?

Warping happens thanks to the way that metal expands as it heats up. Flimsier pans are more likely to warp, but even a good pan can warp in the oven. Pro tip: Spread food evenly over the pan's entire surface to help cut down on warping. Unevenly filled pans will be hotter where there's no food, and thus more likely to warp. If your pans are warping all the time—and critically, if your warped pans don't more or less flatten out again when heated—it may be time to invest in sturdier ones.

Is It Bad If My Sheet Pans Are Dark and Stained?

Heated oil can polymerize and form a dark nonstick layer on your rimmed baking sheets just as it can on your skillet (when done intentionally, this process is known as seasoning). This can make your pans look blotchy or even nearly completely blackened—but it's not necessarily a bad thing. In fact, darker pans are better at browning food because they absorb more heat than shiny new pans. Just know that darker pans run hotter, so check your food on the earlier end of any cooking time ranges. If you prefer to avoid too much browning, use a lighter pan if you have one, or give your darkened pan a scrub with Bar Keepers Friend to restore its lighter surface.

Hannah Says . . .

A rimmed baking sheet and a wire cooling rack: Name a more iconic duo. The rack elevates food so air can circulate underneath for even cooking and cooling, and the baking sheet below contains any mess. We also use them to hold food before and after frying, and (bonus!) a wire rack makes a handy cooling trivet for a hot-from-the-oven baking sheet.

Are Insulated Baking Sheets Any Good? What About Nonstick Sheets?

Give us a plain old uninsulated, non-nonstick baking sheet any day. These added "features" actually make baking sheets less versatile. Instead of buying an insulated sheet (one with a layer of air sandwiched between two thin sheets of metal) when you want to cook food extra gently, you can create your own insulated sheet by stacking two regular baking sheets. The stacked sheets will trap a layer of insulating air between them.

As for nonstick baking sheets, they come with all the durability issues of any other piece of nonstick cookware. In most cases, adding some oil or a layer of parchment paper to a regular baking sheet should be all you need to ensure that your food comes off cleanly. And with time, regular baking sheets can even start to form a darkened, naturally nonstick surface that also helps food get browner and crispier (see "Is It Bad If My Sheet Pans Are Dark and Stained?" at left).

SHEET-PAN HUEVOS RANCHEROS

serves 4

Stacking two rimmed baking sheets traps a layer of insulating air in between, which helps the eggs cook gently and evenly in the oven. We like our eggs slightly runny; if you prefer your yolks cooked a little more, cook them to the end of the time range in step 4. Serve with hot sauce.

2	(28-ounce) cans diced tomatoes
1	tablespoon packed brown sugar
1	tablespoon lime juice
1	onion, chopped
½	cup canned chopped green chiles
¼	cup extra-virgin olive oil
3	tablespoons chili powder
4	garlic cloves, sliced thin
½	teaspoon table salt
4	ounces pepper Jack cheese, shredded (1 cup)
8	large eggs
1	avocado, halved, pitted, and diced
2	scallions, sliced thin
¼	cup minced fresh cilantro
8	(6-inch) corn tortillas, warmed

1 Adjust oven racks to lowest and middle positions and heat oven to 500 degrees. Drain tomatoes in fine-mesh strainer set over bowl, pressing with rubber spatula to extract as much juice as possible. Combine 1¾ cups drained tomato juice, sugar, and lime juice in bowl and set aside; discard extra drained juice.

2 Combine tomatoes, onion, chiles, oil, chili powder, garlic, and salt in bowl, then spread mixture out evenly on rimmed baking sheet. Place sheet with tomato mixture on upper rack and roast until charred in spots, 35 to 40 minutes, stirring and redistributing into even layer halfway through roasting.

3 Remove sheet from oven and place inside second rimmed baking sheet. Carefully stir reserved tomato juice mixture into roasted vegetables, season with salt and pepper to taste, and spread into even layer. Sprinkle pepper Jack over top and, using back of spoon, hollow out eight 3-inch-wide holes in mixture. Crack 1 egg into each hole and season with salt and pepper.

4 Bake until whites are just beginning to set but still have some movement when sheet is shaken, 7 to 8 minutes for slightly runny yolks or 9 to 10 minutes for soft-cooked yolks, rotating sheet halfway through baking.

5 Remove sheet from oven and top with avocado, scallions, and cilantro. To serve, slide spatula underneath eggs and sauce and gently transfer to warm tortillas.

Feeling Saucy

Saucepans don't get enough appreciation for all they do in the kitchen. It's time to change that—and give a little love to their lesser-known cousins too.

What's the Difference Between a Sauté Pan, a Saucepan, and a Saucier?

A sauté pan (above photo, left) is like a cross between a saucepan and a skillet, with a broad cooking surface and L-shaped sides. We don't consider them a must-have, but they're a good choice for braising, shallow frying, or wilting≈large amounts of greens. (Skillets are sometimes erroneously labeled as sauté pans, but they are in fact two distinct pan types.)

A saucepan (above photo, middle) is a long-handled pot with relatively high, straight sides. We use them for making everything from small batches of soup and pasta to pudding—anything liquidy or saucy (ha!) that doesn't merit pulling out a heavy Dutch oven.

A saucier (above photo, right) is a bowl-like saucepan with a wider mouth and flared walls. They can do everything a saucepan can do, but they excel at cooking foods that require a lot of stirring (think custard, oatmeal, risotto, and polenta) because their cornerless design allows utensils to move around uninhibited and leaves nowhere for food to get lodged and burn. Their wide-mouthed design also promotes evaporation, making them good for reducing sauces.

How Many Saucepans Do I Need?

Every kitchen should be equipped with two saucepans: one that holds 3 to 4 quarts and one with a 2-quart capacity. The larger size works great for cooking macaroni and cheese, steaming vegetables, making soft- and hard-cooked eggs, and more. For smaller households, a large saucepan can be used instead of a Dutch oven or stockpot for cooking pasta as well as soups, stews, and chili. The smaller saucepan comes in handy for making custard, melting butter, and reheating a few servings of soup or boiling a few eggs.

Should I Opt for Nonstick?

It's a case of suiting the material to the job. Nonstick saucepans excel at any cooking task where cleanup could be an issue, such as making pastry cream or rice. Given that these are the kind of recipes that can be made in a smaller pot, it makes sense to make your 2-quart saucepan a nonstick model. A large saucepan, on the other hand, is often used for dishes that involve browning, which is easier to monitor against the light finish of a regular tri-ply pot. With a saucepan of each type, you'll have the best of both worlds.

ALL-PURPOSE CARAMEL SAUCE

makes 2 cups

Caramel is notorious for going from perfectly caramelized to burnt in seconds. Making it in a highly conductive stainless steel (or even better, copper) saucepan reduces the risk that residual heat from the pan will cause it to burn once removed from the heat. In addition to a good pan, you'll want an instant-read thermometer (see page 93) to assess the caramel's doneness. Serve this sauce over ice cream, cake, or fresh fruit.

1¾	cups (12¼ ounces) granulated sugar
½	cup water
¼	cup light corn syrup
1	cup heavy cream
1	teaspoon vanilla extract
¼	teaspoon table salt

1 Bring sugar, water, and corn syrup to boil in large heavy-bottomed saucepan over medium-high heat. Cook, without stirring, until mixture is straw-colored, 6 to 8 minutes. Reduce heat to low and continue to cook, swirling saucepan occasionally, until mixture is amber-colored and registers between 360 and 370 degrees, 2 to 5 minutes longer.

2 Off heat, quickly but carefully stir in cream, vanilla, and salt (mixture will bubble and steam). Continue to stir until sauce is smooth. (Sauce can be refrigerated for up to 2 weeks. Reheat in microwave, stirring frequently, until warm and smooth.)

Pan Out

We can almost guarantee you're underutilizing some of the pans in your kitchen—and holding on to others that aren't worth the cabinet space. But which is which?

anatomy of

A GOOD ROASTING PAN

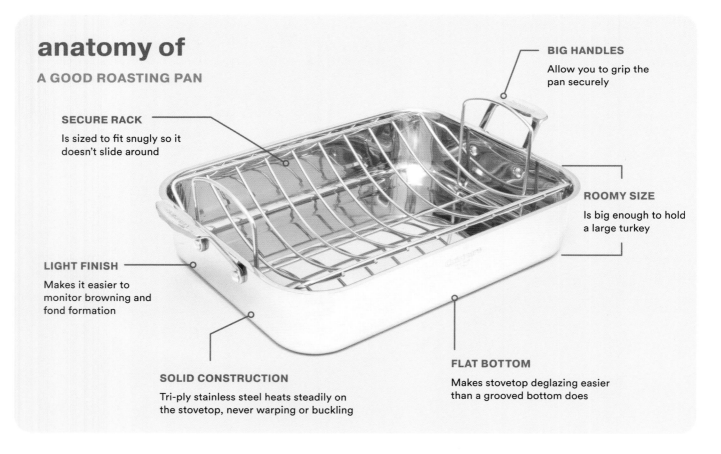

SECURE RACK

Is sized to fit snugly so it doesn't slide around

BIG HANDLES

Allow you to grip the pan securely

ROOMY SIZE

Is big enough to hold a large turkey

LIGHT FINISH

Makes it easier to monitor browning and fond formation

SOLID CONSTRUCTION

Tri-ply stainless steel heats steadily on the stovetop, never warping or buckling

FLAT BOTTOM

Makes stovetop deglazing easier than a grooved bottom does

Is a Stovetop Griddle a Good Idea?

Stovetop griddles offer a large expanse of flat cooking space perfect for making mega batches of pancakes or eggs or burgers. But in order to do that, these pans—little more than flat pieces of metal—have to rely on heat from your stove, and that's where things get tricky. Because these pans are so big (that's the whole point!) they don't fit atop one burner. Instead, they have to straddle at least two, which creates hot spots directly above the burners and cooler spots in between. Not exactly ideal for evenly cooked pancakes.

If you really love to throw weekend pancake brunches, you're probably better off getting an electric griddle (see page 139) instead. These have just as much surface area as the stovetop kind, but their integrated heating elements distribute heat more evenly across the entire surface.

If you simply must stick with the stovetop kind, be sure to preheat the griddle for at least a few minutes before adding any food to minimize the difference between the hotter and cooler zones.

What Else Is It Good For?

The "it" here may be different for each of us, but we all have it: that one pan that lives in the dark recesses of your most inaccessible cabinet and gets used maybe once a year. This state of affairs likely exists because you associate that pan with one very particular use and aren't sure what else, if anything, you can do with it. Check out the chart for some novel ways to put those lesser-used pans to work.

Hannah Says . . .

A roasting rack is a useful companion to a roasting pan. It elevates roasts so they don't sit in their own fat and also allows the hot air to circulate around the roast, which is important for even cooking and a perfectly browned exterior.

USE THIS . . .	TO DO THIS . . .	AND ALSO TO DO THIS!
Grill pan	Create imitation grill marks on food cooked indoors	• **Use as a makeshift panini press:** Press a sandwich between a heated grill pan and a heavy grill press or Dutch oven
Paella Pan	Cook paella	• **Substitute for a griddle or wok:** Make grilled cheese sandwiches, pancakes, or fried rice • Shallow-fry food • Substitute for a roasting pan • Substitute for a plancha or griddle on the grill
Roasting Pan	Roast turkey	• Cook other roasts such as pork loin or chuck roast • **Make hearty one-pan meals:** Cook a side beneath your protein (such as our Peruvian Roast Chicken with Swiss Chard and Sweet Potatoes on page 64) and let the vegetable soak up the yummy drippings • **Make lots of soup or stew:** Straddle the pan across two burners • Make big batches of roasted vegetables

PERUVIAN ROAST CHICKEN WITH SWISS CHARD AND SWEET POTATOES

serves 6

The roomy roasting pan provides ample space for cooking a complete one-pan meal for six. Arranging a side of sweet potatoes on the bottom of the pan, below the chicken, lets them soak up the drippings for excellent flavor. The pan is then transferred from oven to stovetop to finish a quick side of chard. Some leg quarters are sold with backbone attached; removing it (with a heavy chef's knife) before cooking makes the chicken easier to serve.

¼	cup fresh mint leaves
10	garlic cloves (5 chopped, 5 sliced)
¼	cup extra-virgin olive oil, divided
1	tablespoon ground cumin
1	tablespoon honey
2	teaspoons smoked paprika
2	teaspoons dried oregano
2	teaspoons grated lime zest plus ¼ cup juice (2 limes), plus lime wedges for serving
2	teaspoons pepper
1¾	teaspoons table salt, divided
1	teaspoon minced habanero chile
6	(10-ounce) chicken leg quarters, trimmed
3	pounds sweet potatoes, peeled, ends squared off, and sliced into 1-inch-thick rounds
4	pounds Swiss chard, stemmed and cut into 1-inch pieces
2	tablespoons minced fresh cilantro

1 Adjust oven rack to middle position and heat oven to 425 degrees. Process mint, chopped garlic, 1 tablespoon oil, cumin, honey, paprika, oregano, lime zest and juice, pepper, 1 teaspoon salt, and habanero in blender until smooth, about 20 seconds.

2 Using your fingers, gently loosen skin covering thighs and drumsticks and spread half of paste directly on meat. Spread remaining half of paste over exterior of chicken. Place chicken in 1-gallon zipper-lock bag and refrigerate for at least 1 hour or up to 24 hours.

3 Toss potatoes with 1 tablespoon oil and ½ teaspoon salt in bowl. Heat remaining 2 tablespoons oil in 16 by 12-inch roasting pan over medium-high heat (over 2 burners, if possible) until shimmering. Add potatoes, cut side down, and cook until well browned on bottom, 6 to 8 minutes.

4 Off heat, flip potatoes. Lay chicken, skin side up, on top. Roast until thighs and drumsticks register 175 degrees and potatoes are tender, 40 to 50 minutes, rotating pan halfway through roasting.

5 Remove pan from oven. Transfer potatoes and chicken to platter, tent with aluminum foil, and let rest for 10 minutes. Being careful of hot pan handles, pour off all but ¼ cup liquid left in pan. Add sliced garlic and cook over high heat (over 2 burners, if possible) until fragrant, about 30 seconds. Add chard and remaining ¼ teaspoon salt and cook, stirring constantly, until chard is wilted and tender, about 8 minutes; transfer to serving bowl.

6 Sprinkle cilantro over chicken and potatoes and serve with chard and lime wedges.

I'm Scared to Put My Baking Dish Under the Broiler. Will It Explode?

It's relatively rare for a baking dish to shatter, but it can happen when tempered glassware such as Pyrex is exposed to sudden temperature changes (known as thermal shock), extremely high heat (over 425 degrees—the kind food is exposed to during broiling), or direct heat. There are steps you can take to reduce the chances of this happening, such as never moving a glass dish from the freezer to the oven or vice versa. But there's an even more foolproof option: Use a broiler-safe ceramic baking dish for all your broiling needs. These dishes are designed to be used at high temperatures and even under the broiler, so you can go ahead and toast those bread crumbs atop your mac and cheese, brown the potatoes on a shepherd's pie, or melt that cheese topping on your lasagna without fear.

I'm Overwhelmed by All These Choices. Can I Just Buy a Cookware Set and Call It A Day?

You certainly can buy a prepackaged cookware set, but we prefer to create our own customized à la carte set. This lets us focus our resources on what we need most, right away, and gives us the opportunity to build out our set with those nonessential but nice-to-have pans later on. Many prepackaged sets offer relatively puny pans, which saves the manufacturers money but makes it harder for you to cook without overcrowding or spilling. And because lids count as "pieces," an "eight-piece set" is likely to consist of four pans with their lids—not as irresistible a bargain as it looks at first glance. (For more information about stocking your kitchen with the essentials, see page 9.)

head to head

BAKING DISHES AND PANS

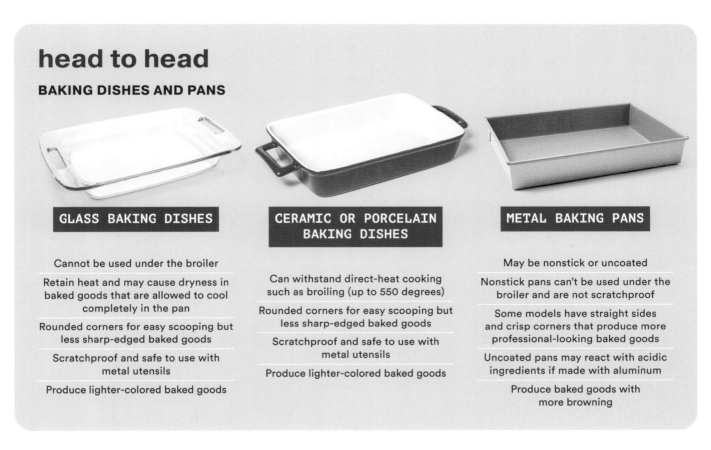

GLASS BAKING DISHES	CERAMIC OR PORCELAIN BAKING DISHES	METAL BAKING PANS
Cannot be used under the broiler	Can withstand direct-heat cooking such as broiling (up to 550 degrees)	May be nonstick or uncoated
Retain heat and may cause dryness in baked goods that are allowed to cool completely in the pan	Rounded corners for easy scooping but less sharp-edged baked goods	Nonstick pans can't be used under the broiler and are not scratchproof
Rounded corners for easy scooping but less sharp-edged baked goods	Scratchproof and safe to use with metal utensils	Some models have straight sides and crisp corners that produce more professional-looking baked goods
Scratchproof and safe to use with metal utensils	Produce lighter-colored baked goods	Uncoated pans may react with acidic ingredients if made with aluminum
Produce lighter-colored baked goods		Produce baked goods with more browning

do your prep work

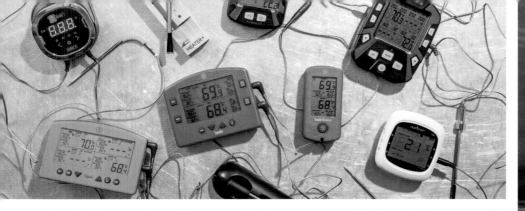

Don't Try This at Home

Testing equipment often calls for breaking the rules, and one rule we break a lot is "Don't play with knives." We often use knives a little creatively over the course of testing. When testing the effectiveness of honing rods, for instance, we first needed some dull knives. Enter an item that we normally wouldn't let within 10 feet of a good chef's knife: a glass cutting board. Slicing several brand-new knives against the hard board just five to seven times each—all the while gritting our teeth at the wrongness of this action—gave us perfectly dull test subjects for our honing rods.

Our search for the best knife sharpeners also required dull knives—but not just run-of-the-mill, normal-use dull. To see how well the sharpeners could repair major damage, we needed blades that were in truly sorry shape. So we ran each knife against the hard surface of a whetstone in a slicing motion—a highly effective way to damage the cutting edge—and even went as far as to cut small notches in the blades meant to simulate the chips a knife can acquire from cutting very hard or frozen foods.

When playing with knives threatens to turn into work, we get a little help from . . . robots. Yeah, you read that right. Years ago, testing how different cutting board materials affected knife sharpness required us to make up to 1,000 slices with a new knife against each board. Lisa, who had the (dis) honor of doing this test, developed blisters and recalls, "It took a week of my life. Test cooks kept coming up, pausing to watch and gently pointing out, 'You know you're not actually cutting any food, right?'" So when it was time to retest boards, our colleague and resident knife expert Miye Bromberg teamed up with the Autodesk Technology Center in Boston to customize a robot that would make 5,000 cuts on every board with a brand-new, factory-sharpened knife. Each cut was programmed to use about 7 pounds of force, about the amount you'd use to break down a chicken, and the bot automatically paused every 200 cuts to test the sharpness of the blade. By the end of this robot chopping marathon we had a much better understanding of how cutting board material affects knives—and a lot fewer blisters.

Knives Out

Good knives should let you prep food safely, comfortably, and effectively—and that doesn't always mean using the biggest or the most expensive ones you can buy.

the three knives everyone should own

KNIFE		WHY YOU NEED IT
Chef's Knife/ Santoku/ Gyutou		A Western-style chef's knife is an all-purpose workhorse: Rely on it for all kinds of prep from mincing garlic to chopping piles of greens to slicing meat. Japanese santoku knives are a good option if you like a slightly smaller but no less versatile tool. Gyutou knives feature a fusion of Japanese and Western knife design and are light, supersharp, and precise. Whichever style you choose, this will likely be the most hardworking all-purpose knife in your collection.
Paring Knife		This sharp, nimble knife is invaluable for jobs that require precision, such as scoring chicken skin or peeling fruits and vegetables.
Serrated Knife		This surprisingly versatile knife, also known as a bread knife, is the best choice not only for cutting bread, slicing sandwiches, and splitting cake layers, but also for slicing into tomatoes, watermelons, and pineapples and even finely chopping chocolate.

What Size Chef's Knife Should I Buy?

You can buy chef's knives with blades from 6 inches up to 14 inches. The size knife you choose will depend on what feels most comfortable to you, but for most adult cooks we recommend an 8-inch knife. It's big enough to handle a multitude of kitchen tasks—mincing, dicing, chopping, and slicing—while also being small enough that it's comfortable to work with.

For young cooks, those who are new to cooking, or those who prefer a more agile blade, a 6-inch knife can be a good choice. Its blade is more nimble than that of an 8-inch knife, which makes it suitable for tasks requiring some dexterity, such as breaking down a whole chicken. But it also requires more force to use, so tasks like mincing and chopping take longer.

A 10-inch knife can feel more substantial when breaking down large cuts of meat or cutting through tough vegetables such as butternut squash, but the longer blade can be harder to manage, especially for tasks that require more dexterity. And its extra weight can lead to fatigue. (We don't see any reason most home cooks would want a 12- or 14-inch knife.)

Are Forged Knives Better than Stamped Knives?

Ah, this question takes us back: It used to be the subject of many a knife snob debate, with many people staunchly holding that forged knives were superior in quality to stamped knives. But as we've found while reviewing knives, the overall quality of a knife has a whole lot more to do with manufacturing techniques and the combination of metals used to create the blade's steel alloy than it does with whether the knife was forged or stamped.

The steel used to make both stamped knives and forged knives is made of a mixture of metals, called an alloy. Each type of steel has its own recipe of ingredients and therefore different degrees of strength, flexibility, hardness, edge retention, resistance to rust and corrosion, and the ability to be made into a fine grain versus a coarse grain. To make stamped knives, a sheet of metal is heated and then rolled out by very heavy rollers; this helps to work-harden it, similar to how forged steel is work-hardened by being struck with a hammer. Stamped knives are then stamped out of this sheet of metal like cookies being cut with a cookie cutter. The main difference between stamped and forged knives is that for stamped knives the whole knife will have the same properties from edge to edge, whereas forging allows the maker to fine-tune different parts of the blade, such as making the edge harder than the spine. But while this sounds like a big deal, in practice a well-made stamped knife works every bit as well as a good forged knife, and the quality of both kinds of knives runs the gamut.

The takeaway: Whether a knife is stamped or forged shouldn't be the deciding factor when choosing a knife.

> **Lisa Says . . .**
> Don't buy a knife that's so fancy you're afraid to use it. A kitchen knife should feel very comfortable when in use, and you should be willing to use it every day. If you save up to buy a special knife only to keep it tucked away in its little box, it's not doing you any favors. Remember, it's a tool, not a treasure.

Can I Use a Santoku Knife as a Replacement for a Western-Style Chef's Knife?

Santoku knives appeared in Japan after World War II as a home cook–friendly all-purpose knife. Santokus have slightly shorter blades than the average Western-style chef's knife or its equivalent, the gyutou—5 to 7 inches versus 8 to 10 inches—and their tips are rounded instead of pointed. If you prefer a smaller blade, a santoku might suit you just fine as your go-to knife. But if you like a longer, more pointed blade for daily use, you might want to consider a santoku as an addition to your arsenal, not as a replacement.

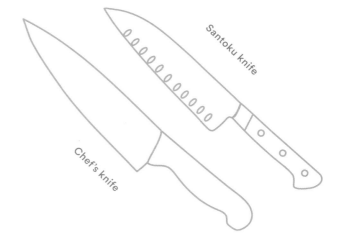

Are Knives with Full Tangs Better?

The part of the blade that extends into the handle is called the tang. Some knives sport a full tang, which runs the entire length (and sometimes the breadth) of the handle and is attached to the sides of the handle with metal rivets. All that metal makes for knives that are on the heavier side, but also more evenly balanced. Knives with partial tangs have tangs that extend only partway into the handle. Because knives with partial tangs contain less metal overall, they tend to be lighter, with a balance that tilts slightly toward the blade.

But is one style better than the other? Ultimately, it's all about personal preference. Some people love the lightness of knives with partial tangs, while others prefer the heft and balance of knives with full tangs. The best knife for you is the one you enjoy and feel comfortable using.

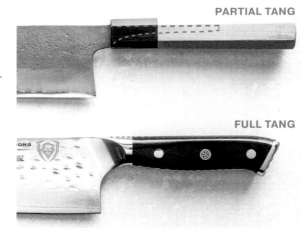

PARTIAL TANG

FULL TANG

Are Carbon-Steel Knives Better than Stainless-Steel?

Many chefs and knife enthusiasts are fans of carbon steel because it is believed to be harder and stronger and able to take on—and retain—a keener edge. But carbon steel is also a high-maintenance metal that rusts if not kept dry.

When we compared our favorite carbon-steel knife to that of our favorite stainless-steel knife, we found that the performance of the two knives was almost identical. The carbon-steel model very slightly edged out the stainless when slicing tomatoes, but both knives sliced onions with ease. Their near-identical performance was borne out in magnified images taken of the two knives: The metals' grain structures looked similarly fine and tight, indicating strong, durable blades. The images supported our hunch that how the metal is manufactured is more important than whether it's carbon or stainless.

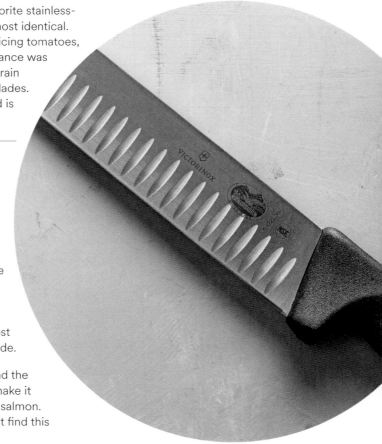

What's with These Shallow Indentations Along the Side of My Knife?

Santoku and slicing knives often feature oval hollows carved into the sides of their blades. Many sources claim that this innovation, often referred to as a "Granton edge" after the company that patented the design, prevents food from clinging to the blade. However, the Granton edge has an additional purpose: The scallops make the blade thinner and lighter to help it slide through food while maintaining some rigidity at the spine for control. The hollows are especially effective on Granton-brand knives, whose deep scallops are carved down through the cutting edge on alternate sides, unlike those of most imitators, which are symmetrical, shallower, and set higher on the blade.

We've tested dozens of Granton-edge knives over the years and found the hollows valuable on slicing knives because they reduce friction and make it easier to carve even slices, whether from a roast or a delicate side of salmon. But on Santoku knives, with their relatively short, thin blades, we don't find this feature necessary.

the wide world of specialized knives

We may not consider them as essential as our top three knives (see page 70), but these specialized knives excel at the tasks they're made for.

KNIFE		BLADE PROFILE	GREAT FOR
Cleaver		Heavy, tall, and fairly long, with a relatively thick spine and subtly curved edge	Chopping through whole chickens or large squashes, mincing raw meat, breaking down bone-in meat for stock, cracking open coconuts
Nakiri		Thin, light, and rectangular, with a relatively straight edge and a blunted tip	Chopping large bunches of vegetables, such as leeks or carrots, with an up-and-down motion
Granton-Edge Slicing Knife		Long and straight with a rounded tip and scalloped indentations along the sides	Slicing roasts smoothly and evenly
Boning Knife		Thin, narrow, and razor-like; flexible	Carving around or removing bones, removing silverskin, frenching racks of lamb
Petty Knife/ Utility Knife		Moderate length; straight triangular shape or slightly curved edge	Detailed prep work such as mincing shallots, trimming fat
Serrated Utility Knife		Moderate length; straight triangular shape	Biting into and slicing smaller or narrower foods such as tomatoes, baguettes, or salami
Bird's Beak Paring Knife		Short and curved with a sharp, narrow tip	Hulling strawberries, removing eyes from pineapples, peeling garlic and shallots, slicing peaches on the pit
Serrated Paring Knife		Short and thin, with sharp serrations	Slicing tomatoes, peeling and segmenting citrus fruits
Steak Knife		Smooth-edged (serrations can mangle meat) and narrow	Slicing steaks, chops, and other meat at the table

How Do I Use a Meat Cleaver?

This somewhat medieval-looking knife can seem intimidating, but it's not that hard to use. Here are some tips from our resident knife expert Miye to help you cut safely and correctly.

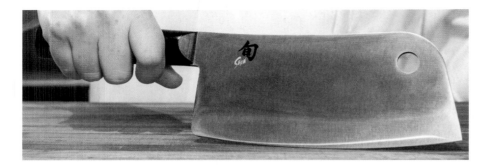

Set up your cutting board: Make sure your cutting board is flat (not warped) and stable; anchor it with a damp towel or cutting board stabilizer so it doesn't move around on the counter. If you're using a wood cutting board with a one-way grain, make sure to cut perpendicular to or at a slight angle to the grain—otherwise you risk splitting the cutting board when you chop.

Use a pinch grip for slicing through dense foods and a power grip for chopping poultry or meat: For slicing, use a slight rocking motion rather than a hacking motion. For chopping, keep your nondominant hand out of the way, raise your arm slightly from the elbow, and then bring it down on the food, using your wrist to direct the knife and apply force. (See "Use the Right Grip" for more information about pinch and power grips.)

Slice all the way through: If the cleaver gets stuck halfway through the item you're cutting, place your nondominant hand on the spine of the knife and apply pressure to drive the knife downward and finish the cut.

I'm Overwhelmed. Can I Just Buy a Knife Block Set and Be Done?

An all-in-one knife set—complete with a block that keeps everything neatly housed and within easy reach—seems like a nice convenience: Why go to the effort of evaluating and choosing knives one by one if you can let someone else do all that work for you?

It's simple: Most knife block sets are loaded with superfluous, impractical, or even downright useless pieces. And not every manufacturer makes an ideal version of every type of knife, so the quality of the knives, even within a single set, can be a mixed bag. Plus, retailers like to sell sets with an impressive-sounding number of pieces, but the quality of each piece often suffers in order to achieve a certain price point.

Putting together your own à la carte set means you have complete control over the knives that make it into your collection, so you can ensure that the knives you buy are of good quality—and that you'll actually use them.

real talk with hannah

"AFFORDANCE" HAS NOTHING TO DO WITH PRICE

One of my favorite expert consultations ever was with Dr. Jack Dennerlein, professor of Physical Therapy, Movement, and Rehabilitation Sciences at Northeastern University in Boston. To find out why some knife handles are more comfortable to grip than others, I chucked a bunch of knives into a large bag and hopped on a train to see him at the university. (Luckily they weren't searching bags that day!) Dr. Dennerlein told me that the difference came down to something called "affordance," or the way the design of an object dictates how it can be used. A good knife handle affords you several different comfortable grip options, allowing you to choke up on the handle for control and just as easily to hold it farther back in a power grip. The best knives in my bag had relatively streamlined handles with rounded edges that didn't limit our grip options. The least comfortable handles had grooves or designs that forced our hands into singular or uncomfortable positions. Affordance applies to far more than knives—we've since applied the concept to our research on everything from pan handles to rubber spatulas. Thanks, Dr. Dennerlein!

3 Knife Skills
All Cooks Should Know

Knives may just be the most important tools in your kitchen. Using good knife technique gives you better results (poorly cut food will not cook evenly or properly) and also makes kitchen prep safer and faster.

1 USE THE RIGHT GRIP

For the most control, choke up on the knife handle, with your thumb and index finger actually pinching the heel of the blade; this is called a pinch grip. If you need to use extra force when cutting through hard foods, hold just the handle; this is known as a power grip.

2 KEEP YOUR FINGER-TIPS SAFE

Make a "bear claw" shape with your non-knife hand, tucking your fingertips away from the knife to hold the food in place. Rest your knuckles against the blade of the knife to provide guidance. During the upward motion of slicing, reposition your guiding hand for the next cut.

3 USE THE RIGHT CUT FOR THE JOB

To cut small items, push blade forward and down, using its curve to make smooth strokes. With each cut, move knife (not food). Blade should touch board at all times.

To cut large items such as eggplant, lift entire blade off board to help make smooth strokes.

To cut through tough foods, use one hand to grip handle and place your flat palm on top of blade. Cut straight down, pushing blade gently. Make sure your hands and knife are both dry to prevent slippage.

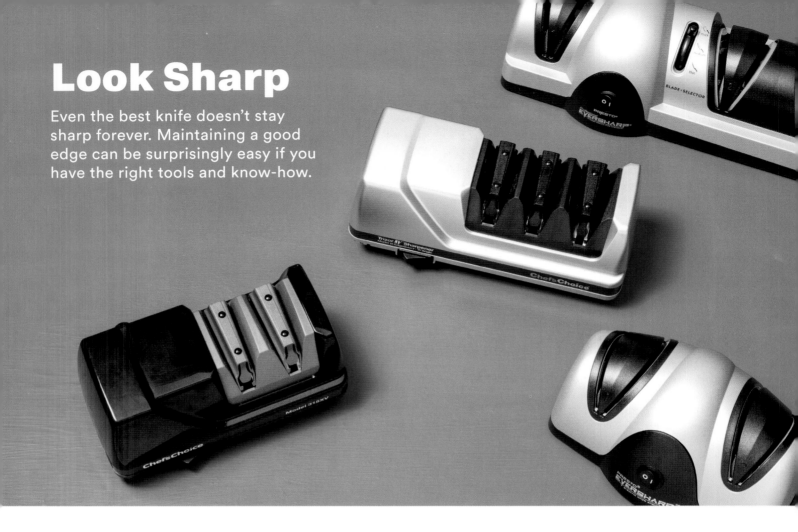

Look Sharp

Even the best knife doesn't stay sharp forever. Maintaining a good edge can be surprisingly easy if you have the right tools and know-how.

Can a Knife Be Too Sharp?

Simply put, the sharper the knife, the better it works and the safer it is to use. A dull blade forces you to push harder to get the job done, which makes it easy for the blade to slip and miss the mark, sending the knife toward your hand. With a sharp knife, the blade does the work—and the razor-like edge is far less likely to slip. So from both safety and performance perspectives, a knife can never be too sharp.

Some people worry that repeated sharpening can wear down a knife over time. Electric sharpeners do take off a small amount of metal each time you grind your knife, especially if you're using a coarse-grind setting to sharpen a very dull knife. But your knife won't suffer excessive metal loss if you use a well-designed sharpener with multiple options for sharpening—such as coarse, fine, and a nonmotorized stropping disk—and if you follow the instructions carefully. The fine slot is the one you'll use most often just to polish up a barely dull knife. Because you'll be maintaining the sharpness of your knife with the lightest of the sharpening options rather than giving it an intense regrinding with the coarse slot, there's no need to worry about metal loss from "oversharpening."

real talk with hannah

ONE REASON YOUR KNIVES MAY BE DULL

I was at a dinner party thrown by my friend Louise, chatting with a couple I didn't know, when one of them said, "Oh, you test kitchen equipment? We have a mystery to ask you about." They had done a house swap with a family from England and when they returned home their knives were incredibly dull. What could have done that kind of damage to them in such a short time? Like a cool-headed detective nailing a perp, I immediately said, "Do you have a glass cutting board?" They did. They kept it for display only and never used it themselves—but upon reflection, they *had* noticed that it was in a different place upon their return home. Case closed. Glass is fragile in the sense that it can shatter, but it's also an extremely hard surface that wreaks havoc on knife blades; we actually use them to purposely dull knives for certain tests. My advice: If you have a glass cutting board, use it as a serving tray instead of a cutting surface, and for the love of sharp, safe knives everywhere, don't buy or gift any more of them.

Can a Serrated Knife Be Sharpened?

Knives with serrated edges stay sharp longer than smooth-bladed knives: Their pointed teeth do most of the work so the edges endure less friction. But you can (and should!) sharpen your serrated knife if you notice a decline in its cutting precision. The good news: You don't need a superspecialized tool or painstaking technique. If you own a regular knife sharpener you may already have the right tool for the job. Manual knife sharpeners can ride up and down the different serrations (pointed, scalloped, and saw toothed), sharpening not only the edges and tips, but the deep valleys too.

Not all electric knife sharpeners will work on serrated blades, but our favorite sharpener (see page 370) can sharpen serrated blades, using what the company calls its "stropping" disk. The rotating disks in this slot are made from a material that is flexible enough to get into the valleys on the blade's edge.

How Can I Tell Whether My Knives Should Be Honed or Sharpened?

Whenever you feel your knife is less sharp than it should be, try honing first. Honing is a gentle way to extend the time between sharpening sessions; it pushes the cutting edge of the blade back into alignment while removing a very small amount of metal from the blade's edge. If you don't own a honing rod (sometimes incorrectly referred to as a honing steel or sharpening steel), you can use the fine-grit slot of a manual or electric sharpener for touching up the blade to achieve similar results.

If you find that honing the blade doesn't make much of a difference, it's time to get out the sharpener. The angle control, power, and progressive stages (from rough to fine to a final polish) offered by a good sharpener can bring even the dullest blade back to a brand-new, razor-sharp condition in minutes.

Hannah Says . . .

For easy and precise honing, we don't recommend slashing the rod and the knife together up in the air, as pros do. Instead, plant the top of the rod on a folded, slightly damp dish towel to anchor it securely, so the only moving part will be your knife. This helps you keep a consistent motion, which is important for good results.

Lisa Says . . .

When we tested honing rods, we found that diamond-coated rods are way too rough on knife edges. They not only removed too much metal but also left the blade edge badly scratched and chewed-up looking.

Learn proper honing and sharpening technique from Lisa and Hannah in this video.

test it yourself

IS IT TIME TO SHARPEN YOUR KNIFE?

Owning a knife sharpener makes it easy to tune up your knives, but how do you know when it's time? The best way to tell if a knife is sharp is to put it to the paper test. Holding a sheet of paper (basic printer/copy paper is best) firmly at the top with one hand, draw the blade down through the paper, heel to tip, with your other hand. The knife should glide through the paper and require only minimal pushing. If it snags, try realigning the blade's edge using a honing rod and then repeat the test. If the knife still doesn't cut the paper cleanly, use your sharpener. Repeat the paper test to make sure the knife is properly sharpened; if it catches on the paper, note where on the blade the snagging happens. You can minimize the amount of metal removed from the knife by focusing on just this section of the blade to fine-tune the sharpening (just make sure you don't overdo it and end up making the blade uneven).

head to head

SHARPENERS

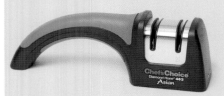

MANUAL SHARPENERS	ELECTRIC SHARPENERS	WHETSTONES
Tall walls hold the knife steady so that the user can draw the blade through the chamber at the correct angle	Spring-loaded guides restrict the knife's movement so that the entire edge makes steady contact with the abrasive at a precise angle	Extremely adaptable; because the cook holds the knife at a specified angle to match the edge angle, whetstones can be used to sharpen any knife
Have a smaller footprint; easily stow in a drawer, making them more convenient for routine upkeep	Typically have multiple grinding slots, each with a different coarseness of blade to control the amount of sharpening	Most feature a coarse side and a fine side, which determine the amount of sharpening at each pass
Effective and quick at sharpening most kitchen knives	Can quickly repair extensive damage	Take practice to master; require holding the knife at the correct angle to ensure a proper edge
Can't repair extensive damage to a blade (such as removing notches)	Cannot be used to sharpen blades with a full bolster, as the entire blade cannot be drawn through the sharpener	Can take a lot of time to restore a very dull blade
Cannot be used to sharpen blades with a full bolster, as the entire blade cannot be drawn through the sharpener	Relatively expensive	Can sharpen blades with a full bolster
Less expensive than electric sharpeners		Relatively inexpensive

---

FREQUENTLY ASKED QUESTIONS: KNIFE SHARPENING EDITION

Q: What can I use to sharpen a knife with a full bolster?

A: Knives with full bolsters feature thick ridges between the blade and the handle that extend all the way to the bottom of the blade, which can complicate sharpening. You must be able to pull a knife completely through the slots of a manual or electric sharpener (otherwise the blade will be unevenly shaped), and a thick full bolster prevents this. If you have a knife with a full bolster, you'll need to sharpen it using a whetstone—or get it professionally sharpened if you're not confident in your skill.

Q: What about single-bevel knives?

A: Single-bevel knives have a sharp angle (a bevel) on just one side of the blade, as opposed to double-bevel knives, which have a sharp angle on both sides of the blade. Most sharpeners are designed for double-bevel knives and will damage the blade of a single-bevel knife. Look for a sharpener that works with single-bevel knives, such as our favorite electric sharpener (page 370), which enables you to pull the knife through a single slot to sharpen just one side. Alternatively, use a whetstone or have these knives professionally sharpened.

Q: Do I need to know my knife's edge angle before sharpening? How can I find that out?

A: Older Western-style knives typically had edge angles of 20–22 degrees, but these days knives are typically 15 degrees. It's important to know your knife's edge angle before sharpening, as some sharpeners are made to sharpen to 20 degrees and some to 15. If you're not sure what your knife's edge angle is, check with the manufacturer. (Note that some electric sharpeners are powerful enough to regrind a 20-degree edge angle to 15 degrees.)

Lisa Says . . .

If you want to take the time to learn how to sharpen on a whetstone, that's great. If not, our favorite electric sharpener does a fantastic job in a few minutes, with no skill or preparation needed. Just follow the steps in the manual, and you'll be back to chopping and slicing—with a wickedly sharp edge—in less than 5 minutes. After all, that's the whole point: You want to spend your time cooking, not sharpening.

PAN-SEARED SESAME-CRUSTED TUNA STEAKS

serves 4

The delicate sesame crust on these tuna steaks will put your knife's edge to the test: Sharp knives will slice right through, but dull knives will tear the crust apart. For tuna steaks cooked medium, observe the timing for medium-rare, then tent the steaks with foil for 5 minutes before slicing. If you prefer tuna steaks cooked so rare that they are still cold in the center, try to purchase steaks that are 1½ inches thick and cook them according to the timing below for rare steaks. Bear in mind, though, that the cooking times below are estimates; check for doneness by nicking the fish with a paring knife.

¾	cup sesame seeds
4	tuna steaks, 8 ounces each and about 1 inch thick
2	tablespoons vegetable oil, divided
½	teaspoon table salt
¼	teaspoon pepper

1 Spread sesame seeds in shallow baking dish or pie plate. Pat tuna steaks dry with paper towels; use 1 tablespoon oil to rub both sides of steaks, then sprinkle with salt and pepper. Press both sides of each steak in sesame seeds to coat.

2 Heat remaining 1 tablespoon oil in 12-inch nonstick skillet over high heat until just smoking; swirl to coat pan. Add tuna steaks and cook 30 seconds without moving steaks. Reduce heat to medium-high and continue to cook until seeds are golden brown, about 1½ minutes. Using tongs, carefully flip tuna steaks; cook, without moving steaks, until golden brown on second side, opaque at perimeters, and translucent red and cool at center when checked with tip of paring knife and registering 110 degrees (for rare), about 1½ minutes, or until opaque at perimeters and reddish pink at center and registering 125 degrees (for medium-rare), about 3 minutes. Slice steaks ¼ inch thick and serve.

On Board

A good cutting board can be the difference between uncomfortable, awkward food prep and a truly enjoyable prepping experience.

Does My Cutting Board's Material Matter?

Cutting boards come in a range of materials including bamboo, both hard and soft woods, plastic, wood fiber composite, and glass. Aside from glass, which will damage your knife edge and should never be used to cut on, all of these materials have some good things going for them. Here's a quick breakdown of some of the more common materials used to make cutting boards.

Wood and Bamboo: Handsome Heavyweights

In general, wood and bamboo are good choices for larger boards; their slightly textured surface makes for a pleasant cutting experience and they offer heft and stability for heavy-duty tasks. But what about hard wood versus soft wood? Is one type better?

Soft woods such as **hinoki** (Japanese cypress) feel pleasant to cut on and are initially very gentle on knives, but we noticed that after making several thousand cuts on these boards our knives started to dull faster. This is likely because softer wood is more easily damaged by the knife; its surface becomes scored and irregular, which in turn causes wear on the knife.

Counterintuitively, harder woods such as **maple** or **cherry**, as well as **bamboo**, are gentle on knives in the long run, although the cutting experience is less cushy.

Teak is a happy medium: It's soft enough to provide a luxurious cutting experience but hard enough to be relatively durable. One caveat with teak: Embedded in its grain are microscopic bits of silica (a mineral component of sand) that can potentially wear down your blade if you're repeatedly sinking your knife deep into the wood. On the plus side, teak contains natural resins that help keep it moisturized and less likely to crack than other wood or bamboo boards.

Plastic and Composite: Fuss-Free Utility

Plastic and **composite** boards make a lot of sense for small to mid-size boards. Unlike wood cutting boards, plastic and composite boards require no maintenance. They're thin and relatively lightweight, and what's more, they resist stains and odors better than wood and bamboo and they can be thrown in the dishwasher. And best of all, they're comparatively inexpensive, making them accessible to most cooks and easy to replace in the event that they crack or warp. Knives generally stay as sharp when used on composite boards and plastic boards as they do on wood and bamboo; however, composite boards tend to have a smooth, hard surface, making them less pleasant to cut on than textured plastic.

Lisa Says . . .

The only thing a glass cutting board is good for is display, or perhaps serving snacks. Their hard surface will dull your knife within a few slices. (See Hannah's Real Talk on page 76 for more about that.)

Can My Cutting Board Go in the Dishwasher?

Don't put your good wood or bamboo boards in the dishwasher! The dishwasher environment is too harsh for these boards; detergent wears away the finish you build up through oiling, and water soaking into the wood will eventually cause the boards to warp and crack at their joints. Plastic and composite boards are dishwasher-safe, so opt for one of these if you really don't want to wash by hand. (Note that thinner plastic boards can warp due to heat.)

Why Did My Board Warp?

For wood and bamboo boards, moisture is the enemy: The more water they absorb, the more vulnerable they are to damage, including warping. For composite and plastic boards, temperature is the culprit: Even though these boards are touted as dishwasher-safe, the heat of the dishwasher can cause them to warp. Prevention is key: Once a board is warped, there's not much you can do to straighten it out.

To lessen the risk of warping, you should maintain your wood board by oiling it regularly; this helps minimize its water absorption. Make sure to use only food-safe mineral oil (not cooking oil). And when buying a plastic board, choose one that's at least ½ inch thick, as thinner boards are more prone to warping.

Eww . . . Is That Mold?

It happens to the best of us: You take your wood or bamboo cutting board, carving board, or baking peel out of the cabinet and realize it's developed a dank mildewy odor. You might even see mildew or mold growing on it. (Maybe you put it away damp or left a few traces of food on it.) Don't despair! You can get rid of that mildew by thoroughly sanitizing the board.

The USDA's Food Safety and Inspection Service recommends using a dilute bleach solution: 1 tablespoon of unscented, liquid chlorine bleach to 1 gallon of water. Flood the surface of the board with the solution and let it stand for a few minutes. Let the solution drain off and then flip the board and apply more solution to the other side. Rinse the whole board with clean water and pat it dry with paper towels.

And remember: Prevention is always the best option. Try to keep all your cutting boards as dry as possible after use, never leave them sitting in a puddle (we beg you!), and store them in a well-ventilated area to prevent new mold or mildew from forming.

real talk with hannah

TAKE CARE OF YOUR BOARDS

My husband and I received no fewer than eight cutting boards as wedding gifts. I have loved and used every one of them, but my wealth of cutting boards has led me to bad habits: I don't regularly oil my cutting boards, and *someone* in my household leaves them sopping wet after washing. Of our eight, one has split in two, one is so warped it rocks like a rocking chair, and another has deep cracks prone to mold. So please do as I say, not as I do, and let my mistakes be your gain. Wash your wooden and bamboo cutting boards with hot, soapy water, pat them dry, and always store them in a position that maximizes air flow. And when your board looks dry and ashy and water sinks into it rather than beads up on top, it's time to season it: Rub it all over with mineral oil, let the oil sink in overnight, and then buff off any excess.

Which Is Better: End-Grain or Edge-Grain Boards?

A cutting board's grain is determined by the way it's constructed. End-grain boards are made by gluing together blocks of wood, each with the grain running vertically. Edge-grain boards are made by gluing together long planks of wood, each with the grain running horizontally. Some people think end-grain boards are gentler on knives because the knife slices with the blocks' exposed grain. But is this true, and does it mean end-grain cutting boards are better than edge-grain boards?

No on both counts. Our tests showed no correlation between knife sharpness and cutting board grain. (You should be sharpening your knife regularly, anyway.) And we actually have several reasons for preferring edge-grain boards. For one thing, fewer exposed wood joints in edge-grain boards means they're less likely to split and crack with use than end-grain boards. End-grain boards absorb more water than edge-grain boards, which causes the wood to expand and contract and puts stress on all those glued joints. End-grain boards also require more oil to maintain than edge-grain boards.

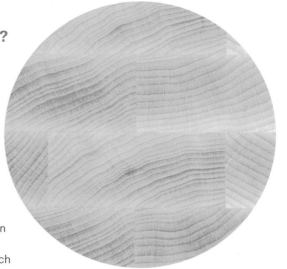

End-grain board

How Many Boards Do I Need?

It doesn't have to be complicated. Every kitchen should have a full-size, all-purpose cutting board; get the biggest board that your counter and sink will allow—and that you're able to lift comfortably. Additional boards can be nice to have, but you definitely don't need them to complete your equipment collection.

Compact boards are easy to maneuver and clean, so they come in handy for small jobs or when cooking in cramped spaces. It's nice to have a plastic board that you can throw in the dishwasher (see page 81 for more on why you shouldn't put wood boards in the dishwasher). If your primary cutting board is plastic, you might still want to have a good-looking wood board that you can leave out on your counter or use as a cheese board. If you cook roasts even a few times a year, a carving board is worth the space in your kitchen. And a set of flexible cutting mats requires minimal storage space and provides maximum real estate for chopping.

Edge-grain board

Lisa Says . . .

Get the biggest cutting board you can manage. With room to spread out as you prep food, the whole task becomes exponentially easier and more pleasant. Food stays on the board (you're not chasing carrots that roll away as you slice them). Give yourself space to do the job, get a sharp knife, turn on some tunes, and chopping food becomes—dare I say it?—a pleasure.

Is It OK to Work with Raw Meat on a Wooden Board?

It's fine—as long as you clean the used board properly. This means scrubbing it thoroughly with hot, soapy water after each use, or alternatively, using a diluted bleach solution of about 1 tablespoon of bleach per 1 gallon of water. It's easiest to do this in the sink, but if your board is very big or very heavy, it's okay to clean it where it sits (admittedly, a messy task). You can't simply wipe it down with a wet sponge and call it a day, though: Scrub the cutting board well on all sides, including the bottom, with a hot, soapy washcloth. After you've washed the board, don't let it drip dry; instead, pat off as much moisture as you can with a clean dish towel. Store it upright or in a position that maximizes airflow and prevents moisture from being trapped between the board and the counter.

Do I Really Need a Carving Board?

A carving board may seem like a luxury when you pull it out only a few times a year—but anyone who's tried carving a roast on a flat cutting board knows what a disaster that can be, with juices dribbling onto the counter from all sides. Carving boards are designed to avoid this mess, traditionally by relying on a perimeter trench to trap liquid. The most effective carving boards trap at least ½ cup of liquid, roughly the amount released by a midsize turkey as it rests. But you can also hack your own DIY version: Simply set an ordinary cutting board inside of a rimmed baking sheet (make sure your board will fit first). The rimmed baking sheet will capture any juices that run off the board just as effectively as an actual carving board.

real talk with lisa

A FLEXIBLE CUTTING MAT AND A CUTTING BOARD: A MATCH MADE IN HEAVEN

You might think that when it comes to owning a flexible cutting mat or a cutting board it's an either-or choice, but you'd be wrong. I use both tools all the time—and often at the same time. When I'm cutting up or prepping raw meat, for example, I like to do it on a flexible cutting mat placed on top of my cutting board. When I'm done, I remove the mat, wash it in the sink in hot, soapy water, clean the knife the same way, and check that no juices got onto the board beneath. This makes it so much easier to clean up and to control where bacteria can spread. I do the same thing when I'm cutting up something juicy and messy, like a watermelon, or prepping foods that are spicy or prone to staining (think chipotle chiles in adobo).

worth it

CUTTING BOARD STABILIZER

At some point or another, you've probably had a cutting board slip on the counter while you were preparing a meal. While this disconcerting problem is more common with boards that are lightweight or lacking rubber grips, it can occasionally occur even with sturdier boards. One solution: Wet a dish towel or paper towel and stick it under your cutting board before chopping to help anchor the board in place. But a dedicated cutting board stabilizer promises to work even better and with less fuss: Just pull it out, place it under the board, and go. No more boards skidding across the counter, no more worries. For the peace of mind it'll give you during even the most vigorous chopping or pounding sessions, we think a stabilizer is worth it.

Blades Abound

Knives aren't the only sharp tools in the kitchen. When it comes to peeling, slicing, grating, and more, there's a whole world of blades to choose from.

Why Can't I Find a Really Good Can Opener?

After testing and retesting can openers, our colleague Miye finally had to admit that the perfect one-size-fits-all can opener just doesn't exist. Some people prefer safety can openers because they leave behind a smooth edge and ensure that you never need to go fishing for a sharp lid. Others find that traditional openers are easier to use. Plus, in our experience, most can openers of either style just don't seem built to last. Over time handle grips loosen or fall off, the tension and alignment of arms or gears shift, metal parts rust, and like all bladed tools, cutting wheels dull. The takeaway: The best can opener for you will depend on your personal preferences—and you should be prepared to replace it when it inevitably starts to fail.

Am I Using My Can Opener Wrong?

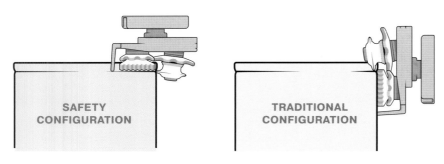

SAFETY CONFIGURATION

TRADITIONAL CONFIGURATION

There's more than one way to open a can. Traditional can openers puncture the top of a can and cut the lid inside the can's rim. So-called safety can openers cut into the side of the can and remove both the metal lid and the rim itself; this creates a smoother edge as well as a loose lid that sits on top rather than sinks into the can. But you might not know that most traditional can openers can also be used as safety openers: Place the can opener on top of the can, on the left-hand side, with the cutting wheel on the outside of the can and the gear on the inside rim. Turn the driving handle clockwise and the opener will cut through the side of the can, severing the lid below the rim. One caveat: While the lid will be smooth, the top of the can will be sharp and slightly jagged, unlike when using an actual safety opener.

Does the Shape of a Vegetable Peeler Matter?

Vegetable peelers come in two basic shapes: Some have a blade that extends in a straight line from the handle, while others look like a "Y," with a blade running perpendicular to the handle. In practice, they function similarly: You can both whittle away from yourself and pare toward yourself, so it really doesn't matter which shape you use: Choose whichever kind you're more comfortable with.

anatomy of

GOOD KITCHEN SHEARS

MEDIUM-SIZE FINGER BOWS
Easy to use with any size hand

MEDIUM TENSION BETWEEN BLADES
Loose enough to open and close easily, but stiff enough to power through cuts

LONG BLADES
Make longer, smoother strokes

EASILY SEPARATED BLADES
For convenient and thorough cleaning

AMBIDEXTROUS
Can be used regardless of handedness

CRISPY ROAST BUTTERFLIED CHICKEN WITH ROSEMARY AND GARLIC

serves 4

Using a strong pair of kitchen shears to cut through the bones on either side of the backbone makes the process of butterflying a chicken easier, faster, and safer. Although the chicken may slightly overhang the skillet at first, it will shrink to fit. Don't use a chicken larger than 4 pounds.

2	tablespoons extra-virgin olive oil, divided
1	teaspoon minced fresh rosemary
1	garlic clove, minced
1	(3½- to 4-pound) whole chicken, giblets discarded
¾	teaspoon table salt
¾	teaspoon pepper
	Lemon wedges

1 Adjust oven rack to lowest position, place 12-inch cast-iron skillet on rack, and heat oven to 500 degrees. Meanwhile, combine 1 tablespoon oil, rosemary, and garlic in bowl; set aside.

2 With chicken breast side down, use kitchen shears to cut through bones on either side of backbone; discard backbone. Flip chicken over, tuck wingtips behind back, and press firmly on breastbone to flatten. Pat chicken dry with paper towels, then rub with remaining 1 tablespoon oil and sprinkle with salt and pepper.

3 When oven reaches 500 degrees, carefully place chicken breast side down in hot skillet. Reduce oven temperature to 450 degrees and roast chicken until well browned, about 30 minutes.

4 Using pot holders, remove skillet from oven. Being careful of hot skillet handle, gently flip chicken breast side up. Brush chicken with oil mixture, return skillet to oven, and continue to roast chicken until breast registers 160 degrees and thighs register 175 degrees, about 10 minutes. Transfer chicken to carving board, tent loosely with aluminum foil, and let rest for 15 minutes. Carve chicken and serve with lemon wedges.

Do I Really Need Seafood Scissors?

Kitchen shears are ideal for butterflying chicken and snipping herbs but not so great for thick, curvy seafood shells. If you cook lobster, crab, or shrimp on a regular basis, you'll appreciate having seafood scissors, which are designed to open shells without marring the seafood within. Look for scissors with gently arched, very slightly serrated blades for snipping through tough lobster claws and delicate shrimp shells.

SHRIMP MOZAMBIQUE

serves 4

Seafood scissors make it a breeze to remove the shells from shrimp, something we prefer to do ourselves since shell-on shrimp are cheaper and usually in better shape than peeled ones. If possible, choose untreated shrimp—those without added sodium or preservatives such as sodium tripolyphosphate (STPP). Most frozen E-Z peel shrimp have been treated (the ingredient list should tell you). If you're using treated shrimp, do not sprinkle the shrimp with salt in step 2.

SAUCE

2	tablespoons Frank's RedHot Original Cayenne Pepper Sauce
2	tablespoons extra-virgin olive oil
2	tablespoons water
¼	slice hearty white sandwich bread, torn into small pieces
1	tablespoon chopped fresh parsley
2	garlic cloves, chopped
2	teaspoons paprika
½	teaspoon pepper

SHRIMP

2	pounds extra-large shrimp (21 to 25 per pound), peeled, deveined, and tails removed
1	teaspoon table salt, divided
¼	teaspoon pepper
1	tablespoon extra-virgin olive oil
½	cup finely chopped onion
3	garlic cloves, sliced thin
1	cup dry white wine
2	tablespoons unsalted butter, cut into 2 pieces
2	tablespoons chopped fresh parsley

1 for the sauce Process all ingredients in blender until smooth, about 2 minutes, scraping down sides of blender jar as needed.

2 for the shrimp Sprinkle shrimp with ½ teaspoon salt and pepper; set aside. Heat oil in 12-inch nonstick skillet over medium heat until shimmering. Add onion and remaining ½ teaspoon salt and cook until softened, about 5 minutes. Add garlic and cook until fragrant, about 1 minute. Add wine and bring to boil. Cook until reduced by half, about 4 minutes.

3 Add shrimp and cook, stirring occasionally, until opaque and just cooked through, about 4 minutes. Stir in butter and sauce and cook until butter is melted and sauce is heated through, about 1 minute. Season with salt and pepper to taste. Sprinkle with parsley and serve.

Are All The Holes on a Box Grater Good for Something?

Most box graters feature three different-size sets of holes plus a set of wide slicing slots, but we admit that we mostly use just one of those options: the large holes. These are best for grating vegetables and soft cheeses such as mozzarella or Monterey Jack. The medium holes provide a finer shred on firmer cheeses such as cheddar or Gruyère. For tasks such as zesting citrus and finely grating hard cheeses like Parmesan or Romano, we prefer to use a rasp-style grater such as a Microplane rather than the smallest holes of a box grater. And as for those wide slicing slots, there are a host of other kitchen blades that work just as well, or even better. In the test kitchen we've actually found that the large holes on a single-sided paddle-style grater plus the fine holes on a rasp-style grater cover all our grating needs. That said, even if you use only one or two of the holes on the grater, the shape of a box grater itself has some upsides, allowing it to sit securely on a cutting board and helping to contain shredded food so it doesn't go flying all over the counter.

Will My Food Processor's Shredding Disk Work Just as Well as a Grater?

A good food processor's shredding disk can make quick work of shredding a whole pile of vegetables or a block of cheese with very little waste. Unless we have only a very small amount of food to grate, we'll happily pull out our processor to do the job. (For more about food processors, see page 134.)

I'm Always Skinning My Knuckles on My Grater. Is There A Better Way?

We shred a whole lot of food in the test kitchen. Over the years, we've learned a few things about how to grate food without grating our fingers. Here are our top tips for easier, safer grating.

1 Go slow.

2 If you're worried about injuries, wear cut-resistant gloves (see page 340) to add a layer of protection.

3 Use longer strokes for faster grating.

4 Place cheese in the freezer for 30 minutes prior to grating; it'll be firmer and easier to grate.

5 Coat the surface of the grater with nonstick spray to prevent sticking.

6 Apply pressure on the downward stroke only; the upward stroke won't shred anything.

7 Replace the grater as needed; graters can dull over time and cannot be sharpened. Just like knives, sharp graters are safest.

Are Mandolines as Dangerous as People Say?

Mandolines are notorious for being dangerous if not handled properly. Lightweight or poorly anchored mandolines can skitter across counters unexpectedly; the razor-sharp blades are exposed and all too happy to nip fingers; the hand guards that ship with them can often be next to useless. But to be fair, any bladed tool, whether it's a knife or a grater, can be dangerous. And as proven by the fact that our colleague Miye, who spent weeks testing mandolines both good and bad, still has all her fingers, when used correctly a mandoline is just another tool in a cook's arsenal.

Follow these simple directions for safely and efficiently slicing with a mandoline, and soon you'll be turning out produce that looks like it's been cut by a chef from a three-star restaurant in record time.

1 Work on a flat, dry surface so the mandoline doesn't slip.

2 Wear a cut-resistant glove (see page 340) to keep your fingers safe, even if you're using a guide. The mandoline works faster than you might expect and very soon you'll be working close to your hand.

3 Cut foods in half so that they have a flat surface that can sit flat on the platform.

4 Slice at a moderate pace, but don't go too slowly or you won't have enough momentum to push the food through the blade.

5 Position food toward the side(s), where the platform is less likely to flex.

6 Clear food from under the mandoline as you work so it doesn't obstruct the blade.

7 Don't try to force food through. If necessary, use the handle of a knife or a wooden spoon to gently knock the food back off the blades.

8 Replace your mandoline as needed. Don't keep a dull mandoline around; it'll struggle to cut food but bite your fingers willingly.

Hannah Says . . .

Badly designed hand guards may be the number-one cause of mandoline-related injuries. Many just don't work as intended: They either have too-short prongs that don't securely hold on to food, or they get in the way and prevent us from completely slicing food, resulting in waste. But while ditching a bad guard and going it alone may be tempting, that's where the real danger lies: You can be slicing along just fine, but one slip-up is all it takes. That's why we recommend wearing cut-resistant gloves while using a mandoline: They offer protection without the drawbacks of a bad hand guard. And even if your guard is relatively good, a second layer of protection never hurts.

Mix and Measure

Measuring cups and mixing bowls may seem too basic to fuss over, but the right design can make a big difference.

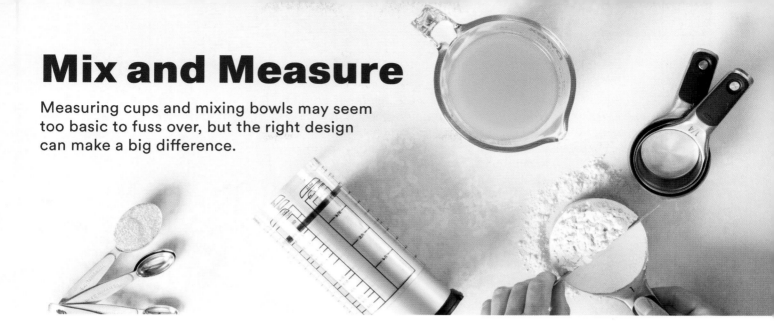

How Many Bowls Do I Need?

A basic set of three bowls—one small (1 to 1½ quarts), one medium (2½ to 3 quarts), and one large (4 to 6 quarts)—will see you through most kitchen tasks. But if you have the space, it's useful to own each size bowl in both stainless steel and glass. Why? Stainless steel bowls are lightweight and durable, while transparent tempered glass ones offer better visibility and can go in the microwave. We like the convenience of being able to switch between both types depending on what we're cooking. (Plastic and ceramic bowls aren't as practical: The former's porous surface scratches and retains oils, while the latter is quite heavy.) In addition to these six basic mixing bowls, you might want a set of small bowls to hold prepped ingredients (sometimes called mise bowls, for "mise en place," a French term that means "to put everything in its place").

TALL & WIDE

Does the Shape of My Bowl Matter?

While material and size are important, there's another factor to consider when it comes to picking a mixing bowl: shape. Depending on what you're mixing, the shape of your bowl can make your work faster, easier, and neater—or just the opposite.

Tall and wide: A wide bowl provides plenty of room for your hands and tools to work comfortably within the bowl without limiting your range of motion, while tall walls contain flyaways during vigorous mixing. Use these for tasks such as mixing batter by hand; emulsifying vinaigrettes; and whisking cream, egg whites, and dry ingredients.

TALL & NARROW

Tall and narrow: Steep sides contain splatters and make it easier to tell when a dough has doubled. The narrow bottom corrals food, helping beaters work more effectively. Its narrow footprint is also ideal for storage. Use these to proof dough, beat food with a hand mixer, and store food.

WIDE & SHALLOW

Wide and shallow: A roomy, shallow bowl makes it easier to toss foods and allows for the big, broad mixing motions needed for combining ingredients gently and in just a few strokes. Use these for tossing salads, seasoning foods, and folding together light, airy batters.

Can I Use a Liquid Measuring Cup to Measure Dry Ingredients (or Vice Versa)?

Say you need to measure some all-purpose flour, but all your dry measuring cups are in the dishwasher. Can you use a liquid measuring cup? We found that when we asked a group of people to measure a cup of flour in dry measuring cups, results between different testers varied by as much as 13 percent. When a liquid measuring cup was used for the flour, the difference jumped to 26 percent. When we repeated the tests using a cup of water, the dry cup results varied by 23 percent, while the liquid cup varied by only 10 percent. So for the best shot at accurate results (without a scale), use the cup intended for what you're measuring.

Hannah Says . . .

The dip and sweep might sound like a funky dance but it's actually our preferred method for measuring dry ingredients by volume. You dip a dry measuring cup into a dry ingredient such as flour or sugar and then scrape across the top with a straight edge (such as a bench scraper or the back of a butter knife) to remove the excess. A scale is always going to be the most accurate measuring method, but the dip and sweep is the most accurate way to measure dry ingredients without one.

Lisa Says . . .

If you're measuring liquid in a liquid measuring cup, there is one important step you shouldn't skip. Set the cup on a level surface, then bend down and look at the top of the liquid at eye level. Not only is this good exercise, but you'll get a much more accurate measurement. If you can't bend, choose a measuring cup with an angled ramp inside designed to be read from a standing position.

How Should I Measure Thick, Sticky Ingredients?

It can be a pain to measure sticky and/or semisolid ingredients such as mayonnaise, peanut butter, and honey in either a dry measuring cup or a liquid one. But there's a third option: the adjustable measuring cup.

An adjustable measuring cup has a clear cylinder with volume markings and a plunger insert. You withdraw the plunger to the desired measurement and then fill the cylinder, level it off, and plunge to empty it. The plunger scrapes out the ingredient, and one additional swipe of a rubber spatula over the plunger is all that is needed to empty the measuring cup completely.

This design makes it easy to level ingredients (thus getting an accurate measurement) and then push out every last bit of the ingredient. If you don't own an adjustable measuring cup, a dry measuring cup is the next most consistent tool.

converting teaspoons to tablespoons to cups

TEASPOONS	TABLESPOONS	CUPS
3	1	¹⁄₁₆
6	2	⅛
12	4	¼
16	5 tablespoons plus 1 teaspoon	⅓
24	8	½
32	10 tablespoons plus 2 teaspoons	⅔
36	12	¾
48	16	1

Isn't Weighing Ingredients More Accurate?

Plenty of recipes will work fine if you carefully measure the ingredients using liquid and dry measuring cups, which is why we continue to include volume measurements in our ingredient lists. (If weighing is crucial to a recipe's outcome, we let you know.) That said, a digital scale can be a game changer in the kitchen. For baking recipes, where measuring dry ingredients by weight is the only way to guarantee accuracy, using a scale versus using measuring cups can mean the difference between a cake that's fluffy and tender or one that's squat and dense. For bread recipes, we often weigh water and other liquids too. Scales also have many applications in cooking: Using one to portion burgers, for example, means no more guessing if the patties are the same size and will thus cook at the same rate. And a scale's tare function resets the displayed weight to zero, letting you measure out multiple ingredients using just one bowl rather than multiple measuring cups. Fewer things to clean? Score! Once you get used to using a scale, you'll likely find yourself reaching for it instead of your measuring cups.

test it yourself

HOW ACCURATE ARE YOUR MEASURING CUPS?

Want to know if your measuring cups are accurate? Test them yourself using a kitchen scale. One by one, weigh the empty cup, hit the tare button, and then fill the cup with sugar (for dry measuring cups) or water (for liquid measuring cups). Then weigh the filled cup and compare its weight to the weights in the chart below. The closer your weights are to those in the chart, the more accurate your cups.

AMOUNT	TARGET WEIGHT (SUGAR)	TARGET WEIGHT (WATER)
1 cup	7.00 ounces or 198 grams	8.34 ounces or 236 grams
½ cup	3.50 ounces or 99 grams	4.17 ounces or 118 grams
⅓ cup	2.33 ounces or 66 grams	2.78 ounces or 79 grams
¼ cup	1.75 ounces or 50 grams	2.09 ounces or 59 grams

Temp and Time

After all the effort you put into prepping and cooking your meal or dessert, the last thing you want is for it to burn—or just as bad, to be raw inside. Keeping a good thermometer and timer on hand can help prevent disaster.

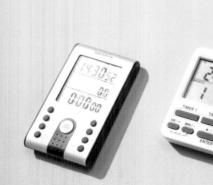

How Do I Temp That?

Not sure exactly how you should be temping tricky foods such as caramel and bone-in roasts? Fret no more. Here's how to do it the right way.

Bread in a loaf pan
Insert the thermometer from the side, just above the pan edge, and direct it at a downward angle into the center of the loaf.

Free-form bread
Tip the loaf (protect your hand with a dish towel) and insert the probe through the bottom crust into the center.

Cheesecake
If possible, insert the thermometer into the side of the cheesecake where it rises above the pan and angle it toward the center (otherwise, insert it into the center of the cake).

Caramel
Swirl the caramel to even out any hot spots. Tilt the pot so that the caramel pools 1 to 2 inches deep and move the thermometer back and forth in the caramel for about 5 seconds before taking a reading.

Steaks, chops, and poultry parts
Hold the steak, chop, or poultry with tongs and insert the thermometer through the side of the meat.

Burgers
Leaving the burger in the pan (or on the grill), slide the tip of the thermometer into the top edge and push it toward the center, making sure to avoid hitting the pan or cooking grate.

Roasts
Insert the thermometer at an angle, pushing the probe deep into the thickest part of the roast (avoid any bones), and then slowly draw it out. Look for the lowest temperature to find the center of the meat.

Whole poultry (breast)
Insert the thermometer from the neck end, holding it parallel to the bird. (Avoid hitting the bone, which can result in an inaccurate reading.)

Whole poultry (thigh)
Insert the thermometer into the area between the drumstick and breast, avoiding the thigh bone.

Whole stuffed poultry
In addition to taking the temperature of white and dark meat, insert the thermometer directly into the center of the cavity to take the temperature of the stuffing.

the right thermometer for the job

A thermometer takes temperatures. Simple, right? Well, depending on just what you're temping (say, barbecue or caramel or even the inside of your fridge), the right thermometer for the job can vary. Here are the ones we find most useful in the kitchen.

THERMOMETER		WHAT IT DOES	USE IT FOR
Digital Instant-Read Thermometer		Takes internal temperature of food in seconds	• All-purpose use: checking the doneness of meat, poultry, fish, sauces, custards, bread, and some vegetables • Checking temperature of frying oil (in a pinch)
Clip-On Probe Thermometer		Clips on to cooking vessel and takes continuous temperature readings	• Tracking internal temperature of food or oil over longer periods of time • Roasting, smoking, deep-frying, candy making
Remote Probe Thermometer		Same as clip-on probe thermometer, but also sends readings to your phone or a portable receiver	• Long, slow cooking such as barbecuing, where the ability to walk away from the food is helpful
Infrared Thermometer		Quickly gives surface temperature readings without needing to make contact	• Measuring surface temperature of bakeware • Finding hot or cold spots in your fridge or freezer or on a griddle, skillet, or other cookware
Refrigerator/Freezer Thermometer		Monitors temperature of refrigerator and/or freezer over time	• Determining if the interior of your refrigerator and/or freezer is cold enough to keep foods at a safe temperature
Oven Thermometer		Measures ambient temperature inside oven	• Determining if your oven is running hot or cold (some clip-on probe thermometers come with ambient temperature probes that can also do this)

test it yourself

HOW ACCURATE IS YOUR THERMOMETER?

Even the best thermometers should be periodically checked for accuracy and recalibrated if necessary. To test your thermometer's accuracy, fill a glass completely with ice. Add just enough cold water to fill in most of the gaps in the ice (you don't want to add so much water that the ice floats). Stir the ice mixture and let it sit for 60 seconds to allow the temperature to even out. Then submerge the probe 2 to 3 inches into the ice water and hold it in place for 60 seconds. (Don't let the probe touch the sides or bottom of the glass.) Once the 60 seconds is up, the thermometer should read between 31 and 33 degrees Fahrenheit. If it doesn't, refer to the manufacturer's instructions on how to recalibrate it or contact the manufacturer for help.

Hannah Says . . .

Don't bother using old-fashioned dial-face thermometers to temp your food; they can't produce readings fast enough. When you're dealing with temperature- and time-sensitive foods such as caramel or a perfectly medium-rare steak, seconds can matter. Trust me, an instant-read thermometer really is the way to go.

Does It Matter What Kind of Timer I Use?

You can use the timers on your smartphone, smart speaker, oven, or microwave—but there are good reasons to have a dedicated kitchen timer. Unlike some of the alternatives, a timer can be carried into another room so that it's always visible and within earshot. A kitchen timer is also often easier to set than the timers on appliances, and you don't have to worry about dirtying your phone with food. We prefer digital models to old-fashioned dial-face timers because they tend to be more precise, easier to set, and easier to read.

kitchen timers to avoid

DIAL-FACE TIMERS

These old-fashioned models are less precise than digital models, are hard to read from a distance, and often can't be set for more than an hour.

TIMERS THAT MAX OUT AT 100 MINUTES OR LESS

That's not enough time to braise a brisket, let alone roast a Thanksgiving turkey or proof a batch of bread dough.

MODELS WITHOUT SECONDS SETTINGS

Some models can be set for only whole hours or minutes, which isn't precise enough for quick-cooking foods such as soft-cooked eggs.

What a Crock

Some tools are so handy and used so often, it's not practical to hide them away in a drawer.

What Should I Keep in My Crock?

There are a lot of kitchen utensils that can go in a crock, but should they? Many crocks can only fit 10 to 15 items comfortably, so as a general rule we think this valuable space should be reserved for the tools you reach for most often during cooking. (Just *please* don't keep your knives in a crock—all that jostling and scraping will dull them faster than you can blink.) Here is a list of the tools we like to keep in our crocks at all times.

All-purpose whisk: Emulsifies sauces, whips cream, blends dry ingredients, and more. Of all the different types out there, we think a balloon whisk is the best all-purpose option. (That's not to say that other types aren't handy for certain tasks; see page 96 for more about what the other styles are good for.)

Large silicone spatula: Nimble and flexible, this can be used to fold batters, mix ingredients, scrape bowls and pans, scramble eggs, and much more.

Fish spatula: Our go-to spatula for all our food-flipping needs. (See page 97 for more about why we prefer this type over conventional turners.)

Kitchen tongs: Grab and manipulate small or awkward foods with ease; toss and portion long-strand pasta such as spaghetti with more control than with a pasta fork.

Wooden spoon: Offers more leverage than a softer silicone spatula; ideal for mixing stiff doughs, stirring soup, breaking up ground meat, and more.

Slotted spoon: Easily drains and removes small or delicate foods, such as peas, poached eggs, or meatballs, from liquid.

Lisa Says . . .

I always used to have trouble pouring liquids from a ladle or from one vessel to another. Then a test cook told me, "Commit to the pour." It really works! If you just go for it, you'll have fewer dribbles.

Ladle: Neatly scoops up and pours liquids. Moderately angled handle makes it easy to dip into pots and helps keep hands away from steam.

Pasta fork: Good for serving shaped pastas that aren't easily picked up with tongs.

Spider skimmer: Gently and efficiently removes food, such as ravioli or fried chicken pieces, from hot oil or boiling water.

Potato masher: Mashes potatoes and other soft foods.

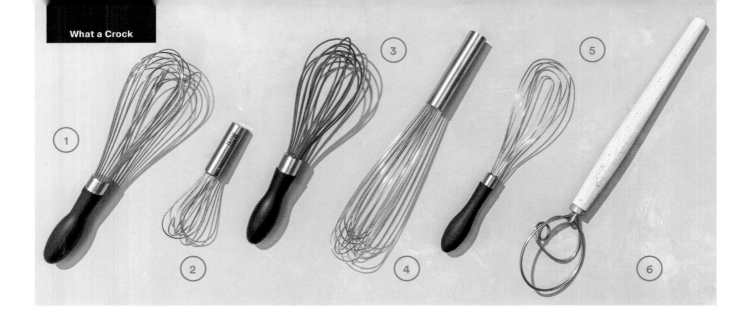

What Are All These Whisks Good For?

Whisks have a handle at one end and wires at the other. It's those wires that set the many varieties apart, coming in a wide variety of lengths, thicknesses, and configurations that make different styles better suited to certain tasks.

Bulbous **balloon whisks** (1) are great at whipping cream and egg whites and quickly combining dry ingredients; they're our favorite all-purpose whisk. **Mini** versions (2) whisk a single egg or make vinaigrette for two, while versions with **silicone-coated** tines (3) keep nonstick cookware scratch-free.

Narrow **sauce whisks** (4), also called French whisks, have lightweight tines that are great for making pan sauces.

Shoehorn-shaped **flat whisks** (5) reach into the corners of a skillet and can be used to whisk shallow gravies and rouxs.

The curlicue wire of **dough whisks** (6) splits the difference between a whisk and a spatula; it scrapes through stiff dough to eliminate flour pockets without getting all gummed up or overworking the dough.

Am I Whisking the Right Way?

When whisking, some people prefer side-to-side strokes, others use circular stirring, and others like the looping action of beating that takes the whisk up and out of the bowl. We tested each of these motions to see if one was more effective than the others.

Side-to-side won handily. Because it's an easier motion to execute quickly and aggressively, you can carry out more and harder motions per minute. It also applies more of what scientists call "shear force" to a liquid. As the whisk moves in one direction across the bowl, the liquid starts to move with it. But then the whisk is dragged in the opposite direction, exerting force against the rest of the liquid still moving toward it. Because stirring and beating take the liquid in the same direction of the whisk, they produce less shear force.

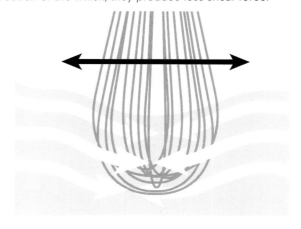

Beating does have a slight advantage when it comes to egg whites: The viscous whites cling to the tines, which allows the whisk to create wider channels that trap more air; pulling the whisk out of the mixture preserves those channels.

Which Kind of Spatula Is Best for Flipping Food?

A single spatula can cover all your food turning and flipping needs, but it might not be the kind you think: It's a fish spatula. While the name makes it sound like it does only one thing, we think these spatulas are actually the best all-purpose turners out there and prefer them to conventional turners for a whole host of reasons.

head to head
SPATULAS FOR FLIPPING

FISH SPATULAS

Long, moderately flexible heads securely support large foods and scoot under food easily

Narrow heads are easier to maneuver in tight spaces

Shorter handles offer superior control

Subtly curved edges give leverage for lifting food

CONVENTIONAL SPATULAS

Short, thick heads can't accommodate large foods and push food instead of sliding cleanly under it

Wide heads are hard to maneuver in tight spaces

Long handles put hands farther away from food

Flat edges provide no added leverage for lifting food

How Many Rubber Spatulas Does One Person Need?

A large (about 12-inch) spatula—we prefer silicone—is one of the busiest tools in any kitchen, so it's not a bad idea to have two. While not essential, a spoonula (combination spoon and spatula) is handy for folding, scraping, and scooping. And a jar spatula, designed to maneuver in tight spaces, is a worthwhile purchase for the ability to get at that last drop of molasses or marinara.

anatomy of
GOOD KITCHEN TONGS

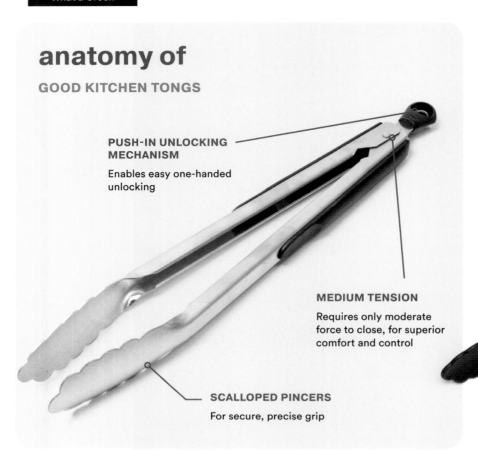

PUSH-IN UNLOCKING MECHANISM

Enables easy one-handed unlocking

MEDIUM TENSION

Requires only moderate force to close, for superior comfort and control

SCALLOPED PINCERS

For secure, precise grip

Should I Buy Silicone-Coated Kitchen Tongs?

We generally prefer the precision and control of tongs with uncoated metal pincers, finding that silicone- or plastic-coated pincers tend to be thicker and a little less precise. That said, coated pincers are safe for use with nonstick cookware, so if you often cook with nonstick pots and pans, tongs with coated pincers might be the right choice for you.

What's the Best Way to Clean a Fine-Mesh Strainer?

While it may always be a drudgery to get your fine-mesh strainer sparkling clean, there are a few things you can do to make the work lighter. First, scrape a clean spatula on the underside of the strainer's basket, as that's where most of the separated stuff will cling. Be sure to wash your strainer right after using it—you don't want to let any grainy bits dry and cling tighter to the mesh. And to dislodge any stuck-on grit, scrub the strainer with a dish-cleaning brush and use your faucet's spray attachment to "blast" it out.

Why Are My Mashed Potatoes So Lumpy?

There are two main kinds of potato mashers—those with perforated mashing plates and those with wave-shaped wires—and they are not created equal. Mashers with perforated plates make smoother potatoes with less effort; the larger gaps in wavy mashers can leave lumps of untouched potato, and their blocky footprints make it difficult to navigate the circular edges of pans, especially in smaller saucepans. But if achieving supersmooth and supremely fluffy mashed potatoes is your goal, a potato ricer is the best tool for the job. Potato ricers look and work just like giant garlic presses: You put the cooked potatoes in a hopper and squeeze the handles to force the spuds through a perforated disk.

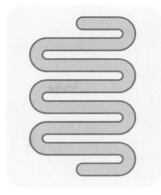

Larger gaps in wave-style mashers leave lumps of untouched potato.

Perforated mashing plates make a smoother mash.

What's So Complicated About a Wooden Spoon?

As simple as they are, wooden spoons are subject to a lot of subtle and not-so-subtle differences that affect how they perform. The biggest factor in determining how well a spoon works is the shape of its head. Overall, wider heads are more effective than narrower heads. Spoons with thinner front edges are easier to slip underneath food to scrape or scoop than those with thick front edges. Scoop-shaped spoons can lift and move more food at a time than flatter, paddle-style models. Most traditional round- or oval-headed spoons need to be held at an angle to scrape a pot effectively. Wide flat-edged, spatula-shaped spoons work well to scrape up fond and move food using a minimum number of strokes, and to transfer food efficiently.

Gadgets Galore

There's a gadget out there to scratch every cooking itch. Not all of them are winners—but we think assembling a collection that matches your cooking personality can be a lot of fun.

Are One-Task Tools Ever Worthwhile?

Multitasking kitchen tools rightly get a lot of praise, but a tool can deserve space in your kitchen even if it does only one thing. Consider: Where would we be without can openers, or corkscrews? If you're trying to decide whether to spring for a so-called "unitasker," think about how often you engage in that task, how easy it is to do the task without that particular tool, and how effective the tool is at accomplishing the task. Will it save you time? Will it make the job more enjoyable (or at least less tedious)? Even seemingly oddball gadgets can be worthwhile: If you love fresh pineapple, a pineapple corer (yes, that's a thing) could make you a very happy cook.

real talk with hannah

A CASE FOR SPECIALIZED GADGETS

Single-use or specialized gadgets get a lot of guff. Some folks say you can do everything you need with a knife and a cast-iron skillet. I'd argue specialized tools are worth it—if they're worth it to you. Take a tomato corer: These little devices quickly and efficiently scoop out the stem and core of tomatoes. Sure, a knife works, but a corer works even *better*. Take it from me: Prepping 25 pounds of tomatoes for canning without a corer, as I did last year after forgetting to buy myself a new one, is no fun. I was mentally kicking myself the entire time I was slowly carving out the stems and cores with a paring knife. Our teammate Carolyn's family cans 425 pounds of tomatoes (yes, you read that right) every single year, and Carolyn told me that ever since they bought a few corers the process has hummed right along. I've already ordered my corer for next August.

FREQUENTLY ASKED QUESTIONS: GARLIC PRESS EDITION

Q: Is there any difference between garlic that's been pressed and garlic that's been minced by hand?

A: No. Both produce a fine mince with pungent flavor. In the test kitchen, we like using a garlic press instead of mincing tricky, tiny garlic cloves with a knife. If you've got the knife skills (and the patience), go for it—but we love that a garlic press creates finely minced, equal-size pieces in a matter of seconds.

Q: Should I peel garlic cloves before pressing them?

A: It depends on your garlic press. Most garlic presses struggle with unpeeled cloves; the fibrous skin is harder to get through, and the minced garlic tends to spray in different directions as it emerges from the press. If this is the case for your press, use the side of a chef's knife to smash and peel the cloves before pressing. Even if your press can handle unpeeled cloves, it's helpful to trim off the tip or halve the clove to break the tension in the skin.

Q: How do I get my garlic press clean?

A: There's no fancy method: Just be sure to wash or soak the press immediately. Garlic quickly turns into garlicky cement if allowed to dry on, meaning you'll be working with fewer and fewer holes in your press over time. So if you don't have time to wash your press right away, at least soak it until you do. (And if you're still in the market for a press, you can make cleaning easier by choosing one that doesn't have a lot of parts to take apart and put back together.)

DIY alternatives to single-use gadgets

INSTEAD OF USING THIS . . .	DO THIS!
Egg separator	Hold your hand over bowl with your fingers slightly separated and pour cracked egg into your hand; white will flow through while yolk stays in your hand.
Jar opener	Place rubber band around jar lid for better grip.
Garlic peeler	Place garlic cloves in 2-cup wide-mouth Mason jar, screw on lid, and shake jar for 30 seconds. Pour out cloves and inspect; if any still have skins, put them back in jar and repeat.
Cherry pitter	Place cherry on mouth of empty wine or beer bottle and use drinking straw to push pit through (bottle catches pits and juices for easy cleanup).

more uses for common gadgets

Even if these handy gadgets have already earned their place in your kitchen, chances are you could be making them work even harder for you.

USE THIS . . .	TO DO THIS!
Apple corer	Coring pears; cutting potatoes or onions into wedges
Colander	Draining old, runny egg whites; draining watery fruits and vegetables
Potato masher	Mashing lemons for lemonade, tomatoes for sauce, and avocados for guacamole
Ricer	Juicing citrus; peeling and mashing roasted garlic; squeezing excess moisture out of spinach

Am I Using My Salad Spinner Wrong?

If you place your greens, herbs, or vegetables in the perforated basket of your salad spinner and run it under water in the sink before returning the insert to the salad spinner's bowl to spin it dry, you're not getting your food as clean as it could be. For squeaky-clean greens and vegetables, do this instead.

Watch Lisa and Hannah show off their favorite fruit prep gadgets (as well as some that didn't make the cut).

1 Place food inside basket. Keeping filled basket inside outer bowl, fill bowl with water to thoroughly soak contents.

2 Lift out basket, let water drain, and empty outer bowl. Repeat until food is free of dirt and grit.

3 Return filled basket to empty bowl and spin its contents dry. If large amount of water comes off food, remove basket, dump water, and spin again.

PURSLANE AND WATERMELON SALAD

serves 4 to 6

Draining the moisture-rich watermelon in a colander before assembling this salad prevents it from turning into a soupy mess. This salad benefits from a liberal sprinkling of salt and pepper, so don't be shy when seasoning the salad at the end of step 2.

4	cups watermelon cut into 1-inch pieces
2	teaspoons sugar
2	tablespoons extra-virgin olive oil, plus extra for drizzling
1	tablespoon cider vinegar
½	teaspoon grated lemon zest plus 1 tablespoon juice
½	teaspoon table salt
¼	teaspoon pepper
6	ounces purslane, trimmed and torn into 1½-inch pieces (6 cups)
¼	cup fresh basil or parsley leaves, torn
1	shallot, sliced thin
6	ounces fresh mozzarella cheese, torn into 1-inch pieces

1 Toss watermelon with sugar in colander set over bowl; set aside and let sit for 30 minutes.

2 Whisk oil, vinegar, lemon zest and juice, salt, and pepper together in large bowl. Add purslane, basil, shallot, and drained watermelon and toss gently to combine. Transfer to serving platter and scatter mozzarella over top. Drizzle with extra oil and season with salt and pepper to taste. Serve.

PASTA WITH RAW TOMATO SAUCE

serves 4

Taking a potato masher to raw peak-season tomatoes yields a ridiculously easy no-cook sauce that tastes like summer. Use the ripest tomatoes you can find for this recipe.

2	pounds very ripe tomatoes, cored and cut into ½-inch pieces
2	teaspoons plus 2 tablespoons extra-virgin olive oil, divided, plus extra for serving
1½	tablespoons chopped fresh oregano
2	garlic cloves, minced
1½	teaspoons table salt
¼	teaspoon sugar
3	cups water plus extra as needed
1	pound short pasta, such as campanelle, busiate, penne, or fusilli
½	cup fresh basil leaves, torn
1	ounce Parmesan cheese, grated (½ cup), plus extra for serving

1 Combine tomatoes, 2 teaspoons oil, oregano, garlic, salt, and sugar in large bowl. Let sit until tomatoes soften and release their juice, at least 1 hour or up to 3 hours.

2 Drain tomato mixture in fine-mesh strainer set over bowl, reserving juice. (You should have 1 cup tomato juice; if not, add water as needed to equal 1 cup.) Divide tomato mixture evenly between 2 bowls. Using potato masher, mash 1 bowl of tomato mixture to pulp.

3 Combine water, pasta, and reserved tomato juice in Dutch oven. Cover; place over medium-high heat; and cook at vigorous simmer, stirring often, until pasta is al dente and liquid has nearly evaporated, 12 to 15 minutes. Off heat, stir in basil, Parmesan, mashed and unmashed tomato mixtures, and remaining 2 tablespoons oil. Season with salt and pepper to taste. Serve, passing extra oil and extra Parmesan separately.

gadget alignment chart

From the weirdly useful to the downright wacky, here are just a few of the more noteworthy gadgets we've tested over the years.

MORE USEFUL

TOMATO CORER
One scoop and done

BEAR PAW MEAT HANDLERS
Shred hot meat—and feel like
Wolverine while you're at it

CHERRY PITTER
Does what it says on the tin—fast

CORN STRIPPER
No more errant kernels

PINEAPPLE CORER
Cores, slices, and removes the
eyes all in one go

PEANUT BUTTER MIXER
A must-have for lovers of
natural peanut butter

LESS WACKY

MORE WACKY

MANUAL SPICE GRINDER
Gets the job done, but is slow
and arduous

AVOCADO SLICER
Safely removes pits, but mangles the
delicate slices

LETTUCE KNIFE
Less effective at preventing
browning than tearing the
lettuce with your hands

WATERMELON SLICER
No less messy, and you still need a
knife to cut through the rind

EGG SEPARATOR
Just use your hands

EGGIES
Expectation: easy hard-cooked
shell-less eggs; Reality: a mess

LESS USEFUL

plug it in

RECIPES

Don't Try This at Home

One thing we've learned through years of testing equipment is not to make any assumptions.

Just because an appliance has been around in one form or another for decades doesn't mean it has all the kinks worked out. Take toasters, for example. They have one job to do, and it's a seemingly simple one: heat a slice of bread until it's evenly crispy and brown. But when we reviewed long-slot toasters, we had to burn through 1,500 slices of bread (plus a bundle of bagels) to find one that makes a decent piece of toast. We were left with mountains of more-or-less browned bread. We're all about going to great lengths to get results, but even for us, that's . . . a lot.

How did we get there? First, we made toast in our 10 contenders at light, medium, and dark settings, and then we filled each toaster to capacity and made full batches of toast in rapid succession. Finally, we chose our top three models and toasted 365 consecutive pieces of bread—a year's worth of toast—in each of them. (As if that wasn't enough toasting for a lifetime, when we reviewed toaster ovens we did it all over again, racking up another 860 slices of toast.) Along the way we learned how long each toaster took to do its job, how hot the exterior became, and of course how evenly and accurately it toasted. And yes, all that toasting did help us find models of both types of toaster that turned out toast we were happy to spread with jam and call breakfast— just as soon as we were ready to face eating toast again.

The Big Three

It's easy to take your refrigerator, freezer, and dishwasher for granted, but taking the time to get to know these built-ins a little better pays off big.

How Cold Should My Refrigerator Be?

To prevent the growth of harmful bacteria, all areas of your fridge should be at or below 40 degrees Fahrenheit but above 32 degrees (the coldest setting on your fridge is often too cold). You can and should buy a refrigerator/freezer thermometer (see page 93) to monitor temperature. The best ones alert you if the temperature strays from the safe zone. But if you don't have one of these thermometers, you can use your instant-read thermometer to do a quick check by temping the food in your fridge. Provided your food has been in the fridge a while, it'll have the same temperature as the fridge. Liquids such as your carton of milk or orange juice are easiest to temp, but you can temp anything, from leftover mashed potatoes to cranberry sauce to marmalade.

 Lisa Says . . .

If you put hot food in the fridge, it will raise the overall temperature and shorten the lifespan of the food in it. It also makes your fridge work harder. It's OK to transfer food into a storage container and let it sit at room temperature for a short period of time. But short is the operative word: Bacteria can multiply in the "danger zone" between 40 and 140 degrees. About 30 minutes should lower the food's temperature sufficiently but keep it within the safe temperature range. Set the kitchen timer to remind you to put it away!

your refrigerator's microclimates

Even a properly running refrigerator has different temperature zones. To keep your food at its best, know what to store where.

COLD ZONE

Located at the back of the fridge, from top to bottom. Also includes the shelves at the bottom of the fridge door.

Best for storing prepared foods, left-overs, meat, dairy, and produce that is not prone to chilling injury, such as apples, cherries, grapes, and cabbage.

HUMID ZONE

Located within the crisper drawer.

Best for storing produce with a high water content, such as artichokes, asparagus, beets, broccoli, carrots, cauliflower, celery, chiles, cucumbers, eggplant, fresh herbs, green beans, leafy greens, leeks, lettuce, mushrooms, peppers, radishes, and scallions.

MODERATE ZONE

Located at the front of the fridge, from top to bottom. Also includes the shelves at the top of the fridge door.

Best for storing beverages, condiments, eggs, butter, and produce that is sensitive to chilling injury, such as berries and melons.

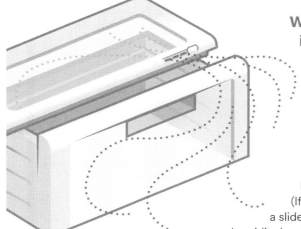

Why Is My Food Going Bad in the Crisper Drawer?

The humid environment of the crisper drawer is designed to protect produce from shriveling and rotting. But too much humidity can cause water to accumulate, hastening spoilage. You can fix this problem by adjusting the vents; the more cold air that is let in, the less humid the environment will be. (If your crisper drawer doesn't have a slide control, it is always at the highest humidity level of which it is capable.)

What's the Safest Way to Store Meat in the Refrigerator?

Meat should always be stored in the coldest part of your refrigerator—that's toward the back—and in its original packaging. Whether the meat is fresh or you're defrosting it, set it on a rimmed plate or quarter sheet pan to collect any juices. Never set meat on top of produce or anything you'd eat raw.

How Can I Get Rid of That Funky Fridge Smell?

If you, like many people, keep a box of baking soda in the fridge to neutralize odors, you may have noticed that some smells still linger. That's because baking soda only absorbs acidic molecules. Most foods are slightly acidic, but not all are. To really clear the air, you're better off using charcoal briquettes or activated charcoal pellets. Charcoal is made almost entirely of carbon, a substance that absorbs all organic compounds (aka smelly food particles), and it's porous, with lots of nooks and crannies for trapping those odors. Charcoal briquettes (yes, the same kind used for grilling) are widely available; you can buy activated charcoal at pet and aquarium supply stores. For a full-size refrigerator, place 2 cups in an open container in the back of the fridge near an air vent. It should work for at least a month.

But here's another thought: That funky smell might be telling you it's time to get rid of last week's leftovers. A good clean-out should help your fridge smell fresh again.

Can My Freezer Be Too Cold?

Unlike your refrigerator, the colder your freezer is, the better. Make sure your freezer is at the coldest possible setting and use a thermometer to check the temperature; you want it to register 0 degrees Fahrenheit or colder. Keep food away from freezer vents so it doesn't block cold air coming in. To help your freezer (and fridge) do its job of chilling efficiently, vacuum the filters and coils periodically to remove dust and grime. (Just be sure to unplug it first.)

Is My Freezer Overcrowded?

A full freezer is an efficient one; when you open the door of an empty-ish freezer, warm air rushes in and the freezer needs to work to cool it down. If the freezer is full of already frozen items, it has less work to do. So it's a good idea to take advantage of your freezer's full capacity, as long as you're not blocking the air vents. (The more quickly you freeze food, the better its quality once defrosted, and good airflow allows for a quicker freeze.) But if you've got so many things piled in your freezer that it's hard to find what you want, you may be overcrowding your freezer. Adding some wire shelving can help organize your freezer and enable better airflow.

How (and How Often) Should I Defrost?

If you notice ice that's ¼ inch thick or more lining your freezer walls, it's time to defrost. Putting if off will only make the defrosting take longer when you eventually do it; plus, your freezer will run less efficiently in the meantime.

Before you start, turn off or unplug your freezer and transfer all the food to coolers. (If you have a fridge/freezer combo, be careful not to open the refrigerator door while it's unplugged in order to maintain the fridge's temperature.) If your freezer has a drainage hose, place the end in a low bucket. Leave the freezer door open so warm air can reach the inside. To speed things up, place a bowl of hot water on a folded towel in your freezer and replace it every 15 minutes or so. As the ice melts, use large towels or rags to mop up the water. Resist the urge to chip away at the ice with a metal knife or ice pick, as this can risk puncturing the freezer; if you want, you can use a wooden spoon or plastic spatula. Once all the ice has melted, clean your freezer with warm, soapy water and wipe it dry. Wipe the gasket clean too. Turn the freezer back on and wait for it to reach the proper temperature. While you're waiting, sort through your frozen food and get rid of items that are past their prime. Then repack your freezer, making sure you don't block the vents.

8 things you may not know you can freeze

BREAD

To freeze: Wrap sliced loaves tightly in plastic wrap, or wrap unsliced loaves in foil, then seal in zipper-lock bag.

To use: Thaw individual slices at room temperature; no need to thaw slices before toasting. Place frozen loaves, still wrapped in foil, in 450-degree oven for 10 to 15 minutes, then remove foil and return loaves to oven for 1 to 2 minutes to crisp crust.

BUTTER

To freeze: Freeze butter in its wrapper.

To use: Transfer to refrigerator as needed. To soften frozen butter quickly, cut into small pieces or place in zipper-lock bag and pound to desired consistency with rolling pin.

CANNED CHIPOTLE CHILES IN ADOBO

To freeze: Spoon chiles, each with a couple teaspoons of adobo sauce, onto different areas of baking sheet lined with parchment paper and freeze. Transfer frozen chiles to zipper-lock bag for long-term storage.

To use: Use in any recipe that calls for canned chipotle chiles in adobo; no need to thaw before using.

CHEESE

To freeze: Wrap hard and semifirm cheeses such as Parmesan, cheddar, and Brie tightly in plastic wrap; seal in zipper-lock bag; and freeze for up to two months.

To use: Defrost cheese in refrigerator before use.

CITRUS ZEST

To freeze: Remove zest from entire fruit. Deposit grated zest on plate in ½-teaspoon piles and freeze. Once piles are frozen, transfer them to zipper-lock bag and return to freezer.

To use: Add frozen zest to any recipe that calls for citrus zest; no need to thaw before using.

EGG WHITES

To freeze: Pour egg whites (never yolks) into each well of ice cube tray and freeze.

To use: Use paring knife or small spatula to remove each frozen egg white cube and defrost in small bowl in refrigerator as needed.

HERBS

To freeze: Place 2 tablespoons chopped fresh hardy herbs such as rosemary, sage, parsley, or thyme in each well of ice cube tray. And water to cover (about 1 tablespoon per well) and freeze. Once cubes are frozen, transfer to zipper-lock bag for long-term storage.

To use: Add frozen herb cubes directly to sauces, soups, or stews; no need to thaw before using.

WINE

To freeze: Pour 1 tablespoon wine into each well of ice cube tray and freeze.

To use: Use paring knife or small spatula to remove each frozen wine cube and add as desired to pan sauces; no need to thaw before using.

worth it

COUNTERTOP ICE MAKER

If your freezer doesn't have a built-in ice maker, and if you're fed up with the small capacities of ice trays and the hassle of using them, a countertop ice maker could be a worthwhile purchase. They're also a more portable option for home bars, dorm rooms, and studios, as well as boats and RVs. You can use one 24/7 to always have ice on hand, or reserve it for parties or trips and store it when it's not in use. One important note: Ice makers are not freezers in and of themselves; as unused ice in the bins begins to melt, the water collects under the bins and is recirculated to make more ice.

Does Running a Dishwasher Really Use Less Water than Washing Dishes by Hand?

All those splashing and gurgling sounds a dishwasher makes as it goes through a cycle make it seem like a lot of water is being used, but the amount is actually less than you might think. Any standard-size model made since 2013 uses no more than 5 gallons per cycle, and current Energy Star–rated models use 3½ gallons or less. By contrast, because faucets run at 1½ to 2 gallons per minute, hand-washing dishes under running water for 5 minutes can add up to 10 gallons of water down the drain. If you do wash dishes by hand, filling your sink or a dishtub with hot, soapy water will cut down on your water usage. You can also install an aerator in your faucet if it doesn't already have one to cut back on water output. And if you use a dishwasher, stick to scraping your dishes before loading them in the washer rather than prerinsing them so you don't offset the water savings too much. (See page 114 for more about why you might want to reconsider prerinsing.)

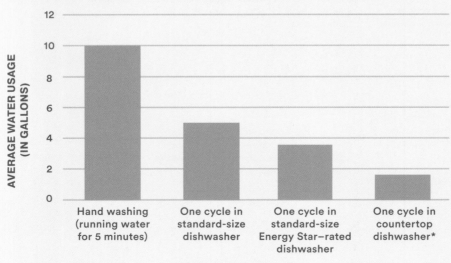

dish-washing water usage at a glance

Chart: AVERAGE WATER USAGE (IN GALLONS) vs. DISHWASHING METHOD

- Hand washing (running water for 5 minutes): 10
- One cycle in standard-size dishwasher: 5
- One cycle in standard-size Energy Star–rated dishwasher: ~3.5
- One cycle in countertop dishwasher*: ~1.6

* Most countertop dishwashers hold two to four place settings; water savings may be offset by more frequent use

Why Aren't My Dishes Getting as Clean as They Used To?

When your dishwasher is busy cleaning all your dirty dishes, it can't clean itself. Minerals from your tap water, soap residue, and grease can build up over time, and the filter can become clogged with food scraps (see page 115 for more on cleaning the filter), leading to spots, streaks, and food traces on your just-washed dishes. To keep your dishwasher cleaning effectively, you should run a cleaning cycle to deep-clean its interior about once a month.

Dishwasher cleaning products such as Affresh or Finish are designed to scrub and descale the machine. Alternatively, you can do a DIY clean with vinegar: Place a sturdy glass or dishwasher-safe measuring cup containing 2 cups of distilled white vinegar on the bottom rack. Without adding any detergent, run the dishwasher through a complete wash cycle, using an air-dry or an energy-saving dry option.

Just don't go overboard and do this cleaning cycle more than once per month: Vinegar is an acid, and too much can damage your dishwasher, even if its interior is made of stainless steel. And definitely don't be tempted to use chlorine bleach, which will damage the machine.

Lisa Says . . .

Need a little more space for taller dishes? Many dishwashers have an adjustable top rack; check for two latches on either side of the rack or two sets of rollers.

Hannah Says . . .

The top rack of a dishwasher tends to receive less heat, so if an item specifies that it's "top-rack dishwasher-safe only" it's probably a bit more delicate and less heat-resistant. Plastic food storage containers and breakable glassware are often best on the top rack, whereas sturdier items such as plates and bowls are fine on the bottom.

Are Countertop Dishwashers Any Good?

If you're ready to quit hand-washing dishes, but can't install (or don't need) a full-size dishwasher, a countertop dishwasher might be a good solution. They use regular dish detergent and reach safe temperatures for effective cleaning, and they require less energy and cost less to run than full-size dishwashers. Smaller models call for pouring a set amount of water into them before running, and wash about two place settings at a time. Larger models, which handle about four place settings, hook up to the kitchen faucet. One drawback: They claim a lot of counter real estate, so consider storing yours on a rolling cart, if you have one.

6 Pro Tips for Getting Dishes Squeaky Clean

To prerinse or not to prerinse? Should cutlery be loaded handle up or handle down? It's time to put all those contentious dishwashing debates to bed.

1 LOAD THE DISHWASHER THE RIGHT WAY

Yes, there is a right way to load the dishwasher. Loading your dishes correctly (and taking care not to overcrowd them) helps get them cleaner by preventing dishes from nesting into one another, trapping water and food, and by allowing your dishwasher to effectively circulate water and soap and wash away food scraps.

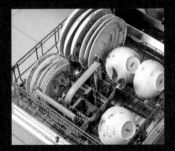   

Put delicate items such as glassware and plastic containers on top rack. Put sturdier items that can withstand higher heat, such as plates or bowls, on bottom rack. Leave some space between items to allow water and soap to circulate.

Load cup-shaped items such as bowls, glasses, mugs, and colanders upside down to prevent water pooling inside.

Place butter knives in baskets handle-side up. Place forks and spoons in baskets handle-side down. Separate similar items to prevent utensils from nesting and trapping food.

Before you start wash cycle, spin spray arm (usually located beneath top rack). If it gets stuck on anything, you need to do some reconfiguring.

2 DON'T PRERINSE

You'll definitely want to scrape off huge chunks of meatloaf, spaghetti, or whatever you had for dinner before you load the dishwasher, but it isn't necessary to rinse the dish until it looks clean. Dishwasher detergents actually need some food traces to cling to while the enzymes in the detergent gobble up starches and proteins and fats.

3 EMPTY THE FILTER

If your dishwasher is starting to smell a little funky, the filter trap at the bottom of the dishwasher is most likely the culprit. It should be cleaned at least once a month, depending on how often you use it. Getting food residue out of the trap will leave dishes cleaner and help the dishwasher drain.

Pull out filter and empty it.

Gently scrub with old toothbrush or soft bottle brush.

Rinse well and carefully put filter back in place.

4 USE THE RIGHT DETERGENT

Never use soap meant for handwashing dishes in your dishwasher—it's formulated very differently from dishwasher detergent. Dish soap creates foamy bubbles as you clean; if you add it to your dishwasher the likely outcome is a river of foam escaping the machine. Dishwasher detergents, whether liquid or pods, use enzymes to clean food from dishes and produce few to no bubbles.

5 CONSIDER A RINSE AID

A dishwasher rinse aid is a liquid containing surfactants that reduce the surface tension of water so that it can't cling to dishes and glassware. We've found that it makes dishes come out of the dishwasher a bit cleaner and much drier, and it leaves flatware and glassware shiny and spotless. Be sure to check your dishwasher's manual to make sure a rinse aid is compatible with your model, and use only the amount recommended.

6 KNOW WHICH ITEMS YOU SHOULD HAND-WASH

A dishwasher is too harsh an environment for some kitchenware. Chef's knives and other kitchen prep knives, wooden spoons and cutting boards, nonstick cookware, copper cookware, sterling silver or silver-plated flatware, and delicate china should all be washed by hand. And while some pots and pans say they're dishwasher-safe, many are not; for space economy alone we typically prefer to wash pots and pans by hand.

Zap It

Whether it's warming up coffee or cooking a whole meal, the microwave oven has become a valuable team player in the kitchen.

How Do Microwaves Work?

Microwave ovens are powered by a vacuum tube called a magnetron that uses an electric current and magnets to generate electromagnetic waves called microwaves. The waves can pass right through glass, paper, plastic, and similar materials—but they're absorbed by food. They make the food's water molecules (and to a lesser extent, the fat molecules) vibrate, which produces heat that cooks the food.

Microwaves don't penetrate very deeply; they only reach the outer layer of the item you are cooking. The rest of the food warms by conduction as the heat spreads inward from the hot surface. Microwave ovens typically cycle power on and off as they work. (You'll hear a fan whirring continuously, while a slightly louder hum switches on and off; that's the magnetron kicking in.) Some use inverter technology, where the power doesn't cycle on and off like a typical microwave, but stays on, even at lower settings, for what manufacturers claim to be more precise cooking.

Why Can't Metal Go in the Microwave?

Microwaves don't pass through metal the way they pass through glass, paper, plastic, and other materials (including food). Instead, much of the microwave energy bounces off the metal, which can damage the oven's circuitry.

That said, you *can* actually sometimes put metal in the microwave. What distinguishes microwave-safe metal from metal that will spark or "arc" (i.e. create what looks like a bolt of lightning between the metal and the walls of the microwave) is the type of metal, its thickness, and its shape. For example, gold is highly conductive, so putting your vintage tea cups with thin gold filigree in the microwave would be a no-go. Metal with sharp corners, such as forks, will also spark because the electricity can jump from one point to a nearby one easily. On the other hand, the smooth, rounded, thick metal components in some microwaveable cookware is specifically designed not to cause issues. Bottom line: You shouldn't put metal in the microwave . . . unless the manufacturer has designated it safe to do so.

How Can I Get More Even Results?

Have you ever bitten into a morsel of microwaved food to find it hardly heated at all, only to burn your mouth on another piece moments later? These tips can help with that.

Use a lower power setting: This allows heat to spread through and cook food more slowly without scorching.

Stop and stir or flip food: Edges warm up faster than the interior and the underside gets hotter than the top. Stirring or flipping the food helps redistribute the heat.

Place food off-center: Food positioned at the center of a turntable doesn't move relative to the magnetron. If food is placed off-center, it passes steadily through both heavier and lighter regions of microwave radiation for more even exposure.

Let it stand: When you're done microwaving your food, let it rest for anywhere from 2 to 15 minutes, depending on its size and quantity, so that hotter and cooler spots can even out.

When Should I Use One of Those Food Covers?

To prevent soup splatters, rice fireworks, and butter explosions, it's a good idea to cover your food when microwaving it. Lots of people reach for plastic wrap, but the FDA recommends only using wrap marked microwave-safe and leaving several inches of room between the food and the plastic wrap during microwaving. This is particularly important if the food is high in fat or oil since most of the suspect chemicals in plastic wrap are fat-soluble rather than water-soluble. A safer and more durable option is a flat silicone cover. But the easiest solution is something you already have on hand: an overturned microwave-safe bowl or plate.

is this microwave-safe?

NO	USE WITH CAUTION	YES
• Recycled paper bags	• Glass jars and bowls: may overheat and shatter if microwaved at high temperatures, especially if scratched or damaged in any way	• Ceramics, including stoneware and porcelain
• Paper towels with synthetic fibers		• Tempered glass, such as Pyrex
• Recycled paper towels	• Mason jars: check to see if they are labeled microwave-safe; microwave at low power for short amounts of time	• Borosilicate glass
• Melamine		• Containers marked "microwave-safe"
• Most metals, including aluminum foil, metal handles on takeout containers, and dinnerware with metal trim	• Plastic containers: check to make sure they are labeled microwave-safe, otherwise they may melt or burn	
• Baby bottles		
• Styrofoam		
• Paper cups		

real talk with lisa

HIGHER WATTAGE DOESN'T MEAN A BETTER MICROWAVE

You might assume higher wattage means better performance, but this is not the case with microwave ovens. With high-wattage ovens you'll only get good results if you nearly always run them on lower power settings such as 50 percent. Otherwise you risk overcooked, shriveled food and exploding butter. Very low-wattage ovens take longer, and you'll have to keep adding cooking time—although if you ask me, this is still better than over-zapping food with a high-wattage oven. Ideally, you should get a microwave oven with a moderate power level of 900 to 1,000 watts; these work efficiently with fewer adjustments and just-right results.

FREQUENTLY ASKED QUESTIONS: MICROWAVE EDITION

Q: Why do microwave ovens have turntables?

A: The microwaves within the oven vary in intensity, which makes for uneven cooking and can lead to hot and cold spots within food. By moving food around the microwave oven, the rotating turntable helps even out the heating process.

Q: Why is there mesh on the door?

A: The mesh on the door of your microwave has holes large enough to let wavelengths of visible light out (so you can see inside) but small enough to reflect microwaves, which are larger, back in so that they can't cook anything outside the microwave.

Q: Is it dangerous to stand close to a running microwave?

A: Microwave ovens are highly regulated and required to have fail-safe features, such as double gaskets and locking mechanisms to prevent leaks, as well as automatic shutoff when the door opens. The level of radiation emitted from them is less than that emitted from a cell phone. While it's probably not a great idea to stand with your nose pressed to the window for the entire cooking time, there's no need to worry about standing near the microwave or checking on food as it cooks.

Q: How should I clean my microwave?

A: You don't need a fancy microwave cleaning gadget. Just use this DIY method: Microwave a mixture of ¼ cup water, ¼ cup distilled white vinegar, and a squeeze of lemon juice in a microwave-safe bowl at full power for 7 minutes. Without opening the door, let the mixture sit for 2 minutes longer. The steam will loosen dried, stuck-on food on the interior walls, so you can just wipe them clean.

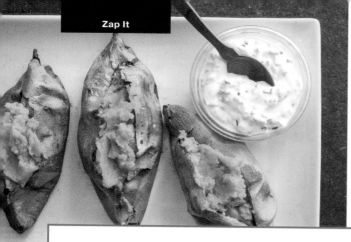

BEST BAKED SWEET POTATOES

serves 4

For baked sweet potatoes that don't take hours to cook, we jump-start their cooking in the microwave before transferring them to the oven. Buy potatoes of uniform size; we prefer bright orange-fleshed varieties such as Garnet.

> 4   small sweet potatoes (8 ounces each), unpeeled, each lightly pricked with fork in 3 places

1   Adjust oven rack to middle position and heat oven to 425 degrees. Place potatoes on large plate and microwave until potatoes yield to gentle pressure and centers register 200 degrees, 6 to 9 minutes, flipping potatoes every 3 minutes.

2   Set wire rack in aluminum foil–lined rimmed baking sheet and spray rack with vegetable oil spray. Using tongs, transfer potatoes to prepared rack and bake for 1 hour (exteriors of potatoes will be lightly browned and potatoes will feel very soft when squeezed).

3   Slit each potato lengthwise; using clean dish towel, hold ends and squeeze slightly to push flesh up and out. Transfer potatoes to serving platter. Season with salt and pepper to taste. Serve.

real talk with hannah

BUY YOURSELF A MICROWAVE ALREADY!

I don't want to out myself as a total hippie, but I was anti-microwave for a while. I just figured the stove was fine—and it is! But microwaves are so convenient. You can fry up some crispy shallots without turning your stovetop into a splatter-y mess. You can melt chocolate without a double boiler set up. Never mind the everyday tasks it makes easier, such as reheating leftovers or zapping a cup of coffee back to life. I'm not gonna say it's my favorite cooking appliance (#ToasterOvensForLife) but it's darn handy and I don't miss the counter space one bit.

What Else Can I Do with My Microwave?

Microwaves may reign supreme when it comes to quickly reheating food, but that's far from all they can do. Here are a few of our favorite microwave hacks.

Toast nuts, coconut, whole spices, or bread crumbs: Spread ingredient into thin, even layer in shallow bowl or glass pie plate. Microwave, stirring and checking color every minute. When ingredient starts to color, microwave in 30-second increments until golden brown.

Temper chocolate: Place three-quarters of chocolate, chopped fine, in bowl. Microwave at 50 percent power, stirring every 15 seconds, until melted and a little cooler than body temperature, about 93 degrees. Add remaining one-quarter of chocolate, grated, and stir until smooth, microwaving for no more than 5 seconds at a time, if necessary, to finish melting.

Mellow garlic: Place unpeeled garlic cloves in small bowl. Microwave at full power for 15 seconds or until cloves are warm to touch but not cooked. Mince or otherwise prep garlic as called for in raw applications such as pesto, hummus, and dressings.

Dry herbs: Place hardy herbs such as sage, rosemary, thyme, oregano, or marjoram in single layer between 2 paper towels on microwave turntable. Microwave at full power for 1 to 3 minutes until leaves turn brittle and fall easily from stems.

more helpful appliances

CRISPY EGGPLANT SALAD WITH TOMATOES, HERBS, AND FRIED SHALLOTS

serves 2 to 3

Microwaving the eggplant for this salad quickly dehydrates it, allowing it to soak up the savory sauce. We prefer Japanese eggplant here, but globe eggplant can be substituted. Italian basil makes a fine substitute for the Thai basil. Depending on the size of your microwave, you may need to microwave the eggplant in two batches in step 2; if the eggplant is piled up, it will steam rather than dehydrate.

2	tablespoons fish sauce
2	tablespoons unseasoned rice vinegar
2	tablespoons lime juice
2	tablespoons palm sugar or packed light brown sugar
1	(1-inch piece) ginger, peeled and chopped coarse
2	garlic cloves, chopped coarse
½	red Thai chile, seeded and sliced thin
6	ounces cherry tomatoes, halved
2	large Japanese eggplants (1½ pounds), halved lengthwise, then cut crosswise into 1½-inch pieces
1	teaspoon kosher salt
2	cups vegetable oil for frying
1½	cups mixed fresh cilantro leaves, mint leaves, and Thai basil leaves
1	recipe Microwave-Fried Shallots

1 Process fish sauce, vinegar, lime juice, sugar, ginger, garlic, and Thai chile in blender on high speed until ginger, garlic, and sugar are broken down and dressing is mostly smooth, about 1 minute. Transfer to medium serving bowl and stir in tomatoes. Set aside while preparing eggplant.

2 Toss eggplant and salt together in medium bowl. Line entire surface of large microwave-safe dish with double layer of coffee filters and lightly spray with vegetable oil spray. Spread eggplant in even layer over coffee filters. Microwave until eggplant feels dry and pieces shrink to about 1 inch, about 10 minutes, flipping pieces halfway through microwaving to dry sides evenly. Remove plate from microwave and immediately transfer eggplant to paper towel–lined plate.

3 Line rimmed baking sheet or plate with triple layer of paper towels. Add oil to large Dutch oven and heat over medium-high heat to 375 degrees. Fry eggplant, stirring occasionally, until flesh is deep golden brown and edges are crispy, 5 to 7 minutes. Transfer to prepared sheet and blot to remove excess oil. Transfer to bowl with tomatoes and toss to evenly dress.

4 Thoroughly fold half of herb mixture into eggplant. Top eggplant mixture with remaining cilantro mixture and sprinkle with shallots. Serve.

MICROWAVE-FRIED SHALLOTS

serves 4 to 6 (Makes about ½ cup)

Microwaving shallots in oil turns them into a crispy garnish in minutes, with no fuss or mess.

3	shallots, sliced thin
½	cup vegetable oil

1 Combine shallots and oil in medium bowl. Microwave for 5 minutes. Stir and continue to microwave 2 minutes longer. Repeat stirring and microwaving in 2-minute increments until beginning to brown (4 to 6 minutes). Repeat stirring and microwaving in 30-second increments until deep golden brown (30 seconds to 2 minutes).

2 Using slotted spoon, transfer shallots to paper towel–lined plate; season with salt to taste. Let drain and crisp, about 5 minutes. (Shallots can be stored in airtight container for up to 1 month.)

IN THIS SECTION . . .

Toasters
Toaster ovens
Small rimmed baking sheets
Air fryers
Smart ovens
Steam ovens

Your Satellite Ovens

Sometimes heating up your main oven is overkill. The right countertop helpers can take over a lot of smaller oven tasks.

I Just Want Toast. Is a Toaster a Better Choice than a Toaster Oven?

Buying the more specialized appliance doesn't guarantee better results. Both toasters and toaster ovens can struggle with making perfect toast; we've come across plenty of losers in both categories, but, we've also found toasters and toaster ovens that can actually produce good toast. If you're not interested in any of the other functions of a toaster oven, you may prefer a toaster because of its smaller size and (generally) lower price. Another big toaster upside: They toast a lot faster than toaster ovens. If you do buy a dedicated toaster, look for one with a wide, long slot to give you the most versatility, especially if you like to make toast from large artisanal loaves.

Do I Need to Preheat My Toaster Oven?

Conventional ovens take a while to come up to temperature and then even out (see page 23). The beauty of a modern toaster oven is that it does not require much preheating. Due to its small size, a toaster oven heats up much faster than a regular oven—in just about 5 minutes as opposed to around 15 minutes or more for most full-size ovens.

How Do I Get That Gross Gunk off the Window?

Over time, grease that builds up on the glass door of a toaster oven becomes baked on, developing into a thin, dark film that makes it hard to see inside. You can easily remove this layer by scrubbing the window with warm water and a Mr. Clean Magic Eraser. The same method works to clean the rest of the toaster oven too.

worth it

SMALL RIMMED BAKING SHEETS

We love a full-size rimmed baking sheet, otherwise known as a half-sheet pan. But when it comes to cooking within the confines of a toaster oven, you need a smaller version: either a quarter-sheet pan (which measures 9½ by 13 inches) or an eighth-sheet pan (which measures 7 by 10 inches). While many toaster ovens come with their own baking sheets, we don't like any of these included pans as much as our favorites from Nordic Ware. You can use these mini sheets in your regular oven, too, or as convenient prep surfaces for tasks such as letting cooked meats rest, organizing ingredients, and drying out herbs and greens on paper towels.

What Do All of My Toaster Oven's Functions Do?

Understanding your toaster oven's functions will help you use it to the fullest.

Warm Turns on both heating elements to 200 degrees or less: ideal for warming bread or keeping something hot while you finish getting the meal on the table.

Toast Uses both heating elements at the maximum temperature. "Light," "medium," and "dark" settings generally reference how long the food spends in the oven.

Bake or Roast Uses the bottom heating element to provide most of the heat, with the top element on at a reduced wattage, similar to a conventional oven.

Broil Uses only the top heating element, at full power. This function is great for giving food a final blast of heat to melt cheese or give spotty brown color.

Convection or Air-Fry Employs a fan to circulate the hot air inside, speeding evaporation and giving food a crispy or crunchy exterior.

Is My Toaster Oven Big Enough to Make a Complete Meal?

Your toaster oven's interior measurements determine whether certain pans or foods will fit inside. To be able to handle many standard recipes for four—say, a whole 4-pound roast chicken—the dimensions should be at least 12½ inches (inside wall to inside wall) by 9½ inches (back wall to door) by 4½ inches (from lowest rack position to top heating element). If your toaster oven is smaller than that, you may need to scale down your recipes.

TOASTER-OVEN MANICOTTI

serves 6 to 8

A baked pasta dish that uses the toaster oven, so it doesn't heat up the whole kitchen? Yes, please. Note that some no-boil lasagna noodle packages contain only 12 noodles; this recipe requires 16 noodles. Before starting this recipe, confirm that a 13 by 9-inch baking pan fits in your toaster oven and has at least 2 inches of space between the pan and the top heating element. Depending on your toaster oven, you may need to lower the rack position.

1½	pounds (3 cups) whole-milk or part-skim ricotta cheese
8	ounces whole-milk mozzarella cheese, shredded (2 cups)
4	ounces Parmesan cheese, grated (2 cups), divided
2	large eggs, lightly beaten
2	tablespoons minced fresh parsley
2	tablespoons chopped fresh basil
¾	teaspoon table salt
½	teaspoon pepper
16	no-boil lasagna noodles
6	cups jarred marinara sauce, divided

1 Combine ricotta, mozzarella, 1 cup Parmesan, eggs, parsley, basil, salt, and pepper in bowl.

2 Pour 1 inch of boiling water into 13 by 9-inch baking pan. Slip noodles into water, one at a time. Let noodles soak, separating them with tip of knife to prevent sticking, until pliable, about 5 minutes. Remove noodles from water and place in single layer on clean dish towels. Discard water and dry baking dish.

3 Adjust toaster oven rack to middle position and heat oven to 400 degrees. Spread 1½ cups sauce over bottom of now-empty pan. Working with several noodles at a time, spread ¼ cup ricotta mixture evenly over bottom three-quarters of each noodle. Roll noodles up around filling, then arrange seam side down in dish. Spread remaining sauce over manicotti.

4 Sprinkle manicotti with remaining 1 cup Parmesan, cover pan tightly with greased aluminum foil, place on foil-lined small rimmed baking sheet, and bake until bubbling, 40 to 45 minutes, rotating pan halfway through baking. Remove foil and continue to bake until top is spotty brown, 10 to 15 minutes. Transfer pan to wire rack and let cool for 15 minutes before serving.

Do Air Fryers Actually Fry?

Despite their name, air fryers don't fry your food. They're essentially small convection ovens (see page 25) with powerful fans that circulate hot air around the food to approximate the crispy-juicy results of deep frying. They require less oil—mere tablespoons as opposed to quarts—and are less messy than deep frying. While even the best models can't achieve the perfect golden crispiness that deep frying offers, some come impressively close. Because they're basically miniature ovens, this faux-frying is only a fraction of what air fryers can do. So don't think of air fryers just as replacements for deep frying. Instead, think of them as an often faster and more convenient alternative to cooking in a conventional oven.

head to head

AIR FRYERS

DRAWER-STYLE AIR FRYERS

Drawer-like basket slides into appliance that contains heating element and fan

Maneuverable basket is easy to clean and provides large amount of cooking space

Require little to no preheating

INSTANT POT AIR-FRYER LIDS

Lid with heating element locks into place on certain Instant Pot multicookers to turn multicooker into an air fryer

Convenient option if you already have certain Instant Pot models, but don't work with our favorite model

Have relatively limited amount of cooking space

OVEN-STYLE AIR FRYERS

Designed like a miniature oven, with outward-opening door and multiple cooking racks and baskets

Have less space for cooking than drawer-style air fryers

Upper rack blocks heat from reaching the lower one, resulting in unevenly cooked food

AIR-FRYER TOASTER OVENS

Combine the functions of a toaster oven and an air fryer

Larger than drawer-style air fryers and can accommodate more food, but often need preheating and cook more slowly

Generally more expensive than other air fryer styles

What Else Can I Make in My Air Fryer?

Just because it's called an air "fryer" doesn't mean that it produces only crispy fried food such as fish sticks and French fries. You can use it to roast or bake hearty main dishes such as crab cakes and glazed salmon, vegetable sides such as brussels sprouts and butternut squash, and even breakfast foods like scones and muffins. Using a foil sling can make your air fryer even more versatile by allowing you to gently lower and remove delicate foods. Here's how to make one.

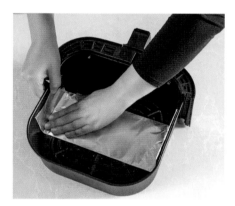

Fold one long sheet of aluminum foil so it is 4 inches wide. Lay sheet of foil widthwise across air-fryer basket, pressing it into and up sides of basket. Fold excess foil as needed so that edges of foil are flush with top of basket.

Hannah Says . . .

Most air-fryer baskets are nonstick and thus easy to clean, so are air-fryer liners, which promise to make cleanup even easier, ever worth buying? We tested a bunch and found that while they're definitely not essential, a good liner made from a solid (non-perforated) layer of parchment or thin silicone can in fact streamline cleanup. If you decide to use a liner, make sure to get the right size for your air fryer so you can take advantage of the basket's full capacity.

AIR-FRYER ORANGE-MUSTARD GLAZED SALMON

serves 2

An air fryer is an ideal way to make glazed salmon; the direct heat from above caramelizes the glaze's sugars while the circulated air cooks the fish from all sides. If using wild salmon, cook it until it registers 120 degrees.

- 1 tablespoon orange marmalade
- ¼ teaspoon grated orange zest plus 1 tablespoon juice
- 2 teaspoons whole-grain mustard
- 2 (8-ounce) skin-on salmon fillets, 1½ inches thick

1 Make foil sling for air-fryer basket by folding 1 long sheet of aluminum foil so it is 4 inches wide. Lay sheet of foil widthwise across basket, pressing foil into and up sides of basket. Fold excess foil as needed so that edges of foil are flush with top of basket. Lightly spray foil and basket with vegetable oil spray.

2 Combine marmalade, orange zest and juice, and mustard in bowl. Pat salmon dry with paper towels and season with salt and pepper. Brush tops and sides of fillets evenly with glaze. Arrange fillets skin side down on sling in prepared basket, spaced evenly apart. Place basket in air fryer and set temperature to 400 degrees. Cook salmon until center is still translucent when checked with tip of paring knife and registers 125 degrees (for medium-rare), 10 to 14 minutes, using sling to rotate fillets halfway through cooking.

3 Using sling, carefully remove salmon from air fryer. Slide fish spatula along under-side of fillets and transfer to individual serving plates, leaving skin behind. Serve.

AIR-FRYER CRISPY BREADED CHICKEN BREASTS WITH APPLE-FENNEL SALAD

serves 2

The convection heat of the air fryer quickly produces golden-brown breaded chicken breasts that crisp up with very little oil. If your fennel does not have fronds, substitute 1 tablespoon fresh chopped dill or parsley. This recipe can be easily doubled.

1	cup panko bread crumbs
2	tablespoons extra-virgin olive oil
1	large egg
4	teaspoons Dijon mustard, divided
1	tablespoon all-purpose flour
¼	teaspoon table salt
2	(6-ounce) boneless, skinless chicken breasts, trimmed
1	tablespoon plain yogurt
1	teaspoon lemon juice
1	teaspoon capers, rinsed, plus 1 teaspoon brine
1	fennel bulb, 1 tablespoon fronds minced, stalks discarded, bulb halved, cored, and sliced thin
1	apple, cored and cut into 2-inch-long matchsticks

1 Toss panko with oil in shallow dish until evenly coated. Microwave, stirring frequently, until light golden brown, 1 to 3 minutes; let cool slightly. Whisk egg, 1 tablespoon mustard, flour, and salt together in second shallow dish.

2 Pound chicken between 2 sheets of plastic wrap to uniform thickness. Pat dry with paper towels. Working with 1 breast at a time, dredge in egg mixture, letting excess drip off, then coat with panko, pressing gently to adhere.

3 Lightly spray bottom of air-fryer basket with vegetable oil spray. Arrange breasts in prepared basket, spaced evenly apart, alternating ends. Place basket into air fryer and set temperature to 400 degrees. Cook until chicken is crisp and registers 160 degrees, 12 to 18 minutes, flipping and rotating breasts halfway through cooking.

4 Whisk yogurt, lemon juice, caper brine, fennel fronds, and remaining 1 teaspoon mustard together in large bowl. Add apple, fennel bulb, and capers and toss to combine. Season with salt and pepper to taste. Serve chicken with salad.

AIR-FRIED BRUSSELS SPROUTS

serves 4

The air fryer makes crispy "fried" brussels sprouts that taste as decadent as their messy deep-fried counterparts. If you are buying loose brussels sprouts, select those that are about 1½ inches long. Quarter brussels sprouts longer than 2½ inches.

LEMON-CHIVE DIPPING SAUCE

¼	cup mayonnaise
1	tablespoon minced fresh chives
½	teaspoon grated lemon zest plus 2 teaspoons juice
½	teaspoon Worcestershire sauce
½	teaspoon Dijon mustard
¼	teaspoon garlic powder

BRUSSELS SPROUTS

1	pound brussels sprouts, trimmed and halved
1	tablespoon extra-virgin olive oil
¼	teaspoon table salt
⅛	teaspoon pepper
	Lemon wedges

1 for the lemon-chive dipping sauce Whisk all ingredients together in small bowl and set aside.

2 for the brussels sprouts Toss brussels sprouts with oil, salt, and pepper in bowl; transfer to air-fryer basket. Place basket in air fryer and set temperature to 350 degrees. Cook brussels sprouts until tender, well browned, and crispy, 20 to 25 minutes, tossing halfway through cooking. Season with salt and pepper to taste. Serve with dipping sauce and lemon wedges.

What Makes Smart Ovens "Smart"?

Smart ovens claim to produce expertly cooked food with hands-off convenience, so you can kick your old toaster oven to the curb—and maybe your conventional oven, your microwave, and a few other appliances too. They have apps that let you control cooking through your phone, laptop, or tablet, and most can also be operated by voice. They use sophisticated software and sometimes cameras to identify the foods you put in them, and built-in temperature probes to detect the internal temperature of the food and ensure that it's cooked to the ideal degree of doneness.

Some models offer helpful videos and tips, transmit images or graphs of your cooking progress on their apps or displays, and scan packaged retail foods or the company's own meal kits for one-step preparation. Smart ovens also periodically update software and add features, just like your phone or laptop does.

One big caveat: Some smart ovens are a lot smarter than others. While all make big claims, only some actually deliver on them: Brand really matters here. The June oven (see page 378) is the best we've tested in an admittedly actively evolving field.

Are Steam Ovens the New High-End Must-Have?

Steam ovens, long a staple of commercial kitchens, are now crossing over to home use. Countertop steam ovens resemble toaster ovens but differ in a key way: They inject steam into the oven cavity during cooking. Steam speeds up the cooking process and is especially useful when proofing and baking bread, preparing large cuts of meat, or steaming vegetables or fish. These ovens can steam, convection bake, or do a combination of the two, which is why they're sometimes referred to as "combi ovens." Overall, we think they're promising, but some models struggle with basic tasks and all require some trial and error to make the most of their advanced features and customizability.

Set and Forget

Pressure cookers, multicookers, slow cookers, and sous vide machines make great kitchen assistants. The better you understand these appliances, the more they can do for you.

Is an Instant Pot the Same Thing as a Pressure Cooker?

There are two main types of pressure cookers: electric and stovetop. An Instant Pot is a very popular brand of electric pressure cooker, also known as a multicooker. Although pressure cooking is arguably foremost among its many functions, manufacturers have added more features to boost the "multi" aspect of this small appliance's name, with some models purporting to slow-cook, sous vide, ferment, make rice, make yogurt, and even adjust their capabilities to accommodate cooking at high altitudes. Stovetop pressure cookers, on the other hand, are designed simply for pressure cooking.

Have Multicookers Made Stovetop Pressure Cookers Obsolete?

Stovetop pressure cookers have been used in home kitchens for decades, but they've changed with the times and are far from obsolete. Modern pressure cookers are quieter and simpler and have many more safety features than early ones did. Today's models use spring-loaded valves, which are silent and don't vent when pressurized. As with a multicooker, you can sauté and simmer food in a pressure cooker—and because you're using your stovetop, you actually have more control than you would using the sauté or browning function on a multicooker. Stovetop pressure cookers are surprisingly simple to use and in less than an hour can produce food that tastes as if you spent all day over the stove: tender beans, creamy risotto, fork-tender pot roast, or savory stew. If pressure cooking is your main goal, a stovetop cooker is a little more hands on but every bit as useful as a multicooker.

real talk with hannah

YOUR MULTICOOKER CAN DO MORE

When I first tested multicookers it was all about meat and beans, beans and meat. Which is fine! But I don't eat meat, and a person can consume only so many beans. It wasn't until I was working next to cooks developing recipes for our book *Mediterranean Instant Pot* that I was convinced a multicooker was a must-have for me. The dishes that went by—mussels, steamed fish, barley salad, rigatoni—opened my eyes to the potential of these machines. That book is now published, my copy sitting dog-eared and splattered on my shelf. And true story: My Instant Pot is spluttering away on my counter as I write, cooking up one of my new go-to recipes, a farro and leek soup.

FREQUENTLY ASKED QUESTIONS: MULTICOOKER EDITION

Q: Do all those buttons actually do anything?

A: Every multicooker varies in the buttons it offers and how to set each function, but all will have an option (or two) for pressure cooking, slow cooking, and browning and/or sautéing. The control panel will also show you when the pot comes up to pressure and allow you to set a cook timer. Some multicookers offer specific settings for food such as meat, soup, and risotto. Usually, these are just variations on the pressure or slow settings, sometimes with built-in timing. These settings vary by appliance and therefore are not as reliable as using the regular pressure or slow settings when you're following a recipe.

Q: When should I use quick-release versus natural release?

A: Natural release is preferred when you want to gently finish cooking food through, since food will continue to cook in the residual heat as the pressure drops. For dishes such as pot roast, beef ribs, or lamb chops, this gentle cooking at the end helps ensure tender meat. Use quick release to stop the cooking right away for foods that can easily overcook (think chicken breasts or fish). If you're in a hurry, you can also use quick release simply because it's faster, as long as a gentle finish isn't important.

Q: The sear function burns my food. What gives?

A: If you find that food is burning while you're sautéing in an uncovered pot, try adding a small amount of liquid to slow down the cooking.

Q: I keep getting the dreaded "burn" error message. What should I do?

A: Avoid this problem in the future by taking care to scrape up all the browned bits left in the pot after sautéing food and before closing the lid. In addition, make sure there's enough liquid in the pot.

Q: Can a pressure cooker explode?

A: Multicookers have multiple fail-safes in place to prevent explosions and other mishaps during pressure cooking. But even though a multicooker is a far cry from your grandmother's pressure cooker, there are still right and wrong ways to use it. Before you start cooking, be sure to read your multicooker's manual for model-specific recommendations regarding safety and proper use.

PRESSURE-COOKER CREAMY SPRING VEGETABLE LINGUINE

serves 4 to 6

Using a pressure cooker for pasta gives you perfectly cooked al dente noodles with a silky sauce and a vibrant mix of vegetables and flavors in a single pot. Do not substitute other pasta shapes here, as they require different liquid amounts. We prefer the flavor and texture of jarred whole baby artichoke hearts in this recipe, but you can substitute 6 ounces frozen artichoke hearts, thawed and patted dry.

1	pound linguine
5	cups water, plus extra as needed
1	tablespoon extra-virgin olive oil
1	teaspoon table salt
1	cup jarred whole baby artichokes packed in water, drained and quartered
1	cup frozen peas, thawed
4	ounces Pecorino Romano cheese, grated (2 cups), plus extra for serving
½	teaspoon pepper
2	teaspoons grated lemon zest
2	tablespoons chopped fresh tarragon

1 Loosely wrap half of pasta in dish towel, then press bundle against corner of counter to break noodles into 6-inch lengths; repeat with remaining pasta.

2 Add pasta, water, oil, and salt to electric pressure cooker, making sure pasta is completely submerged. Lock lid in place and close pressure release valve. Select high pressure cook function and cook for 4 minutes. Turn off pressure cooker and quick-release pressure. Carefully remove lid, allowing steam to escape away from you.

3 Stir artichokes and peas into pasta, cover, and let sit until heated through, about 3 minutes. Gently stir in Pecorino and pepper until cheese is melted and fully combined, 1 to 2 minutes. Adjust consistency with extra water as needed. Stir in lemon zest and tarragon, and season with salt and pepper to taste. Serve, passing extra Pecorino separately.

PRESSURE-COOKER MUSSELS WITH RED CURRY AND COCONUT RICE

serves 4 to 6

Using a pressure cooker to cook mussels ensures they are evenly surrounded with steam, resulting in a pot full of tender, plump mussels in just 1 minute of cooking time. You can substitute 3 pounds of littleneck clams for the mussels; increase the cooking time to 2 minutes. Discard any raw mussels with an unpleasant odor or with a cracked or broken shell or a shell that won't close. This recipe will only work in an electric pressure cooker.

1	tablespoon canola oil
3	tablespoons red curry paste
6	garlic cloves, minced
1½	cups water, divided, plus extra as needed
1	cup canned coconut milk, divided
1	green bell pepper, stemmed, seeded, and cut into 1-inch pieces
1	tomato, cored and cut into ½-inch pieces
2	pounds mussels, scrubbed and debearded
1	teaspoon grated fresh ginger
1	teaspoon grated lime zest, plus lime wedges for serving
1½	cups long-grain brown rice, rinsed
1	tablespoon sugar
½	cup fresh cilantro leaves

1 Using highest sauté function, heat oil until shimmering. Add curry paste and garlic and cook, stirring frequently, until fragrant, about 30 seconds. Stir in 1 cup water and ½ cup coconut milk, scraping up any browned bits, then stir in bell pepper and tomato. Arrange mussels evenly in pot.

2 Lock lid into place and close pressure-release valve. Select high pressure-cook function and set cook time for 1 minute. Once Instant Pot has reached pressure, immediately turn off pot and quick-release pressure. Carefully remove lid, allowing steam to escape away from you.

3 Transfer mussels to large bowl, discarding any that have not opened. Strain broth through fine-mesh strainer into 2-cup liquid measuring cup (you should have 1½ cups broth; if necessary, add extra water to equal 1½ cups). Stir ginger and lime zest into broth. Transfer solids to bowl with mussels and cover to keep warm.

4 Return broth to now-empty pot. Stir in rice, sugar, remaining ½ cup water, and remaining ½ cup coconut milk. Lock lid into place and close pressure-release valve. Select high pressure-cook function and cook for 24 minutes. Turn off Instant Pot and quick-release pressure. Carefully remove lid, allowing steam to escape away from you. Fluff rice gently with fork. Lay clean dish towel over pot, replace lid, and let sit for 5 minutes.

5 Divide mussels among individual serving bowls and sprinkle with cilantro leaves. Serve mussels with rice and lime wedges.

Why Do Some Slow-Cooker Recipes Have Cooking Time Ranges That Span Hours?

Many of our slow-cooker recipes include cooking time ranges of an hour or more, calling for cooking "on low for 6 to 7 hours" or "on high for 4 to 5 hours." In most recipes, an hour more or less of cooking time is likely to result in a meal that's either still raw or practically turned to charcoal. Is cooking in a slow cooker just that much more forgiving?

Actually, not really. While the low temperatures involved in slow cooking may provide a little more leeway, the real reason for these large cooking time ranges is to account for the variability between slow cookers. Some slow cookers run hotter or cooler than others, meaning that they may cook the same recipe a good deal faster or slower than another model. If your cooker runs hot, you should expect your recipes to be ready at the earlier end of the range, and vice versa if your cooker runs cooler. If you don't know yet where your slow cooker falls on this scale, you should check all recipes at the beginning of the time range but allow yourself some extra time to cook food longer if necessary.

```
FREQUENTLY ASKED QUESTIONS:
SLOW-COOKER EDITION
```

Q: Which shape is better: round or oval?

A: For some recipes the shape of the slow cooker doesn't matter as long as it has the right volume capacity, but oval slow cookers are more versatile due to their greater surface area. For example, an oval slow cooker allows for more even cooking of rice and grains because the rice or grain is more spread out. Casseroles and braised vegetable dishes also turn out more successfully in an oval cooker for this reason. And racks of ribs and some roasts just won't fit in a round slow cooker.

Q: Does it matter if my slow cooker has a metal or ceramic crock?

A: Some slow cookers use an aluminum pot insert while others use a heavy ceramic crock. There are advantages and disadvantages to both. Aluminum inserts are lighter and more durable than ceramic inserts, and most are nonstick. In the slow cooker, they sit directly on a hot plate, giving you the ability to sauté and brown right in the slow cooker—something you can't do with a ceramic insert. However, slow cookers with aluminum inserts tend to cook hotter and faster than slow cookers with ceramic inserts, which isn't necessarily a plus, and the handles can become too hot to touch. Slow cookers with ceramic inserts usually have a heating element that circles the crock. This configuration can cause hot spots if the machine isn't well insulated. On the upside, the thick ceramic allows for gentle cooking and, provided the handles are large enough, you can grip them without worrying about burning yourself.

Q: Is it safe to cook food in a slow cooker?

A: Using a slow cooker is a safe way to cook food as long as you follow a few common-sense practices. First, make sure your slow cooker and your utensils have been properly cleaned. Don't let meat or fish sit out on the counter for any length of time before adding them to the slow cooker. Never put frozen food into your slow cooker, as this greatly increases the risk that your food will not reach a safe bacteria-killing temperature. And finally, check to make sure that your food has cooked to the proper temperature if the recipe specifies one.

How Does Sous Vide Cooking Work, Anyway?

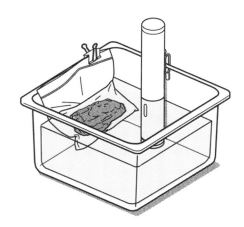

A sous vide immersion circulator is a stick-like appliance that heats water in a vessel to a desired temperature and then maintains that temperature to cook food immersed in the water bath. The food, which is typically sealed in plastic or reusable silicone bags (eggs can be cooked right in their shells, and you can also cook sous vide in glass jars), eventually reaches the same temperature as the water, so it can't overcook. With meat, poultry, and fish, you usually follow up with a quick sear in a skillet for surface browning.

The benefits of sous vide cooking are perfectly and uniformly cooked food with minimal cleanup required. As a gentle cooking method, sous vide is slow, but it's largely hands-off and the window of time for doneness is very forgiving; for instance, most common cuts of pork, beef, and poultry will be fully cooked in about 1 hour and can stay in the bath for about 4 hours without much change to texture.

What Kind of Vessel Is Best for Sous Vide Cooking?

You can sous vide in a variety of vessels. We often turn either to our favorite large plastic food storage container (see page 400) or a Dutch oven (see page 48), both of which have ample room for the water and food. A large saucepan will also work.

Do I Need to Cover the Water Bath?

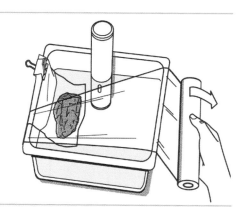

Covering the water bath isn't always necessary, but it is often helpful. When preheating, the water will come up to temperature more quickly if it's covered. During longer sous vide cooking sessions, covering helps prevent too much water from evaporating. (If the water level drops below the necessary minimum, the machine will shut down automatically. Most will also sound an alarm or, if they have an app, send a notification to add water.) We've tested and like reusable sous vide lids, but you can also simply use a few sheets of plastic wrap to cover the bath, or cut a 3- to 4-inch slit in the middle of one side of a square of plastic so that we can wrap the cut edges snugly around the device and seal off the entire surface of the water bath.

Do I Need a Vacuum Sealer for Sous Vide Cooking?

A good vacuum sealer is really helpful to have when sous vide cooking because it extracts all the air from the plastic bag, enabling food to cook more evenly (any air pockets will block contact between the heated water and the food). But if you don't have a vacuum sealer, you can use a regular zipper-lock bag. For the best results, you'll want to remove as much air as possible to prevent air pockets.

Here's how to do it: Fill the bag and zip it partly closed, then submerge most of the bag in the water, allowing the water to help squeeze out any air from the bag before you zip it fully closed. We sometimes double-bag foods with sharp edges, such as bone-in chops or veal shanks, to prevent the edges from poking through the bag or ripping a seam. You can use the same water-displacement trick to remove air from the second bag too.

SOUS VIDE THICK-CUT HALIBUT FILLETS WITH LEMON BROWNED BUTTER

serves 4

Halibut is easily overcooked; cooking it sous vide guarantees a moist and tender piece of fish without the need for stovetop babysitting. We prefer to prepare this recipe with halibut, but you can substitute a firm-fleshed white fish such as cod or hake that is between 1 and 1½ inches thick.

FISH
2	teaspoons table salt
2	teaspoons sugar
4	6- to 8-ounce skinless halibut fillets, 1 to 1½ inches thick
1	tablespoon vegetable oil

BROWNED BUTTER
1	lemon
4	tablespoons unsalted butter, cut into 4 pieces
1	small shallot, minced
2	tablespoons capers, rinsed
2	tablespoons chopped fresh parsley

1 Combine salt and sugar in small bowl. Sprinkle halibut evenly on all sides with salt mixture and place on wire rack set in rimmed baking sheet. Refrigerate for at least 30 minutes and up to 45 minutes.

2 for the fish Using sous vide circulator, bring water to 120 degrees F/49 degrees C in 7-quart container. (If you prefer your fish to be fully opaque, set your sous vide bath to 135 degrees F/57 degrees C.)

3 Pat halibut dry with paper towels and brush with oil on all sides. Individually wrap each fillet with plastic wrap, then arrange in single layer in 1-gallon zipper-lock freezer bag. Seal bag, pressing out as much air as possible. Gently lower bag into prepared water bath until fillets are fully submerged, then clip top corner of bag to side of water bath container, allowing remaining air bubbles to rise to top of bag. Reopen 1 corner of zipper, release remaining air bubbles, and seal bag fully. Cover and cook for at least 30 minutes or up to 45 minutes.

4 for the browned butter Cut away peel and pith from lemon. Holding fruit over small bowl, use paring knife to slice between membranes to release segments. Cut segments crosswise into ½-inch pieces. Squeeze membranes over bowl to release juice; discard membranes and seeds.

5 Cook butter in small saucepan over medium heat, swirling constantly, until butter melts and turns dark golden brown and has nutty aroma, 4 to 5 minutes. Stir in shallot and cook until fragrant, about 30 seconds. Off heat, stir in capers, parsley, and lemon segments and juice. Season with salt and pepper to taste; cover to keep warm.

6 Gently transfer halibut to cutting board and discard plastic. Pat fillets dry with paper towels and transfer to dinner plates. Spoon sauce over fillets and serve.

SOUS VIDE SOFT-POACHED EGGS

makes 1 to 16 eggs

Eggs are the poster child for sous vide cooking, and there's perhaps no better or easier way to learn how to use your new machine than by making the perfect soft-poached egg. Be sure to use large eggs that have no cracks and are cold from the refrigerator. Fresher eggs have tighter egg whites and are better suited for this recipe.

1–16 large eggs, chilled

1 Using sous vide circulator, bring water to 167 degrees F/75 degrees C in 7-quart container. Using slotted spoon, gently lower eggs into prepared water bath, cover, and cook for 12 minutes.

2 Meanwhile, fill large bowl halfway with ice and water. Using slotted spoon, transfer eggs to ice bath and let sit until cool enough to touch, about 1 minute. To serve, crack eggs into individual bowls and season with salt and pepper to taste. (Eggs can be rapidly chilled in ice bath for 10 minutes and then refrigerated for up to 5 days. To reheat, lower eggs into water bath set to 140 degrees F/60 degrees C and cook until heated through, at least 15 minutes or up to 60 minutes. Crack into bowls as directed.)

Blend, Chop, and Mix

Blenders, food processors, and mixers do what you do with a knife or a spoon, only faster. A lot faster.

What's With All My Blender's Buttons and Speed Settings?

Many blenders come with multiple speed settings meant to give you more control over the consistency of your food. Slower speeds are helpful for ensuring that ingredients combine without excessive splattering; a too-high speed can simply fling food around the jar rather than actually blending it. So even if your aim is to make a supersmooth puree, start the blender on a slower speed and work your way up to a higher one to progressively process the food. This will protect the motor too.

Many blenders also include several preset buttons, most commonly for smoothies, crushed ice, cleaning, frozen desserts, hot soup, and juicing. These buttons are designed to make certain tasks more hands-off, but we don't find any of them helpful enough to be absolutely necessary. "Self-cleaning" modes, for example, typically just run the machine on high for 60 seconds, something you can easily do manually, and definitely not something worth forking over more money for.

Are Personal Blenders Any Good?

Personal blenders offer promising perks, such as smaller footprints, lower price tags, and lids that allow them to transition neatly from pitchers to travel cups. The best ones consistently whir hard-frozen and fibrous ingredients into a cohesive blend in less than a minute. Their travel lids snap right onto the jar, so you don't have to transfer your smoothie after making it. While not a necessity, this style of blender might be worth purchasing if you're a smoothie enthusiast.

Should I Spring for a High-End Blender?

A good high-end blender more than earns its high price tag, but these workhorses are definitely a luxury rather than a necessity. Their powerful motors easily make dense, velvety smoothies out of tough fibrous ingredients such as kale and pineapple. They're also adept at making hummus, nut butter, mayonnaise, and crushed ice. But what you're really paying for here is longevity. High-end models typically have warranties in the five- to seven-year range, and if properly cared for, will last even longer. Less expensive models usually have limited one- to two-year warranties.

If you don't want to spend $450-plus and don't intend to put your blender through regular heavy-duty use, you might be happy with a lower-priced blender. These tend to be lighter weight with less adjustable, noisier motors. Some struggle to make nut butter, but they do well with crushing ice and making smoothies (although their smoothies might not be *quite* as, ahem, smooth).

Why Do Blenders Puree Better than Food Processors?

A blender's jar makes it ideally suited to the task of making smooth purees. In the narrow confines of a blender jar (as opposed to the wide bowl of a food processor), the food forms a vortex, a spiral motion that keeps it in near-constant contact with the blades. As the blades spin, the food is drawn down into the blades and back up again before being drawn back down into the blades at a high speed. All this blade action results in more uniformly smooth results than a food processor can achieve.

Hannah Says . . .

Most people associate blenders with smoothies and soups, but these machines can do so much more. In the test kitchen we use them to make granita, ice cream, waffle batter, pancake batter, farrotto, corn spoonbread dough, Brazilian cheese bread roll dough, all kinds of non-dairy milks, almond butter, pesto, hummus, crushed ice, and on and on. Don't limit yourself to smoothies—put your blender to work!

real talk with lisa

USE YOUR BLENDER SAFELY

Blenders are great tools, but there are a few things you should know to use them safely. First, never open the lid when the blender is running or you'll get a faceful of smoothie. Don't stick a tool such as a wooden spoon into the jar unless you want wood chips in your hummus. Turn off the blender before stopping to scrape down the sides. (Some blenders come with "tamper" tools that look like stubby baseball bats. If you take a close look at them, you'll see that they're just long enough to push foods towards the blades without danger of reaching all the way to the blades themselves.) Hot foods such as soup can be dangerous to blend; they can build up pressure and blow the lid off. Keep amounts small if you're blending hot food, and use a folded dish towel to hold down the lid while it's running. For cleaning and handling, stay away from the blades. Add a small amount of warm water and a drop of dish soap, put the lid on and run the blender. It will scrub itself! And before cleaning an immersion blender, always be sure to detach the blades from the motor first.

worth it

IMMERSION BLENDER

Anyone who has pureed hot soup in a countertop blender knows it can be a hassle. It often has to be done in batches, which requires an extra pot or bowl. You also have to let the soup cool down a little so that pressure doesn't build up inside the blender and cause the lid to pop off. An immersion blender (also called a hand blender or stick blender) gets the job done efficiently, tidily, and safely, since all the blending is done directly in the pot. We think an immersion blender is worth owning even if you use it only a few times a year, but you can also use one for many of the tasks you'd lug out your regular blender to do, including making smoothies, emulsifying salad dressings, and blending sauces and marinades. If you want a little whipped cream in a hurry, an immersion blender will do the trick. They're also generally easier to clean and store than countertop blenders, and they often cost less.

head to head

BLENDERS AND FOOD PROCESSORS

BLENDERS

Sealed jar won't leak when processing liquids, even in large amounts

Short, upturned blades and narrow jar shape are designed to make smooth purees and batters

Most can't mix dough or chop vegetables

FOOD PROCESSORS

Hole in the middle and lack of seal around the lid allow leakage if processing large amounts of liquids

Wider bowl and additional cutting blades provide more space and cutting options for grinding meat, slicing and shredding food, and making dips and pesto

Long, sharp blades chop vegetables effectively

Powerful motor can mix pizza, bread, and pie dough

Does the Capacity of My Food Processor Matter?

For different reasons, opting for either a large food processor or a small one makes more sense than choosing a medium-capacity processor. If you're going to buy a full-size processor, go for a 14-cup model. A large-capacity food processor allows you not only to chop, slice, or shred large quantities of vegetables, but also to make large batches of dough. These processors have more powerful motors than their slightly smaller siblings. For the sake of versatility, the position of the blade is as important as the size of the bowl: If the blade sits too high above the bowl's bottom, it won't engage properly with smaller amounts of food.

Smaller processors can't handle doughs as well; their work-bowls are too small and their motors too weak. But a good small food processor can excel at mayonnaises, dressings, dips, marinades, and sauces—projects that would otherwise require serious muscle or a blender. They can also handle a smaller quantity of mincing, grinding, and dicing. If money or space is limited, you prefer a knife for most food prep, or you only plan to make smaller quantities, a 3.5- or 4-cup model is ideal: compact yet large enough to handle a range of projects.

Some large-capacity processors come with an additional mini-bowl, giving you the best of both worlds.

What Do All These Blades Do?

Most food processors come with an S-shaped multipurpose blade as well as a disk with raised holes and/or a disk with a raised cutting edge. The S-shaped blade is fitted in the bowl before adding food; it's used for chopping, mixing, and blending. To use the disk for shredding (raised holes) or slicing (raised edge), you position it in the bowl, secure the lid, and push food through the vertical feed tube onto the spinning disk. Some processors come with different-sized slicing and shredding disks, and some also come with a plastic dough blade. (We've found that the processor's regular blade works better for bread dough than the dough blade.)

How Do I Get My Food Processor Clean?

As with any blade, you should wash your food processor blade carefully by hand. Let it air dry or pat it dry gently. The processor bowl and lid can go in the dishwasher, but note that they may get cloudy over time.

FOOD-PROCESSOR POUND CAKE

serves 8

Adding hot butter to the processor while the blade spins emulsifies all the liquid ingredients before they can curdle. Our preferred loaf pan measures 8½ by 4½ inches; if you use a 9 by 5-inch loaf pan, start checking for doneness 5 minutes early.

- 1½   cups (6 ounces) cake flour
- 1   teaspoon baking powder
- ½   teaspoon table salt
- 1¼   cups (8¾ ounces) sugar
- 4   large eggs, room temperature
- 1½   teaspoons vanilla extract
- 16   tablespoons unsalted butter, melted and hot

1 Adjust oven rack to middle position and heat oven to 350 degrees. Grease and flour 8½ by 4½-inch loaf pan. Whisk flour, baking powder, and salt together in bowl.

2 Process sugar, eggs, and vanilla in food processor until combined, about 10 seconds. With processor running, add hot melted butter in steady stream until incorporated. Pour mixture into large bowl.

3 Sift flour mixture over egg mixture in 3 additions, whisking to combine after each addition until few streaks of flour remain. Continue to whisk batter gently until almost no lumps remain (do not overmix).

4 Transfer batter to prepared pan, smooth top, and gently tap pan on counter to settle batter. Bake cake until toothpick inserted in center comes out with few moist crumbs attached, 50 minutes to 1 hour, rotating pan halfway through baking.

5 Let cake cool in pan for 10 minutes. Run paring knife around edge of cake to loosen. Gently turn cake out onto wire rack and let cool completely, about 2 hours. Serve.

VARIATION
Food-Processor Lemon Pound Cake

Add 2 tablespoons grated lemon zest (2 lemons) and 2 teaspoons juice to processor with sugar.

real talk with lisa

MAKE YOUR FOOD PROCESSOR WORK HARDER FOR YOU

There are so many things you can do with a great food processor. I love to use mine to make salsa in the summer using fresh tomatoes, tomatillos, and chiles, or to make pie dough, since the processor cuts cold butter into flour perfectly in just a few seconds. You can shred a heap of cheese without risking your knuckles on a box grater. You can make thin-crust pizza dough *and* its delicious sauce in minutes. Turn basil from the garden into pesto. Make cauliflower rice. And don't get me started on fresh mayonnaise. I had no idea simple mayonnaise could be so great and so easy. So don't be intimidated—put your processor to work for you.

Do I Have to Pay Hundreds for a Good Stand Mixer?

A reliable and powerful stand mixer will set you back a couple hundred dollars, but it's a solid investment and still much less than you'd pay for a top-of-the-line model. High-end stand mixers have large bowls and powerful motors—and hefty price tags. The bowl size on pricey mixers—up to 8 quarts—may make you feel like you're getting more for your money, but we've found that the 4½-quart bowl on a more budget-minded mixer is large enough for most jobs, including bread dough. As for the motor, in testing mixers all along the price spectrum we found that more horsepower doesn't always mean more powerful performance. A mixer's power also depends on the machine's torque. Torque, or rotational force, provides leverage: The more torque a machine has the more effectively it will not only push on dough but also rotate it in the bowl. A well-designed mixer doesn't need to be super-expensive to take advantage of this, and it will serve you well.

Which Mixer Attachments Are Worth It?

KitchenAid, the company that makes some of our favorite stand mixers, also makes a variety of attachments that fit in the "hub" at the front of each machine. If you own a KitchenAid stand mixer, these attachments can save space, but some work better than others.

Pasta roller: Requires a bit of a learning curve, but is easy to attach and adjust and makes pasta fast (see page 259).

Pasta extruder: Works slowly and pinches the end of the pasta shapes; is also tedious to clean. (For more about pasta extruders, see page 260.)

Meat grinder: Works quickly, with little waste.

Spiralizer: Has handy blades and is easy to clean, but is fussy to use and produces a lot of waste.

Ice cream maker: Yields decent results but is difficult to use.

head to head

MIXERS

STAND MIXERS

Powerful motor can mix dense bread and pizza doughs

Larger and heavier; require counter space

Provide hands-off mixing

Come with their own bowl

More expensive

HAND MIXERS

Less powerful motor; most can't handle bread or pizza dough

Lighter and smaller; many can fit in a drawer

Require hands-on mixing and can be tiring

Use any bowl

Less expensive

Am I Mixing at the Right Speed?

If the recipe says to mix on medium speed and your settings go from 1 to 10, that means you should set your mixer to 5 and go, right? Not so fast.

First of all, you should always start low and crank up the speed gradually to avoid sending flour flying all over your kitchen. You should also watch what's happening in the bowl; mixers are powerful and more efficient than you might expect, so you should rely on visual cues as much or even more than the times and settings listed in a recipe.

And finally, even if a recipe says to mix on high speed, you probably don't need to take your mixer all the way up to its highest setting. KitchenAid mixer manuals, for instance, recommend using the highest speed only for light tasks such as whipping cream or egg whites. Prolonged high-speed mixing or lower-speed kneading of stiffer, heavier doughs can take a toll on even the powerful motors of some high-end stand mixers: KitchenAid recommends not exceeding speed 2 when kneading dough with the dough hook, not to knead for more than 2 minutes at a time, and limiting the total mixing and kneading time to 4 to 6 minutes.

Hannah Says . . .

We use stand mixers with glass bowls on our TV shows for a very specific reason: so viewers can see what's going on inside the bowl. Unless you're cooking for an audience, we recommend sticking with stainless steel bowls. Glass bowls are heavier and more fragile, making them harder to handle and potentially much more short-lived.

Can I Use a Hand Mixer to Knead Bread Dough?

Even if your hand mixer comes with dough hooks, we don't recommend using it for breadmaking. Hand-mixer dough hooks are much smaller than a stand mixer's standard dough hook, so they engage less dough as they rotate. Anchoring the dough in the mixing bowl and getting the dough hooks to dig in and knead it require a lot of hand and arm strength; much more so than kneading by hand. And even sturdy hand mixers are taxed by the heavy-duty work of kneading dough, putting the motor in danger of overheating. A stand mixer is much better suited to the task.

I've Heard Good Things About All-In-One Machines. Do They Live Up to the Hype?

So-called all-in-one kitchen machines promise to replace every small appliance in your kitchen. Similar in size and appearance to a stand mixer, all-in-one machines have a workbowl that sits atop a base containing a concealed heating element and motor. Inside the workbowl is a chopping and mixing blade (which is removable in some models). They come with an assortment of attachments, including steamer baskets, spatulas, and interchangeable blades. Fans of these machines claim you can use one to cook an entire multicourse meal.

We tested several models, including the Thermomix, which is incredibly popular in Europe. Most fell short of being truly all-in-one: They don't slow-cook or cook sous vide effectively, they struggle with basic tasks such as browning food and boiling water, and they can be frustratingly difficult to use. But while these machines are pricey and not truly all-in-one, if you have a very small kitchen one may well be worth considering in lieu of a blender, stand mixer, and food processor. An all-in-one machine can also be an asset in situations where kitchen space is nonexistent, such as on a boat, in an RV, or in some dorm rooms.

More Countertop Contenders

Depending on what you like to cook and how often you like to cook it, specialty appliances such as waffle makers, electric griddles, and rice cookers can be a worthwhile addition to your kitchen.

Why Are My Waffles So Pale?

Preheating a waffle iron is key to producing crispy, evenly browned waffles, and it's not as simple as waiting for the preheat indicator light to signal that the iron is ready. Preheat indicators rely on a simple sensor that tells you when only one particular area of the iron plate has reached the desired temperature—not when the cooking surface is uniformly hot. For a cooking surface that is heated evenly from edge to edge, we recommend preheating the waffle iron (no matter the brand) for at least 10 minutes (or up to 20 minutes if you have the time) before using it. And between batches, give your waffle iron 1 to 2 minutes to rebound to its proper temperature so every waffle will turn out just right.

Love a good brownie edge? Check out how Hannah makes crispy-chewy almost-all-edge brownies using a waffle maker.

How Can I Keep the First Waffles Hot Until the Last Ones are Ready?

All you need to do is preheat your oven to 200 degrees, place a wire rack inside a rimmed baking sheet, and set the sheet on the middle oven rack. As you're cooking, simply transfer each finished waffle from your waffle maker to the wire rack. The low temperature of the oven will keep the waffles warm and crispy without burning them and the elevation of the rack in the baking sheet helps keep away sogginess. The result? Hot, still-crispy waffles that taste as fresh as they would straight from the waffle iron.

Why Does My Electric Griddle Cook Food So Unevenly?

A spacious electric griddle that cooks a big batch of flapjacks or burgers evenly is a boon when you're cooking for a crowd since, unlike a stovetop griddle, it frees up your burners for other tasks. If you're experiencing uneven cooking, your griddle may be too thin. A thin sheet of metal heats quickly but doesn't have the mass to hold on to that heat, creating hot spots. In some cases, you can actually see the outline of the heating coil that's beneath the griddle charred into the pancakes. By contrast, the extra mass of thicker metal means it's slower to heat up but also disperses the heat more evenly and holds on to the heat longer, which means more even cooking.

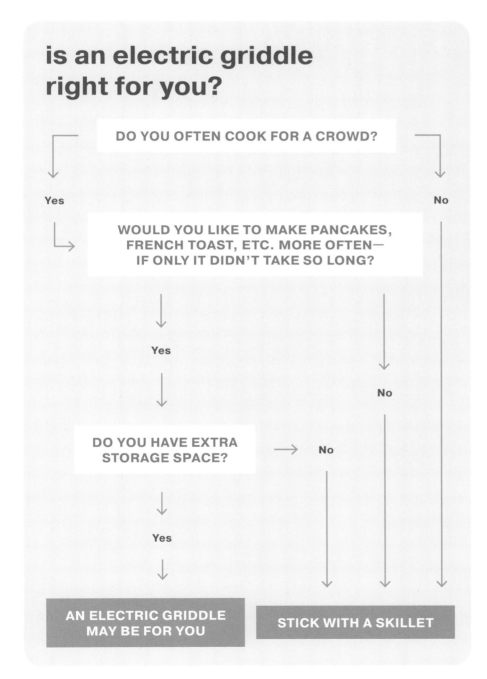

is an electric griddle right for you?

DO YOU OFTEN COOK FOR A CROWD?

Yes → **WOULD YOU LIKE TO MAKE PANCAKES, FRENCH TOAST, ETC. MORE OFTEN— IF ONLY IT DIDN'T TAKE SO LONG?**

Yes → **DO YOU HAVE EXTRA STORAGE SPACE?** → No

No → **AN ELECTRIC GRIDDLE MAY BE FOR YOU**

Yes → **AN ELECTRIC GRIDDLE MAY BE FOR YOU**

No → **STICK WITH A SKILLET**

worth it
RICE COOKER

Cooking rice to the perfect texture can be tricky. If you struggle to turn out fluffy, tender rice or if you cook rice often, a good rice cooker will make life easier. All you need to do is rinse the rice and then add it to the cooker with some water; proper amounts are marked in the cooker bowl. With rice cookers that use an operating strategy known as "fuzzy logic," which allows them to adjust cooking time and temperature throughout the cooking process, you don't have to worry about over- or undercooking the rice. Once the rice is done, the machine automatically switches to a hold setting that keeps the rice at a safe temperature until you're ready to eat—up to 12 hours in some models. As a bonus, these cookers are also versatile: You can use them to prepare all kinds of rice, including brown rice, as well as other grains such as quinoa, barley, and bulgur.

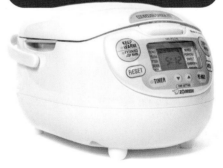

Watch this video to find out which budget-friendly appliances Hannah and Lisa think deserve a place in your kitchen.

take it outside

RECIPES

Don't Try This at Home

Sometimes testing equipment is as simple as making pots of coffee or whisking egg whites, and sometimes it involves protective eyewear, power saws, and shards of broken glass. Take our cooler testing: Measuring the thickness of the walls got us only so far toward figuring out why some coolers keep food cold better than others. We wondered if the stuff between those walls was making the difference. So we bought an electric saw, strapped on our safety goggles, and ripped our way through every model in the lineup. After the racket died down, we found ourselves facing not only 10 now-useless coolers but also the key to a good cooler's cold-preserving ability: an interior construction of thick foam full of visible air bubbles. Because air is a poor conductor of heat, this airy layer keeps the heat out and the cold in.

On another exciting day in the test kitchen, we put glass drinking bottles through a battery of tests that included dropping them on the floor to test their likelihood of shattering. We dropped filled water bottles from counter height onto the floor, holding them at three different angles (upright, sideways, and upside down). If they survived, we took them outside and dropped them onto concrete. This straightforward experiment yielded some telling results. A glass bottle's likelihood of breaking varies depending on how the glass itself was processed, how thick it is, and the shape it's formed into. (And of course the thickness of the protective sleeve matters too.) This knowledge helped us identify two traits—a more rounded bottom edge and thicker walls—that give some bottles the edge.

Sometimes you just have to bust up the equipment to find out what works best.

When Food Meets Fire

If you like cooking and eating your food in the great outdoors, you have more choices than ever. You can make just about anything you're hungry for—from breakfast to dessert—outside.

Can You Taste the Difference Between Foods Cooked Over Charcoal Versus Gas?

Many fans of charcoal grilling staunchly believe that it's the only way to get real grilled flavor. Is this true? That depends on what you're cooking. What we think of as "grilled" flavor comes from a few sources: the smoke that bathes food when its fat hits the heat source and sizzles; the dark char created by high heat; and the smoke from the fire, as well as from wood chips or chunks set on the flames or coals. While gas burns without smoking, charcoal smokes as it burns, which gives charcoal grills a slight edge for producing smoky flavor. If you want to give gas-grilled foods a bit of woodsy flavor you can place a packet of wood chips on top of one of the burners.

Charcoal grills also have an advantage when it comes to charring. This deep, flavorful browning is produced by scorching radiant heat (think heat from the sun). Burning charcoal emits almost all radiant heat, but gas grills cook mainly through convection (the circulation of hot air), which is less intense. To compensate, many gas grills feature ceramic rods that absorb and radiate heat; however, only the most powerful gas grills can approximate the dark, crusty exterior of char-grilled foods. Finally, there's that sizzle effect: When foods such as hamburgers are cooked directly over the flames, dripping fat creates smoke no matter the type of grill. But when using indirect heat, as you would for a roast, flavor comes from the smoke being drawn across the food as it cooks, a process at which charcoal grills excel (see page 145). Quick-cooking foods such as boneless chicken breasts, kebabs, or vegetables don't spend enough time on the grill to produce an appreciable difference. But for longer-cooking foods such as whole chickens, roasts, and ribs, charcoal has the flavor edge.

head to head

GRILLS

CHARCOAL GRILLS

Messier and more labor-intensive; heat fades over time unless charcoal is replenished

Lower charcoal grate holds lit coals, which can be arranged to suit the type of food being cooked

Better control of heat and airflow thanks to adjustable vents in base and lid

Can produce stronger charred, smoky flavor in longer-cooking foods

Ash catcher must be emptied periodically

GAS GRILLS

Easier to use and provide steady heat

Propane tank must be returned to store for refills; propane level should be checked before grilling

Multiple burners can be adjusted or turned off to create different cooking configurations

Little to no control over heat and airflow due to non-adjustable vent

Produce less pronounced charred, smoky flavor, especially in longer-cooking foods

Grease tray must be emptied periodically

How Can I Create Different Heat Zones on My Grill?

For basic backyard fare such as burgers and dogs, all you need is even heat: coals spread across the grill or gas burners turned to high. (How you position and how far you open a charcoal grill's vents is important too; see page 157 for more.) But what if you want to cook a whole chicken, mammoth racks of ribs, or a protein and a vegetable side? This is where different grill setups come into play. By piling lit coals into different arrangements on a charcoal grill, you can create hotter or cooler temperature zones for grilling food of any size or shape. (Gas grill burners can be adjusted to mimic most charcoal setups.) These are the grill setups we use most often.

SINGLE-LEVEL FIRE

Purpose: Delivers uniform level of heat across entire cooking surface

Good for: Small, quick-cooking pieces of food such as shrimp, fish fillets, and some vegetables

Charcoal method: Distribute lit coals in even layer across bottom of grill

Gas method: After preheating grill, turn all burners to desired heat setting (low, medium, or high)

CONCENTRATED FIRE

Purpose: Creates contained area of intense heat to sear quick-cooking foods

Good for: Burgers; scallops

Charcoal method: Poke holes in bottom of disposable aluminum roasting pan and set in center of charcoal grate, pour lit coals into disposable pan

Gas method: After preheating grill, leave all burners on high

TWO-LEVEL FIRE

Purpose: Creates two cooking zones: hotter zone for searing and slightly cooler zone for gentler cooking

Good for: Thick chops; bone-in poultry pieces; recipes with multiple foods that require different heat levels

Charcoal method: Evenly distribute two-thirds of lit coals over half of grill, then distribute remainder of coals in even layer over other half

Gas method: After preheating grill, leave primary burner on high and turn other burner(s) to medium

HALF-GRILL FIRE

Purpose: Creates two cooking zones with greater difference between heat levels than two-level fire, with one side intensely hot and other side comparatively cool

Good for: Large cuts of meat such as porterhouse steaks and pork tenderloin; bone-in poultry pieces; foods that need both searing and gentle cooking

Charcoal method: Distribute lit coals over half of grill, piling them in even layer; leave other half of grill free of coals

Gas method: After preheating grill, adjust primary burner to desired heat level and turn off other burner(s)

BANKED FIRE

Purpose: Concentrates heat in even smaller area than in half-grill fire; large flame-free or coal-free area can accommodate pan of water to prevent food from drying out

Good for: Large foods such as brisket, pork shoulder, or whole poultry; foods that need both browning and indirect cooking

Charcoal method: Bank lit coals steeply against one side of grill, leaving rest of grill free of coals

Gas method: After preheating grill, adjust primary burner to desired heat level and turn off other burner(s)

DOUBLE-BANKED FIRE

Purpose: Creates cool area between two heat sources so that food cooks evenly without needing to be rotated; ideal setup for using grill rotisserie

Good for: Rotisserie chicken or leg of lamb; small roasts

Charcoal method: Divide lit coals into two steeply banked piles on opposite sides of grill, leaving center free of coals

Gas method (requires at least 3 burners): After preheating grill, leave primary burner and burner at opposite end of grill on medium-high or medium and turn off center burner(s)

When and How Should I Clean My Grill?

Exactly how you should clean your grill depends on what kind of grill you have.

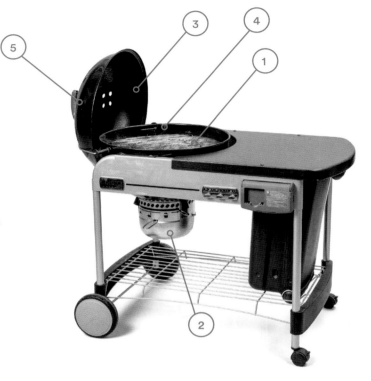

CHARCOAL

Cooking grate (1): Before each use, once the grill is hot, scrub with a grill brush and then wipe with oil. Periodically inspect for deep rust, which may mean the grate needs to be replaced. (If you clean and oil the grate every time, rust shouldn't be a problem.)

Ash catcher (2): Check after every few grilling sessions and empty when full.

Inside lid (3): Every couple of months or so, depending on how much you use your grill, scrape off any built-up carbon (black, flaky paint-like material) using a grill brush.

Inside grill bowl (4): Every couple of months, use a plastic scraper to clean any gunk or buildup, paying attention to the blades.

Exterior (5): Periodically inspect for surface rust around the welded joints; use grill cleaner or nonacidic oil such as WD-40 to remove it and then wash the exterior with warm, soapy water.

GAS

Cooking grate and flavorizer bars (1): Before each use, once the grill is hot, scrub with a grill brush and then wipe with oil. If the bars are particularly dirty, remove and soak in warm, soapy water as needed and then rinse.

Cookbox interior and burner tubes (2): At least once per season (before storing the grill), scrape off buildup, starting from the top down, and then scrub with a bristle brush or with steel wool. Gently clean the igniters.

Grease tray, disposable drip pan (if there is one) (3): Empty and wipe out the grease tray frequently (ideally after every use). At least once per season, or whenever it's full, scrape the tray down and then scrub in soapy water. Replace the disposable pan.

Exterior (4): Periodically inspect for surface rust around the welded joints; use grill cleaner or nonacidic oil such as WD-40 to remove it and then wash the exterior with warm, soapy water; remove the knobs for better access.

Cooking with Charcoal

Charcoal grills are not only relatively inexpensive, they also allow you to customize your heat setup to cook just about any kind of food to perfection. Cooking with charcoal is more of an art form than cooking with gas, but for many backyard pitmasters, that's part of the appeal.

What's Better: Lump Charcoal or Charcoal Briquettes?

There are two types of charcoal: lump (also known as hardwood) and briquettes, both of which produce great-tasting food. Lump resembles the wood it comes from. Briquettes are compact pucks made from sawdust and other materials. Both briquettes and lump charcoal are great for direct, fast grilling. If you're grilling something that takes more than 40 minutes to cook or you're planning to grill several items over a period of time, go for briquettes, since they stay hot longer. In our testing, a chimney full of briquettes gave us 2½ to 3½ hours of grilling time (meaning that's how long grill temperatures remained above 300 degrees). A chimney full of lump charcoal, on the other hand, gave us 40 minutes to 2 hours of cooking time.

Charcoal briquettes (top) and lump charcoal (bottom)

Can I Reuse Charcoal?

Sometimes the food is done but the coals are not. You can save them and replace up to half of the fresh coals called for in a recipe with used coals. Here's how:

As soon as you're finished grilling, cover the grill and close the vents. Once the coals are cool enough to handle, dump them into a small, lidded metal container such as a garbage can.

Before you light a new fire, place your previously used, cooled briquettes into a charcoal chimney starter and shake and rap it over the trash to dislodge ash which would keep the coals from properly igniting. Temporarily remove the coals from the chimney starter. Then, to maximize airflow, place 1 part of fresh coals in the chimney first and top them with 1 part of the used coals. Don't try to build a new fire with only used coals; because they pack together more tightly than new coals, they can be difficult to start.

Cooking with Gas

Gas grills make cooking outdoors accessible. They heat up quickly so you can fit a grilled meal into a busy schedule, and, unlike charcoal, they maintain an even heat level so they're ready when you are.

Is a Higher BTU Number Better?

British Thermal Units, or BTUs, are a measurement of heat output meant to indicate a grill's firepower. But this number doesn't tell the whole story. In addition to producing significant heat, a great grill retains that heat and spreads it across the grates. When we tested gas grills, one grill rated at 30,000 BTUs outperformed another rated at 55,000 BTUs thanks to its superior ability to hold on to and disperse heat.

In general, grills with a tight-fitting lid (1), vents that are on the small side (2), heat diffusers between the burners (3), and a thick-walled cookbox (4) will heat more evenly and better hold on to that heat—a much surer mark of a good grill than the BTU number alone.

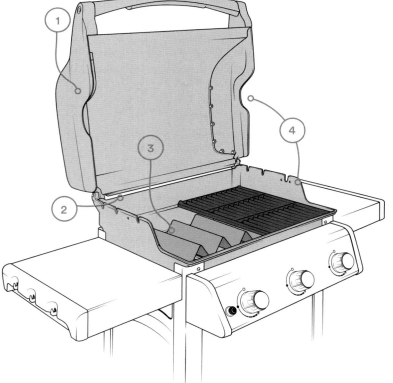

Can I Trust My Grill's Built-In Thermometer?

Your grill thermometer may measure temperature accurately, but what temperature, exactly, is it measuring? If the thermometer (and therefore its sensor) is in the lid, that number on its dial tells you how hot the air near the lid is, not how hot the cooking surface is. The difference between the two can be as much as 50 to 100 degrees Fahrenheit, not to mention that it can vary when you open and close the lid. As long as you remember this, you can use a built-in thermometer to gauge whether your burners are working as they usually do. But for the best outcome, use a remote probe thermometer (see page 93) to monitor the temperature of the food itself.

Yikes! My Grill Caught on Fire! What Do I Do?

A buildup of old grease drippings on the bottom of your gas grill is a real safety hazard, which is why you should check the interior and clean it regularly (see page 148). But if you've neglected this chore and your grill suddenly fills with fire when you light it, calmly shut the lid, turn off the gas both at the grill knobs and at the tank, and wait for the fire to go out. Then clean up the greasy interior before reigniting the grill.

I Don't Have Outdoor Space for a Grill. Can I Fake It Indoors?

There's no substitute for the kiss of smoke or intense sear that an outdoor grill gives food, but if you want good browning with some attractive grill marks, a grill pan is worth a little space in your kitchen. Grill pans are essentially skillets with ridges across the cooking surface that mimic the cooking grates of a grill. The pan's hot ridges sear grill marks onto the surfaces of food while radiant heat cooks the food, and any fat drains away to the channels between the ridges. (To learn what else you can make with a grill pan, see page 63.)

Q: How can I tell how much propane is left in the tank?

A: In general, you should get between 10 and 20 hours of cooking time from a 20-pound tank of propane (the larger the grill, the faster it uses up fuel). But before you start grilling, it's a good idea to find out if your tank will see the project through. This low-tech method is surprisingly accurate: Pour hot water down the side of a tank and note the tank's temperature in different spots. The empty portion of the tank will be warm to the touch, while the full portion of the tank will feel cool. Why? Under pressure (as in a propane tank), propane is both a liquid and a gas. The usable, liquid portion sits at the bottom of the tank, and the gas portion is at the top. Because gas doesn't conduct heat well, hot water poured over the side of the tank will stay hot when it meets the top portion of the tank, making the tank feel warm. The liquid in the bottom, meanwhile, will conduct heat away from the side of the tank, making it cool to the touch.

Q: I haven't used my propane tank in . . . a while. Is it still safe to use?

A: Propane has an indefinite shelf life; the container it's stored in is another story. In the United States, steel propane cylinders have to be inspected and recertified 12 years after manufacture, and every five years after that. To find the date of manufacture, look for numbers stamped on the collar at the top of the tank; 02 23 means the tank was manufactured in February, 2023. Once you've determined that your tank hasn't expired, take a careful look. If it's free from dents and rust, it's good to go. But if you see signs of damage, regardless of the tank's age, you should dispose of it properly by trading it in at your propane dealer or hardware store.

Q. What about the hose?

A: The fuel hose can deteriorate (or be chewed on by critters), so don't forget to inspect it for signs of wear and tear. To be sure the hose is leak-free, you can do a bubble test: Turn on the fuel supply and apply a half-and-half solution of liquid dishwasher soap and water to the various junctions connecting the propane tank to the burner. If bubbles appear, there's a leak. Turn off the fuel and tighten the connections. Wait at least 5 minutes for any gas fumes to dissipate before checking again and proceeding. If you still see bubbles, you've got a leak. Turn off the gas and contact a service technician; you may need to replace the hose or valve. If the leak appears to be coming from the tank, don't try to move or transport it. Turn off the valve, leave the area, and call the fire department.

Can a Small Gas Grill Cook as Well as a Full-Size Version?

Tabletop propane grills hold a lot of appeal if your yard—or your household—is small or if you like the idea of grilling away from home. While they tend to have a reputation for wimpy heat output and uneven cooking, you can get excellent results from a small grill if you choose wisely. The best-performing models have a substantial steel grate that spreads heat uniformly and allows for those all-important dark grill marks on food. A thick body and lid and a low, narrow vent offer optimum heat retention. Finally, while they don't have the capacity of a standard grill, many compact grills can accommodate eight to 10 burgers at a time. If you want to cook larger foods, look for a model with a domed lid.

Which Grills Are Best for Traveling?

Portable grills are meant to be ideal for picnics, tailgating, and camping, but when we tested them we found that some were more portable than others. Weight is one factor; we think 20 pounds is about the limit of what you want to carry. But the placement and configuration of the handles, along with the shape of the grill once lifted, is just as important. A truly portable grill should close securely and compactly and feel balanced when you lift it. Unbalanced, irregularly shaped grills are awkward and poky to carry. (One of our favorite small grills is relatively heavy and uses a 20-pound propane tank, making it a great choice for a small backyard or balcony but not for a road trip.)

SHRIMP SKEWERS WITH CHILI CRISP AND NAPA CABBAGE SLAW

serves 4

A hot single-level fire cooks shrimp in just a few minutes so they brown beautifully but don't have time to dry out. You will need four 12-inch metal skewers for this recipe.

2	pounds jumbo shrimp (16 to 20 per pound), peeled and deveined
¼	cup vegetable oil, divided
¼	teaspoon pepper
¼	cup chili crisp, plus extra for serving
2	tablespoons white wine vinegar
½	teaspoon table salt
1	small head napa cabbage (1½ pounds), cored and sliced thin
4	scallions, sliced thin on bias
1	cup fresh cilantro leaves
¼	cup salted dry-roasted peanuts, chopped

1 Thread shrimp tightly onto four 12-inch metal skewers, alternating direction of heads and tails. Pat shrimp dry with paper towels, then brush with 1 tablespoon oil and sprinkle with pepper.

2A for a charcoal grill Open bottom vent completely. Light large chimney starter mounded with charcoal briquettes (7 quarts). When top coals are partially covered with ash, pour evenly over grill. Set cooking grate in place, cover, and open lid vent completely. Heat grill until hot, about 5 minutes.

2B for a gas grill Turn all burners to high; cover; and heat grill until hot, about 15 minutes. Leave all burners on high.

3 Clean and oil cooking grate. Grill shrimp (covered if using gas) until lightly charred and opaque throughout, about 4 minutes, flipping halfway through grilling. Using tongs, slide shrimp off skewers onto serving platter and brush with chili crisp.

4 Whisk remaining 3 tablespoons oil, vinegar, and salt together in large bowl. Add cabbage, scallions, and cilantro and toss to coat. Season with salt and pepper to taste. Sprinkle with peanuts and serve with shrimp, passing extra chili crisp separately.

real talk with lisa

STOP CHECKING ON YOUR FOOD SO OFTEN

The lid of your grill is such an important tool. It keeps heat around your food, helping it cook. If you're grilling in cold weather, or any time when the aim is to cook the food low and slow, leaving the lid on is absolutely critical. Every time you lift the lid to take a peek, the temperature around your food drops dramatically, messing with your results. As our barbecue expert Morgan Bolling says, "If you're looking, you ain't cooking." Your best bet? Use a remote probe thermometer (see page 93 for more about those) to keep tabs on your food so you can monitor progress and leave the lid on!

PAPRIKA AND LIME-RUBBED CHICKEN WITH VEGETABLE SUCCOTASH

serves 4

A two-level fire lets you cook a whole meal on the grill at once. Here, bone-in chicken pieces do best over indirect heat, where their insides can cook through without the outsides burning. Quick-cooking corn, onion, and tomatoes pick up color and flavorful charring over high heat. You will need four 12-inch metal skewers for this recipe.

12	ounces cherry tomatoes
1	red onion, sliced into ½-inch-thick rounds
3	ears corn, husks and silk removed
¼	cup extra-virgin olive oil, divided
1	teaspoon table salt, divided
¾	teaspoon pepper, divided
1	tablespoon plus ½ teaspoon smoked hot paprika, divided
4	teaspoons grated lime zest, divided, plus 2 tablespoons juice (2 limes), plus lime wedges for serving
1½	teaspoons packed dark brown sugar
1	teaspoon ground cumin
3	pounds bone-in chicken pieces (split breasts cut in half crosswise, drumsticks, and/or thighs), trimmed
3	tablespoons minced fresh cilantro, divided
2	garlic cloves, minced
1	(15-ounce) can butter beans, rinsed

1 Thread tomatoes onto four 12-inch metal skewers. Push toothpick horizontally through each onion round to keep rings intact while grilling. Brush corn, onion, and tomato skewers with 2 tablespoons oil and sprinkle with ½ teaspoon salt and ¼ teaspoon pepper.

2 Combine 1 tablespoon paprika, 1 tablespoon lime zest, sugar, cumin, remaining ½ teaspoon salt, and remaining ½ teaspoon pepper together in large bowl. Pat chicken dry with paper towels, transfer to bowl with spice mixture, and stir to coat evenly.

3A for a charcoal grill Open bottom vent completely. Light large chimney starter filled with charcoal briquettes (6 quarts). When top coals are partially covered with ash, pour two-thirds evenly over half of grill, then pour remaining coals over other half of grill. Set cooking grate in place, cover, and open lid vent completely. Heat grill until hot, about 5 minutes.

3B for a gas grill Turn all burners to high; cover; and heat grill until hot, about 15 minutes. Leave primary burner on high and turn other burner(s) to low.

4 Clean and oil cooking grate. Place chicken, skin side down, on cooler side of grill. Cover and cook until skin is well browned and slightly charred and breasts register 160 degrees and drumsticks/thighs register 175 degrees, 20 to 30 minutes, flipping and rearranging as needed so all pieces get equal exposure to heat source. Transfer chicken pieces to serving platter as they finish cooking, tent with aluminum foil, and let rest.

5 While chicken cooks, place corn, onion, and tomato skewers on hotter side of grill. Cook vegetables covered, flipping as needed, until tomato skins blister, about 2 minutes, and corn and onion are lightly charred, 8 to 10 minutes. Transfer to cutting board as they finish cooking.

6 Remove toothpicks from onion rings. Chop grilled onions and cut corn kernels from cobs. Whisk remaining 1 teaspoon lime zest, lime juice, 2 tablespoons cilantro, garlic, remaining ½ teaspoon paprika, and remaining 2 tablespoons oil together in large bowl. Add beans, tomatoes, chopped onion, and corn to bowl and toss to combine. Season with salt and pepper to taste. Sprinkle remaining 1 tablespoon cilantro over chicken. Serve with succotash and lime wedges.

THICK-CUT PORTERHOUSE STEAKS

serves 6

Starting these superthick steaks over the hotter side of a half-grill fire lets them pick up beautiful char. We then transfer them to the cooler side of the grill to allow the insides to cook gently to a rosy medium-rare.

- 2 (2½- to 3-pound) porterhouse steaks, 2 inches thick, fat trimmed to ¼ inch
- 4¼ teaspoons kosher salt, divided
- 4 teaspoons olive oil (if using gas)
- 2 teaspoons pepper
- 3 tablespoons unsalted butter, melted

1 Pat steaks dry with paper towels and sprinkle each side of each steak with 1 teaspoon salt. Transfer steaks to large plate and refrigerate, uncovered, for at least 1 hour or up to 24 hours.

2A for a charcoal grill Open bottom vent completely. Light large chimney starter filled with charcoal briquettes (6 quarts). When top coals are partially covered with ash, pour evenly over half of grill. Set cooking grate in place, cover, and open lid vent completely. Heat grill until hot, about 5 minutes.

2B for a gas grill Turn all burners to high; cover; and heat grill until hot, about 15 minutes. Leave primary burner on high and turn off other burner(s). (Adjust primary burner [or, if using three-burner grill, primary burner and second burner] as needed to maintain grill temperature of 450 degrees.)

3 Pat steaks dry with paper towels. If using gas, brush each side of each steak with 1 teaspoon oil. Sprinkle each side of each steak with ½ teaspoon pepper.

4 Clean and oil cooking grate. Place steaks on hotter side of grill, with tenderloins facing cooler side. Cook (covered if using gas) until evenly charred on first side, 6 to 8 minutes. Flip steaks and position so tenderloins are still facing cooler side of grill. Continue to cook (covered if using gas) until evenly charred on second side, 6 to 8 minutes longer.

5 Flip steaks and transfer to cooler side of grill, with bone side facing fire. Cover and cook until thermometer inserted 3 inches from tip of strip side of steak registers 115 to 120 degrees (for medium-rare), 8 to 12 minutes, flipping halfway through cooking. Transfer steaks to wire rack set in rimmed baking sheet, tent with aluminum foil, and let rest for 10 minutes.

6 Stir remaining ¼ teaspoon salt into melted butter. Transfer steaks to carving board. Carve strips and tenderloins from bones. Place bones on platter. Slice steaks thin against grain, then reassemble sliced steaks around bones. Drizzle with melted butter and season with salt and pepper to taste. Serve.

Hannah Says . . .

Cleaning and oiling your grill grate means your food will be less prone to sticking, you get better grill marks, and you avoid getting all those old carbonized bits on your food. I keep a roll of paper towels, a container of vegetable oil, and a set of tongs next to my grill so I'm always ready to go.

SALMON FILLETS

serves 4

A clean and well-oiled cooking grate is the key to salmon fillets that release cleanly with gorgeously distinct grill marks. Patience is key when cooking the fillets; if you try to turn a piece of fish before it develops char marks, it's more likely to stick.

SAUCE

½	cup mayonnaise
2	tablespoons extra-virgin olive oil
1	tablespoon lemon juice
1	garlic clove, minced
¼	teaspoon kosher salt
	Pinch cayenne pepper

SALMON

1	(2- to 2¼-pound) center-cut skin-on salmon fillet, about 1½ inches thick
1	teaspoon kosher salt
½	teaspoon pepper
	Vegetable oil

1 for the sauce Whisk all ingredients together in bowl. Cover with plastic wrap and refrigerate while preparing salmon.

2 for the salmon Trim away and discard thinner bottom 1 inch of salmon to make salmon more consistent thickness. Cut salmon crosswise into 4 equal fillets. Dry fillets thoroughly with paper towels and refrigerate while preparing grill. Combine salt and pepper in bowl; set aside.

3A for a charcoal grill Open bottom vent completely. Light large chimney starter filled with charcoal briquettes (6 quarts). When top coals are partially covered with ash, pour evenly over grill. Set cooking grate in place, cover, and open lid vent completely. Heat grill until hot, about 5 minutes.

3B for a gas grill Turn all burners to high; cover; and heat grill until hot, about 15 minutes. Leave all burners on high.

4 Clean cooking grate, then repeatedly brush grate with well-oiled paper towels until grate is black and glossy, 5 to 10 times.

5 Using pastry brush, brush flesh and skin sides of fillets with thin coat of oil. Sprinkle flesh sides all over with salt mixture. Place fillets on grill, flesh side down, perpendicular to grate bars, about 3 inches apart on all sides. Cover grill (reduce heat to medium if using gas) and cook, without moving fillets, until flesh side is well marked and releases easily from grill, 4 to 5 minutes.

6 Using fish spatula, gently push each fillet to roll it over onto skin side. (If fillets don't lift cleanly off grill, cover and continue to cook 1 minute longer, at which point they should release.) Continue to cook, covered, until centers of fillets are opaque and register 125 degrees, 4 to 5 minutes longer. Using tongs to stabilize fillets, slide spatula under fillets and transfer to platter. (If skin sticks to grill, slide spatula between fillet and skin and lift fillet away from skin.) Serve with sauce.

How Can I Keep Fish (and Other Delicate Foods) from Sticking to the Grill?

A dramatically char-striped fillet of fish is a thing of beauty, but if it sticks to the grate, you'll wind up with a ragged mess. Fortunately there's an easy way to avoid this tragedy: Get into the good habit of cleaning and oiling your cooking grate every time you cook.

First, preheat the grill to loosen the gunk on the grates (hot grates also produce better char marks, which help food to release cleanly). Use a sturdy grill brush to scrape the cooking grate clean. Next, use grill tongs to hold a wadded rag (or paper towels), dip it in vegetable oil, and wipe the grate until the bars are dark and glossy.

Fish (or other delicate foods) still sticking? Before adding it to the grill, make sure the food is dry and brush it with a thin coat of oil. The drier the food, the more apt it is to develop a crust instead of just steaming on the grill. The oil provides added insurance against sticking.

5 Things Grilling Experts Know (That You Might Not)

How well do you really know your grill? Here are some hows, whens, and whys you can use to become a better griller.

1 WHEN TO USE DIRECT VERSUS INDIRECT HEAT

When you want to put dark char marks on thin, quick-cooking boneless chicken breasts, cooking over direct heat (placing the food right over the fire) is the way to go. But if you treat bone-in, skin-on chicken parts or a whole bird the same way, the outside can incinerate before the inside is safe to eat. Many foods need a bit more TLC than a ripping-hot grill can provide, and that's where cooking with indirect heat (placing the food adjacent to, not directly over, the fire) comes in. Some grill setups provide both indirect and direct heat. It may seem complicated but it's actually a pretty simple way to get the best of both worlds—thick steaks, chops, or roasts that are perfectly cooked inside and beautifully bronzed outside. With two heat zones at your disposal, you're in control: Slide the food over the flames for more color, or set it aside to slow things down. Combination grill setups also let you cook a variety of foods at the same time. (See page 146 for more about direct and indirect heat grill setups.)

2 WHEN TO COOK WITH THE LID UP VERSUS DOWN

An uncovered grill loses a lot of heat; only the side of the food facing the flames gets hot. This is OK for thin, fast-cooking foods such as burgers, but for many dishes, trapping heat by keeping the lid down makes for more efficient cooking. A good recipe should tell you whether to leave the lid up or put it down, but in general, heat loss is less of a problem with charcoal grills because they run hotter than gas grills. For that reason, the same recipe might call for covering a gas grill while leaving a charcoal grill uncovered. The lid on a charcoal grill is mostly used for low-and-slow cooking and smoking. One major exception: If you're grilling in cold or windy weather, you should cook with the lid down regardless of what type of grill you're using, or you'll be wasting gas or burning through charcoal as the heat gets whisked away.

3 WHEN THE GRILL IS HOT ENOUGH

Gas grills have dials that let you cook at your chosen temperature, but you still need to give the grill enough time to preheat. We recommend preheating charcoal grills for 5 minutes, but when it comes to gas grills, 15 minutes is better. Since gas flames don't produce as much radiant heat (which cooks the portions of food between the grill grate) as hot coals, gas grills need the extra time to convert the heat of the flames into radiant heat, and produces better results when it comes to your food.

4

WHEN TO OPEN OR CLOSE THE VENTS

Grill vents are like the dials on your stovetop: They allow you to manipulate how hot the fire gets and how the food cooks. Charcoal grills have a vent in the lid and a vent on the underside of the basin. In general, opening the vents completely allows more oxygen to reach the fire so that it burns hotter and faster, while partially closing the vents lowers the temperature and prolongs the fire's duration. The bottom vent is always at least partially open when cooking; air drawn through the bottom vent feeds the fire. Because heat and smoke rise from the coals and are drawn out through the top vent, you can position the lid to minimize or maximize heat and smoke contact with the food you're grilling. Shutting the top and bottom vents will kill charcoal fires quickly and even lets you save any unburned charcoal for the next time you grill. Gas grills have vents, too, but they are not adjustable; when the lid is closed, hot air and smoke flow straight out the back of the grill. That's why it's important to choose a gas grill with a narrow vent and a thick, heat-retaining body.

5

HOW TO KEEP FOOD FROM FALLING THROUGH THE GRATE

One way to grill small foods without losing them to the flames is to use a plancha (see page 168). But if you want grill marks, here are a few ways to prep the food to make it easier to handle and keep it on top of the grate where it belongs.

Insert toothpick or skewer into side of onion slices to keep rings from separating as they cook.

Thread bite-size pieces onto skewers.

Slice vegetables such as zucchini and eggplant lengthwise into planks rather than crosswise into small rounds.

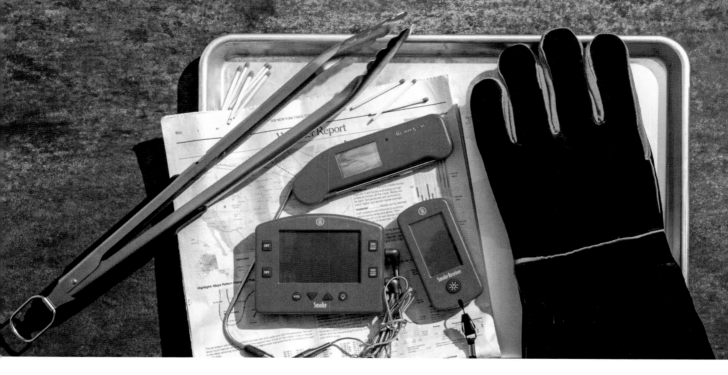

Grill Accessories

Choosing the right equipment for outdoor cooking doesn't end with your grill. The quality and design of small tools and accessories can mean the difference between grilling fun and grilling frustration.

real talk with hannah & lisa

 HC

DISPOSABLE ALUMINUM PANS ARE A GRILLER'S BEST FRIEND

Disposable aluminum roasting pans are a handy grill accessory. We like moderately deep 13 by 9-inch ones because they can be used in so many ways. As drip trays under the cooking grate on a charcoal grill, they reduce flare-ups. They can also hold water to add humidity to a cooking environment or corral a pile of lit briquettes for a concentrated fire. You can use them to braise on the grill, and on a flat-top grill, they make a great lid for trapping heat and moisture to melt cheese or cook eggs. While they are disposable, you can get several uses out of them. I use mine either until they're totally charred or somehow get punctured.

LM

MY GRILL PREP STATION

Good organization makes grilling easy. I use a rimmed baking sheet as a tray to corral all my gear, including my 16-inch tongs (long enough to keep me safe from the heat, but short enough for good leverage and control); a small bowl of vegetable oil and wad of paper towels to oil the clean grates; matches or a lighter; sheets of newspaper for the chimney starter; my remote-probe thermometer and my instant-read thermometer for quick checkups; and a digital timer. I also make sure to include sturdy grill gloves and potholders. I use a second baking sheet to hold raw food and a third to collect cooked food, keeping them well separated to prevent cross-contamination. And of course I store my chimney starter, charcoal, and grill brush outside with my grill, so I'm always ready to cook!

Should I Be Worried About Metal Grill Brush Bristles Winding Up in My Food?

Durability is an important quality in a grill brush, not only because you want it to last but also because you want those bristles to stay embedded in the brush and not in your food. The Centers for Disease Control and Prevention cautions grillers who use a wire bristle brush to carefully check the grill's surface before placing food on it—sound advice. That said, the metal brushes we tested didn't show evidence of broken or detached bristles even after vigorous scrubbing; in fact, they were more durable than brushes that used palmyra fibers or steel wool. However, if you have concerns about using a brush with metal bristles, you may consider opting for a brush that uses stainless-steel coils instead of bristles.

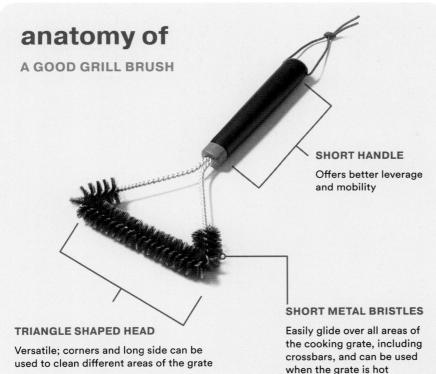

anatomy of
A GOOD GRILL BRUSH

SHORT HANDLE

Offers better leverage and mobility

TRIANGLE SHAPED HEAD

Versatile; corners and long side can be used to clean different areas of the grate

SHORT METAL BRISTLES

Easily glide over all areas of the cooking grate, including crossbars, and can be used when the grate is hot

Lisa Says . . .

A grill is not the place to use nonstick cookware. Grills routinely reach temperatures of 600 degrees or more, much hotter than nonstick coatings can withstand without breaking down and releasing harmful fumes. Even though you're outdoors, you don't want to breathe those in as you cook. What's more, the nonstick ability of that cookware degrades quickly in high heat, so it doesn't even work as intended. It's just not worth it!

Why Are Grill Tongs Often So . . . Bad?

Long-handled grill tongs should work like an extension of your hands, keeping you well away from the heat while enabling you to deftly grab, lift, and turn food. But you're not imagining it: Many (far too many!) grill tongs are just plain bad, and it all comes down to construction. They often come with misaligned pincers and are either huge and unwieldy or too light and flimsy. Either way, bad tongs make grilling harder than it should be, as they force you to fight for control over the food you're cooking.

The best grill tongs are lightweight to cut down on fatigue, but not lightly built; they need to be tough enough to lift and flip heavy whole chickens and slabs of ribs. Shallow, scalloped pincers with narrow tips and a slight curve offer precision so you can grasp a variety of foods gently and securely. And while you might think that longer means safer, we've found that 16-inch tongs provide the perfect balance of protection from heat and optimum control.

What's the Best Way to Light Coals Quickly?

We get it: You want dinner now. But resist the urge to reach for lighter fluid, or that dinner will wind up tasting like chemicals. Instead, use a chimney starter. It takes just about 20 minutes to properly heat coals using this method. You'll know the coals are fully lit and hot when they're covered with a thin layer of ash; don't be tempted to pour out the coals prematurely or you'll be left with unlit coals at the bottom of the pile that may never ignite, as well as a cooler fire.

Fill the bottom of chimney starter with two sheets of loosely crumpled newspaper or a charcoal lighter cube, set it on the charcoal grate (make sure the bottom vent is open), and then fill the top with charcoal as the recipe directs. Light the newspaper or cube and allow the charcoal to burn until the briquettes on top are partially covered with a thin layer of gray ash.

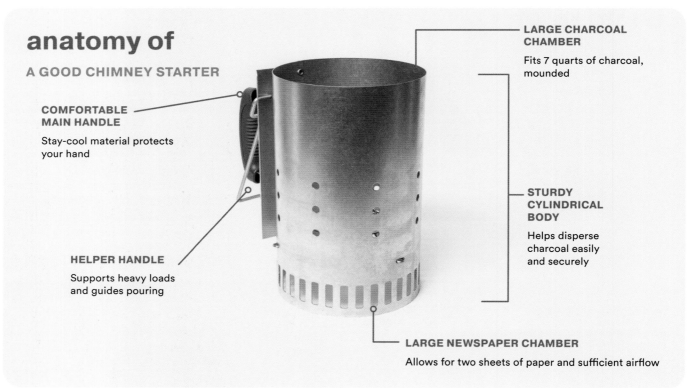

anatomy of
A GOOD CHIMNEY STARTER

COMFORTABLE MAIN HANDLE
Stay-cool material protects your hand

HELPER HANDLE
Supports heavy loads and guides pouring

LARGE CHARCOAL CHAMBER
Fits 7 quarts of charcoal, mounded

STURDY CYLINDRICAL BODY
Helps disperse charcoal easily and securely

LARGE NEWSPAPER CHAMBER
Allows for two sheets of paper and sufficient airflow

Hannah Says . . .

If you don't have a chimney starter, don't use instant-light charcoal: It can impart gross flavors to food. Instead, open the grill's bottom vent and place eight sheets of balled-up newspaper beneath the charcoal grate. Pile the charcoal in the middle of the grate and light the paper. After about 20 minutes the coals should be covered with gray ash and ready for cooking. If you don't have newspaper, charcoal lighter cubes are a handy sub; they produce a good-size flame instantly, and because they're made from paraffin, they'll burn for a few minutes, ensuring that your charcoal will ignite, without adding any off flavors.

GLAZED ROTISSERIE PINEAPPLE WITH SALTED RUM BUTTERSCOTCH SAUCE

serves 6 to 8

This stunning dessert really shows off what a motorized grill rotisserie can do: Turning a ripe pineapple over a hot fire caramelizes its surface to a golden brown and brings out an irresistible aroma reminiscent of a tropical cocktail. Be careful when threading the rotisserie skewer through the pineapple, as it takes some pressure to push the skewer through the core. If using a charcoal grill, you will need a 13 by 9-inch disposable aluminum roasting pan. Our gas grill instructions are for a three-burner grill. If using a two-burner grill, turn both burners to medium.

1	cup packed (7 ounces) light brown sugar
½	cup heavy cream
8	tablespoons unsalted butter, cut into 8 pieces and chilled, divided
½	teaspoon table salt
2	tablespoons dark rum
½	teaspoon vanilla extract
1	pineapple

1 Cook sugar, cream, 4 tablespoons butter, and salt in medium saucepan over medium-high heat, stirring often with rubber spatula, until large bubbles burst on surface of sauce, about 4 minutes. Off heat, carefully stir in remaining 4 tablespoons butter until fully combined, about 1 minute. Stir in rum and vanilla. Transfer sauce to bowl and let cool for 30 minutes (sauce will thicken as it cools). (Sauce can be refrigerated for up to 1 week; reheat in microwave before serving.)

2 Using sharp knife, slice off crown and bottom of pineapple. Holding pineapple upright, pare off rind from top to bottom as thin as possible. Lay fruit on 1 side. Working around pineapple, cut shallow, diagonal V-shaped grooves just deep enough to remove eyes, following their natural spiral pattern.

3 Set pineapple upright on cutting board. Center beveled tip of rotisserie skewer on top of pineapple and carefully push skewer down through core of pineapple. Turn pineapple on its side and continue to thread it onto center of skewer. Attach rotisserie forks to skewer and insert tines into pineapple; secure forks by tightening screws.

4A for a charcoal grill Open bottom vent completely and place disposable pan in center of grill. Light large chimney starter mounded with charcoal briquettes (7 quarts). When top coals are partially covered with ash, pour into 2 even piles on either side of disposable pan. Position rotisserie motor attachment on grill so that skewer runs parallel to coals. Cover, open lid vent completely, and heat grill until hot, about 5 minutes.

4B for a gas grill Remove cooking grate. Position rotisserie motor attachment on grill and turn all burners to high. Cover and heat grill until hot, about 15 minutes. Turn outside burners to medium-high and turn off center burner. (Adjust outside burners as needed to maintain grill temperature between 450 and 500 degrees.)

5 Brush pineapple with ¼ cup sauce. Attach rotisserie skewer to motor and start motor. Cover and cook for 30 minutes.

6 Brush pineapple with ¼ cup sauce and continue to cook, covered, until tender and lightly charred, 15 to 30 minutes. Transfer pineapple, still on skewer, to cutting board. Using large wad of paper towels in each hand, carefully remove rotisserie forks and skewer from pineapple. Slice pineapple thin and serve with remaining sauce.

worth it

GRILL ROTISSERIE

If you often grill roasts such as whole chicken, leg of lamb, prime rib, and pork loin (or if you'd like to), a motorized rotisserie kit makes a practical addition to your grill. As the motor turns the food, juices and seasonings stay mostly inside it and on it, so the result is extra-juicy, crisp, well browned, and slightly smoky. For charcoal grills, the kit consists of a metal ring that rests on the rim of a kettle-style grill and supports a spit, while a small electric motor turns the spit continuously. Rotisseries for gas grills are similar, but without the metal ring.

All Things Smoke

Backyard cooking holds all kinds of appeal, but for some of us, it comes down to the allure of smoke. Fortunately, you've got plenty of options for imbuing your food with that tantalizing smoky flavor.

Can I Make Real Barbecue Using Just My Grill?

If you have a charcoal grill, you can produce seriously good ribs, brisket, smoked turkey, and pulled pork with the help of a charcoal snake. This grill setup calls for lining the perimeter of the charcoal grate with briquettes in a "C" shape, two rows wide and two rows high. The C is lit at one end and burns gradually, for the low and slow heat that great barbecue requires. Adding a disposable aluminum roasting pan filled with water in the center of the grate keeps the temperature even. Wood chunks evenly spaced along the C provide sustained smoke.

While authentic-tasting barbecue is harder to pull off with a gas grill, a packet of wood chips can add nice smoky flavor to ribs, wings, and more.

But for real barbecue aficionados, there are a few reasons to invest in a dedicated smoker (see right). Most good smokers can better maintain the low-and-slow temperature range barbecue experts recommend for turning tough cuts of meat tender without drying them out. Many also have larger fuel capacities (unlimited with electric models), so you won't have to worry as much about running out of heat during long cooking times.

head to head

SMOKERS

CHARCOAL SMOKERS

Standout flavor makes them worth the effort

Produce superior tasting, smoky barbecue

Create more and better smoke than other smoker types

Air intake vents must be adjusted periodically to maintain low heat

Charcoal is a somewhat messy and fussy fuel to use

Easy to assemble and maintain, with fewer parts that can break or get damaged

GAS SMOKERS

Trade some flavor for convenience

Food just isn't as richly flavored or intensely smoky as food cooked in a charcoal smoker

Good at maintaining low temperatures, so food is tender and moist

Easy to use; relatively hands-off

Achieve and maintain temperature with little to no adjustment needed

Can be hard to assemble

ELECTRIC SMOKERS

Only worthwhile if space or fire hazards are issues

Food has little to no smoke flavor

Good at maintaining low temperatures, so food is tender and moist

Unlimited fuel supply; just plug it in

Easy to set up

Are Wood Chips or Wood Chunks Better for Smoking?

In the test kitchen, we use both wood chips and wood chunks for adding smoky flavor to food. Wood chips can be used on gas grills and charcoal grills, while wood chunks are used only with charcoal grills. Chips are smaller and burn faster than chunks, so they're better for adding flavor to foods that cook more quickly. Wood chunks (most are roughly the size of a tennis ball) work well for long-cooked foods. For most recipes there's no need to soak wood chips or chunks in water before you use them. Simply place wood chips inside a foil pouch with holes cut into it for ventilation; place wood chunks directly on the coals for long, slow-smoked recipes.

our favorite woods for smoking

Beyond the straightforward smokiness, the wood you use for smoking contributes its own unique flavor to food. Here are some of our favorite choices.

WOOD TYPE	FLAVOR NOTES
Fruit (Apple and Cherry)	Lightly sweet, mild smoke; great for seafood and poultry
Hickory	Balanced though intense smoke that works with almost any food
Maple	Relatively mild and tasty smoke on pork and poultry; can taste somewhat "resiny" on salmon
Mesquite	Strong smoke that works best with stronger-tasting cuts of beef, pork, lamb, and game
Oak	Nutty and well-balanced smoke; the traditional choice for many pitmasters

Lisa Says . . .

If you love smokiness and want to add smoky flavor without grilling, try a portable smoke infuser. These gadgets, which have a small chamber to burn wood chips (or spices or herbs) and a battery-powered fan to blow the smoke toward the food, are supersimple to operate, and you can use them to infuse foods such as popcorn, cheese, and even cocktails with smoky flavor.

SMOKED NACHOS

serves 6 to 8

Cooking nachos in a cast-iron skillet on your grill lets you put a smoky, charry spin on this indoor favorite. If you'd like to use wood chunks instead of wood chips when using a charcoal grill, substitute two medium wood chunks for the wood chip packet. You will need a 12-inch cast-iron skillet for this recipe.

2	cups wood chips
2	ears corn, husks and silk removed
2	teaspoons vegetable oil
2	poblano chiles, stemmed, halved, and seeded
4	Fresno or jalapeño chiles, stemmed, halved, and seeded
1	(15-ounce) can black beans, rinsed
8	ounces Monterey Jack cheese, shredded (2 cups)
8	ounces sharp cheddar cheese, shredded (2 cups)
12	ounces tortilla chips
2	scallions, sliced thin
	Lime wedges

1 Using large piece of heavy-duty aluminum foil, wrap chips in 8 by 4½-inch foil packet. (Make sure chips do not poke holes in sides or bottom of packet. If using gas, make sure there are no more than 2 layers of foil on bottom of packet.) Cut 2 evenly spaced 2-inch slits in top of packet.

2A for a charcoal grill Open bottom vent halfway. Light large chimney starter mounded with charcoal briquettes (7 quarts). When top coals are partially covered with ash, pour two-thirds evenly over half of grill, then pour remaining coals over other half of grill. Place wood chip packet along 1 side of grill near border between hotter and cooler coals. Set cooking grate in place, cover, and open lid vent halfway. Heat grill until hot and wood chips are smoking, about 5 minutes.

2B for a gas grill Remove cooking grate and place wood chip packet directly on primary burner. Set cooking grate in place and turn primary burner to medium and turn other burner(s) to high. Cover and heat grill until hot, about 15 minutes. Leave primary burner on medium and other burner(s) on high.

3 Clean and oil cooking grate. Brush corn with oil. Grill corn, poblanos, and Fresnos on hotter side of grill (covered if using gas) until corn is charred on all sides and poblanos and Fresnos are well blistered, 5 to 10 minutes. As poblanos and Fresnos finish cooking, transfer to bowl, cover tightly with aluminum foil, and let sit until skins soften, about 5 minutes. Transfer corn to cutting board. Turn all burners to medium (if using gas).

4 Cut corn kernels from cobs. Using paper towels, peel away skin from poblanos and Fresnos. Slice poblanos into ¼-inch-thick strips and thinly slice Fresnos. Combine corn, poblanos, Fresnos, black beans, Monterey Jack, and cheddar in bowl.

5 Spread one-quarter of tortilla chips evenly in 12-inch cast iron skillet. Sprinkle with one-quarter of vegetable-cheese mixture. Repeat layering of chips and vegetable-cheese mixture 3 more times. Arrange skillet on cooler side of grill (if using charcoal), cover, and cook until cheese is melted, 15 to 30 minutes. Sprinkle with scallions and serve with lime wedges.

real talk with hannah

GO AHEAD: USE POTS AND PANS ON THE GRILL

I love using cast-iron cookware to expand what I can cook on the grill. I use my cast-iron skillet and Dutch oven (both unenameled—that's key for live-fire cooking!) for things such as green beans that might fall between the grates and for foods that I want to accompany my grilled food that are not grill-friendly, like a pot of chili, cornbread, or fried eggs.

Other Backyard Big Shots

Fire pits and outdoor fryers expand the limits of what it's possible to cook outside.

Can I Use My Fire Pit to Cook Food That's Actually Good?

Campfire cooking is outdoor cuisine at its most primal. You can indeed use a fire pit to cook great food in much the same way as you would using a charcoal grill, albeit with a bit more improvisation and less predictability than a grill provides. Here's how to set up a fire pit for cooking; once the majority of the logs have carbonized (burned down into coals) you can spread them over the grill in an even layer for a single-level fire or over half the grill for a half-grill fire.

1 Arrange small bundle of tinder in center of grill. Lean thinnest pieces of kindling against each other over tinder to form cone shape. Continue leaning larger pieces of kindling on top, making sure to leave gaps for air to circulate. Arrange 2 largest pieces of fuel wood on either side of cone, parallel to each other.

2 Stack next 2 largest pieces on top of and perpendicular to the first two. Repeat once more with next 2 largest pieces to create log cabin shape. Ignite tinder and let kindling and logs catch fire.

3 As fire burns, use fire tongs or poker to concentrate burnt logs that begin to break down into center. Allow to burn until most logs have carbonized and broken down into large coals.

What Kind of Wood Should I Use?

To create a hot, clean-burning fire, you need dry, seasoned wood. Green wood will burn poorly, creating excess smoke and unnecessary pollution. The ideal wood for a cooking fire is hardwood such as oak, ash, birch, or maple. We like to use fuel wood that's about 12 inches long, split into 2-inch-thick pieces in order to quickly create usable coals. You'll need tinder, such as a small bundle of crumpled newspaper, wood shavings, dryer lint, or torn-up cardboard egg cartons, to get your fire started. Charcoal lighter cubes make a great option, too. And you'll need kindling to bridge the gap between the burning tinder and the larger logs. Small sticks between ½ and 1 inch thick catch fire easily and keep burning for a while.

Are Outdoor Fryers as Dangerous as They Say?

There's no getting around it: Frying a turkey is dangerous. As our colleague Miye found out when testing outdoor fryers, the National Fire Protection Association discourages the use of outdoor fryers because of the risk of accidents due to user error, and some state and local fire agencies specifically warn against frying turkeys. (Miye actually collaborated with her local Lexington, Kentucky fire department to make sure her tests were completed safely.)

But there's also no denying that fried turkey (or, let's face it, anything deep-fried) is seriously delicious. And it *is* possible to use an outdoor fryer safely—as long as you follow a long list of dos and don'ts to the letter.

DO	DON'T
Thaw your bird completely and dry it thoroughly before putting it in the hot oil. Water and ice contacting hot oil can cause a fire or even an explosion.	Fry food (such as a turkey) that has not been completely thawed and thoroughly dried.
Place your fryer on a flat, level surface, such as a patio or concrete driveway, that's at least 10 feet away from any walls or structures.	Fry when it's raining, snowing, or windy.
Leave at least 2 feet between the propane tank and the burner.	Fry under a tree or over-hang such as a roof, awning, porch, etc.
Check your propane tank for leaks (see page 151).	Overfill the fryer.
Have an ABC fire extinguisher standing by.	Let the flames lick up the sides of the fryer.
Measure how much oil you need before you fry.	Attempt to move the fryer once the oil is hot.
Keep pets and children far away.	Leave the fryer unattended.
Turn the propane burner off before adding or removing food.	
If frying turkey, lower and raise the bird slowly.	
Let the oil cool completely before cleaning up.	

How Much Oil Should I Use?

If you're frying a turkey, you want to make sure the bird is just covered by the oil; to measure out exactly how much oil that will take, you can follow these steps. First, place the turkey (frozen is fine; just be sure to thaw it before cooking!) and rack into the stockpot, then fill the pot with water until it covers the turkey by about half an inch, keeping track of how much you've used as you go. (If the turkey floats due to air bubbles inside the package, you'll need to take it out of the package and try again.) Mark this line and make sure it is at least 6 inches from the top of the pot. Empty the water and dry the pot thoroughly before you fry.

What Else Can I Make in My Fryer?

The large capacity of an outdoor fryer makes it a good choice for big-batch frying; it can produce a whole lot of fried chicken, mozzarella sticks, beignets, or onion rings in a hurry. Invite a bunch of folks over and let the fryer turn out enough fish fillets and hushpuppies for all. You can also use your fryer to steam and boil; use it to steam enough tamales for everyone at your cookout to take some home. Crawfish boils, low-country boils, crab boils—the fryer is ideal for all of these. Or think of the fryer as a supersize stockpot, perfect for making and holding lots of chili or soup.

 Want Hannah to walk you through all the steps involved in safely deep-frying a turkey? Check out this video.

anatomy of

A GOOD OUTDOOR FRYER

ROOMY STAINLESS-STEEL POT

Is sturdy, durable, and big enough to hold a large bird

LARGE STEAMER BASKET

Allows fryer to be used for seafood boils, tamales, and more

FLAT-BOTTOMED, PERFORATED TURKEY RACK

Holds turkey securely

PREASSEMBLED PROPANE BURNER

Provides plenty of power for maintaining cooking temperature and is easy to set up

worth it

FLAT-TOP GRILL

Peek into the kitchen at any busy diner and you'll likely see a short-order cook standing in front of a flat-top griddle, employing every inch of its wide, flat cooking surface to churn out batch after batch of fried eggs, pancakes, bacon, grilled cheese sandwiches, burgers, and more. A flat-top grill is a scaled-down version of this diner appliance that replaces a grill's grates with a flat sheet of carbon steel. Like traditional gas grills, flat-top grills are propane powered, have multiple heat zones, and are designed exclusively for outdoor use. But flat-top grills can't be used for barbecuing or smoking foods. Instead, they're meant for cooking foods that are typically cooked on a griddle—pancakes and fried eggs—as well as foods that are typically grilled but are flattop-friendly—steak, burgers, and sliced vegetables. And since flat-top grills have multiple burners, they also have multiple heat zones, so you can sear burgers in one zone while toasting burger buns in another. If you regularly cook for crowds, or if you enjoy cooking on a griddle indoors and want to bring that experience outdoors, a flat-top grill is a good investment. And if you like the idea but not the expense, try a plancha (see left).

Do I Need One of Those Vegetable Grill Mats?

Perforated metal grill pans, also called grill toppers or griddles, are designed to cook smaller, more fragile foods without losing any through the grates, but there's another grill accessory that works great for small foods and offers more versatility: a plancha. Popular in Spanish cooking, a plancha is a griddle, usually made of cast iron, that sits on top of charcoal or gas grill grates. Its flat surface prevents small foods from falling through the grate; plus, it puts a great sear on food. (Regular cast-iron griddles and cast-iron pans will work too.)

DINER-STYLE BREAKFAST

serves 4

The wide, flat surface of a plancha makes it easy to cook an entire diner-worthy breakfast on the grill. You'll need a plancha that measures at least 20 by 10 inches. If you don't have a round biscuit or cookie cutter, cut the toast holes with a sturdy drinking glass.

1	pound ground pork	1	pound Yukon Gold potatoes, unpeeled, shredded
1	tablespoon pure maple syrup		
2	garlic cloves, minced	½	red bell pepper, cut into 1-inch-long matchsticks
1½	teaspoons dried sage		
1	teaspoon pepper, divided	3	scallions, sliced thin on bias
¾	teaspoon table salt, divided	4	(½-inch-thick) slices hearty sandwich bread
½	teaspoon dried thyme		
	Pinch cayenne pepper	3	tablespoons extra-virgin olive oil, divided
		4	large eggs

1 Mix pork, maple syrup, garlic, sage, ¾ teaspoon pepper, ½ teaspoon salt, thyme, and cayenne in large bowl until thoroughly combined. Using lightly moistened hands, divide mixture into 8 portions, shape into lightly packed balls, and flatten each ball into ½-inch-thick patty. Press center of each patty with your fingertip to create ¼-inch-deep depression; set aside.

2 Place potatoes in center of clean dish towel. Gather ends of towel and twist tightly to wring out excess moisture from potatoes. Transfer potatoes to large bowl and toss with bell pepper, scallions, remaining ¼ teaspoon pepper, and remaining ¼ teaspoon salt; set aside. Using 2½-inch round cutter, cut out and remove circle from center of each slice of bread. Brush 2 tablespoons oil evenly over both sides of bread.

3A for a charcoal grill Open bottom vent completely. Light large chimney starter three-quarters filled with charcoal briquettes (4½ quarts). When top coals are partially covered with ash, pour evenly over grill. Set cooking grate in place, center plancha on grill, cover, and open lid vent completely. Heat grill with plancha until hot, about 5 minutes.

3B for a gas grill Turn all burners to high, cover, and heat grill until hot, about 15 minutes. Center plancha on grill, cover, and heat for an additional 5 minutes. Turn all burners to medium-high.

4 Brush plancha with well-oiled paper towels. Place patties on one half of plancha. Spread potato mixture in even layer on other half of plancha and lightly pack down. Cook until sausage is browned and registers 160 degrees, 3 to 5 minutes per side. Cook hash until golden brown and crisp on first side, 6 to 8 minutes. Transfer sausage to platter and tent with aluminum foil. Drizzle remaining 1 tablespoon oil over now-empty side of plancha. Flip spatula-size portions of hash onto oiled side of plancha and cook until golden brown and crisp on second side, 6 to 8 minutes. Transfer hash to platter with sausage and tent with foil.

5 Clean plancha and reduce burners to medium-low (if using gas). Arrange bread on now-empty plancha and cook until golden brown on first side, about 3 minutes. Flip bread and, working quickly, crack 1 egg into each bread hole. Cover and cook until bread is golden brown on second side and egg whites are set, about 4 minutes. Transfer toast to platter with sausage and hash. Serve.

VARIATION

Flat-Top Grill Diner-Style Breakfast

Turn all burners to medium-high and heat griddle until hot, about 10 minutes. Turn all burners to medium, then clean griddle. Proceed with recipe from step 4, cooking sausage, hash, and toast with eggs on griddle at same time. Use 13 by 9-inch disposable aluminum pan to cover toast while eggs cook.

Keep Your Cool

A cooler is indispensable for camping trips and picnics, sure, but it's also darn handy to have on hand when tailgating, for field days, and for hot-weather grocery runs.

How Much Do I Need to Spend on a Cooler?

In recent years, premium coolers costing hundreds of dollars have shaken up the consumer market. Certified bear-proof, and "virtually indestructible," Yeti coolers in particular have inspired a cultlike following. But here's the thing: For most people, a bear-proof, virtually indestructible cooler is probably overkill. Before you spend cold hard cash on a cooler, think about how often you'll likely use it and what you use it for. Higher prices generally correspond with better cold preservation and sturdier construction, but also with increased weight and reduced capacity. So a lightweight cooler that keeps ice frozen for two or three days may work fine if you're planning to haul it to the beach for picnics or use it for weekend camping trips. And by the way, soft-sided coolers do not necessarily cost less than hard coolers; in both categories, you pay for improved insulation.

Hannah Says . . .

I was so excited about my new Costco membership, but I learned a tough lesson on my first trip. It started when I bought everything I needed to stock up my freezer . . . on a blazing day in July. When I got home all my lovely frozen goodies had turned soupy. Now I always stow a soft cooler or cooler bag in the trunk of my car before heading to the store or farmers' market—you gotta protect that investment!

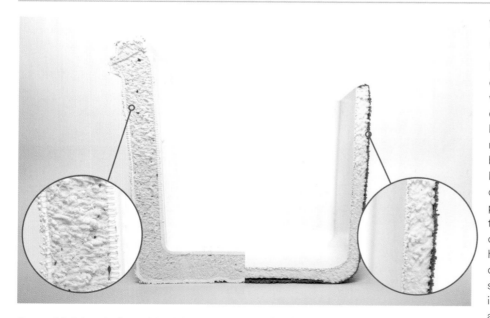

Extra-thick insulation with visible air bubbles (left) keeps food colder longer than thinner, denser insulation (right).

Why Are Those Premium Coolers Sooo Heavy?

In a word: insulation. While cheaper coolers often have thinly insulated walls and hollow lids, the walls and lids of high-end coolers sandwich a thick layer of foam insulation. The foam is responsible for superior cold retention, but the downside is a heavier cooler. Interestingly, though, this correlation only holds up to a point. When we cut premium coolers open, we noticed that the insulation in our best-performing cooler was less dense than that of a heavier model. Air is a poor conductor of heat, especially when it's immobile, so it's the air inside the foam that really insulates. The airier foam was not only a better insulator, but also a bit lighter than the denser foam.

head to head

COOLERS

SOFT COOLERS

Lighter and smaller than hard coolers; good for
a day at the beach or a short camping trip

Some models can keep ice frozen for up to three days

Zip closed

HARD COOLERS

Heavier and bulkier than soft coolers but also
available with larger capacity

Some models can keep ice frozen for up to nine days

Latch closed

Hard exterior protects food

Should I Empty the Water from My Cooler as the Ice Melts?

There's no need; the ice water is still
quite cold, so keeping it helps keep
food cold. Just make sure to pack your
food in watertight containers.

Power tools and
coolers collide as
Lisa and Hannah
take a deep dive into
how coolers keep
food fresh.

real talk with hannah

GET THE RIGHT-SIZE COOLER FOR YOU

I made a mistake when I bought my Yeti cooler: I considered its overall dimensions
rather than its interior ones. The thick walls that make these coolers work so well
eat into their interior space, which means my large-looking cooler is much smaller
on the inside than I expected. It fits enough food for a picnic or overnight trip but
not a full weekend away. I still love it, but these days I'm the happy owner of both a
Yeti and a large soft cooler. Yetis are heavy, so the soft cooler is a better option for
when I've got some walking to do or need a little extra capacity. I use the Yeti for
outdoor parties at home. On a camping trip I bring both: I pack the Yeti with things
such as meat, eggs, and milk and fill the soft cooler with drinks and vegetables.

Campsite Cooking

Roasted hot dogs and marshmallows on a stick are classics, but if you've got the proper gear, campfire cuisine can be so much more.

Can I Use My Regular Pots and Pans on a Camp Stove?

You can absolutely take your kitchen pots and pans camping, with a few caveats. Although some car-camping stoves can accommodate 12-inch skillets side by side, the burners are typically fairly close together, so you'll want to try your cookware out for size before bringing it along. You might also want to leave your more expensive cookware at home, since cooking in the wild can involve soot, stuck-on food, and the occasional mishap with a rock.

Using regular pots and pans on a backpacking stove is trickier, for a few reasons: weight, space, and balance. When you're carrying your kitchen on your back, you don't want pots and pans to weigh you down. Backpacking cookware sets are lightweight and compact; most can be nested together and feature detachable handles. That last point is important because each pot or pan needs to perch atop a backpacking stove; a heavy handle could make your dinner plans collapse—literally. So for backpacking, a sturdy set of camping cookware is a wise investment, and you might also want to consider the purchase if space is an issue when you're car camping.

head to head

CAMP STOVES

BACKPACKING STOVES	CAR-CAMPING STOVES
Lighter and more compact than car-camping stoves	More heavily built than backpacking stoves
Somewhat delicate	Two burners enable more varied food prep
Pot must balance on burner	Grate over burners adds stability
Single burner limits use	Built-in windscreen
Windscreen sold separately	Propane canisters are somewhat heavier
Lightweight butane or isobutane fuel canisters	

How Do I Set Up and Care for a Gas Canister Backpacking Stove?

It's a smart idea to practice assembling and starting your stove before you head out. First, check to make sure that the fuel-adjuster knob is set to the closed position. This usually means turning it as far clockwise as you can. Next, remove the tab on the gas canister and screw the stove onto the fuel, making sure it's tightly secured. You may hear some gas escape from the canister when you do this, but it should stop once the stove is fully attached.

To light the stove, first turn the fuel-adjuster knob counterclockwise, listening until you hear a whoosh of fuel being released. If the stove has a built-in igniter, push it until the flame appears. If the stove doesn't have a built-in igniter, use a lighter to carefully ignite the fuel near the burner. Turn the fuel-adjuster knob to adjust the heat level to your needs.

When you've finished cooking, turn the fuel-adjuster knob fully clockwise until the flame extinguishes and the sound of gas stops. After the stove cools down, unscrew it from the canister and put the cap back on the canister.

Pssst! One reminder: Never use your stove inside an enclosed space. If it looks like it will be rainy during your backpacking trip, consider bringing an umbrella or tarp or food that doesn't need to be cooked.

Q: I've heard some stoves don't work in cold temperatures or at high altitudes. Is that true?

A: Most backpacking stoves use a blend of isobutane and propane gases that's designed both to be lightweight and to function in adverse conditions, including cold temperatures and high altitudes. Still, very high altitudes (over 10,000 feet) can negatively affect a stove's ability to perform; as with any kind of cooking, the decreased air pressure leads to a decreased water boiling point and longer cooking times. Higher elevations also correspond to lower temperatures, and frigid conditions can reduce the internal pressure of a fuel canister, making it harder to light the stove and slower to heat up food. One hack to make your setup work better in the cold: Climb into your sleeping bag with your fuel tank to warm it up. Really!

Q: What's the difference between backpacking stoves that use liquid fuel versus gas canister fuel?

A: Liquid fuel stoves come with empty fuel bottles that can be filled with a variety of liquid fuels, including white gas, kerosene, and gasoline. Gas canister stoves rely on nonrefillable gas fuel canisters that contain a blend of isobutane and propane. Gas fuel canisters weigh less than liquid fuel canisters (important when backpacking) and are easier to connect to the stove. Liquid fuel stoves are usually bigger than gas canister–fueled models and often more work to set up and maintain, so they can be intimidating to a novice backpacker. However, liquid fuel stoves are worth considering if you're looking for a stove to use internationally, since the empty fuel bottle can be packed and then filled with whatever liquid fuel is available at your destination.

Q: How can I tell how much fuel is left in a gas canister?

A: While backpacking stoves that use gas canisters are great, it can be hard to tell if you're running low on fuel—and it's no fun if you run out of fuel in the middle of meal prep. To measure how much fuel is left in used gas canisters before you head out into the wild, weigh a full (unused) canister of the same size and brand on a kitchen scale, and then weigh your used canister and note the difference.

Q. My stove is taking forever to boil water. What can I do?

A: First, make sure you're set up in a sheltered area, away from the elements as much as possible: think behind a boulder rather than on a scenic open hilltop. And for added insurance, get yourself a windscreen and heat reflector: These simple, bendable metal pieces keep heat in and wind out, cutting down the time it takes to boil water significantly, even against 8-mile-per-hour winds.

Freeze-Dried Backpacking Meals Are Expensive. Can I Make My Own?

A dehydrator (see page 285) comes in handy for making your own backpack-able meals, but even if you don't have one, some smart shopping will have you dining al fresco in style. Build your meals with these components:

Starch or grain base: Bread, especially tortillas and pita, is a great lightweight base for a meal. Instant ramen, mashed potatoes, rice, couscous, and packets of soup all cook up fast with the addition of hot water. Pasta is another great base, though it does take longer to cook.

Protein: Shelf-stable options include fish or meat packed in water; cured meats such as Spanish chorizo, smoked fish, and various jerkies; TVP (textured vegetable protein); and some quick-cooking legumes such as red lentils and split peas. Opt for items sold in packages and pouches; leave the cans at home.

Vegetables: Some fresh vegetables, including carrots, spinach, kale, brussels sprouts, snap peas, and broccoli, can be kept for about three days without refrigeration. To prepare larger vegetables such as broccoli, cut florets into small pieces and store them in zipper-lock bags.

Flavor boosters: With a little creativity you can make your meals tasty as well as filling. Nonrefrigerated pickles are a great way to boost flavor (you can find some amazing options at Asian grocery stores), as are nori, nuts, seeds, and preportioned seasoning packets.

more homemade backpacking meals

Tuna Salad Pita Pockets
Water-packed tuna + mayonnaise packets + relish packets + salt and pepper + pita

Loaded Ranch Mashed Potatoes
Instant mashed potatoes + ranch seasoning packet + bacon bits + store-bought fried shallots

Broccoli Bonanza Pasta
Pasta + chicken and broccoli pasta seasoning packet + broccoli florets + Parmesan cheese

GROCERY-STORE BACKPACKER ALFREDO WITH MUSHROOMS AND SUN-DRIED TOMATOES

serves 2

This easy meal made with grocery-store ingredients can be cooked on any camp stove. Do not use sun-dried tomatoes packed in oil here; they are not shelf-stable. It's most efficient to cook one serving at a time, because most backpacking pots are rather small.

1	packet Knorr Alfredo Sauce Mix or Knorr Parma Rosa Sauce Mix
½	cup dried porcini mushroom slices, broken into pieces
1	teaspoon red pepper flakes
1	teaspoon dried basil
1	teaspoon dried oregano
½	cup dehydrated sun-dried tomatoes, chopped coarse
8	ounces linguine, broken in half
2	(⅜-fluid-ounce) packets olive oil
2	ounces Parmesan cheese, grated (1 cup)
3	cups water, divided

1 Combine sauce mix, mushrooms, pepper flakes, basil, and oregano in bowl; divide mixture evenly between 2 zipper-lock bags. Divide pasta into two 4-ounce portions and place 1 portion in each bag. Place 1 oil packet (unopened) into each bag. Place Parmesan, salt, and pepper into separate zipper-lock bags.

2 to cook Empty contents of 1 spice-mixture bag and 1 oil packet into pot . Cover with 1½ cups water (this should be enough to cover pasta). Bring to boil over high heat. Lower heat to maintain simmer and cook, stirring frequently, for about 14 minutes. Add ½ cup Parmesan and salt and pepper to taste. Transfer to serving bowl. Repeat with remaining ingredients. Serve.

Lisa Says . . .

To me, a huge appeal of camping and backpacking is cooking outdoors and seeing what you can make despite the restrictions imposed by your site and supplies. It's a fun puzzle to figure out before you go. And being outdoors makes everyone hungrier, so the food tastes amazing!

Out and About

When you're taking your food on the road, little things can make a big difference in keeping it looking and tasting its best.

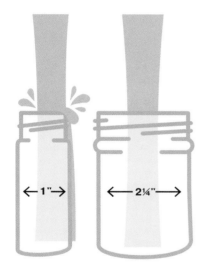

Water bottles with wider mouths are easier to fill without spilling.

What's So Complicated About a Water Bottle?

A good water bottle should be easy to open, fill, close, carry, sip from, and clean, but those qualities don't need to make it complicated. There are just a few design factors we consider to be key to a good water bottle: a screw-on lid to prevent leaks, a body that's narrow enough to grip comfortably, and a mouth that's wide enough for easy filling. The material of the bottle depends on your personal preferences; plastic is lightweight and durable, but glass bottles are good options if you don't want to drink from plastic. We also like the bottles to be dishwasher-safe for easy cleanup—and the fewer individual parts, the better. Bottles that come with lots of extra parts or bells and whistles are likely just overengineered and unnecessarily complicated.

Hannah Says . . .

According to experts, you do have to clean your water bottle every day. A test of reusable water bottles found more than 300,000 colony-forming units of bacteria per square centimeter, roughly the same as a pet bowl—yikes! Just get a bottle brush and use it to reach down into the bottle and clean every last inch. Using hot soapy water is also a must.

Lisa Says . . .

I love, love, love our favorite travel mug, which keeps tea or coffee ripping hot for hours. It's light and easy to carry even when full. But it almost works *too* well—it's hard to sip from until the contents cool down, and who wants to wait? I pack a small, lightweight, unbreakable heatproof cup and feel very fancy when I'm pouring my tea while sitting in the park, out on a hike, or at the beach on a chilly day.

How Long Will an Insulated Travel Mug Keep Beverages at a Safe Temperature?

A good travel mug should keep your drinks out of the danger zone (defined by the U.S. Department of Agriculture's Food Safety and Inspection Service as 40 to 140 degrees Fahrenheit) for a reasonable amount of time. The travel mugs we tested with double-walled insulation all kept coffee hot and out of the danger zone for at least 3½ hours; some held the heat for about 10 hours. As a rule of thumb, any decent travel mug ought to be able to keep your beverages safe to drink for at least a few hours, but if your drink is tepid or if you can't remember exactly how long it's been since you poured it into the mug, you're best off throwing it out.

I'm Going on a Picnic. What Am I Forgetting?

So you've got your picnic blanket tucked under your arm; food and drinks in the cooler; dishes, glasses, and utensils in a basket. Before you carry that basket out to the car, add these handy items: a small cutting board, a paring knife (with sheath!), dish towels, bug spray, hand sanitizer or wipes, and garbage bags (plural). And you might want to trade those glasses for insulated tumblers (see page 179) to keep the cold in and bugs out. Is there still some room in there? A portable speaker and solar-powered lights will keep the picnic fun going into the evening.

Which pieces of outdoor gear do Lisa and Hannah personally swear by? Check out our video to find out.

ITALIAN PASTA SALAD

serves 8 to 10

This pasta salad is perfect for a picnic as it's designed to be made well ahead of time. We prefer a small, individually packaged, dry Italian-style salami such as Genoa or soppressata, but unsliced deli salami can be used. If the salad is not being eaten right away, don't add the arugula and basil until just before serving.

1	pound fusilli
	Table salt for cooking pasta
¼	cup extra-virgin olive oil
3	garlic cloves, minced
3	anchovy fillets, rinsed, patted dry, and minced
¼	teaspoon red pepper flakes
1	cup pepperoncini, stemmed, plus 2 tablespoons brine
2	tablespoons capers, rinsed
2	ounces (2 cups) baby arugula
1	cup chopped fresh basil
½	cup oil-packed sun-dried tomatoes, sliced thin
½	cup pitted kalamata olives, quartered
8	ounces salami, cut into ⅜-inch dice
8	ounces fresh mozzarella cheese, cut into ⅜-inch dice and patted dry

1 Bring 4 quarts water to boil in large pot. Add pasta and 1 tablespoon salt and cook, stirring often, until pasta is tender throughout, 2 to 3 minutes past al dente. Drain pasta and rinse under cold water until chilled. Drain well and transfer to large bowl.

2 Meanwhile, combine oil, garlic, anchovies, and pepper flakes in liquid measuring cup. Cover and microwave until bubbling and fragrant, 30 to 60 seconds. Set aside.

3 Slice half of pepperoncini into thin rings and set aside. Transfer remaining pepperoncini to food processor. Add capers and pulse until finely chopped, 8 to 10 pulses, scraping down sides of bowl as needed. Add pepperoncini brine and warm oil mixture and process until combined, about 20 seconds.

4 Add dressing to pasta and toss to combine. Add arugula, basil, tomatoes, olives, salami, mozzarella, and reserved pepperoncini and toss well. Season with salt and pepper to taste. Serve. (Salad can be refrigerated for up to 3 days. Let come to room temperature before serving.)

TURKEY PICNIC SANDWICH WITH SUN-DRIED TOMATO SPREAD

serves 4

This colorful and shareable turkey sandwich is a picnicker's dream since the flavor improves as the sandwich sits. Pressing the sandwich makes it sturdier for travel and helps the flavors meld; plus, the compact profile is easier to bite into.

SPREAD

¾	cup oil-packed sun-dried tomatoes, drained and patted dry
¼	cup sliced almonds, toasted
¼	cup capers, rinsed
1	teaspoon lemon juice
1	small garlic clove, minced
¼	teaspoon table salt
¼	teaspoon red pepper flakes
6	tablespoons extra-virgin olive oil

SANDWICH

1	large round loaf Italian bread or French bread (about 9-inch diameter)
4	ounces sliced Muenster cheese
8	ounces thinly sliced deli turkey
½	cup fresh parsley leaves
1¼	cups jarred roasted red peppers, drained and patted dry

1 for the spread Process tomatoes, almonds, capers, lemon juice, garlic, salt, and pepper flakes in food processor until finely chopped, about 20 seconds, scraping down sides of bowl as needed. Transfer to bowl and stir in oil. (Spread can be refrigerated for up to 3 days.)

2 for the sandwich Slice bread in half horizontally. Spread tomato spread evenly on cut sides of bread (use all of it). Layer Muenster, turkey, parsley, and red peppers on bread bottom. Cap with bread top and wrap sandwich tightly in double layer of plastic.

3 Place Dutch oven on top of sandwich and let sit at room temperature for 1 hour. (Pressed sandwich can be refrigerated for up to 24 hours; let come to room temperature before serving. Sandwich can be kept unrefrigerated for up to 2 hours.) Unwrap sandwich, cut into 8 wedges, and serve.

5 Tips for Flawless Food Transportation

Preparing delicious potluck or picnic fare is only half the battle; to make it a truly movable feast, you need to pack foods and beverages securely.

1 KEEP FRAGILE FOODS SAFELY SUPPORTED

A luscious layer cake or flaky, juicy pie elevates any picnic or potluck, but getting your painstakingly made dessert to its destination unscathed can be nerve-wracking. Safe, secure transport is what dessert carriers are all about. Practicality trumps looks: Old-fashioned pie baskets are lovely but plastic, dishwasher-safe carriers are airtight and easy to clean. Look for a molded or grippy base to keep your dessert stable and a large dome to accommodate a layer cakes or mile-high meringue pie. Bonus points if the carrier has features that let it convert to hold two pies, or other foods such as deviled eggs.

2 KEEP IT HOT (OR COLD)

Whether you're toting mac and cheese or tiramisu, an insulated carrier will help ensure it arrives ready to eat and safe to serve. The best carriers hold a baking dish (usually 13 by 9 inches) snugly and have generous insulation to keep the temperature as hot or as cold as it should be. Sturdy straps are important, and extra compartments come in handy for bringing along serving utensils.

3 MAKE THE MOST OF YOUR COOLER

Prechill the items you pack in your cooler and, if the weather is particularly hot, consider prechilling the cooler itself by filling it with an ice bath or at least setting it in a cool basement for a few hours. Coolers work best when they're full, so if you own more than one, choose the cooler that's just big enough to hold your food plus ice. If your food needs to stay cold for a few days, use a ratio of two-thirds ice (or ice packs) to one-third food. To avoid losing your cool while searching for food with the lid open, pack smart by keeping similar foods together: snacks in one section of the cooler, sandwiches in another, and beverages in another. It'll make grabbing what you need much quicker.

4 USE GOOD-QUALITY FOOD STORAGE CONTAINERS

Repurposed yogurt and margarine tubs might be OK for keeping the odd leftover in your fridge, but when you're taking food on the road you want sturdy, packable containers with tight-fitting lids. A leakproof design is crucial, not only to keep food inside from getting out, but also to keep water from melted ice in your cooler from getting in. Rectangular shapes fit together well and take up less space. (For more on our favorite containers, see page 400.)

5 DON'T BREAK THAT BOTTLE

A glass of cold white wine on the patio or at a picnic is one of summer's simple pleasures. But the great outdoors can upset your chill in more ways than one, whether it's bugs on the back porch or a stray football at the beach. Enter wine tumblers: sturdy, insulated cups that promise to keep your wine colder and safer than it would be in a wine glass. The best tumblers have a slim, straight body that's comfortable to hold; a glossy surface, which (surprisingly) allows a more secure grip than a matte surface; and a lid to prevent spills and keep critters out. If the lid has a sliding tab to cover the sipping port, so much the better. You don't need to buy a dedicated wine tumbler; an insulated travel mug works equally as well. Just don't use the same mug that holds your coffee or tea; those beverages tend to leave odors in the mug that will leach into your water or wine.

raise a glass

RECIPES

Don't Try This at Home

It's no secret that at America's Test Kitchen we like to put the equipment we review through the wringer before it wins our approval. Sometimes, that means putting ourselves through the wringer, too. To learn all the ins and outs (not to mention the dos and don'ts and whys) of automatic drip coffee makers, for example, we ended up brewing almost 100 pots of fully-caffeinated coffee using 16 different machines. That may not sound so bad at first—but factor in that some of those pots were described as "watery and sad" and others as having a "pronounced bitterness," and suddenly the picture looks less like getting paid to sip on fancy café-style drinks and more like, well, work. Not that the process didn't have its upsides—such as helping some of us (temporarily) cut down on our trips to the local café.

Other times, we jump through hoops not just to pinpoint the best-designed gadget, but to determine whether you actually need that piece of specialty equipment. Take clear-ice cocktail molds. Sure, there are plenty of products on the market that claim to make it easy to produce the stunning cubes (or spheres) of perfectly clear ice that are so sought after by master mixologists. Some of them even deliver on this promise. But they're also bulky and expensive, often taking up a significant amount of freezer space and requiring the better part of a day to turn out just a few ice cubes. Determined to find a way to make practically clear ice without a specially designed mold and with as little fuss as possible, we first had to go to quite a lot of fuss. This meant filtering, boiling, insulating, and freezing dozens of gallons of water in round after round of tests until we finally hit upon a method that reliably turned out beautiful pieces of nearly-clear ice.

So why, if it's so much trouble, do we go to these lengths just to pick a good coffee maker or craft a nice-looking block of ice? For us, the answer is easy: so you don't have to.

Morning Joe

Sometimes, a cup of coffee is just a means to an end, a purely utilitarian way to get yourself going in the morning. But if you, like us, take pleasure in sipping an expertly crafted cup at your leisure, it pays to know a little more about how it gets made.

How Does an Automatic Drip Coffee Maker Work?

Automatic drip coffee makers are everywhere, and good ones can make coffee every bit as satisfying as trendier brewing systems. They work by mimicking the technique used to make handmade pour-over coffee (see page 187), but the machine takes care of heating the water and distributing it over the coffee grounds for you. A metal heating element warms the water in the machine's reservoir, creating steam that forces the hot water up a narrow tube, through a one-way valve, and out over the coffee grounds in the brewing basket. The hot water extracts flavor compounds, oils, and tiny coffee particles from the grounds and then drips down through the filter, out of the basket, and into the carafe. This method can quickly produce a whole pot of strong, smooth-tasting coffee.

Sometimes My Coffee Maker Overflows. What Gives?

It's important to use the right ratio of coffee grounds to water (see page 186). Some coffee makers have brewing baskets that are too small to match their large water tanks. The brewing basket on the left is adequately sized to hold the right proportion of coffee when brewing a full pot. Coffee overflowed in the basket on the right, which is too small.

Do I Really Need to Care About Water Temperature and Brewing Time?

Simple answer: Yes! According to the Specialty Coffee Association, the best drip coffee is made with water heated to between 194 and 205 degrees Fahrenheit. The amount of time coffee and hot water interact is critical to extracting only the good flavor compounds for your morning brew. For the best extraction, a good machine should take 4 to 8 minutes to brew your coffee.

Hannah Says . . .

Your coffee maker's hot plate can burn your coffee. Turn it off and replace your glass coffee carafe with a thermal one to keep your precious brew hotter (and tastier) longer.

Lisa Says . . .

Do you often use the coffee carafe to fill your coffee maker's water tank? Stop right there. Doing this transfers coffee residue from the pot to your brewing water, discoloring the water reservoir over time. And trust me: Those dregs aren't going to make your coffee taste any better.

USE A(N) . . .		IF YOU . . .
Automatic Drip Coffee Maker		• Love "regular" coffee with medium body and smooth flavor • Don't mind having an appliance take up some of your counter space • Sometimes need to brew enough coffee to serve a crowd • Don't mind spending a little extra on the right machine • Have less than 10 minutes to dedicate to making coffee in the morning • Want a coffee-making method that's mostly hands-off
French Press		• Want rich, strong, full-bodied coffee • Don't have a lot of counter space or extra outlets • Want to brew anywhere from 1 to 8 cups at a time • Don't want to spend a lot of money • Like to keep things simple • Have less than 10 minutes to dedicate to making coffee in the morning
Portable Single-Serve Coffee Maker		• Love a clean, concentrated cup of richly flavored coffee • Only ever need to make 1 or 2 cups at a time • Want something that's easy to use and incredibly compact • Don't want to spend a lot of money • Want to take your coffee maker with you for great coffee whether you're traveling or at the office • Have a way to heat water separately
Cold-Brew Coffee Maker		• Like smooth coffee with low acidity • Can dedicate some counter space to your coffee maker while brewing • Don't want to spend a lot of money • Like both iced and hot coffee • Don't mind prepping ahead
Pour-Over Coffee Maker		• Are either a bare-bones kind of coffee drinker or are highly particular about your coffee • Don't have a lot of counter space or extra outlets • Only ever need to make 1 or 2 cups at a time • Don't want to spend a lot of money • Have a way to heat water separately
Moka Pot		• Want strong, complex, full-bodied, fierce-tasting coffee reminiscent of espresso • Don't have a lot of counter space or extra outlets • Don't want to spend a lot of money • Want your coffee fast and fuss-free
Espresso Machine		• Love rich, intense flavor • Don't mind having an appliance take up some of your counter space • Don't mind spending a few hundred for the right machine • Want to enjoy a quick shot of espresso on weekdays and fool around doing latte art on weekends

FREQUENTLY ASKED QUESTIONS: COFFEE EDITION

Q: How much coffee should I use to brew one pot?

A: Coffee specialists recommend you use 55 grams of medium to medium-fine ground coffee per liter of water. Measuring by volume can give inaccurate results depending on factors like how the beans were roasted and ground. This is one reason why we love coffee scales (see page 188).

Q: Should I be using filtered water?

A: It depends. A cup of coffee is about 98 percent water. If your tap water tastes bad or has strong mineral flavors, your coffee will, too, so filtering it is a good idea. If you like the taste of your tap water, you can skip this step.

Q: Should I descale my coffee maker?

A: Yes. In time, the minerals in hard water can build up and clog a coffee maker's water tubes. A good rule of thumb is to descale your coffee maker once every 100 pots. (Pro tip: Many paper filters come in packs of 100, so if you use paper filters make it a habit to descale your coffee maker each time you open a new package.) Be sure to use a specially formulated descaling product—it's more effective and less corrosive than the DIY vinegar solutions often recommended for descaling.

Q: Why do some coffee makers come with two baskets?

A: Some coffee makers come with both a conical basket and a flat-bottomed basket. Generally, the flat-bottomed basket is for making a full pot, while the cone-shaped basket is better for making half pots (or less). This is because water passes through the deeper, more compact coffee grounds in a cone more slowly than those spread out in a flat basket, so with less coffee you'll keep the water-to-coffee contact at the right pace for good extraction.

Hannah Says . . .

After we reviewed single-serve manual coffee makers, I immediately ordered the travel-size version of our winner, the AeroPress, for myself. Like a miniature French press, it forces ground coffee through hot water, producing a superflavorful brew. I now use it every morning.

Lisa Says . . .

In a French press, the mass of steeped coffee makes a kind of "hockey puck" on top of the water, creating pressure that makes it hard to push down the plunger. But if you lift the top and stir the coffee to break up the puck, pushing the plunger becomes very easy.

My Kitchen Is Tiny. Which Coffee Maker is the Best Fit for Me?

Anyone with limited counter space knows how precious every square foot is. So how can you satisfy your coffee craving without dedicating a third of your prep area to a coffee machine? Consider a French press or a portable single-serve coffee maker. A French press takes up very little space, doesn't need to be plugged in (a boon if you're short on outlets as well as space), and depending on the model can produce up to eight cups at once. A single-serve coffee maker, as the name suggests, makes just one cup at a time but is even more compact than a French press—small enough to pack in your bag if you need to make your own coffee while traveling. One caveat: Both of these options require the use of a separate vessel, such as a kettle, to heat the water (see page 190 for more information about kettles).

Why Does Coffee Made in a French Press Taste Different Than Drip Coffee?

Coffee made using a French press is almost impossible to confuse with drip coffee. A French press uses a piston-like mechanism to force ground coffee through hot water, sending the grounds to the bottom of the press. The metal mesh filter allows more of the beans' oils and fine particulates to pass through than a paper filter, resulting in a brew that's noticeably more oily (in a good way!) and thick-bodied. And because this method effectively steeps the grounds for several minutes rather than quickly filtering water through them, the coffee also has a deeper, bolder flavor.

Is It True That a French Press Can Explode?

It can happen. Attempting to force the filter down after meeting more than mild resistance can build pressure that can ultimately cause glass-sided presses to shatter. That's one reason we prefer steel French presses over glass. The other? Insulated steel models keep the coffee hotter for longer.

Can I Make Pour-Over Coffee Without Fancy Equipment?

Pour-over is perhaps the most hands-on coffee-making method, offering the maker precise control over both water temperature and steeping time. There are plenty of coffee makers out there specifically designed for making pour-over coffee, but do you need one of them? Not really. We found that you can make a cup of great pour-over coffee with just four pieces of equipment you likely already have on hand: a funnel, a cup, a cone-shaped coffee filter, and a vessel (such as a kettle) for boiling water. Here's how.

Find out what coffee-related gear Lisa and Hannah keep in their own kitchens.

1 Bring 1 cup water to boil. (The act of pouring the water will bring its temperature down to the ideal 194- to 205-degree Fahrenheit range for brewing coffee, so once it boils you're good to go.)

2 Place filter in funnel, place funnel in cup, and add 13 grams coffee grounds. Pour just enough water over grounds to wet them. Wait about 15 seconds. (This opens up the flavor of the coffee.)

3 Slowly pour in rest of water, trying to wet all grounds. If desired, stir grounds with spoon while pouring water to ensure no dry pockets remain. (That's it! Enjoy an amazing cup of coffee.)

COLD-BREW COFFEE CONCENTRATE

makes 1½ cups (Enough for 3 cups iced coffee)

A favorite tool for coffee connoisseurs who love a full-bodied brew, a French press can also be used to make an easy cold-brew coffee concentrate that can be stored for up to a week and diluted to your preferred strength just before drinking. We recommend using a 1:1 ratio of concentrate to water, but you can dilute it more if you like.

> 9 ounces medium-roast coffee beans, ground coarse (3½ cups)
>
> 3½ cups water, room temperature, filtered if desired

1 Stir coffee and water together in large (about 2-quart) French press. Allow raft of ground coffee to form, about 10 minutes, then stir again to recombine. Cover with plastic wrap and let sit at room temperature for 24 hours.

2 Line fine-mesh strainer with coffee filter and set over large liquid measuring cup. Place lid on press and slowly and evenly press plunger down on grounds to separate them from coffee concentrate. Pour concentrate into prepared strainer. Line large bowl with triple layer of cheesecloth, with cheesecloth overhanging edge of bowl. Transfer grounds to cheesecloth. Gather edges of cheesecloth together and twist; then, holding pouch over strainer, firmly squeeze grounds until liquid no longer runs freely from pouch. Discard grounds.

3 Using back of ladle or rubber spatula, gently stir concentrate to help filter it through strainer. (Concentrate can be refrigerated in jar with tight-fitting lid for up to 1 week.)

How Can I Level-Up My Home-Café Game?

There's a lot you can do to take your coffee skills from good to great. Want to maximize the flavor of your beans without fussy time-consuming methods or expensive equipment? Buying whole beans and grinding them yourself just before you plan to use them will result in fresher, more nuanced-tasting coffee than you get when using preground beans. Want to be in complete control of all the coffee-brewing variables? Try your hand at making pour-over. You can do it without fancy equipment (see page 187), but you can get technical if that's your jam; a precision coffee scale with a built-in timer will help ensure exact weights and times for precision pour-over. If you want an espresso-like experience without the expense or hassle of an actual espresso machine, try a moka pot. Or invest in a milk frother and treat yourself to lattes, cappuccinos, and more at a fraction of your local café's prices.

head to head

COFFEE FILTERS

PAPER COFFEE FILTERS	METAL MESH COFFEE FILTERS
Disposable	Reusable
Water takes longer to pass through	Need regular washing
Hold back more oils and particulates for smoother but thinner coffee	Water passes through more quickly
	Let oils and very fine coffee particulates pass through for more full-bodied coffee

How Finely Should I Be Grinding My Beans?

The optimal grind size for coffee differs depending on your preferred brewing method. Generally, coarsely ground coffee is used for French press coffee, medium for drip coffee, and fine for espresso. Because of the way that coffee beans shatter when they're ground, all ground coffee will contain some pieces that are too big for ideal extraction (called "boulders") and some that are tiny and dust-like (called "fines"). But a good coffee grinder will produce mostly ideal-size pieces.

If you have a burr grinder, you can choose your setting and let the machine take care of the rest. With a blade grinder you'll need to periodically shake the grinder to redistribute the beans and visually inspect the coffee to see if it has reached the right consistency, but you can get properly-ground coffee with either model.

BOULDERS   **IDEAL-SIZE PIECES**   **FINES**

real talk with hannah & lisa

HC — **WHY I USE A BURR GRINDER**

In our coffee grinder testing, even coffee experts couldn't tell a difference between coffee made with beans ground in a blade grinder versus those ground in a burr grinder. That said, I still prefer a burr grinder. They're more hands-off and more consistent. You load your beans, choose how finely you want them ground (easily toggling between different settings for different brewing methods), select the number of cups, and then let the machine do the rest.

LM — **WHY I USE A BLADE GRINDER**

As Hannah said, coffee experts could not tell the difference between coffee made from beans ground in a blade grinder versus beans ground in a burr grinder. That's all I needed to hear to become an unapologetic blade grinder advocate. I can see the coffee texture through the lid as I grind, and I know what I want it to look like, so why spend more for a burr grinder? They're also more compact, which is great for my limited counter space.

worth it

MILK FROTHER

Love the idea of making specialty coffee drinks at home, but don't love the thought of laying down hundreds of dollars for an espresso machine with an attached steam wand? Consider a stand-alone milk frother. These machines heat and aerate milk (including dairy and plant-based varieties) for lattes, cappuccinos, and more.

We found that both handheld wand–style frothers and countertop models are capable of whipping up hot and cold foams and can even control the foams' texture—airy and voluminous for cappuccinos, or looser and silkier for lattes.

How Much Should I Spend on an Espresso Machine?

Espresso machine prices can reach into the stratosphere, but you don't need to spend thousands to bring one to your kitchen. You can get a perfectly good machine—complete with a built-in grinder and milk frother—for a few hundred dollars. These relatively modestly priced machines still offer customization, allowing you to experiment with temperature, strength, and volume until you achieve your ideal espresso shot.

Teatime

Simply pouring hot water over your tea leaves and hoping for the best is a recipe for tannic, bitter, overbrewed tea. To make a first-rate cup of tea, it helps to slow down a little and use the right tools.

What's So Complicated About Boiling Water?

Boiling water isn't complicated: All you really need is a heat source and a cooking vessel. But a good kettle will do the job faster and—this is important when dealing with piping-hot water—more safely than any old saucepan you have lying around. Many electric kettles have features that prevent them from turning on when empty and cause them to shut off once the water boils to prevent overheating. A kettle's spout is designed to pour water in a controlled way, without splashes or drips. And whether you opt for an electric or stovetop model, a kettle can bring enough water for several cups of tea up to temperature at once.

Lisa Says . . .

It sounds fussy, but I use a timer and instant-read thermometer when I make tea. Different teas need different temperatures and steeping times, and I was amazed at how much more—and better—flavor I got from tea when I actually followed those recommendations.

best practices for brewing tea

TEA TYPE	AMOUNT*	TEMPERATURE	STEEP TIME	NOTES
black tea	*1 teaspoon*	212 degrees	3 to 5 minutes	Using too much tea to make iced black tea results in cloudiness from the tea's caffeine and tannins.
white tea	*2 teaspoons*	180 to 185 degrees	4 to 5 minutes	White tea leaves are more delicate and therefore less dense and compact, so they require a larger quantity than some tea types.
Earl Grey tea	*1 teaspoon*	208 degrees	3 to 5 minutes	Using boiling water pulls out too much citrus oil from the bergamot, leaving the tea overly bitter.
green tea	*1 teaspoon*	175 degrees	3 to 5 minutes	Green tea leaves are not oxidized like black leaves, so you should never use boiling water as it will burn the leaves and taint the flavor profile.
gunpowder green tea	*1 teaspoon*	212 degrees	An initial rinse, then drain and steep for 5 to 6 minutes	Gunpowder green tea is rinsed with boiling water to help wash away particulates and bitterness before steeping.
herbal tea blend	*1 tablespoon*	212 degrees	10 minutes	A 10-minute steep is the sweet spot for fully extracting flavor from herbal tea.
herbal tea blend with chamomile	*1 tablespoon*	212 degrees	5 to 7 minutes	Chamomile becomes overextracted and bitter if steeped longer than 5 to 7 minutes.

* Tea amounts are per 8 ounces of water.

Does the Design of My Tea Infuser Matter?

It's tempting to prioritize aesthetics when it comes to tea infusers. Those spherical infusers embellished to look like squat little bees or hedgehogs look so cute peeping over the rim of your mug, and surely the difference between models is minimal, right? Not so. A good tea infuser needs to be able to contain loose tea leaves and prevent any odd bits from escaping into your cup while also yielding a full-bodied cup of tea, and unfortunately most spherical varieties fail on both accounts.

The reason? Tea infusers need to be relatively roomy so that water can circulate to extract the fullest flavor even as the leaves soak and expand, leaving less room for water to move around. Ideally they should also be made of superfine metal mesh, which confines particulates better than perforated metal baskets. Most spherical infusers are much too small, and their designs allow stray leaves to escape into your cup. Instead, we opt for a basket-style infuser. While they might not be quite as adorable as the spherical kind, the bottom line is that they're easier to use and they make better tea.

Do I Need Specialized Tools to Make Matcha?

Matcha is traditionally prepared by using a chawan (tea bowl) and chasen (bamboo whisk). The chawan holds the matcha and is just big enough to accommodate the prongs of the chasen, which is used to aerate the matcha. If you like matcha enough to make it at home regularly, we strongly encourage you to use both of these tools, which we've found produce smoother, creamier matcha with a much thicker foam. But in a pinch, you can substitute a small ceramic or glass soup bowl for the chawan and a small wire whisk or milk frother for the chasen.

MATCHA

serves 1

If you can't find ceremonial-grade matcha powder, you can use premium-grade.

- 1½ teaspoons ceremonial-grade matcha powder
- 1 cup hot water (175 degrees), divided

1 Sift matcha powder into chawan or small soup bowl. Using chasen or small whisk, whisk 2 tablespoons hot water into sifted powder until dissolved. Add another 2 tablespoons hot water and quickly whisk using a zigzag motion until a thick layer of small bubbles form on surface of matcha, about 30 seconds.

2 Stir remaining ¾ cup hot water into matcha. Serve immediately in chawan or teacup.

worth it

TEA MACHINE

If you're the type to drink a pot of tea a day, a tea machine—essentially an electric kettle with a removable brew basket—might be worth the splurge. After the kettle heats water to a specified temperature, the tea basket is lowered into the water to steep and then raised once the tea has brewed. The best models include extra features such as a programmable timer, adjustable temperature settings for different teas, a keep-warm function, and automatic steeping for a truly set-it-and-forget-it tea brewing experience.

Get Juiced

Juicing is one of the easiest and most enjoyable ways to work extra fruits and vegetables into your weekly routine. But juicers themselves can be intimidating. Here's what you should know.

head to head

JUICERS

MASTICATING JUICERS

Work by grinding produce to a pulp and forcing it through a fine-mesh filtration screen

More expensive

Slower

More efficient with leafy greens

Smaller feed tubes require more food prep

Quieter and less messy

CENTRIFUGAL JUICERS

Work by shredding produce into a pulp and flinging it against the sides of a finely perforated filter basket

Less expensive

Faster

More efficient with dense foods

Wider feed tubes require less food prep

Can be loud and messy

Often produce foamy juice

Q: Don't centrifugal juicers make warm, oxidized juice?

A: We tested the claim about warm juice by measuring the internal temperature of carrots before using them to make juice with both centrifugal and masticating juicers. Centrifugal juicers did not produce notably warmer juice than their masticating counterparts; all temperature changes were within 3 degrees. As to the claim that centrifugal juicers produce more oxidized and therefore less nutritious juice, studies comparing the nutritional content of juices made with both types of juicers have been inconclusive.

Q: How am I supposed to get these machines clean?

A: Juicers have to be disassembled and their pieces washed thoroughly after every use. A good soak will loosen up stuck pulp and plant fiber, but you'll still likely need to break out a scrub brush and spend time scouring the nooks and crannies. Best practice: Wash your machine right away so the pulp doesn't have time to dry out and stick.

When Should I Be Using High Versus Low Speed?

Most juicers offer the option to juice at either high or low speed. The speed you choose should depend on the produce you're juicing. Leafy greens and denser foods, such as root vegetables, should be juiced at high speed. For softer, less dense foods like many fruits, low speed works better. The chart below offers a more complete breakdown.

Apples, cored	High		Kale	High
Apricots, pitted	Low		Kiwis, peeled	Low
Arugula	High		Lemon slice	Low
Beets	High		Lime slice	Low
Berries Blueberries, strawberries, and raspberries	Low		Mangos, peeled and pitted	Low
			Melons, peeled	Low
Broccoli	Low		Nectarines, pitted	Low
Cabbage	Low		Oranges	Low or High
Carrots	High		Parsnips	Low
Celery	High		Peaches, pitted	Low
Cherries, pitted	Low		Pears, cored	Low or High
Cranberries	High			
Cucumbers	High		Peppers, bell, seeded	High
Eggplants	High		Pineapple, peeled	High
Fennel	High		Plums, pitted	Low
Ginger	High		Romaine lettuce	High
Grapefruit	Low		Spinach	High
Grapes, seedless	Low		Sweet potatoes	High
Herbs Parsley, thyme, sage, tarragon, cilantro, mint, and basil	High		Swiss chard	High
			Tomatoes	Low
Horseradish root	Low		Turmeric	High
Jicama	High		Watercress	High
			Watermelon, seedless	Low

Lisa Says . . .

When we tested electric juicers, we ground 95 pounds of produce and learned a few things nobody tells you in the instruction manuals. My biggest pro tip: Juice lighter foods first, heavier foods last. The heavier, denser foods help press the light foods, such as leafy greens, through the grinder, so you'll extract much more juice!

Want to see our favorite juicers in action? Check out our video.

Hannah Says . . .

Some people claim that juice made with masticating juicers stays fresh longer than juice made with centrifugal juicers. When we put this to the test by storing carrot juice made using each juicer style in the fridge and monitoring them for several days, we didn't notice a difference. Both juices darkened and dulled in flavor after just a couple days.

DAILY GREENS JUICE

serves 1 to 2

Packed with leafy greens—including the nemesis of many a juicer, kale—this is a great juice for putting a masticating juicer through its paces.

1	(¼-inch-thick) slice lemon
1	(½-inch) piece fresh ginger
½	cup fresh parsley and tender stems
4	ounces lacinato kale
½	green apple, cored
2	celery ribs

On low speed, process lemon through juicer into storage container or serving glass. Increase speed to high. In order listed, process remaining ingredients. Stir to combine before serving.

BEET SUNSET JUICE

serves 1 to 2

The dense root vegetables in this juice make it a good candidate for the centrifugal juicer treatment.

- 1 (1-inch) piece turmeric
- 5 ounces golden beets, unpeeled, trimmed
- 4 ounces carrots, unpeeled
- 6 ounces peeled pineapple

On high speed and in order listed, process all ingredients through juicer into storage container or serving glass. Stir to combine before serving.

How Can I Extract More Juice from Citrus?

We squeezed a dozen lemons—cold, rolled, and warm—and found that each yielded the same amount of juice. The only difference: Warm and room-temperature lemons were softer and therefore easier to squeeze than the cold lemons. Much more important to the juice yield is using a quality juicer. But to quickly warm a cold lemon, you can heat it in the microwave until it's warm to the touch.

Do I Need an Electric Citrus Juicer?

Allow us to answer your question with another question: How often do you like to enjoy fresh-squeezed orange juice, a pitcher of lemonade, or any other refreshment that requires a cup or more of citrus juice? If you don't intend to use your citrus juicer to yield multiple servings of juice at least once a week, you probably don't need an electric one. These machines are expensive and bulky, and for smaller or less frequent citrus juicing jobs, we think a manual juicer gives better bang for your buck.

FRESH MARGARITAS

serves 4 to 6

These margaritas use a total of 1 cup of lime and lemon juices, so whipping them up is a delicious and fun way to test the juicing power of your citrus juicer. To serve the margaritas immediately, omit the zest and skip the steeping process in step 1.

- 4 teaspoons finely grated lime zest plus ½ cup juice (4 limes)
- 4 teaspoons finely grated lemon zest plus ½ cup juice (3 lemons)
- ¼ cup superfine sugar
  Pinch table salt
- 2 cups crushed ice
- 1 cup 100 percent agave tequila, preferably reposado
- 1 cup triple sec

1 Combine lime zest and juice, lemon zest and juice, sugar, and salt in 2-cup liquid measuring cup; cover; and refrigerate until flavors meld, at least 4 hours or up to 1 day.

2 Divide 1 cup ice among 4 to 6 margarita or double old-fashioned glasses. Strain juice mixture through fine-mesh strainer into 1-quart pitcher or cocktail shaker; discard solids. Add tequila, triple sec, and remaining 1 cup ice. Stir or shake until thoroughly combined and chilled, 20 to 60 seconds. Strain into ice-filled glasses and serve immediately.

Unsteady giant

Too-small bowl

Efficient but uncomfortable

Tiny and messy

Blunt and tippy

Bare-bones reamer

Stable and simple

Perfect press

Strange little spout

Sorry seed catcher

Why Do Manual Citrus Juicers Come in So Many Styles?

The sheer variety of styles when it comes to citrus juicers can make these simple little tools seem much more intimidating than they should. When you're juicing citrus, you want three things: to be able to wring as much juice as possible out of the fruit, to catch the juice somewhere relatively mess-free, and ideally, to capture seeds.

Some models, such as the reamers with attached bowls, try to solve all three problems: You press the citrus against the pointy, ridged reamer to extract its juice, which then flows into the collection bowl while a perforated drain catches the seeds. Others, like stand-alone reamers, do only one job: extract juice. You'll need to hold them over a bowl as you work to catch the juice, and you'll likely have to go fishing for seeds once you're done. Press-style juicers also require a separate bowl for catching the juice, but they both extract juice and do a pretty good job of keeping seeds contained. We prefer press-style juicers, which are both easy to use and great at getting the maximum amount of juice out of each piece of fruit. But ultimately, most styles work fine. (Just stay away from that quirky little spout-like juicer unless you have lots of time and very, very strong forearms.)

Get Fizzy

A so-called soda maker isn't just for soda—in fact, many people skip the soda syrup altogether and use them purely for making sparkling seltzer.

Will a Soda Maker Save Me Money?

The short answer is probably not—or at least not much.

When you factor in the cost of the carbon dioxide (CO_2) canister, the amount of CO_2 you're using per liter (which can be greater if you like highly-carbonated beverages with lots of bubbles), and any added flavorings, the price per liter can be roughly on par with store-bought sparkling waters and sodas. But if you drink carbonated beverages often, you may find that the other pros make up for this. With a soda maker, you won't have to haul home cases of sparkling water from the store. You also won't have to deal with as many empty plastic bottles or aluminum cans—a plus for both you and the environment.

FREQUENTLY ASKED QUESTIONS: SODA MAKER EDITION

Q: Can I carbonate liquids besides water?

A: It depends on which model you buy. Some can be used only with water, but others are marketed as safe for use with everything from juice to tea to wine, so check your model's instructions. In our experience, though, liquids other than water foamed so much that we could only carbonate a small amount of them at a time.

Q: How (and how often) should I clean the bottles?

A: If you have dishwasher-safe bottles, just run them through a dishwasher cycle in between uses. If your bottles aren't dishwasher safe or if you don't have a dishwasher, rinse the bottles with warm water after every use. Every four or five uses, fill them with warm, soapy water, use a bottle brush to give them a good scrub, and then let them dry completely on a dish rack or bottle drying rack.

Q: How can I get the fizziest water possible?

A: Gas, such as the CO_2 used to carbonate water, dissolves better in colder liquids, so start with the coldest water possible. We like to keep a bottle of flat water in the fridge so it's ready to go whenever.

Q: How often should I replace the CO_2 canister?

A: You'll know that your CO_2 canister is running out of gas when it fails to properly carbonate water. But if you want to double-check how much CO_2 is left, you can weigh your canister. A full CO_2 canister weighs about 1,167 grams (about 2 pounds, 9 ounces); an empty canister weighs about 750 grams (about 1 pound, 9 ounces).

PEAR AND VANILLA SPRITZER

serves 4

Using just vanilla bean, pears, and carbonated water (also known as seltzer), this recipe makes a refreshing sparkling drink reminiscent of cream soda, minus the added sugar.

- ½   vanilla bean
- 2   Bosc pears, peeled, halved, and cored
- 3   cups seltzer, chilled

1 Cut vanilla bean in half lengthwise. Using tip of paring knife, scrape out seeds; discard empty pod. Process pears and vanilla seeds in food processor until smooth, scraping down sides of bowl as needed, about 90 seconds. Strain mixture through fine-mesh strainer into pitcher. (Puree can also be stored in airtight container in refrigerator for up to 2 days; transfer puree to pitcher before proceeding.)

2 Just before serving, gently stir seltzer into puree until combined. Pour into ice-filled glasses. (You can also make a single portion by combining ¼ cup puree and ¾ cup seltzer in glass before adding ice.)

CITRUS SODA SYRUP

makes 1 cup (Enough for 16 sodas)

Combine one of these syrups with freshly carbonated water (also known as seltzer) to make a completely homemade soda.

- ¾   cup sugar
- ⅔   cup water
- 2   teaspoons grated grapefruit, lemon, lime, or orange zest

Heat sugar, water, and zest in small saucepan over medium heat, whisking often, until sugar has dissolved, about 5 minutes; do not boil. Let cool completely, about 30 minutes. Strain syrup through fine-mesh strainer into airtight container; discard solids. (Syrup can be refrigerated for up to 1 month.)

to make flavored soda Add 1 cup seltzer and 1 to 2 tablespoons flavored syrup to ice-filled glass and stir gently to combine.

VARIATIONS
Berry Soda Syrup

Substitute 1 cup mashed blueberries, raspberries, or strawberries for citrus zest.

Ginger Soda Syrup

Substitute 2 tablespoons grated fresh ginger for citrus zest.

The Bar Cart

There's no one right way to stock a bar cart, but there are a few tools we think no bar cart should be without.

real talk with hannah & lisa

HC

HOW I STOCK MY MINIMALIST BAR CART

If I'm enjoying an alcoholic beverage, it's typically white wine—with one exception. I live for a dirty martini, and no one ever makes it dirty enough for me when I'm out at a bar, despite me saying "extra dirty, like X-rated" to many a bemused bartender over the years. My super minimal bar cart is tailored to help me get my X-rated martini fix at home. That means it's missing a lot of the accoutrements stocked by more serious home bartenders. You won't find a cocktail mallet or a muddler on my bar cart. Instead, in the place of honor is my Boston-style cocktail shaker (my martinis are always shaken, never stirred). A mixing glass, a bar spoon, and a Hawthorne strainer round out my bar cart and are enough to get by on the rare occasion that I feel like making something other than my beloved martini.

LM

HOW I STOCK MY MAXIMALIST BAR CART

My husband is really, really good (like Stanley Tucci good) at mixing cocktails. So I keep my bar area well stocked with everything I (that is, he) might need. And in this department, I defer to my teammate, Miye Bromberg, who has bartending experience and mixes a fantastic drink. She has also reviewed bar gear for America's Test Kitchen for years, and her choices are impeccable. That's why, in addition to the basics, I always have a tray or two of cocktail ice molds in my freezer, a channel knife/citrus zester combo for making perfect citrus twists on my cart, and a few different types of glassware (see page 205) in my cabinet. As Miye says, "Mixing a drink is pretty similar to cooking a dish: For the best results, you need good ingredients, good equipment, and a good recipe." I think I've got that "good equipment" part down.

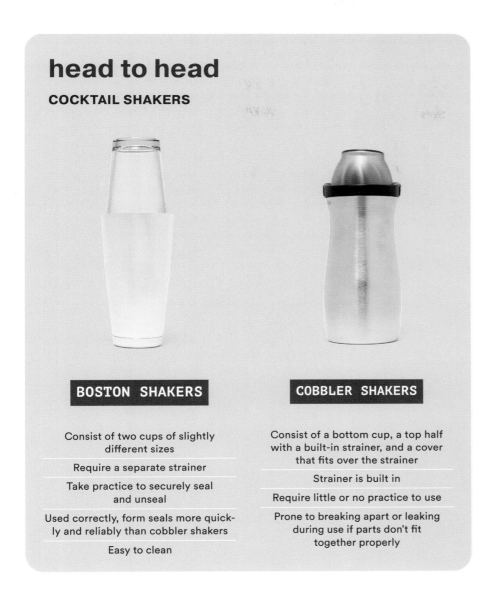

head to head

COCKTAIL SHAKERS

BOSTON SHAKERS

Consist of two cups of slightly different sizes

Require a separate strainer

Take practice to securely seal and unseal

Used correctly, form seals more quickly and reliably than cobbler shakers

Easy to clean

COBBLER SHAKERS

Consist of a bottom cup, a top half with a built-in strainer, and a cover that fits over the strainer

Strainer is built in

Require little or no practice to use

Prone to breaking apart or leaking during use if parts don't fit together properly

NEW-FASHIONED GIN AND TONIC

serves 1

Practice making this twist on a classic cocktail to work on your mixing technique. For information about making large cubes of nearly-clear ice, see pages 200–201.

2	ounces London dry gin
1½	teaspoons tonic syrup
⅛	teaspoon old-fashioned aromatic bitters
	Strip of lime peel

Add gin, tonic syrup, and bitters to mixing glass, then fill three-quarters full with ice. Stir until mixture is just combined and chilled, about 15 seconds. Strain cocktail into chilled old-fashioned glass half-filled with ice or containing 1 large ice cube. Pinch lime peel over drink and rub outer edge of glass with peel, then garnish with lime peel and serve.

Do I Need a Mixing Glass?

Don't even think about trying to cut corners by mixing your stirred cocktails in a cocktail shaker. The unstable, narrow bases of shakers are just begging for a heartbreaking tip-over—trust us on this. If you love a good stirred cocktail, you absolutely need a mixing glass. For one thing, its straight sides and evenly wide circumference allow for optimal ice movement when stirring. As a result, your drink mixes and chills while being diluted with just enough water to allow the flavors of the ingredients to meld. The pouring spout makes it easy to transfer your cocktail to a serving glass without losing a single precious drop. Plus, using a mixing glass just makes you look like you know what you're doing—especially when combined with a bar spoon and the right stirring technique (see page 206).

Do Those Giant Ice Cubes Make for a Better Cocktail?

When shaking or stirring a cocktail, you can use any kind of ice you like as long as it's made from good-tasting water. But for serving, you might want to consider using a perfectly shaped ice cube or sphere to give your drink an especially elegant and polished look. Aside from looking nice, larger ice cubes also provide a small benefit to the taste of your drink. The relatively low surface area to volume ratio means they melt more slowly, which means less risk of your drink becoming overly diluted. We recommend using 1-inch silicone or rubber ice cube trays to make ice for stirring or shaking cocktails and 2-inch trays to make ice for serving.

How Can I Make Clear Ice Cubes Like the Ones from Cocktail Bars?

Ever wondered why the ice cubes you get at a fancy cocktail bar are nearly perfectly clear, while the ones from your freezer are practically opaque? Freezing forces the dissolved air naturally present in water to come out of solution. As the ice freezes from the outside in, air bubbles and trace minerals get trapped in the center, creating that cloudy look. Mixologists often go to great lengths to counter this, but it's possible to get mostly clear ice at home with just a little extra effort.

First, you'll want to start with mineral-free distilled water. Next, you'll need to boil it, which helps drive off much of the dissolved air. And finally, you'll want to insulate the bottom of your ice cube trays. This forces the ice to freeze from the top down rather than from the outside in, forcing any remaining dissolved air into just the bottom layer of the ice cube.

test it yourself

IS CLEAR ICE MORE SHATTER-RESISTANT?

Perfectly clear ice isn't only about aesthetics. One of the reasons bartenders go to such great lengths to make it is because the impurities that cause cloudiness in ice also weaken its crystal lattice, causing the ice to be more prone to shattering while shaking. This creates many unwanted ice shards that will overdilute your cocktail.

Want to test it yourself? Start by making two batches of ice cubes. For the first, simply fill an ice tray with tap water and freeze it as you usually would. For the second, follow our recipe for Practically Clear Ice (right) to create nearly clear ice cubes. Then, one batch at a time, fill a cocktail shaker with the ice cubes, shake, and observe the difference in how each batch breaks into pieces.

Lisa Says . . .

Silicone ice trays and other silicone kitchen tools can hold on to odors that you don't want transferred to your drinks or food. Luckily, there's an easy way to get rid of those weird smells: Just bake the offending tools at 350 degrees Fahrenheit for 1 hour. It's totally fine to do this repeatedly, so you know what to do if those smells ever return.

PRACTICALLY CLEAR ICE

makes about 7 cups

We use silicone ice trays that measure about 6½ inches by 4½ inches here, but rubber ice trays will also work. If your trays are larger, you may be able to fit only one in the baking dish. You can substitute filtered tap water for the distilled water, but the ice will not be quite as clear.

6   cups distilled water

1 Fold 3 dish towels in half widthwise, then stack in 13 by 9-inch baking dish, allowing towels to overhang edges. Arrange two 6½ by 4½-inch silicone ice cube trays in center of prepared dish. Roll up additional towels and tuck into sides of dish as needed to ensure trays are packed snugly.

2 Bring water to boil in large saucepan and let boil for 1 minute. Working in batches, carefully transfer water to 4-cup liquid measuring cup, then pour into trays. Let cool completely, about 30 minutes; you may have extra water. Place baking dish in freezer and let sit, uncovered, until ice is completely frozen, at least 8 hours.

FREQUENTLY ASKED QUESTIONS: COCKTAIL EDITION

Q: What's the best way to measure liquids for cocktails?

A: Because precision is important when it comes to measuring the small amounts of liquid needed for cocktails, we like to measure liquid ingredients in ounces rather than cups. The best tool for doing so is a cocktail jigger, a roughly hourglass-shaped tool with one end designed to measure a larger amount (usually 1½ or 2 ounces) and the other end designed to measure a slightly smaller amount (usually 1 ounce). For measuring out very small amounts of ingredients such as aromatic bitters, we use a teaspoon.

Q: Is it really necessary to chill my cocktail glasses?

A: We think it's worth the effort. Chilling your glasses helps ensure that the drinks you pour into them stay chilly too. It also prevents the ice in your drinks from melting too quickly and overdiluting the cocktails you worked so hard to get just right. There are a few ways to get your glasses frosty-cold: You can leave them in the freezer for at least 30 minutes, or, if your freezer space is limited, at the back of the top shelf of your fridge (the coldest zone) for at least 1 hour. Filling glasses with ice water and letting them sit for at least 5 minutes will also do the trick.

Q: Should I shake or stir?

A: The way you mix a cocktail depends on its contents. If the drink is composed of just spirits, you stir it (unless your name is Hannah or James Bond). Stirred drinks tend to be chilled and diluted slightly less than shaken drinks; this allows the flavors of the liquors themselves to shine. If a drink contains fruit juice, egg, or dairy—ingredients that are a little harder to integrate into liquor— you'll want to shake it. Shaking chills the drink more quickly than stirring and dilutes the alcohol to bring acid, sugar, and alcohol into harmony.

Are Julep Strainers Only for Juleps?

Julep strainers predate the Hawthorne strainer. They were originally developed specifically for use with mint juleps, where they'd be used in the serving cup to hold back the crushed ice and mint as revelers drank.

That said, these simple strainers—shaped somewhat like large perforated metal spoons—can be used to make much more than their eponymous drink. They fit well into a mixing glass, so we often turn to this model when straining stirred cocktails.

When it comes to shaken cocktails, however, we generally prefer to use a Hawthorne strainer. The tightly packed coils catch even tiny fragments of ice and other ingredients, and the wider shape is ideal for fitting over the mouths of most cocktail shakers.

anatomy of
A GOOD HAWTHORNE STRAINER

LARGE WINGS

Fit securely on vessels of different sizes

SMALL HANDLE

Keeps the whole unit well-balanced

CLOSELY PACKED COILS

Dense coils with moderate tension make for finer, cleaner straining

FINGER TAB

Makes it easy to keep your grip on the strainer and adjust how finely you strain

worth it

BAR SPOON

The elegant long-handled bar spoon not only looks dramatic, it also allows you to stir cocktails efficiently with just a few flicks of your wrist. With a relatively long handle and a small, slender bowl, it's designed for stirring drinks in mixing glasses and for fishing garnishes such as olives and cherries out of their jars. It can even be used to crack ice or to make layered cocktails by carefully pouring spirits over the back of the spoon to create a striped effect.

MOJITO

serves 1

Making a few batches of this iconic drink is a great way to practice your shaking and straining techniques.

⅓	cup fresh mint leaves, plus mint sprig for garnishing
1	ounce simple syrup
2	ounces white rum
¾	ounce lime juice
4	ounces seltzer, chilled

1 Add mint leaves and simple syrup to base of cocktail shaker and muddle until fragrant, about 30 seconds. Add rum and lime juice, then fill shaker with ice. Shake mixture until just combined and chilled, about 5 seconds.

2 Double-strain cocktail into chilled collins glass half-filled with ice. Add seltzer and, using bar spoon, gently lift rum mixture from bottom of glass to top to combine. Top with additional ice and garnish with mint sprig. Serve.

test it yourself

DO YOU REALLY NEED TO DOUBLE-STRAIN?

Double straining involves straining a cocktail through either a built-in strainer (for a cobbler shaker) or a hand-held strainer (for a Boston shaker) before then pouring it through a second, small conical strainer set over the serving glass. It may seem fussy, but there are two situations that make the small extra effort more than worth it. For shaken cocktails served straight up (without ice), double-straining results in beautifully translucent cocktails with no floating ice shards. And for muddled cocktails double-straining prevents chunks of herbs or fruit pulp from making it into the finished drink.

But don't take our word for it: Test it yourself. Try making our Mojito recipe (above) twice—double-straining one cocktail as directed, and straining the other just once. Then take a close look at each cocktail, noting how many stray pieces of ice and crushed mint you see floating in each.

Is It Safe to Drink from Vintage Glassware?

Not to sound alarmist, but those delightfully retro glasses you picked up from the thrift store likely contain lead. As our colleague Valerie discovered while researching vintage glassware, it used to be very common for glass manufacturers to add lead oxide to glass to increase its prismatic brilliancy and make it easier to work with. And when it comes to colorful vintage glassware, the concern goes beyond just lead. Old manufacturing processes incorporated heavy metals such as cadmium or even radioactive uranium oxide to turn glass bright green, red, and other colors.

But do you really need to worry? If you only use your vintage glassware every now and then, it's probably fine—it takes time for exposure to build and for heavy metals to leach out into a drink. But experts warn against storing things (like your nice aged Scotch) in vintage glassware for long periods of time, and advise that children and pregnant women are better off staying away from vintage glassware entirely.

So how can you find out whether or not your glassware contains lead so you can sip your cocktail in peace? First, you can try the tests below. They aren't 100 percent foolproof, but combining two or more of them will give you a more accurate picture than just one. And when in doubt, consider making use of your vintage glasses only on special occasions or, better yet, keeping them in a purely decorative role.

Look for a Rainbow

Lead was added to make glass look prismatic, so a leaded glass will likely look more rainbowy when you shine a white light through it. However, less-harmful modern additives (such as zinc oxide and potassium oxide) can create the same effect, so this is just one of a few precautionary measures you should take.

Listen for a Ringing Sound

Gently tap the glass with a knife or fork and pay attention to the sound. If it makes a relatively high-pitched ringing sound, it's probably lead glass. Lead-free glass should make a lower clinking sound.

Measure the Density of the Glass

Lead oxide is heavier than the lead-free alternatives used in modern glassmaking. For the most definitive way to determine whether your glassware contains lead or not, measure its density. Here's how.

1 Weigh glass (in grams).

2 Sink glass in beaker full of water and measure how much water is displaced, to get volume of glass (in milliliters).

3 Divide weight by volume to get density.

Roughly speaking, if the density is more than about 3 g/ml, the glass likely contains lead.

Why Are There So Many Different Glass Designs?

Glassware choice can be utilitarian. Design differences such as the presence or lack of a stem, the height of the walls, or the width of the base can have functional ramifications that lend themselves particularly well to certain kinds of drinks. But not every detail is strictly functional—glass choice is also about tradition, preference, and the vibe you're going for. Here are some of the glasses we consider essential for any well-stocked bar cart, plus a few that are fun but a little more specialized.

ESSENTIAL

Cocktail Glass
Stem keeps your hand from warming straight-up drinks.

Wine Glass
Wide bowl allows more contact between wine and air, which helps bring out nuanced aromas. Inwardly curved rim concentrates and directs aromas toward your nose. Stem keeps your hand from warming wine.

Old-Fashioned Glass
(also known as a rocks glass)
Short, thick walls allow room for chunky ice cubes and help insulate on-the-rocks cocktails.

Pint Glass
Standard for beer and beer-based cocktails. Streamlined design makes them easy to stack and clean.

Collins Glass (also known as a highball glass)
Tall, straight walls keep seltzer bubbles from dissipating too quickly.

Mug
Heatproof, handled mug keeps your fingers safe from hot drinks.

SPECIALTY

Margarita Glass
Just as iconic as its namesake drink. Stem keeps your hand from warming frozen drinks. Wide rim provides plenty of surface area for salting or sugaring.

Flute Glass
Narrow flute concentrates aromas and keeps bubbles in sparkling wines and sparkling cocktails from dissipating too quickly. Stem keeps your hand from warming drink.

Hurricane Glass
Good alternative to margarita glass and commonly used for frozen and tiki drinks. Stem keeps your hand from warming frozen drinks. Flared rim leaves room for garnishes.

Punch Cup
Inwardly curved rim concentrates and directs aromas toward your nose. Small size encourages more frequent refills (and thus, more socializing at the punch bowl).

Tiki Glass
A quirky, retro must-have for lovers of tiki drinks.

5 Skills That'll Make You a Master Mixologist

A big part of the appeal of making mixed drinks at home is in looking suave in front of your friends. Having all the right tools helps, but you also need to know how to use them if you really want to impress. Keep your cocktail night classy with the following tips.

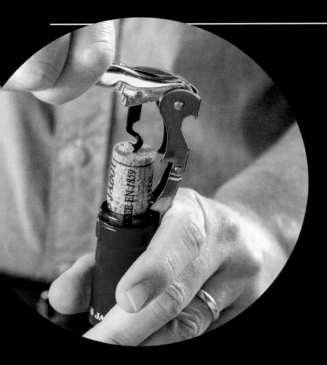

2 STIR A COCKTAIL THE RIGHT WAY

1 Assemble ingredients in mixing glass, then fill glass three-quarters full with ice.

2 Insert bar spoon into mixing glass with outer curved side positioned against wall of glass. Hold base of mixing glass firmly. Loosely grasp stem of spoon with other hand, between thumb, forefinger, and middle finger (similar to how you would hold a pencil).

3 Pivot wrist of hand holding spoon to guide convex side of spoon around wall of glass, allowing stem of spoon to rotate between your fingers until cocktail is combined and chilled, for time specified in recipe; remove spoon.

4 Fit julep or Hawthorne strainer into mixing glass and decant drink into chilled serving glass.

1 USE YOUR WINE OPENER THE RIGHT WAY

It takes a little practice to get the hang of using a waiters' corkscrew, but we think the learning curve is worth it. Not only can this corkscrew open a bottle of wine in seconds, but you can also change up the entry angle and location to remove corks that get broken or stuck in the bottle (it happens). To use one, first insert the worm (that's the spiral part) into the center of the cork and aim it straight down as you turn. Then, with one hand, hold the top notch on the metal arm against the lip of the bottle, using your other hand to lift the handle. After pulling the cork out as far as you can, hold the bottom notch against the bottle lip and again lift the handle. The cork should come right out.

3

CREATE THE PERFECT CITRUS TWIST

Citrus twists are a popular cocktail garnish. The narrow, twisted coil looks elegant floating in the glass or perched on the rim, and it imparts a light floral aroma to the drink's bouquet. All you need to make one is a channel knife (the larger blade built into many citrus zesters). Here's how.

1 Use channel knife to remove 3- to 4-inch strand, working around circumference of citrus in spiral pattern to ensure continuous piece.

2 Curl strand tightly to establish uniform twist, then place in cocktail or on edge of glass.

4

SEAL YOUR BOSTON-STYLE SHAKER THE RIGHT WAY

The hardest part of learning to use a Boston-style shaker is getting a good seal between the two pieces so your cocktail doesn't go flying all over the room when you start to shake. Luckily, practice makes perfect. Here's how you do it.

Add your drink ingredients to the smaller cup or mixing glass and then add ice to the larger cup until it's about two-thirds full. Holding the larger cup in your nondominant hand, invert the smaller cup over the larger one at a slight angle and pour the drink ingredients into the ice. Finally, firmly tap the smaller cup to form a tight seal with the larger one. (To test the seal, try lifting the whole shaker by the smaller cup. If you can lift the shaker without it falling apart, the seal is good.)

5

SEPARATE A STUCK BOSTON-STYLE SHAKER (WITHOUT LOSING A DROP)

Most of the time, you'll be able to unseal your Boston-style shaker by simply wiggling the top cup back and forth. But if you've got a very tight seal, grip the bottom half of the shaker with your nondominant hand and, using the heel of your dominant hand, firmly tap the bottom cup just under the junction where the two halves meet. (You may have to do this more than once.)

Unfortunately, we've found out the hard way that there's no easy way to get a stuck cobbler-style shaker apart. If pure muscle power and grip strength doesn't do the trick, you might be left with a permanently sealed shaker. Just one more reason we gravitate towards Boston-style shakers in the test kitchen.

bake it
till you
make it

RECIPES

Don't Try This at Home

Durability is important for baking tools and equipment. It should come as no surprise that baked goods are some of the stickiest, messiest, most stubborn recipes to remove remnants of. Washing isn't always easy, and that means it can contribute to some wear and tear over time. We want items that can stand the test of time—and the sink.

To test how well muffin tins stood up to long-term use, for example, we subjected each muffin tin to multiple hand-cleanings. What does multiple cleanings mean exactly? That was 25 washes of *each* muffin tin with an abrasive sponge. We can still feel every tight turn of the rough sponge and the bruised knuckles from this one. In fact, our hands were worse for wear than the pans afterwards. Each muffin tin (except for the one that wasn't nonstick) released baked goods as beautifully at the end of testing as at the beginning.

And that's OK. We really root for everything we test to succeed, and this test was a powerful testament to the quality of nonstick baking coatings these days. And while the process may have been arduous while it lasted, really, how can we complain? Testing baking equipment is pretty sweet.

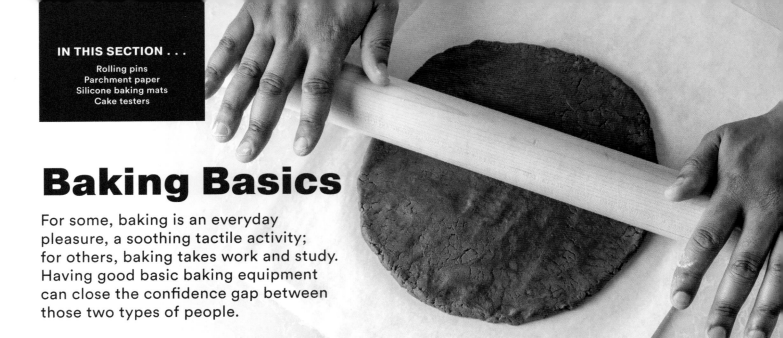

Baking Basics

For some, baking is an everyday pleasure, a soothing tactile activity; for others, baking takes work and study. Having good basic baking equipment can close the confidence gap between those two types of people.

I Want to Start Baking More. What Tools Will I Need?

Congratulations! Chances are that you won't start with shiny tortes or laminated pastries—and thus specialty gear items. Many nuts-and-bolts baking equipment items serve other purposes in your savory cooking.

If we didn't convince you to stock your kitchen with the following items in previous chapters, maybe the prospect of eating a warm, gooey chocolate chip cookie or a jammy homemade pie might sway you. At right is a list of our most-used basic baking gear.

Hannah Says . . .

Rolling pins can be useful for non-baking tasks as well. We use them to crush chips or crackers or cookies into crumbs, pulverize peppercorns and whole spices (cumin seeds, fennel seeds, etc.), and, in a pinch, to crush ice, muddle herbs, and pound out chicken or pork cutlets. Our straight winner from J.K. Adams is basically a club and could also be handy if you were to encounter, say, a rabid squirrel or territorial rooster.

BASIC BAKING GEAR	WHAT IT'S FOR
Mixing Bowls (page 89) (stainless steel and glass)	Containing ingredients as you mix them together
Dry Measuring Cups (page 90)	Measuring dry ingredients
Liquid Measuring Cups (page 90)	Measuring (and mixing and pouring) liquid ingredients
Kitchen Scale (page 91)	Weighing dry ingredients with greater accuracy
Measuring Spoons (page 91)	Measuring small volumes of ingredients
Whisk (page 96)	Combining and aerating ingredients
Rubber Spatula (page 97)	Mixing doughs and folding batters and foams
Hand Mixer or Stand Mixer (page 136)	Mixing or whipping most batters and doughs
Food Processor (page 134)	Everything from chopping ingredients to mixing pie dough
Oven Thermometer (page 93)	Checking oven temperature
Ice Cream Scoop (page 280)	Evenly portioning cookie dough and cake batter

What's the Best Size Liquid Measuring Cup to Own?

Most anything you'll need to measure in baking recipes will fit in a common 2-cup measuring cup. And with a 2-cup measure, you can whisk some ingredients right in the cup and then use the handle and spout to slowly incorporate the contents into your dry ingredients. But owning a 1-cup version is helpful as well. We often call for just a cup of liquids. And the 1-cup measure comes in handy when your 2-cup is occupied.

Does Sifting Actually Do Anything?

Yes, sometimes, but probably not when you think it does.

We sift flour when incorporating it into an egg foam (a whipped mixture of egg whites or whites and yolks that lifts and lightens baked goods) to avoid deflating the delicate whipped mixture before or during folding. For layer cakes and other recipes, however, whisking the flour with other dry ingredients is typically enough to aerate it. Throughout history, some recipes have called for taking the sifting step before measuring the flour to avoid clumps—don't do this! Only sift if a recipe calls for doing so and when it calls for doing so. For example, a cup of flour or confectioners' sugar sifted before measuring can weigh up to 35 percent less than a cup of flour or sugar sifted after measuring—a difference that can make a huge impact on the texture of finished baked goods.

The best way to sift is with a fine-mesh strainer. Add the ingredient(s) and tap the side of the strainer for a light snowfall of powder.

Why Are Most Rolling Pins Made of Wood?

In our testing of rolling pins, metal and silicone pins stuck to and lifted whole swaths of dough off the counter. They also couldn't hold a dusting of flour when needed. Wood is the way to go. But texture matters. Look for slightly rough-textured wood; it holds some flour and grips dough just enough to roll it out nicely.

Which Type of Rolling Pin Is Better: Tapered or Straight?

Do you have space for two pins? Tapered rolling pins are light (but heavy enough to roll out pie dough) and lovely; they offer superb control and maneuverability so you can change rolling direction quickly. That said, you might not want a tapered pin to be your only pin. While the tapered rolling pin is great for some goods, a straight pin offers heft for rolling out big batches of dough efficiently. The straight plane ensures there won't be hills and valleys in the thickness of broader doughs, which can lead to uneven baking.

Isn't It a Waste to Line a Greased Pan with Parchment Paper?

We call for parchment paper in a number of places where you don't want your perfectly prepared baked goods to stick—lining a baking sheet for cookies, fitting into the bottom of a cake pan, and sitting under a freeform tart or pavlova. It might feel less wasteful to just grease the pan more liberally, but let us stress that in many cases you really need to use it. The extra fat from super-greasy pans can cause cookies to spread more and bake unevenly, and can essentially fry the bottom of baked goods to a too-brown color. Sometimes, baked goods are fat-averse; meringue, made of fluffy whipped egg whites, is one, and angel food cake, which needs to grip its pan to rise, is another. It's particularly important to line your pans when working with these recipes.

How Do I Clean the Gunk off My Silicone Baking Mat?

Over time, silicone baking mats can build up a sticky—and often stinky—residue of polymerized fats. Here's how to get rid of it.

1 Place baking mat on wire rack set in rimmed baking sheet. Bake in 450-degree oven until mat no longer smokes, about 1 hour.

2 Using tongs, transfer mat to sink and wash thoroughly with soap and hot water.

3 If oily residue remains, scrub gently with Bar Keepers Friend or similar nonabrasive scrub. (Note: This method will not remove the brown spots that these mats acquire over time.)

FREQUENTLY ASKED QUESTIONS: PARCHMENT PAPER EDITION

Q: Can I substitute waxed paper for parchment paper?

A: Like parchment, waxed paper can be a useful kitchen supply for separating layers of cookies when storing them or wrapping homemade ice cream sandwiches before stashing in the freezer. But do not substitute waxed paper for parchment when it really counts: for baking. Waxed paper can't go in the oven; it's coated with a thin layer of either soybean or paraffin wax so it melts at high temperatures.

Q: Is it OK to reuse parchment paper?

A: Yes! Reduce your waste and cost per bake by using your parchment at least twice (so long as it didn't get overly greasy, messy, or wet with anything that might burn on a second trip to the oven—that won't improve the flavor of your food). We've found that we could make at least five batches of cookies on a single sheet of parchment with no sticking. You can also reuse most parchment with recipes baked at higher temperatures such as rustic breads that bake at 400-plus degrees. Because parchment degrades faster at higher temperatures, its life expectancy is a little shorter there—two uses is about the maximum. You'll know you can't use the parchment any more when it has turned dark and brittle.

Q: Should I oil my parchment paper?
A: Generally there's no need to oil a sheet of parchment paper—it's already coated in a layer of nonstick material and oiling the parchment can make cookies spread too much. But while most baked goods don't require any further barrier, we do like an extra layer of insurance for layer cakes. Our foolproof method of cake pan prep is to grease the pan, line it with parchment paper, and then grease and flour the parchment and pan sides. The parchment guarantees that the cake pulls away from the pan bottom completely; a coat of grease and flour on the parchment and up the pan sides helps the batter cling and rise, and ensures that the parchment pulls away from the cake bottom without removing large crumbs.

Lisa Says . . .

Our favorite parchment paper is precut to precisely the size of our favorite half sheet pan. We love this because parchment that comes in rolls tends to want to stay rolled. It springs up unless you pin it down! By contrast the sheets, sold in packs of 100, slide right into the pan and lie flat. Easy peasy.

head to head

PAN LINERS

SILICONE BAKING MATS

Perfectly nonstick

Endlessly reusable after cleaning

Fit a standard half sheet pan

Weigh 60 to 117 grams so they stay put on a baking sheet

Lay flat for desserts with perfectly flat undersides

Repel fat so cookies can spread more resulting in a crispier final product

PARCHMENT PAPER

Very reliably nonstick

Reusable up to five times

Sold in rolls or in flat sheets to fit standard half sheet pan

Weigh only 4 grams so can move around

Can sometimes roll or wrinkle, leaving desserts with an uneven underside

Results in cookies that spread less for a chewier bite

anatomy of

A GOOD WIRE COOLING RACK

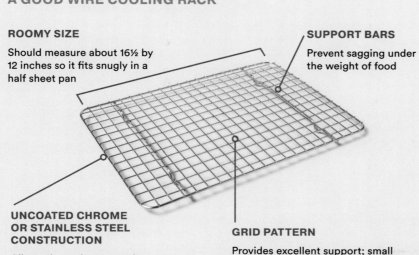

ROOMY SIZE

Should measure about 16½ by 12 inches so it fits snugly in a half sheet pan

SUPPORT BARS

Prevent sagging under the weight of food

UNCOATED CHROME OR STAINLESS STEEL CONSTRUCTION

Allows the rack to go under the broiler (nonstick coatings are not broiler-safe)

GRID PATTERN

Provides excellent support; small foods can fall through the gaps in racks with parallel bars

What's the Easiest Way to Clean a Wire Rack?

All those bars on a cooling rack can really trap food particles that you'll need to dislodge to get it clean. To make this easier, squirt some dish soap into a rimmed baking sheet and fill it with warm water. Invert the rack in the baking sheet and let it soak until particles are loosened. Then, scrub the rack gently in the direction the wires run, crosswise on the top and lengthwise on the underside.

8 More Ways to
Use Your Cooling Rack

While cooling might be in the name, a wire cooling rack can be a useful tool at various points in the baking process. Learn how this lightweight piece of equipment (with a lightweight price tag) can be one of the handiest items in your baking arsenal.

1 FASHION A RESTING PLACE FOR FRIED FOODS

Some of the best "baked" goods aren't baked at all—they're fried. Fritters, doughnuts, and even fried cookies (such as Danish klejner and Greek melomakarona) should be transferred to a wire rack lined with paper towels and set in a rimmed baking sheet. (That goes for savory foods like fried chicken and French fries too.) The rack allows the items to cool and stay crispy rather than sogging out on a flat surface, and the baking sheet catches any drips of oil.

2 CONTAIN A DUSTING OF CONFECTIONERS' SUGAR

A snow shower of confectioners' sugar looks beautiful on baked goods—but not so much sprinkled all over your counter. Place cooled baked goods on a wire rack set in a rimmed baking sheet before dusting them with confectioners' sugar to keep the process sweet. This also prevents a buildup of confectioners' sugar on a serving platter.

3 NEATLY GLAZE CAKES

For cakes that call for a sleek blanket of ganache, dribbles of sugar glaze, or a soaking of simple syrup, it's best to place the cake on a rack set in a baking sheet before embellishing so glazes don't pool at the base of the cake (they'll fall right through the grids).

4 DRY OUT BREAD FOR THE BEST PUDDINGS

For proper custard absorption and bread that doesn't disintegrate, bread pudding recipes call for soaking day-or-more-old bread. If you want bread pudding but your slices are too fresh to soak, you can dry them out by baking them on a wire rack set in a rimmed baking sheet. This allows the warm air to dry out both sides of the slices.

5

TWICE-BAKE AN ICONIC COOKIE

Biscotti literally means "twice baked" and doing so is much more effective on a wire rack than it is on a flat baking sheet. This evenly browns and dries out the crunchy slices.

6

DUNK YOUR DOUGHNUTS

When you dip your doughnuts, some glaze is bound to drip off before it hardens to a sheer, crystalline coating. Place the glazed doughnuts on a wire rack set in a baking sheet and let the glaze drip onto the sheet.

7

SAFELY BROWN MERINGUE

Burnished plumes of sweet meringue top desserts such as lemon meringue pie and baked Alaska. If you're browning meringue under the broiler, the cooling rack–baking sheet setup is important. Broiling on the wire rack allows you to transfer the cooled and topped dessert right to the oven. This is particularly helpful if you're making baked Alaska, which can melt with every bit of handling.

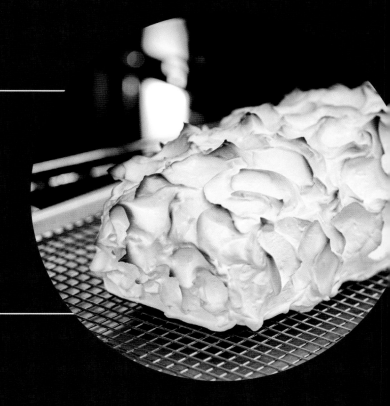

8

BAKE TART CRUSTS

A tart pan is a relatively delicate piece of equipment, and a tart crust is a fragile pastry. Placing a tart pan on a wire rack set in a rimmed baking sheet provides better heat protection for an evenly baked crust that isn't overly browned on the bottom.

Do I Need a Cake Tester?

To test cakes, muffins, and quick breads for doneness, a cake tester or toothpick (or skewer in the case of tall cakes) inserted into the center should come out clean or with a few crumbs attached, depending on the baked good. If batter clings to the tester or skewer, the item needs more time in the oven.

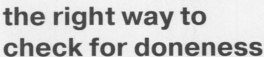

A toothpick is actually our choice for this job. For all kinds of desserts, we found that cake testers came out clean every time—except when the batter was still practically raw inside—so testing was useless. By contrast, bamboo skewers and toothpicks consistently gave us more accurate results, emerging clean when the cakes were fully baked and with crumbs when the interior was still moist. Cake testers have one advantage, and this is it: They leave smaller holes in baked goods than toothpicks or skewers, keeping the baked goods prettier. But here usability definitely beats aesthetics.

the right way to check for doneness

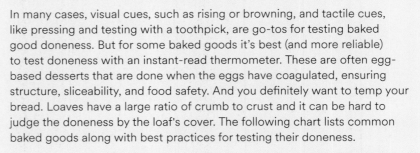

In many cases, visual cues, such as rising or browning, and tactile cues, like pressing and testing with a toothpick, are go-tos for testing baked good doneness. But for some baked goods it's best (and more reliable) to test doneness with an instant-read thermometer. These are often egg-based desserts that are done when the eggs have coagulated, ensuring structure, sliceability, and food safety. And you definitely want to temp your bread. Loaves have a large ratio of crumb to crust and it can be hard to judge the doneness by the loaf's cover. The following chart lists common baked goods along with best practices for testing their doneness.

BAKED GOOD	VISUAL/ TACTILE CUES	INTERNAL TEMPERATURE
Cookies	X	
Brownies & Blondies	X	
Biscuits	X	
Custards		X
Bread Pudding	X	X
Cheesecake		X
Pie Pastry	X	
Fruit Pies	X	
Custard Pies		X
Cakes	X	
Breads	X	X

Sweet Sheet

If you keep only one baking pan on hand, make it a sturdy rimmed baking sheet and use it to turn out cookies, crowd-ready sheet cakes, flexible jelly-roll cakes, breads, and even slab pies. (For more on this pan's uses in savory cooking, see pages 58–59.)

What's the Difference Between a Baking Sheet and a Cookie Sheet?

When it comes to baking, you might casually call the baking sheet a "cookie sheet" for obvious reasons. (Psst: You bake cookies on it.) But a *true* cookie sheet is flat and rimless or has just one or two raised edges. Some true cookie sheets come insulated, others don't; some are thin, some are thick. But we generally call for rimmed baking sheets in all applications—even cookie baking. We haven't found a strong reason to own both. In fact, sometimes cookies brown (and burn) too quickly, before they're baked through, on a cookie sheet since they aren't protected by straight rims. And, despite the claims, insulated sheets don't excel at preventing these problems. Since a cookie sheet performs just one task, and sometimes not as well, we recommend buying more than one multipurpose rimmed baking sheet.

When Should I Rotate and/or Switch Baking Sheets?

For even baking, we rotate most items on baking sheets in the oven halfway through cooking to account for the oven's hotter and cooler zones (see page 23). If you're using just one oven rack (often this is the middle rack when baking) rotating the pan 180 degrees is adequate. If you're using two oven racks (maybe for two cake layers or for two baking sheets of cookies) it's best to rotate both the pans and switch the oven racks they're sitting on for even baking. There are a few exceptions to the rotating rule, mostly for baked goods that get lift from an egg foam. Desserts such as soufflés, meringues, and cream puff shells usually should not be disturbed.

THIN AND CRISPY CHOCOLATE CHIP COOKIES

makes 16 cookies

Baking these thin, crispy, butterscotch-flavored chocolate chip cookies on a sturdy rimmed baking sheet is particularly important—you want them crisp, not burnt. These cookies have a generous bake time: The goal is to dry them out without overcooking them. The right sheet ensures that they bake to an even, deep golden brown.

- 1¼ cups (5 ounces) cake flour
- ¾ teaspoon table salt
- ¼ teaspoon baking soda
- 8 tablespoons unsalted butter, melted and cooled
- ⅓ cup (2⅓ ounces) granulated sugar
- ⅓ cup packed (2⅓ ounces) dark brown sugar
- 2 large egg yolks
- 1½ tablespoons whole milk
- 2 teaspoons vanilla extract
- ¾ cup (4½ ounces) mini semisweet chocolate chips

1 Adjust oven rack to middle position and heat oven to 350 degrees. Line 2 rimmed baking sheets with parchment paper. Whisk flour, salt, and baking soda together in bowl.

2 Using stand mixer fitted with paddle, mix melted butter, granulated sugar, and brown sugar on low speed until fully combined. Increase speed to medium-high and beat until mixture is lightened in color, about 1 minute. Reduce speed to low; add egg yolks, milk, and vanilla; and mix until combined. Slowly add flour mixture and mix until just combined, scraping down bowl as needed. Using rubber spatula, stir in chocolate chips.

3 Using greased 1-tablespoon measure, divide dough into 16 heaping-tablespoon portions on prepared sheets, 8 portions per sheet. Divide any remaining dough evenly among portions. Using your moistened fingers, press dough portions to ½-inch thickness. Bake cookies, 1 sheet at a time, until deep golden brown, 16 to 18 minutes, rotating sheet halfway through baking. Transfer sheet to wire rack and let cookies cool completely before serving.

CARROT LAYER CAKE

serves 12 to 16

This supereasy layer cake requires only one pan: a rimmed baking sheet. We simply bake one thin sheet cake and then cut the cake into quarters once cooled to create thin rectangular layers. Assembling this cake on a cardboard cake round trimmed to a 6 by 8-inch rectangle makes it easy to press the pecans onto the sides of the frosted cake.

CAKE

1¾	cups (8¾ ounces) all-purpose flour
2	teaspoons baking powder
1	teaspoon baking soda
1½	teaspoons ground cinnamon
¾	teaspoon ground nutmeg
½	teaspoon table salt
¼	teaspoon ground cloves
1¼	cups packed (8¾ ounces) light brown sugar
¾	cup vegetable oil
3	large eggs
1	teaspoon vanilla extract
2⅔	cups shredded carrots (4 carrots)
⅔	cup dried currants

FROSTING AND NUTS

16	tablespoons unsalted butter, softened
3	cups (12 ounces) confectioners' sugar
⅓	cup (1 ounce) buttermilk powder
2	teaspoons vanilla extract
¼	teaspoon table salt
12	ounces cream cheese, cut into 12 equal pieces and chilled
2	cups pecans, toasted and chopped coarse

1 for the cake Adjust oven rack to middle position and heat oven to 350 degrees. Grease 18 by 13-inch rimmed baking sheet, line with parchment paper, and grease parchment.

2 Whisk flour, baking powder, baking soda, cinnamon, nutmeg, salt, and cloves together in large bowl. Whisk sugar, oil, eggs, and vanilla in second large bowl until mixture is smooth. Stir in carrots and currants. Add flour mixture and fold with rubber spatula until mixture is just combined.

3 Transfer batter to prepared sheet and smooth top with off-set spatula. Bake until center is firm to touch, 15 to 18 minutes, rotating sheet halfway through baking. Let cake cool in pan on wire rack for 5 minutes. Invert cake onto rack (do not remove parchment), then reinvert onto second rack. Let cake cool completely, about 30 minutes.

4 for the frosting and nuts Using stand mixer fitted with paddle, beat butter, sugar, buttermilk powder, vanilla, and salt on low speed until smooth, about 2 minutes, scraping down bowl as needed. Increase speed to medium-low; add cream cheese, 1 piece at a time; and mix until smooth, about 2 minutes.

5 Transfer cooled cake to cutting board, parchment side down. Using sharp chef's knife, cut cake and parchment in half crosswise, then lengthwise, making 4 equal rectangles, about 8 by 6 inches each.

6 Place 1 cake layer, parchment side up, on 8 by 6-inch cardboard rectangle and carefully remove parchment. Spread ⅔ cup frosting evenly over top, right to edge of cake. Repeat with 2 more cake layers, pressing lightly to adhere and spreading ⅔ cup frosting evenly over each layer. Top with remaining cake layer and spread 1 cup frosting evenly over top. Spread remaining frosting evenly over sides of cake. (It's fine if some crumbs show through frosting on sides, but if you go back to smooth top of cake, be sure that spatula is free of crumbs.)

7 Hold cake with your hand and gently press pecans onto sides with your other hand. Refrigerate for at least 1 hour. Transfer cake to platter and serve. (Cake can be refrigerated for up to 24 hours; bring to room temperature before serving.)

TEXAS SHEET CAKE

serves 12 to 15

Texas sheet cake is an iconic baking sheet cake. This thin, chocolaty, pecan-topped cake is baked in a rimmed baking sheet; topped with a layer of rich chocolate icing while still hot, creating a fudgy middle layer where the icing and hot cake meld; and then served right out of the pan.

CAKE

2	cups (10 ounces) all-purpose flour
2	cups (14 ounces) granulated sugar
½	teaspoon baking soda
½	teaspoon table salt
2	large eggs plus 2 large yolks
¼	cup sour cream
2	teaspoons vanilla extract
8	ounces semisweet chocolate, chopped
¾	cup vegetable oil
¾	cup water
½	cup (1½ ounces) unsweetened cocoa powder
4	tablespoons unsalted butter

ICING

8	tablespoons unsalted butter
½	cup heavy cream
½	cup (1½ ounces) unsweetened cocoa powder
1	tablespoon light corn syrup
3	cups (12 ounces) confectioners' sugar
1	tablespoon vanilla extract
1	cup pecans, toasted and chopped

1 for the cake Adjust oven rack to middle position and heat oven to 350 degrees. Grease 18 by 13-inch rimmed baking sheet. Whisk flour, sugar, baking soda, and salt together in large bowl. Whisk eggs and yolks, sour cream, and vanilla in second bowl until smooth.

2 Heat chocolate, oil, water, cocoa, and butter in large saucepan over medium heat, stirring occasionally, until smooth, 3 to 5 minutes. Whisk chocolate mixture into flour mixture until incorporated. Whisk egg mixture into batter. Transfer batter to prepared sheet. Bake until toothpick inserted in center comes out clean, 18 to 20 minutes, rotating sheet halfway through baking. Transfer sheet to wire rack.

3 for the icing About 5 minutes before cake is done baking, heat butter, cream, cocoa, and corn syrup in large saucepan over medium heat, stirring occasionally, until smooth, about 4 minutes. Off heat, whisk in sugar and vanilla. Spread warm icing evenly over hot cake and sprinkle with pecans. Let cake cool completely in pan on wire rack, about 1 hour, then refrigerate until icing is set, about 1 hour longer. Serve.

TRIPLE-BERRY SLAB PIE WITH GINGER-LEMON STREUSEL

serves 18 to 24

This easily portioned pie is big enough to serve a small army—the result of making it in a rimmed baking sheet rather than a pie plate. We roll a large piece of dough into two rectangles for the bottom crust. By overlapping two smaller pieces, the dough is sturdier and easier to handle. In the mixing stage, this dough will be moister than most, but as it chills it will absorb excess moisture. Be sure to roll the dough on a well-floured counter.

DOUGH

24	tablespoons (3 sticks) unsalted butter, divided
2¾	cups (13¾ ounces) all-purpose flour, divided
2	tablespoons sugar
1	teaspoon table salt
½	cup ice water, divided

STREUSEL

1½	cups (7½ ounces) all-purpose flour
½	cup packed (3½ ounces) light brown sugar
½	cup crystallized ginger, chopped fine
¼	cup (1¾ ounces) granulated sugar
1	tablespoon ground ginger
1	teaspoon grated lemon zest
¼	teaspoon table salt
10	tablespoons unsalted butter, melted and cooled

FILLING

1	cup (7 ounces) granulated sugar
6	tablespoons instant tapioca, ground
1	teaspoon grated lemon zest
¼	teaspoon table salt
1¼	pounds (4 cups) blackberries
1¼	pounds (4 cups) blueberries
1¼	pounds (4 cups) raspberries

1 for the dough Grate 5 tablespoons butter on large holes of box grater and place in freezer. Cut remaining 19 tablespoons butter into ½-inch cubes.

2 Pulse 1¾ cups flour, sugar, and salt in food processor until combined, 2 pulses. Add cubed butter and process until homogeneous paste forms, 40 to 50 seconds. Using your hands, carefully break paste into 2-inch chunks and redistribute evenly around processor blade. Add remaining 1 cup flour and pulse until mixture is broken into pieces no larger than 1 inch (most pieces will be much smaller), 4 to 5 pulses. Transfer mixture to bowl. Add grated butter and toss until all butter pieces are separated and coated with flour.

3 Sprinkle ¼ cup ice water over mixture. Toss with rubber spatula until mixture is evenly moistened. Sprinkle remaining ¼ cup ice water over mixture and toss to combine. Press dough with spatula until dough sticks together. Using spatula, divide dough into 2 equal portions. Transfer each portion to sheet of plastic wrap. Working with 1 portion at a time, draw edges of plastic over dough and press firmly on sides and top to form compact, fissure-free mass. Wrap in plastic and form into 5 by 6-inch rectangle. Refrigerate dough for at least 2 hours or up to 2 days. Let chilled dough sit on counter to soften slightly, about 10 minutes. (Wrapped dough can be frozen for up to 1 month. If frozen, let dough thaw completely on counter before rolling.)

4 Line 18 by 13-inch rimmed baking sheet with parchment paper. Roll each dough square into 16 by 11-inch rectangle on floured counter; stack on prepared sheet, separated by second sheet of parchment. Cover loosely with plastic wrap and refrigerate until dough is firm but still pliable, about 10 minutes.

5 Using parchment as sling, transfer chilled dough rectangles to counter; discard parchment. Wipe sheet clean with paper towels and spray with vegetable oil spray. Starting at short side of 1 dough rectangle, loosely roll around rolling pin, then gently unroll over half of long side of prepared sheet, leaving about 2 inches of dough overhanging 3 edges. Repeat with second dough rectangle, unrolling it over empty side of sheet and overlapping first dough piece by ½ inch.

6 Ease dough into sheet by gently lifting edges of dough with your hand while pressing into sheet bottom with your other hand. Brush overlapping edge of dough rectangles with water and press to seal. Trim overhang to ½ inch beyond edge of sheet. Tuck overhang under itself; folded edge should rest on edge of sheet. Crimp dough evenly around edge of sheet. Cover loosely with plastic and refrigerate until firm, about 30 minutes.

7 for the streusel Meanwhile, adjust oven racks to lower-middle and lowest positions and heat oven to 375 degrees. Combine flour, brown sugar, crystallized ginger, granulated sugar, ground ginger, lemon zest, and salt in bowl. Stir in melted butter until mixture is completely moistened; let sit for 10 minutes.

8 for the filling Whisk sugar, tapioca, lemon zest, and salt together in large bowl. Add blackberries, blueberries, and raspberries and gently toss to combine. Spread berry mixture evenly over chilled dough-lined sheet. Sprinkle streusel evenly over fruit, breaking apart any large chunks. Place large sheet of aluminum foil directly on lower rack (to catch any bubbling juices). Place pie on upper rack and bake until crust and streusel are deep golden brown and juices are bubbling, 45 minutes to 1 hour, rotating sheet halfway through baking. Let pie cool on wire rack until filling has set, about 2 hours. Serve.

All Pans on Deck

Baked goods take a number of shapes and sizes, from petite cupcakes to lofty layer cakes. Such a range of shapes calls for a variety of pans.

Should I Use Nonstick Baking Pans?

We prefer nonstick bakeware. Think of the items you need to remove from it such as delicate cake layers or sticky, sugary cinnamon buns. A nonstick coating also makes cleanup a breeze. That said, some desserts still need extra insurance and you should follow our protocol for greasing and lining those pans (see page 213).

Why Are the Sides of My Cakes Rounded?

You may have noticed that, depending on the cake pan you're using, your cake can emerge with sharp, straight sides, looking like a fancy bakery treat, or it can look more homey (yet equally tasty!) with rounded sides. The difference comes down to how the pans are constructed. With molded pans, a hot sheet of metal is pressed into a mold to create the pan. With folded pans, a metal sheet is folded into the shape of a pan, creating seams. If you like refined cakes, your choice between folded and molded may seem like a no-brainer, but there is a trade-off for the bonus beauty that comes with the folded pans. The folded pans have seams that can trap cake crumbs and so they take more attention to clean. The choice is yours.

Molded pans have rounded edges.

Folded pans have straight, sharp edges.

My Cakes Always Stick to the Pan. What Am I Doing Wrong?

Don't be hard on yourself. Desserts are a sticky situation.

In addition to greasing and lining cake pans (even nonstick ones), there are other steps you can take to ensure your cake comes out cleanly. One that might seem like a given is fully baking your cake. Underbaked cake doesn't have enough structure to come out of the pan cleanly, plus it could have sticky batter spots. (See page 218 for tips on testing different cakes.) Another step is letting a cake cool for some time (usually 10 to 15 minutes but check your recipe) before turning it out of the pan. This allows the cake to set up. Note that some delicate cakes such as angel food cake (see page 228) need to cool completely in the pan before they're turned out since their structure is built by just whipped egg whites. On the other end of the spectrum, some cakes, namely jelly roll cakes, need to be manipulated while warm and so you must remove them from the pan immediately.

Cake baked in an 8½ by 4½-inch loaf pan is lofty.

Cake baked in a 9 by 5-inch loaf pan is squat.

Why Do Some Recipes Specifically Call for Dark or Light Pans?

Our favorite cake pans tend to be lighter in color—golden, specifically. But there is value to owning dark pans for other applications. They radiate heat more intensely so they're great for items you want deep browning on, such as pan pizza and rolls.

If you want only one version of each pan and you're a cake baker, go for a golden or bronze color; it's best for delicate baked goods. We've found that these pans consistently turn out beautiful, evenly golden brown cakes. While cakes baked in these pans require slightly more time in the oven to achieve doneness than in a dark pan, this slower cook time can prevent overbaking and overbrowning. Cakes baked in lighter pans are also much more level. That radiating heat in dark pans? It sets the edges of the cake quickly, causing the still-setting center to rise and create a domed shape.

Cake baked in a gold-colored pan

Cake baked in a dark pan

Hannah Says . . .

With loaf pans we've found a small difference that makes for more gorgeous results. Our winning model's internal dimensions are 8½ by 4½ inches, measured at the top of the pan. This is about ½ inch smaller in each direction than a classic loaf pan, which typically measures 9 by 5 inches. Both sizes hold about 1 pound of dough and are sometimes labeled that way. You may think we're quibbling calling out a ½-inch difference but the slightly narrower dimensions result in loaves that rise higher and have taller, prettier domes.

What Else Can a Cake Pan Do?

We've hinted that cake pans aren't just for cake. They're great for baking rolls and biscuits, which get great height from pushing each other upwards as they rise snug in a pan. New England–style bar pizza is a regional pizza that gets lacy browned edges from being baked in a cake pan. Savory pies, such as Italian Easter pie and deep-dish quiche, also put dinner in these pans. Or you can bake breakfast—enriched breads like cinnamon rolls and sausage buns turn into a delicious pull-apart mass. And if you're willing to add another pan to your collection, a small 6-inch round cake pan can even fit inside your air-fryer for one-pan meals!

CHEWY BROWNIES

makes 24 brownies

You can bake these brownies in a standard pan for a classic chewy, gooey experience, or in one of the pans Lisa recommends below if you're a fan of crispy edges. If you use a glass baking dish instead of a metal baking pan, let the brownies cool for 10 minutes and then remove them promptly from the pan to prevent overbaking.

⅓	cup (1 ounce) Dutch-processed cocoa powder
1½	teaspoons instant espresso powder (optional)
½	cup plus 2 tablespoons boiling water
2	ounces unsweetened chocolate, chopped fine
½	cup plus 2 tablespoons vegetable oil
4	tablespoons unsalted butter, melted
2	large eggs plus 2 large yolks
2	teaspoons vanilla extract
2½	cups (17½ ounces) sugar
1¾	cups (8¾ ounces) all-purpose flour
¾	teaspoon table salt
6	ounces bittersweet chocolate, cut into ½-inch pieces

1 Adjust oven rack to lowest position and heat oven to 350 degrees. Make foil sling for 13 by 9-inch baking pan by folding 2 long sheets of aluminum foil; first sheet should be 13 inches wide and second sheet should be 9 inches wide. Lay sheets of foil in pan perpendicular to each other, with extra foil hanging over edges of pan. Push foil into corners and up sides of pan, smoothing foil flush to pan. Grease foil.

2 Whisk cocoa; espresso powder, if using; and boiling water in large bowl until smooth. Add unsweetened chocolate and whisk until chocolate is melted. Whisk in oil and melted butter. (Mixture may look curdled.) Whisk in eggs and yolks and vanilla until smooth and homogeneous. Whisk in sugar until fully incorporated. Using rubber spatula, stir in flour and salt until combined. Fold in chocolate pieces.

3 Transfer batter to prepared pan and smooth top. Bake until toothpick inserted halfway between edge and center comes out with few moist crumbs attached, 30 to 35 minutes, rotating pan halfway through baking. Let brownies cool in pan on wire rack for 1½ hours. Using foil overhang, remove brownies from pan. Transfer to wire rack and let cool completely, about 1 hour. Cut into 24 pieces before serving.

real talk with lisa

THE EDGE IS THE BEST PART OF A BROWNIE

Some people are all about the gooey brownie middle but I'm first to take the last-in-the-pan edge pieces myself. I have two handy pans that give me so much more of the chewy-crunch and ultradeep flavor of the corners I love. The first is the Baker's Edge pan (see page 233); the maze-like construction sports six more baking surfaces than ordinary pans, so it gives each serving of brownie at least two chewy edges. The second is a mini muffin tin (see page 232), which promises every brownie has a nice crisp crust all the way around, with moist interiors.

OATMEAL DINNER ROLLS

makes 12 rolls

Nestling the dough balls close together in a round cake pan ensures that they support each other in upward, rather than outward, expansion for oatmeal rolls that are more moist and fluffy than average.

¾	cup (2¼ ounces) old-fashioned rolled oats, plus 4 teaspoons for sprinkling
⅔	cup (5⅓ ounces) boiling water, plus ½ cup cold water
2	tablespoons unsalted butter, cut into 4 pieces
1½	cups (8¼ ounces) bread flour
¾	cup (4⅛ ounces) whole-wheat flour
¼	cup molasses
1½	teaspoons instant or rapid-rise yeast
1	teaspoon table salt
1	large egg, beaten with 1 tablespoon water and pinch table salt

1 Stir ¾ cup oats, boiling water, and butter together in bowl of stand mixer and let sit until butter is melted and most of water has been absorbed, about 10 minutes.

2 Add bread flour, whole-wheat flour, cold water, molasses, yeast, and salt. Using dough hook on low speed, mix until flour is moistened, about 1 minute (dough may look dry). Increase speed to medium-low and mix until dough clears sides of bowl (it will still stick to bottom), about 8 minutes, scraping down dough hook halfway through mixing (dough will be sticky). Transfer dough to clean counter and knead by hand to form smooth, round ball, about 30 seconds.

3 Place dough seam side down in lightly greased large bowl or container, cover with plastic wrap, and let rise until doubled in volume, 1 to 1¼ hours.

4 Grease 9-inch round cake pan. Press down on dough to deflate. Transfer dough to lightly floured counter and pat dough gently into 8-inch square. Cut dough into 12 equal pieces and cover loosely with plastic. Working with 1 piece of dough at a time (keep remaining pieces covered), form each piece into rough ball by stretching dough around your thumb and pinching edges together so that top is smooth. Place ball seam side down on clean counter and, using your cupped hand, drag in small circles until dough feels taut and round. Arrange dough balls seam side down in prepared pan, placing 9 dough balls around edge of pan and remaining 3 dough balls in center.

5 Cover with plastic and let rise until doubled in size, no gaps are visible between rolls, and dough springs back minimally when≈poked gently with your finger, 45 minutes to 1 hour.

6 Adjust oven rack to lower-middle position and heat oven to 375 degrees. Gently brush rolls with egg wash and sprinkle with remaining 4 teaspoons oats. Bake until rolls are deep brown and register at least 195 degrees, 25 to 30 minutes. Let rolls cool in pan on wire rack for 3 minutes; invert rolls onto rack, then reinvert. Let rolls cool for 20 minutes. Serve warm or at room temperature.

Why Do Some Pans Have a Hole in the Middle?

The hole in the middle of a tube pan makes for more than an iconic shape. Tube pans help delicate cakes, such as angel food cake and some chiffon cakes, rise. These cakes need help because they're often leavened only by whipped eggs and contain very little flour, and therefore very little gluten. The conical center of the pan provides more heat to the middle of the cake, so as the egg foam heats up the batter clings to and climbs the tube, and the inside of the cake sets at the same rate as the outside. (This is why we don't grease tube pans). The cake also clings to the tube during cooling; sponge cakes cool inverted so they stay fluffy and don't fall under their own weight. (Many tube pans have feet at the top for this reason but you can also put the tube on an upright wine bottle.)

The Bundt pan, the beautifully fluted pan introduced in 1950 by Nordic Ware, encourages this heating as well. The pan's purpose was to emulate the cast-iron pans used in Central Europe to make the yeasted cake kugelhopf. Now many types of cake are baked in Bundt pans, even fine-crumbed pound cake. The inner tube encourages dense cake batters to cook through. You don't want to bake a very delicate cake in a Bundt pan; the deep ridges in this pan would make it hard to extract.

Can Tube Pans and Bundt Pans Be Used Interchangeably?

You can't bake a delicate angel or chiffon cake within the ridges of a Bundt pan, but you can bake a sturdier Bundt cake in a tube pan—with some safe-guarding. If you choose to put a thick Bundt cake batter such as a pound cake, coffee cake, or fudgy chocolate cake batter in a tube pan with a removable bottom, either wrap the exterior of the pan with aluminum foil or place the pan on a baking sheet to prevent a mess from potential batter leakage.

Can I Make Angel Food Cake in a Nonstick Pan?

Angel food cake is baked in an ungreased pan so that it can cling to the pan as it rises and won't slump during baking; the ungreased interior also helps prevent the cake from slipping out of the pan when it's cooling upside down. However, the lack of greasing makes it a challenge to cleanly remove the cake from the pan. For this reason, we like tube pans with nonstick coatings for angel food cake; they make the process easier without being slippery enough to compromise the cake's rise. Another feature that makes getting an angel food cake out of the tube pan easier is a removable bottom. It lets you pull the entire cake out of the pan and then lift it off the base with no fuss. For fixed-bottom pans, you have to use a knife and significant shaking to coax out a cake, resulting in a more ragged appearance.

Cake made in a pan without a removable bottom

Cake made in a pan with a removable bottom

When Should I Use a Springform Pan?

Unlike traditional cake pans (which require the baker to unmold the cake by flipping the pan upside down), springforms consist of two pieces: a round, flat base and a circular collar that latches open and closed. Therefore, these pans are for cakes you can't invert. Think custardy or creamy cheesecakes, flourless chocolate cakes, or nut tortes; cakes that are built in the pan from the bottom up such as ice cream cake and mousse cake; and fruit-packed or -topped cakes such as a French apple cake. You can also use a springform pan simply because you plan on baking a cake too tall for the 2- to 2½-inch sides of a standard cake pan. Just be mindful that batter can leak from these pans.

How Can I Prevent a Springform Pan from Leaking?

Frankly, even the best pans we've found in our years of searching leak! To prevent a mess and a lot of lost batter, we cover the bottom and sides of the pan with two sheets of heavy-duty aluminum foil. This is also helpful for preventing water from seeping into the cake pan if you're baking in a water bath. You can also place the pan on a rimmed baking sheet to catch any leaks.

CHOCOLATE-ORANGE ANGEL FOOD CAKE

serves 12

A tube pan is essential for angel food cake, and we strongly recommend using one with a removable bottom. If your tube pan has a removable bottom, you do not need to line it with parchment. Do not grease the pan. Greasing prevents the cake from climbing up and clinging to the sides as it bakes, producing a disappointingly short cake. Finely grating the chocolate is key here; use either a Microplane grater or the fine holes of a box grater.

¾	cup (3 ounces) cake flour
1½	cups (10½ ounces) sugar, divided
12	large egg whites, room temperature
1	teaspoon cream of tartar
¼	teaspoon table salt
1	tablespoon Grand Marnier
2	teaspoons grated orange zest
½	teaspoon vanilla extract
2	ounces bittersweet chocolate, finely grated

1 Adjust oven rack to lower-middle position and heat oven to 325 degrees. Line 16-cup tube pan with parchment paper but do not grease. Whisk flour and ¾ cup sugar together in bowl; set aside.

2 Using stand mixer fitted with whisk attachment, whip egg whites, cream of tartar, and salt on medium-low speed until foamy, about 1 minute. Increase speed to medium-high and whip to soft, billowy mounds, about 1 minute. Gradually add remaining ¾ cup sugar and whip until soft, glossy peaks form, 1 to 2 minutes. Add Grand Marnier, orange zest, and vanilla and whip until just blended.

3 Sift flour mixture over whites, about 3 tablespoons at a time, gently folding mixture into whites after each addition with large rubber spatula. Gently fold in chocolate.

4 Gently transfer batter to prepared pan and smooth top with rubber spatula. Bake until golden brown and top springs back when pressed firmly, 50 minutes to 1 hour, rotating pan halfway through baking.

5 If pan has prongs around rim for elevating cake, invert pan on them. If not, invert pan over neck of bottle or funnel so that air can circulate all around it. Let cake cool completely in pan, 2 to 3 hours.

6 Run thin knife around edge of pan to loosen cake, then gently tap pan upside down on counter to release cake. Peel off parchment and turn cake right side up onto platter. Serve. (Cake can be stored at room temperature for up to 2 days or refrigerated for up to 4 days.)

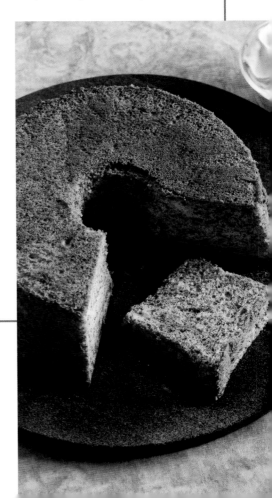

Is It OK to Bake Cupcakes and Muffins in an Unlined Tin?

You can certainly bake cupcakes and muffins in an unlined tin—in fact, we always make muffins this way. We like nonstick muffin tins so a spray of vegetable oil, and a dusting of flour if it's called for, should guarantee you won't be prying out muffins. That said, cupcake liners (paper or foil) cling to the batter and, subsequently, the baked cake, so they prevent the batter from directly touching the pan. This prevents the cake bottoms from forming a browned exterior crust that we love for muffins but that isn't so appropriate for soft cake. (Some cakes are particularly delicate and could be prone to sticking; if a cupcake recipe calls for liners, you should use them.) And, of course, liners can be decorative and fun for parties.

Can I Bake a Half Batch of Cupcakes or Muffins in a Standard Muffin Tin?

Yes, and we're aware that a myth surrounding this exists. Some small-batch bakers contend that you should use a 6-cup muffin tin, and that if you don't own one, you should fill the empty cups in a standard pan with water. The idea is that the water serves two functions: It prevents the pan from warping and acts as a "heat sink" to ensure that cupcakes or muffins next to empty cups heat evenly (avoiding stunted growth or spotty browning). We tested this theory by baking one muffin tin completely filled with batter, one tin in which only half of the 12 cups were filled with batter and the remaining six with water, and one tin in which six of the cups were filled with batter and the other six left empty. The results? All the muffins had the same height, texture, and color and none of the tins warped. This makes sense: In a full 12-cup muffin tin, all but the two center muffins (or cupcakes) are directly exposed to the oven's heat on at least one side to no ill effect.

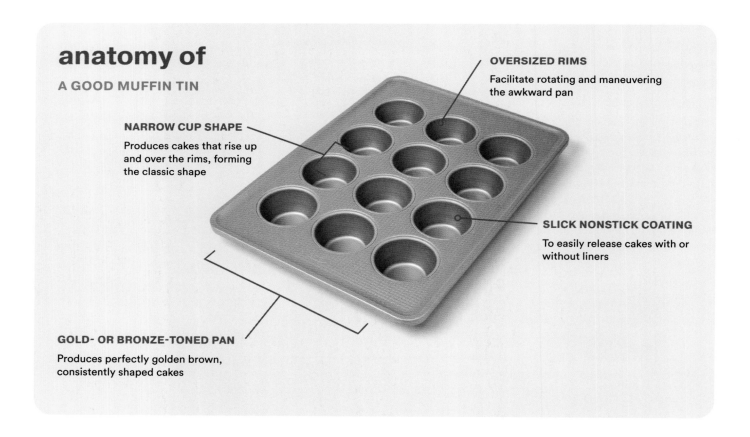

anatomy of
A GOOD MUFFIN TIN

OVERSIZED RIMS
Facilitate rotating and maneuvering the awkward pan

NARROW CUP SHAPE
Produces cakes that rise up and over the rims, forming the classic shape

SLICK NONSTICK COATING
To easily release cakes with or without liners

GOLD- OR BRONZE-TONED PAN
Produces perfectly golden brown, consistently shaped cakes

BUTTER FAN ROLLS

makes 12 rolls

Popping these buttery layered rolls into the cups of a muffin tin to bake gives them their distinctive fanned-out shape as the half that pokes out above the muffin tin expands while the half confined within the cups is kept more compressed.

¾	cup warm milk (110 degrees)
¼	cup (1¾ ounces) sugar
1	large egg plus 1 large yolk, room temperature
1	tablespoon instant or rapid-rise yeast
3½	cups (17½ ounces) all-purpose flour
2	teaspoons table salt
8	tablespoons unsalted butter, cut into 8 pieces and softened, plus 4 tablespoons melted

1 Combine milk, sugar, egg and yolk, and yeast in bowl of stand mixer and let sit until foamy, about 3 minutes. Fit stand mixer with dough hook, add flour and salt, and knead on medium-low speed until dough is shaggy, about 2 minutes.

2 With mixer running, add softened butter, 1 piece at a time, until incorporated. Continue to knead until dough is smooth, about 5 minutes. Transfer dough to greased large bowl. Cover bowl tightly with plastic wrap and let dough rise at room temperature until doubled in size, about 1½ hours.

3 Grease 12-cup muffin tin. Press down on dough to deflate and transfer to lightly floured counter (do not overflour counter). Divide dough in half with bench scraper. Roll 1 half into 15 by 12-inch rectangle with long side parallel to counter's edge.

4 Using pizza wheel, cut dough vertically into six 12 by 2½-inch strips. Brush tops of 5 strips evenly with 1 tablespoon melted butter, leaving 1 strip unbuttered. Stack strips squarely on top of one another, buttered to unbuttered side, finishing with unbuttered strip on top.

5 Using sharp knife, cut stacked dough strips crosswise into 6 equal stacks. Place 1 stack, cut side up, in each of 6 muffin cups. Repeat with remaining dough half and 1 tablespoon melted butter. Cover muffin tin loosely with plastic and let dough rise at room temperature until doubled in size, 1¼ to 1½ hours. Adjust oven rack to upper-middle position and heat oven to 350 degrees.

6 Bake until golden brown, 20 to 25 minutes, rotating muffin tin halfway through baking. Brush rolls with remaining 2 tablespoons melted butter. Let rolls cool in muffin tin on wire rack for 5 minutes. Remove rolls from muffin tin and transfer to wire rack. Serve warm or at room temperature.

real talk with lisa

DO MORE WITH YOUR MUFFIN TINS

You can use the individual cups of a muffin tin to make much more than muffins and cupcakes. They work great for single-serving frittatas, dinner rolls, popovers, mini cheesecakes, and tiny pies, both savory and sweet. You can even use the holes of an empty tin to hold ingredients for your mise en place when cooking. Flipped over, the muffin tin makes a great stand-in for a cooling rack too.

MUFFIN TIN DOUGHNUTS

makes 12 doughnuts

These muffins are cake doughnuts in disguise, with a very tender crumb, a crisp exterior, nutmeg and cinnamon flavors, and a buttery spiced coating. And because they're baked in a muffin tin, there's no rolling, cutting, or hot oil required.

DOUGHNUTS

2¾	cups (13¾ ounces) all-purpose flour
1	cup (7 ounces) sugar
¼	cup (1 ounce) cornstarch
1	tablespoon baking powder
1	teaspoon salt
½	teaspoon ground nutmeg
1	cup buttermilk
8	tablespoons unsalted butter, melted
2	large eggs plus 1 large yolk

COATING

1	cup (7 ounces) sugar
2	teaspoons ground cinnamon
8	tablespoons unsalted butter, melted

1 for the doughnuts Adjust oven rack to middle position and heat oven to 400 degrees. Spray 12-cup muffin tin with vegetable oil spray. Whisk flour, sugar, cornstarch, baking powder, salt, and nutmeg together in bowl. Whisk buttermilk, melted butter, and eggs and yolk together in second bowl. Add buttermilk mixture to flour mixture and stir with rubber spatula until just combined.

2 Using ice cream scoop or large spoon, divide batter evenly among prepared muffin cups. Bake until doughnuts are lightly browned and toothpick inserted in center comes out clean, 19 to 22 minutes, rotating muffin tin halfway through baking. Let doughnuts cool in muffin tin on wire rack for 5 minutes.

3 for the coating Whisk sugar and cinnamon together in bowl. Remove doughnuts from muffin tin. Working with 1 doughnut at a time, brush all over with melted butter, then roll in cinnamon sugar, pressing lightly to adhere. Transfer to wire rack and let cool for 15 minutes before serving.

worth it

MINI MUFFIN TIN

The possibilities for baking with a mini muffin tin go beyond mini muffins. We love petite treats both sweet and savory such as elegant, nutty French financiers and rich two-bite pão de queijo. The pan is ideal for making chocolate candies with a shape to hold rich fillings like peanut butter cups or for molding cookie dough into tassies that feature mousse or nut fillings.

My Pie Crusts Always Come Out Underdone. Is the Pan to Blame?

It could be. You can generally choose from glass, ceramic, and metal pie plates. If you grew up with a Pyrex pie plate, it might be time to move on. While we've found that metal and ceramic plates can produce nicely browned bottom crusts, the pies we've made in glass plates disappoint with softer, paler bottoms. And although ceramic plates can be really pretty, we prefer metal. It's a better conductor of heat than ceramic or especially glass, which heats slowly. Since steel (the typical material) is so strong, metal pie plates can be made thinner than plates of other materials, which helps them heat faster. Gold-colored metal plates are particularly great at turning out crusts that aren't too light or too dark—beautifully golden and crisp. That said, if you're rolling your dough out too thick, making overly watery fillings, or you're not parbaking your single-crust doughs, you might not be able to blame the pan.

Can I Make a Tart in a Pan Without a Removable Bottom?

Good luck. We refuse to use tart pans without removable bottoms. We've done it and we never again want to chisel a delicate tart out of a solid pan. Pans with removable bottoms allow you to remove the rim before sliding the tart off the disk base and onto a serving plate. That said, it's OK to buy individual-size tart pans without removable bottoms—the much smaller tarts pop out easily.

worthwhile one-hit wonders

Single-use kitchen tools such as specialized baking pans have their place. Here are a few we think are worth it—assuming you plan to use them often.

USE THIS . . .	TO DO THIS!
Brioche Pan	Make loaves of traditionally shaped brioche with fluted sides and a slightly conical shape.
Tart Pan	Produce tarts with evenly browned crusts that come out of the pan in one piece thanks to the removable bottom.
Pullman Loaf Pan	Bake squared-off loaves of bread with firm, compact crumbs—perfect for sandwiches.
Soufflé Dish	Allow a finicky soufflé to rise up tall with the help of the soufflé dish's perfectly straight sides.
Baker's Edge Pan	Turn out brownies (or lasagna if that's more your speed) that are nearly all crispy-chewy edge.
Hot Dog Pan	Produce and neatly release 10 perfectly browned hot dog buns.

Finish with Flair

The gorgeous goodies you see behind the glass bakery case benefit from a bit more than just the baking essentials. If you want to level up your baking, take a look at the tools that help finish your goods with flair.

Do I Need Real Biscuit Cutters or Can I Make Do with a Drinking Glass?

Crafty home cooks punch out biscuits with old aluminum cans, overturned glasses, and even Mason jar rings. But using a makeshift cutter with rounded edges can compress the sides of dough, leading to misshapen biscuits. We highly recommend you use actual biscuit cutters, round cutting tools with sharp edges that make even cuts and thus produce tall, symmetrical biscuits.

But even among dedicated cutters are less-than-sharp tools. Look for a sturdy design; flimsy and malleable cutters make misshapen biscuits. Don't fall for handles: They limit your range of motion when cutting the dough. Rounded edges, and not double-sided cutters, are enough to protect your hands. Who knew there could be so much to consider about biscuit cutter design?

Biscuit cut with a metal cutter

Biscuit cut with a drinking glass

Hannah Says . . .

Biscuit cutters are useful for more than biscuits. I use mine in a million different ways. As round cookie cutters. For stamping out mini, individual cakes. For cutting vents or creative dough designs in pie dough. For making the hole in toad in the hole (literally just had this for breakfast). To shape dough for crackers, empanadas, shu mai, and pierogi. To cut out doughnut holes. For shaping ice cream sandwiches. When I want to pretend I am a chef on one of my favorite shows, Below Deck, I use them to shape foods such as crab and avocado salad, scrambled eggs, or rice into fancy-shmancy little towers. Gotta get that tip money, ya know?

POTATO BISCUITS WITH CHIVES

makes 12 biscuits

The potato flakes in this biscuit recipe makes them ultra light and tender. Once you've stamped out the first biscuits with a 2½-inch cutter, you can reroll the scraps and stamp out more without worrying about the biscuits becoming tough.

- 2½ cups (12½ ounces) all-purpose flour
- ¾ cup (1¾ ounces) plain instant mashed potato flakes
- ⅓ cup chopped fresh chives
- 4 teaspoons baking powder
- ½ teaspoon baking soda
- 1 tablespoon sugar
- 1 teaspoon table salt
- 8 tablespoons unsalted butter, cut into ½-inch pieces and chilled, plus 2 tablespoons unsalted butter
- 4 tablespoons vegetable shortening, cut into ½-inch pieces and chilled
- 1¼ cups buttermilk, chilled

1 Adjust oven rack to middle position and heat oven to 450 degrees. Line rimmed baking sheet with parchment paper. Process flour, potato flakes, chives, baking powder, baking soda, sugar, and salt in food processor until combined, about 15 seconds. Add chilled butter and shortening and pulse until mixture resembles coarse crumbs, 7 to 9 pulses.

2 Transfer flour mixture to large bowl. Stir in buttermilk with rubber spatula until combined, turning and pressing dough until no dry flour remains. Turn out dough onto lightly floured counter and knead briefly, 8 to 10 turns, to form smooth, cohesive ball. Roll out dough into 9-inch circle, about ¾ inch thick.

3 Using floured 2½-inch round cutter, stamp out 8 or 9 biscuits and arrange upside down on prepared sheet. Gather dough scraps and gently pat into ¾-inch-thick circle. Stamp out 3 or 4 biscuits and transfer to sheet.

4 Bake until biscuits begin to rise, about 5 minutes, then rotate sheet and reduce oven temperature to 400 degrees. Continue to bake until golden brown, 10 to 12 minutes. Melt remaining 2 tablespoons butter and brush on biscuit tops. Transfer biscuits to wire rack and let cool for 5 minutes before serving.

Do I Need Cake Strips?

Cake strips, also known as magic strips, are engineered to correct uneven baking by applying an insulating layer around the pan. They come in different materials but we prefer silicone. Are you skeptical that something that looks like an exercise band can transform your cakes from dark and domed to even toned and flat? We understand. But without insulation from the oven's heat, the cake's edges can bake more quickly while the center tends to dome, crack, or rise quickly before collapsing. Cake strips work but their effect is noteworthy only if you own dark pans. If you have light or golden-colored pans (see page 225) you can skip the strips.

Note that you can easily get the desired effects with homemade strips: Simply dampen cheesecloth or newspaper, fold it into 2-inch strips of aluminum foil, and tie the strips with twine.

FLUFFY YELLOW LAYER CAKE

serves 10 to 12

This simple but delicious layer cake is the perfect opportunity to practice your cake frosting skills. A rotating cake stand, offset spatula, and a few strategically placed strips of parchment paper make it easy.

CAKE

2½	cups (10 ounces) cake flour
1¼	teaspoons baking powder
¼	teaspoon baking soda
¾	teaspoon table salt
1¾	cups (12¼ ounces) sugar, divided
1	cup buttermilk, room temperature
10	tablespoons unsalted butter, melted and cooled
3	large eggs, separated, plus 3 large yolks, room temperature
3	tablespoons vegetable oil
2	teaspoons vanilla extract
	Pinch cream of tartar

FROSTING

20	tablespoons (2½ sticks) unsalted butter, softened
1	cup (4 ounces) confectioners' sugar
¾	cup (2¼ ounces) Dutch-processed cocoa powder
	Pinch table salt
¾	cup light corn syrup
1	teaspoon vanilla extract
8	ounces milk chocolate, melted and cooled slightly

1 for the cake Adjust oven rack to middle position and heat oven to 350 degrees. Grease two 9-inch round cake pans, line with parchment paper, grease parchment, and flour pans. Whisk flour, baking powder, baking soda, salt, and 1½ cups sugar together in bowl. Whisk buttermilk, melted butter, egg yolks, oil, and vanilla together in second bowl.

2 Using stand mixer fitted with whisk attachment, whip egg whites and cream of tartar on medium-low speed until foamy, about 1 minute. Increase speed to medium-high and whip whites to soft billowy mounds, about 1 minute. Gradually add remaining ¼ cup sugar and whip until glossy, stiff peaks form, 2 to 3 minutes; transfer to third bowl.

3 Add flour mixture to now-empty mixer bowl and mix on low speed, gradually adding buttermilk mixture and mixing until almost incorporated (a few streaks of dry flour will remain), about 15 seconds. Scrape down bowl, then mix on medium-low speed until smooth and fully incorporated, 10 to 15 seconds.

4 Using rubber spatula, stir one-third of whites into batter. Gently fold remaining whites into batter until no white streaks remain. Divide batter evenly between prepared pans and smooth tops with rubber spatula. Gently tap pans on counter to settle batter. Bake until toothpick inserted in center comes out clean, 20 to 22 minutes, switching and rotating pans halfway through baking. Let cakes cool in pans on wire rack for 10 minutes. Remove cakes from pans, discarding parchment, and let cool completely on rack, about 2 hours. (Cake layers can be stored at room temperature for up to 24 hours or frozen for up to 1 month; defrost at room temperature.)

5 for the frosting Process butter, sugar, cocoa, and salt in food processor until smooth, about 30 seconds, scraping down sides of bowl as needed. Add corn syrup and vanilla and process until just combined, 5 to 10 seconds. Scrape down sides of bowl, then add chocolate and process until smooth and creamy, 10 to 15 seconds. (Frosting can be kept at room temperature for up to 3 hours or refrigerated for up to 3 days; if refrigerated, let stand at room temperature for 1 hour and stir before using.)

6 Line edges of cake platter with 4 strips of parchment to keep platter clean. Place 1 cake layer on platter. Spread 1½ cups frosting evenly over top, right to edge of cake. Top with second cake layer, press lightly to adhere, then spread remaining frosting evenly over top and sides of cake. Carefully remove parchment strips before serving.

small tools with big, beautiful returns

Sometimes, the smallest, most inexpensive, or most common tools can assist you in crafting desserts with a professional looking finish. You should definitely add these to your baking drawer.

USE THIS . . .	TO DO THIS!
Small Metal Cookie Cutters	• Cut out cookies with clean edges • Cut a window in the center of a cookie • Act as a stencil that can be filled with sprinkles to decorate cupcakes • Create embellishments for pie crusts
Small Offset Spatula	• Neatly glaze cookies • Frost cupcakes • Scrape away excess chocolate coating • Level custard pie fillings • Create swirls in meringue toppings
Ruler	• Cut dough strips with clean lines for cookies and lattice crusts • Aid in cutting uniform cookies from "slice and bake" rolls • Measure rolled-out pastry and bread dough
Small Kitchen Torch	• Toast meringue • Evenly caramelize crème brûlée coatings • Finish off gratin of fruit and sabayon
Vegetable Peeler	• Make chocolate curls • Zest citrus for candied citrus peel garnishes

Is a Zipper-Lock Bag a Good Substitute for a Pastry Bag?

We prefer disposable plastic pastry bags to reusable cloth bags (we've found them awkward to handle and prone to holding on to stains and odors). Gallon-size freezer bags can be outfitted with a pastry tip in a pinch, but the wider angle of zipper-lock bags makes them prone to ripping when used with thick or heavy fillings such as pate a choux dough.

Why Does the First Slice of Pie Always Fall Apart?

Even if you cool your pie long enough (and this is probably longer than you think—around 3 hours), the first slice usually comes out broken and messy. That's because there isn't any wiggle room in the packed pie plate to help coax out the slice. We've long relied on a simple trick to make the first slice as pretty as the last: We make three cuts before removing the first slice (essentially cutting two pie slices). The extra cut allows for movement in the pie, making it easier to tidily wiggle out the first piece.

Do I Need to Buy Dedicated Pie Weights?

Pie weights go into a raw pie crust during blind baking (partially or fully baking a pie dough before the filling goes in) to prevent the sad slumping that can happen. The weights hold the dough perfectly in place and keep its shape. You can certainly use tried-and-true household pie fillers for blind baking such as dried beans, rice, coins, or sugar. But if you bake pies often, you'll want a stash of weights to do the job every time. Buy them once, and they're infinitely reusable—and a lot easier to wrangle than messy sugar, small grains of rice, or heavy coins.

What's Better: Silicone or Natural Pastry Brush Bristles?

While a silicone brush, with its flexible bristles, can be a helpful tool in the savory kitchen, we recommend you go natural for baking. A pastry brush with natural bristles can apply egg wash or glaze to delicate doughs and pastry, spread butter or oil on paper-thin phyllo dough, and brush crumbs from cake layers without damaging these delicate items or leaving visible lines. Just avoid high heat applications, which can burn bristles and melt the glue that secures them.

Lisa Says . . .

Skip the specialty pie tools. We tested so many silly contraptions for making pie lattices, and they were overly complicated, messy, and not very effective. The best way turned out to be the simplest. Get a ruler and a pizza cutter to cut dough into even, long strips. Lay half of the strips parallel across the pie in a single direction, evenly spaced. Peel back every other strip and lay on a cross piece, and put the strips back. Then peel back the alternate strips and lay on the next piece. Repeat. Voilà, you have made a lattice pie crust!

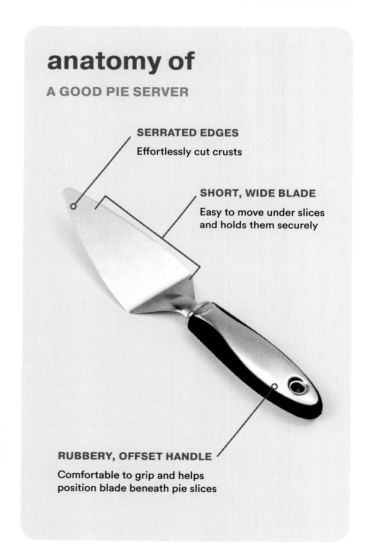

anatomy of

A GOOD PIE SERVER

SERRATED EDGES
Effortlessly cut crusts

SHORT, WIDE BLADE
Easy to move under slices and holds them securely

RUBBERY, OFFSET HANDLE
Comfortable to grip and helps position blade beneath pie slices

ORANGE-CHOCOLATE CUSTARD PIE

serves 8

Pie weights (or a DIY substitute) ensure that this pie's flaky crust doesn't slump during blind baking, and a good pie server plus one simple technique (see page 238) will keep that the first piece looking as good as it tastes. To give the edge of the crust a golden sheen, lightly brush on some egg wash (1 egg lightly beaten with 1 tablespoon of water) with a pastry brush.

DOUGH

10	tablespoons unsalted butter, chilled, divided
1¼	cups (6¼ ounces) all-purpose flour, divided
1	tablespoon sugar
½	teaspoon table salt
¼	cup ice water, divided

FILLING

⅔	cup (4⅔ ounces) sugar
3	large eggs
3	tablespoons cornstarch
1	tablespoon grated orange zest plus 1½ tablespoons juice
⅛	teaspoon table salt
2	cups whole milk
1	cup heavy cream
1	teaspoon vanilla extract
6	ounces bittersweet chocolate, chopped fine

WHIPPED CREAM

1	cup heavy cream, chilled
1	teaspoon orange zest plus 2 tablespoons juice
1	tablespoon sugar
	Pinch table salt
	Chocolate shavings

1 for the dough Grate 2 tablespoons butter on large holes of box grater and place in freezer. Cut remaining 8 tablespoons butter into ½-inch cubes.

2 Pulse ¾ cup flour, sugar, and salt in food processor until combined, 2 pulses. Add cubed butter and process until homogeneous paste forms, about 30 seconds. Using your hands, carefully break paste into 2-inch chunks and redistribute evenly around processor blade. Add remaining ½ cup flour and pulse until mixture is broken into pieces no larger than 1 inch (most pieces will be much smaller), 4 to 5 pulses. Transfer mixture to bowl. Add grated butter and toss until butter pieces are separated and coated with flour.

3 Sprinkle 2 tablespoons ice water over mixture. Toss with rubber spatula until mixture is evenly moistened. Sprinkle remaining 2 tablespoons ice water over mixture and toss to combine. Press dough with spatula until dough sticks together. Transfer dough to sheet of plastic wrap. Draw edges of plastic over dough and press firmly on sides and top to form compact, fissure-free mass. Wrap in plastic and form into 5-inch disk. Refrigerate dough for at least 2 hours or up to 2 days. Let chilled dough sit on counter to soften slightly, about 10 minutes, before rolling. (Wrapped dough can be frozen for up to 1 month. If frozen, let dough thaw completely on counter before rolling.)

4 Roll dough into 12-inch circle on well-floured counter. Roll dough loosely around rolling pin and gently unroll it onto 9-inch pie plate, letting excess dough hang over edge. Ease dough into plate by gently lifting edge of dough with your hand while pressing into plate bottom with your other hand. Trim overhang to ½ inch beyond lip of plate.

5 Tuck overhang under itself; folded edge should be flush with edge of plate. Crimp dough evenly around edge of plate. Wrap dough-lined plate loosely in plastic and refrigerate until firm, about 30 minutes. Adjust oven rack to middle position and heat oven to 350 degrees.

6 Remove plastic and line chilled pie shell with double layer of aluminum foil, covering edges to prevent burning, and fill with pie weights. Bake on foil-lined rimmed baking sheet until edges are set and just beginning to turn golden, 25 to 30 minutes, rotating sheet halfway through baking. Remove foil and weights, rotate sheet, and continue to bake crust until golden brown and crisp, 10 to 15 minutes. Transfer sheet to wire rack. (Crust must still be warm when filling is added.)

7 for the filling While crust bakes, whisk sugar, eggs, cornstarch, orange zest and juice, and salt together in bowl. Bring milk and cream to simmer in large saucepan over medium heat. Slowly whisk 1 cup of hot milk mixture into egg mixture to temper, then slowly whisk tempered egg mixture into remaining milk mixture in saucepan. Cook over medium heat, whisking constantly, until mixture is thickened, bubbling, and registers 180 degrees, 30 to 90 seconds (mixture should have consistency of thick pudding). Strain mixture through fine-mesh strainer into clean bowl, then stir in vanilla. Transfer 1½ cups custard to second bowl; whisk in chocolate until smooth.

8 With pie crust still on sheet, pour chocolate mixture into warm crust, smoothing top with clean spatula into even layer. Gently pour remaining custard over chocolate layer, smoothing top with clean spatula into even layer. Bake until center of pie registers 160 degrees, 14 to 18 minutes. Let pie cool completely on wire rack, about 4 hours.

9 for the whipped cream Using stand mixer fitted with whisk attachment, whip cream, sugar, orange zest and juice, and salt on medium-low speed until foamy, about 1 minute. Increase speed to high and whip until soft peaks form, 1 to 3 minutes. (Whipped cream can be refrigerated in fine-mesh strainer set over small bowl and covered with plastic for up to 8 hours.) Spread whipped cream attractively over pie and sprinkle with chocolate shavings. Serve. (Pie can be wrapped tightly in plastic and refrigerated for up to 2 days.)

6 Tips for Making Cake a Cut Above the Rest

Great looking cake comes from decoration and embellishment, but it also starts with a strong foundation. Learn how to use your tools to make better cakes from building to finishing.

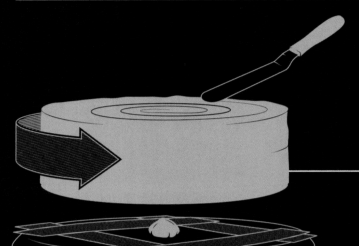

1 ROTATE THE CAKE

A smooth-spinning cake stand feels like a luxury when you're using it, but there are affordable options. Building the cake on one allows you to access all sides with a turn, and makes the frosting process smooth and seamless.

2 LINE THE CAKE BASE

Parchment strikes again. Placing the first cake layer on a square made from four parchment paper strips keeps the stand or platter clean during frosting. When you're done, you can easily slip the strips out from under the cake for a neat presentation.

3 SAW LEVEL SLICES

A cake with more than two layers often requires you to slice a taller layer horizontally. A long serrated knife isn't just for bread and tomatoes; in fact, it's essential here. Well, actually, two knives come in handy. First, use a paring knife to mark the midpoint at several places around the sides of the cake. Next score the entire circumference of the cake with your serrated knife. Following the scored lines, rotate the cake, then run the knife around the cake several times, cutting inward. Once the knife is inside the cake, use a back-and-forth motion to finish slicing.

4 EMPLOY A CAKE LIFTER

Handling cakes can be tricky, whether you're stacking fragile, just-split layers as you frost them or moving a finished cake to a serving platter. These large spatula-like devices slip under and support cakes, preventing breakage.

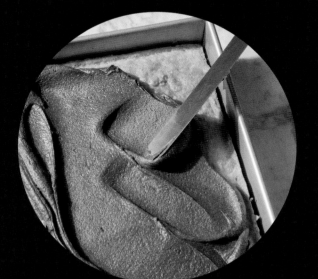

5 NEVER FROST WITH A KNIFE

There is no substitute for a large offset spatula for neatly frosting cakes. The long, narrow blade is ideal for scooping and spreading frosting, and it bends like a stairstep where it meets the handle for better leverage. The blades can be as long as 10 inches, but we've found that 7- and 8-inch lengths are ideal because they can get good coverage on layer cakes but are still maneuverable inside baking pans.

6 USE A BENCH SCRAPER

Hold this rigid tool lightly against the side (or top) of a frosted cake and spin your rotating cake stand to smooth out air bubbles, streaks, and seams.

worth it

BENCH SCRAPER

Bench scrapers are invaluable tools in commercial bakeries and pastry kitchens; they're the baker's version of a pitmaster's tongs or a short-order cook's spatula. But they are also incredibly handy to have at home—and not just for cutting dough or scraping the counter clean. They're awesome for evening out the frosting on the side of a cake. You can push the blade of your bench scraper over a block of chocolate to make decorative curls or use it for portioning butter and cutting that butter into flour for biscuits or pie dough. It's handy for cutting a log of chilled cookie dough into coins for baking or simply scooping and moving chopped ingredients into the mixer or mixing bowl. The humble tool's potential is limitless.

6 Tips for Piping Like a Pro

The ability to pipe neatly isn't an innate skill. To improve, follow these simple tips and practice, practice, practice!

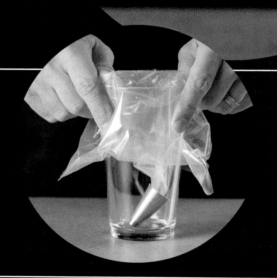

1 PREVENT LEAKS

More than likely, you'll be preparing your piping bag in advance of needing to use it. To avoid prevent leaks during this pause, place your pastry tip in the bag, twist the bag near the tip, and then gently press the twisted portion into the tip to create a temporary barrier before filling the bag. (When you're ready to pipe, pull on the tip to release the barrier.)

2 FILL EFFICIENTLY

If you've ever filled a pastry bag and gotten more filling on your arm than in the bag, this tip's for you. Place the pastry bag in a tall container (a plastic quart container or even a tall drinking glass works) and fold down the sides. Fill the bag just halfway as multiple smaller loads, versus a single big load, are easier to manage, especially if you have small hands. Pipe and repeat.

3 DO THE TWIST

You want your filling to come out the tip of your bag, not the top. To encourage downward motion, twist the upper half of the bag closed to push contents down toward tip. The twisted upper half will allow you to continue exerting pressure on the filling as you pipe.

4 REMOVE AIR BUBBLES

Before piping in earnest, press out a small amount of filling on parchment paper or another surface; this eliminates air bubbles that can cause filling to spurt unevenly.

5 GET EVERY LAST BIT

We hate waste, especially tasty waste. When your pastry bag is almost empty, lay the bag on its side and use a plastic bowl scraper or credit card (avoid a metal tool, since it can tear bag) on the outside of bag to press contents toward the tip.

6 CLEAN AND REUSE

We said we like disposable pastry bags (see page 237), but that doesn't mean you have to dispose of them every time. As long as it isn't punctured, a disposable pastry bag can be reused. To clean the bag, turn it inside out and scrub gently with warm, soapy water; stand up to air-dry.

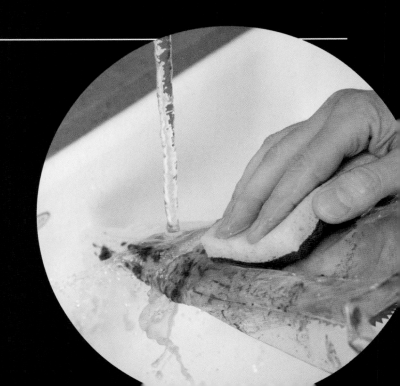

IN THIS SECTION . . .
Bread machines
Bread ovens
Lava rocks
Proofing bins
Couches
Lames
Bannetons

Break Bread

Bread heads weigh the virtues of yeast versus starters, mixing methods, recipe formulations, and proper equipment. We'll tackle the last one here.

Can I Bake Great Bread Without Using Tons of Specialized Equipment?

Just because there's equipment to help you with every bread step doesn't mean you need to own all of it. There are still many bread recipes that you can make with your hands (in fact, some benefit from it; see recipe at right), though we admit owning a stand mixer (see page 136) and food processor (see page 134) will help you efficiently make doughs of all kinds. Here are eight of our favorite tools to get you into the bread game.

BASIC BREAD GEAR	WHAT IT'S FOR
Digital Scale (page 91)	Measuring ingredients accurately
Baking Sheet (page 58)	Baking free-form loaves
Muffin Tin (page 230)	Holding shaped rolls
Cake Pan (page 224)	Baking sweet and savory pull-apart rolls
Loaf Pan (page 225)	Baking sandwich breads
Dutch Oven (page 48)	Baking artisan-quality bread at home
Paring Knife (page 73)	Creating neat slashes in bread dough before baking

What Kind of Vessel Is Best for Letting Dough Rise?

You have mixing bowls, and your dough can certainly rise in them, but we've found a nice trick to help gauge a dough's size. Many recipes call for shaping the dough when it's doubled in size, so we like to put the dough in a clear plastic storage container with volume measurements on the side and a lid (we like these for storing flour as well). The measurements come in handy while monitoring rise, and the lid means that you don't have to use plastic wrap. (These containers are also great for brining.)

NO-KNEAD RUSTIC LOAF

makes 1 loaf

The humid environment of a preheated Dutch oven initiates a dramatic open crumb for a bakery-quality rustic loaf. We use a mild American lager, such as Budweiser; strongly flavored beers will make this bread taste bitter. While we prefer the flavor that beer adds, you can substitute an equal amount of water. You will need a bowl that is at least 9 inches wide and 4 inches deep to cover the dough in step 6.

2¾	cups (15⅛ ounces) bread flour
1½	teaspoons table salt
¼	teaspoon instant or rapid-rise yeast
¾	cup plus 2 tablespoons (7 ounces) water, room temperature
½	cup (4 ounces) mild lager, room temperature
1	tablespoon distilled white vinegar

1 Whisk flour, salt, and yeast together in large bowl. Using rubber spatula, fold water, beer, and vinegar into flour mixture, scraping up dry flour from bottom of bowl and pressing dough until cohesive and shaggy and all flour is incorporated.

2 Cover bowl tightly with plastic wrap and let sit at room temperature for at least 8 hours or up to 18 hours.

3 Using greased bowl scraper or your wet fingertips, fold dough over itself by lifting and folding edge of dough toward middle and pressing to seal. Turn bowl 90 degrees and fold dough again; repeat turning bowl and folding dough 6 more times (for a total of 8 folds). Flip dough seam side down in bowl, cover with plastic, and let rest for 15 minutes.

4 Lay 18 by 12-inch sheet of parchment paper on counter and spray lightly with vegetable oil spray. Transfer dough seam side up onto lightly floured counter and pat into rough 9-inch circle using your lightly floured hands. Using bowl scraper or your floured fingertips, lift and fold edge of dough toward center, pressing to seal. Repeat 5 more times (for a total of 6 folds), evenly spacing folds around circumference of dough. Press down on dough to seal, then use bench scraper to gently flip dough seam side down.

5 Using both hands, cup side of dough farthest away from you and pull dough toward you, keeping pinky fingers and side of palm in contact with counter and applying slight pressure to dough as it drags to create tension. (If dough slides across surface of counter without rolling, remove excess flour. If dough sticks to counter or hands, lightly sprinkle counter or hands with flour.) Rotate dough ball 90 degrees, reposition dough ball at top of counter, and repeat pulling dough until taut round ball forms, at least 4 more times. Using your floured hands or bench scraper, transfer dough seam side down to center of prepared parchment.

6 Cover dough with inverted large bowl. Let rise until dough has doubled in size and springs back minimally when poked gently with your finger, 1 to 2 hours.

7 Thirty minutes before baking, adjust oven rack to middle position, place Dutch oven with lid on rack, and heat oven to 475 degrees. Using sharp knife or single-edge razor blade, make one 6-inch-long, ½-inch-deep slash with swift, fluid motion along top of loaf. Carefully remove hot pot from oven and, using parchment as sling, gently transfer dough to hot pot. Working quickly and reinforcing score in top of loaf if needed, cover pot and return to oven.

8 Reduce oven temperature to 425 degrees and bake loaf in covered pot for 30 minutes. Remove lid and continue to bake until loaf is deep golden brown and registers at least 205 degrees, 10 to 15 minutes. Using parchment sling, carefully remove loaf from hot pot and transfer to wire rack; discard parchment. Let cool completely, about 3 hours, before slicing.

Hannah Says . . .

A dry storage container such as a Cambro is awesome for storing dough while it rises. When a recipe calls for letting dough rise, going away for two hours, and then coming back when the dough's doubled in size, I can never remember what the dough looked like in the first place. With the plastic container, you can leave a mark or a rubber band showing exactly what the dough's starting height was.

WHITE SANDWICH BREAD

makes 1 loaf

The quintessential sandwich loaf is tall and domed, which you can achieve with a good loaf pan with sharply defined edges. The test kitchen's preferred loaf pan measures 8½ by 4½ inches; if you use a 9 by 5-inch loaf pan, increase the shaped rising time and start checking for doneness 10 minutes earlier than advised in the recipe.

2½	cups (13¾ ounces) bread flour
2	teaspoons instant or rapid-rise yeast
1½	teaspoons table salt
¾	cup (6 ounces) whole milk, room temperature
⅓	cup (2⅔ ounces) water, room temperature
2	tablespoons unsalted butter, melted
2	tablespoons honey

1 Whisk flour, yeast, and salt together in bowl of stand mixer. Whisk milk, water, melted butter, and honey in 4-cup liquid measuring cup until honey has dissolved. Fit mixer with dough hook, then slowly add milk mixture to flour mixture and mix on low speed until cohesive dough starts to form and no dry flour remains, about 2 minutes, scraping down bowl as needed. Increase speed to medium-low and knead until dough is smooth and elastic and clears sides of bowl, about 8 minutes. Transfer dough to lightly floured counter and knead by hand to form smooth, round ball, about 30 seconds.

2 Place dough seam side down in lightly greased large bowl or container, cover tightly with plastic wrap, and let rise until doubled in volume, 1½ to 2 hours.

3 Grease 8½ by 4½-inch loaf pan. Press down on dough to deflate. Turn dough out onto lightly floured counter (side of dough that was against bowl should now be facing up). Press and stretch dough into 8 by 6-inch rectangle, with long side parallel to counter edge. Roll dough away from you into firm cylinder, keeping roll taut by tucking it under itself as you go. Pinch seam closed and place loaf seam side down in prepared pan, tucking ends as needed to match size of pan and pressing dough gently into corners.

4 Cover loosely with greased plastic and let rise until loaf reaches 1 inch above lip of pan and dough springs back minimally when poked gently with your finger, 1 to 1½ hours.

5 Adjust oven rack to lower-middle position and heat oven to 350 degrees. Mist loaf with water and bake until deep golden brown and loaf registers at least 205 degrees, 35 to 40 minutes, rotating pan halfway through baking. Let loaf cool in pan for 15 minutes. Remove loaf from pan and let cool completely on wire rack, about 3 hours, before slicing.

CHOCOLATE BABKA

makes 1 loaf

A bench scraper is just the tool to cleanly cut the dough into the separate pieces used to create this bread's iconic swirls. A good loaf pan promotes browning and a good rise.

DOUGH

2¼	cups (12⅓ ounces) bread flour
1½	teaspoons instant or rapid-rise yeast
½	cup (4 ounces) whole milk, room temperature
2	large eggs, room temperature
1	tablespoon grated orange zest (optional)
1	teaspoon vanilla extract
¼	cup (1¾ ounces) granulated sugar
½	teaspoon table salt
6	tablespoons unsalted butter, cut into 6 pieces and softened

FILLING

8	ounces bittersweet chocolate, chopped fine
8	tablespoons unsalted butter
½	cup (2 ounces) confectioners' sugar, sifted
½	cup (1½ ounces) unsweetened cocoa powder, sifted
½	teaspoon table salt

SYRUP

½	cup (3½ ounces) granulated sugar
¼	cup (2 ounces) water

1 for the dough Whisk flour and yeast together in bowl of stand mixer. Whisk milk; eggs; orange zest, if using; and vanilla in 2-cup liquid measuring cup until combined. Fit mixer with dough hook, then slowly add milk mixture to flour mixture and mix on low speed until cohesive dough starts to form and no dry flour remains, about 2 minutes, scraping down bowl as needed. Let rest for 15 minutes.

2 Add sugar and salt and knead on medium-low speed until incorporated, about 30 seconds. Increase speed to medium and, with mixer running, add butter 1 piece at a time, allowing each piece to incorporate before adding next, about 3 minutes total, scraping down bowl and dough hook as needed. Continue to knead on medium-high speed until dough begins to pull away from sides of bowl, 7 to 10 minutes longer. Transfer dough to greased large bowl or container, cover with plastic wrap, and let rise at room temperature until slightly puffy, about 1 hour. Refrigerate until firm, at least 2 hours or up to 24 hours.

3 for the filling Just before removing dough from refrigerator, combine chocolate and butter in medium bowl. Microwave at 50 percent power, stirring often, until chocolate is fully melted and smooth, about 2 minutes. Stir in sugar, cocoa, and salt until combined; set aside.

4 Adjust oven rack to middle position and heat oven to 325 degrees. Grease 8½ by 4½-inch loaf pan. Press down on dough to deflate. Transfer dough to lightly floured counter and press and roll into 18 by 12-inch rectangle, with short side parallel to counter edge. Using offset spatula, spread chocolate mixture evenly over dough, leaving ½-inch border on far edge. Roll dough away from you into even 12-inch cylinder, keeping roll taut by tucking it under itself as you go. Pinch seam to seal and reshape as needed. Arrange dough log so that short side is parallel to counter edge, then use greased bench scraper or sharp knife to cut in half lengthwise. Turn dough halves cut side up and arrange side by side. Pinch top ends together. Forming tight twist, cross left log over right log. Continue twisting, 5 times total, keeping cut sides facing up as much as possible. Pinch bottom ends together and carefully transfer to prepared pan cut sides up, reshaping as needed to fit into pan.

5 Set wire rack in rimmed baking sheet and center loaf pan on wire rack. Bake for 30 minutes. Rotate pan, cover loosely with aluminum foil, and bake until bread registers at least 200 degrees, 50 minutes to 1 hour.

6 for the syrup Meanwhile, combine sugar and water in small saucepan and heat over medium heat until sugar dissolves. Set aside off heat.

7 Remove babka from oven. Leaving babka in loaf pan, brush syrup evenly over entire surface of hot babka (use all of it). Let cool in loaf pan on wire rack for 1 hour. Carefully remove babka from pan and let cool completely on wire rack, about 2 hours. Slice 1 inch thick and serve.

worth it

DOUGH WHISK

When you mix sticky bread dough by hand, the biggest problem is getting it to blend instead of merely clump on your mixing tool. Enter the dough whisk, a thick, looping coil on a wooden handle that blends doughs and batters without clogging. But its utility doesn't stop at bread dough. The whisk works equally well for mixing muffin, cake, pancake, and crepe batters, whether stiff or loose. It also handles polenta, grits, oatmeal, and other porridges with ease, and can fold whipped egg whites into a soufflé base. In all these situations, not only does the dough whisk stir the mixture efficiently and eliminate lumps, but the flat profile of the parallel wire loops makes it great for digging into corners of the pot in a way that a rounded whisk can't.

A balloon whisk can get clogged with batter.

A dough whisk holds on to minimal batter.

Can I Make Really Good Bread With a Bread Machine?

While some might thumb their noses at the idea of a machine taking over the time-honored process of making bread by hand, bread machines can produce a variety of stellar loaves. If you're looking for hands-off convenience, just toss in your ingredients, walk away to do something else, and the house will start smelling like fresh bread. If you're willing to be a little more hands-on, you can venture beyond basic loaves such as white or wheat bread and even make pull-apart breads, dense and chewy rye, babka swirled with chocolate, pizza dough (to be baked in an oven), and more. A bread machine can't braid bread or make individually shaped rolls; however, you can manually braid a loaf or portion a dough into rolls and bake the bread or rolls in the machine. You can also use a machine to knead and proof a dough before baking it in your oven.

Lisa Says . . .

Bread machines often have special settings for making gluten-free bread, which is handy if you need to control the ingredients in your bread. Because gluten is a protein network that provides structure and chew to bread, gluten-free versions are more delicate and may need extra help to set up properly. In a bread machine, the bread mixes and bakes in a single, mostly enclosed pan, so it bakes without slumping.

How Do I Clean My Bread Machine?

The interior of a bread machine consists of a bread pan and at least one kneading paddle (we like two for ideal ingredient integration and even loaf shape). Sometimes after baking it's hard to remove the paddles—dough might work its way between the underside of the kneading paddles and the prongs they stick into. To clean the pan and paddles, fill the pan with water and let it soak for 10 minutes, at which point the kneading paddles should be easy to remove. Make sure you're filling the pan, not the machine; filling the machine can damage it and result in electrocution. To clean the machine, unplug it and use a damp towel or cloth to wipe out the interior, drying it thoroughly and leaving the lip open for air-drying.

Why Do I Need a Dutch Oven for Bread Baking?

In addition to turning out sumptuous suppers, your Dutch oven (see page 48) can deliver loaves of bread as impressive as those from an artisan bakery.

Professional bakers use steam-injected ovens to achieve their results. The moist environment transfers heat more rapidly than dry heat does so the air bubbles inside the dough expand quickly, leading to a more open crumb. It also prevents the bread's exterior from drying out too quickly, which limits rise. And, as steam condenses on the dough, it causes the starches to form a sheath that eventually dries out, giving the finished loaf a shiny, crisp crust. We do like countertop steam ovens for translating the process in your home kitchen, but a common Dutch oven allows you to create and capture steam in much the same way.

A loaf baked in a Dutch oven achieves the two most desired elements of rustic bread: a dramatic open-crumbed structure and a shatteringly crisp crust. As the loaf heats, it gives off steam to create a humid environment inside the pot. The pot traps it and transfers it much like the injected steam in a professional oven. As a test, we baked two loaves, one in a Dutch oven and the other on a preheated baking stone. After 1 minute, the surface temperature of the Dutch oven–baked loaf had risen past 200 degrees, while the other loaf had reached only 135 degrees. As in a professional oven, the steam in the pot condenses on the dough for a glossy, crackly crust.

For nice lofty, evenly baked loaves, we recommend baking in a Dutch oven that holds no less than 4½ quarts (our favorite pot holds 7¼ quarts and works great). You can bake a standard round boule in a round Dutch oven. You can also bake an oval-shaped bâtard if you happen to own an oval one (8 quarts).

worth it

CAST-IRON BREAD OVEN

We love baking bread in our Dutch oven, but if you're an avid baker, you'll appreciate a dedicated oven. This cast-iron bakeware can accommodate both round and oval loaves, and it has short sides so you can avoid grazing the hot pot when lowering in a loaf. Plus, it won't hold residue from yesterday's stew. These ovens are an investment, but they turn out crusts even more blistered and caramelized than those made in a Dutch oven.

Can I Create Steam Without a Bread Oven or a Dutch Oven?

If you don't want to take the plunge on a Dutch oven, bread oven, or countertop steam oven, it is possible to increase the steam in your home oven. Many recipes suggest adding water or ice to the oven; this is helpful but you can do even better. While it won't quite mimic the steamy environment inside of a professional steam-injected oven, you can use lava rocks to make your home oven as steamy as possible. These irregularly shaped rocks (available at many hardware stores for use in gas grills) have a lot of surface area for absorbing and retaining heat, maximizing the amount of steam produced when boiling water is introduced.

To use them, adjust an oven rack to the lowest position. Fill two aluminum pie plates with 1 quart of lava rocks each and place them on the rack before heating the oven. When your bread is ready for the oven, pour ½ cup of boiling water into one of the plates of lava rocks and close the oven door for 1 minute to create an initial burst of steam. Then, working quickly, transfer the loaf to the oven and pour ½ cup of boiling water into the second plate of rocks. This one-two punch ensures that the oven stays steamy for the entire baking time.

Finally, a very easy way to increase steam is to mist your loaf with water using a spray bottle, either before it goes in the oven or at the beginning of baking. This creates enough steam to keep the dough supple and allow it to rise dramatically before the exterior gelatinizes into a crackly crust.

What Does a Proofing Bin Do?

Dough most often rises best at room temperature, but sometimes your room just isn't temperate. If you have a cold, drafty kitchen, proofing bins or boxes provide you with a way to control the temperature for rising your just-kneaded or shaped dough. An enclosed heating element lets you regulate the temperature while a small water pan creates a humid environment. You can mimic this setup by letting your dough rise in a closed oven that contains a 13 by 9-inch baking pan of boiling water. Hardcore bakers who want to splurge may enjoy a proofing bin—or, with a bigger investment, consider a steam oven (see page 125), which also can help with proofing dough as you can calibrate the warmth and humidity to achieve the optimal environment for yeast development.

What Distinguishes a Couche From a Regular Towel?

Professional bakers proof some free-form loaves, often baguettes, in the folds of a piece of heavy linen known as a couche. This isn't just a kitchen towel. The couche has two core jobs: It helps the loaf hold its shape and it wicks away moisture, keeping the dough's surface uniformly dry as it proofs and rises. This helps develop a thin "skin" that bakes up to the perfect crisp, chewy, attractively floured crust. To prepare the couche, we lightly mist the underside with water, drape the couche over an inverted baking sheet, and then dust the couche with flour. Once the dough is shaped, we transfer the dough to the prepared couche seam side up and then pinch the edges of the couche on either side of the loaf into a protective pleat.

Do I Need a Bread Lame?

We like them but you can get by with a paring knife. First and foremost, the slashes on a loaf of bread need to be functional, creating controlled weak points in the loaf's surface that allow it to expand properly in the oven. Without the slashes, the loaf will expand wherever it finds a random weak spot, resulting in an odd shape. Achieving this (appearance aside) is paramount. With a paring knife, make a swift, fluid motion along the top of the loaf. (You can always reinforce your slash if it isn't perfect.)

Do Lames with Curved Blades Really Make More Pronounced "Ears"?

While we say you can use a paring knife instead of a lame to score bread, a lame will make producing an ear—that is, a ridge on the outside of a slash's opening that bakes up deliciously crispy—easier. Traditionally, a sail-like ear is seen as a sign of well-made bread. Professional bakers swear by lames with curved blades, as they can make a slightly more pronounced ear. But in our testing, the difference between ears made by a curved blade and ears made by a straight blade was fairly minor. Straight blades can make good-looking ears, too, and they're far easier to direct and control, making them better for more intricate decorative scoring. Ultimately, however, blade preference—straight or curved—is personal. Our favorite lame is ideal because a simple screw system makes it easy to attach blades in either curved or straight configurations. This innovation allows you to have the best of two worlds, slicing dramatic ears when the blade is curved and making more intricate designs when the blade is straight.

specialized bread tools with DIY alternatives

Maybe you want to buy all the bread things. But there are plenty of ways to make special breads without a bunch of fancy gadgets.

SPECIALIZED BREAD GEAR		DIY OPTION		WHY THIS DIY WORKS
Baking Stone or Steel		Overturned rimmed baking sheet or heavy-duty cookie sheet		It doesn't beat the even heating and heat retention of a baking stone or steel, but a heavy-duty baking sheet can get very hot in a preheated oven and when overturned it has a flat surface.
Pizza Peel		Overturned rimmed baking sheet or cookie sheet		An overturned rimmed baking sheet or cookie sheet dusted with flour will easily transport pizza or bread to the oven.
Steam-Injected Oven		Dutch oven		A closed Dutch oven traps steam from the baking loaf so it heats, and therefore expands, more rapidly for an open crumb. Also, as the steam condenses on the loaf, it forms a starchy sheath that dries to a crisp crust.
Banneton		Towel-lined colander		A rounded colander keeps the loaf's shape and its perforations provide breathability.
Flipping Board		Two 16 by 4-inch pieces of heavy cardboard taped together with packaging tape		Doubling up the cardboard results in a tool sturdy enough to successfully lift and flip proofed bread dough.
Bread Lame		Paring knife		As long as it's sharp, a paring knife slices just deep enough without dragging at the dough.

AUTHENTIC BAGUETTES

makes four 15-inch-long baguettes

Just a few pieces of equipment guarantee success when making bakery-quality baguettes at home. A couche helps maintain the long, pointed shape of the dough; it also gets the delicate proofed loaves to the pizza peel with ease. And a sharp lame ensures beautiful almond-shaped slashes. If you can't find King Arthur all-purpose flour, substitute bread flour. We also add diastatic malt, an enzyme naturally present in flour that converts starches to sugars and ensures a caramelized, well-browned crust. Purchase diastatic malt powder, not plain malt powder or malt syrup. This recipe makes enough dough for four loaves, which can be baked anytime during the 24- to 72-hour window after placing the dough in the fridge.

¼	cup (1⅓ ounces) whole-wheat flour
3	cups (15 ounces) King Arthur all-purpose flour
1½	teaspoons table salt
1	teaspoon instant or rapid-rise yeast
1	teaspoon diastatic malt powder (optional)
1½	cups (12 ounces) water
2	(16 by 12-inch) disposable aluminum roasting pans

1 Sift whole-wheat flour through fine-mesh strainer into bowl of stand mixer; discard bran remaining in strainer. Add all-purpose flour; salt; yeast; and malt powder, if using, to mixer bowl. Fit stand mixer with dough hook, add water, and knead on low speed until cohesive dough forms and no dry flour remains, 5 to 7 minutes. Transfer dough to lightly oiled large bowl, cover with plastic wrap, and let rest at room temperature for 30 minutes.

2 Holding edge of dough with your fingertips, fold dough over itself by gently lifting and folding edge of dough toward center. Turn bowl 45 degrees; fold again. Turn bowl and fold dough 6 more times (total of 8 folds). Cover with plastic and let rise for 30 minutes. Repeat folding and rising every 30 minutes, 3 more times. After fourth set of folds, cover bowl tightly with plastic and refrigerate for at least 24 hours or up to 72 hours.

3 Transfer dough to lightly floured counter, pat into 8-inch square (do not deflate), and divide in half. Return 1 piece of dough to container, wrap tightly with plastic, and refrigerate (dough can be shaped and baked anytime within 72-hour window). Divide remaining dough in half crosswise, transfer to lightly floured rimmed baking sheet, and cover loosely with plastic. Let rest for 45 minutes.

4 On lightly floured counter, roll each piece of dough into loose 3- to 4-inch-long cylinder; return to floured baking sheet and cover with plastic. Let rest at room temperature for 30 minutes.

5 Lightly mist underside of couche with water, drape over inverted baking sheet, and dust with flour. Gently press 1 piece of dough into 6 by 4-inch rectangle on lightly floured counter, with long edge facing you. Fold upper quarter of dough toward center and press gently to seal. Rotate dough 180 degrees and repeat folding step to form 8 by 2-inch rectangle.

6 Fold dough in half toward you, using thumb of your other hand to create crease along center of dough, sealing with heel of your hand as you work your way along the loaf. Without pressing down on loaf, use heel of your hand to reinforce seal (do not seal ends of loaf). Hold your hand over center of dough and roll dough back and forth gently to tighten (it should form dog-bone shape).

7 Starting at center of dough and working toward ends, gently and evenly roll and stretch dough until it measures 15 inches long by 1¼ inches wide. Moving your hands in opposite directions, use back-and-forth motion to roll ends of loaf under your palms to form sharp points.

8 Transfer dough to floured couche, seam side up. On either side of loaf, pinch edges of couche into pleat, then cover loosely with large plastic garbage bag.

9 Repeat steps 4 through 9 with second piece of dough and place on opposite side of pleat. Fold edges of couche over loaves to cover completely, then carefully place sheet inside bag, and tie or fold under to enclose.

10 Let stand until loaves have nearly doubled in size and dough springs back minimally when poked gently with your finger, 45 to 60 minutes. While bread rises, adjust oven rack to middle position, place baking stone on rack, and heat oven to 500 degrees.

11 Line pizza peel with 16 by 12-inch piece of parchment paper with long edge perpendicular to handle. Unfold couche, pulling from ends to remove pleats. Gently pushing with side of flipping board, roll 1 loaf over, away from other loaf, so it is seam side down. Using your hand, hold long edge of flipping board between loaf and couche at 45-degree angle. Then lift couche with your other hand and flip loaf seam side up onto board.

12 Invert loaf onto parchment-lined peel, seam side down, about 2 inches from long edge of parchment, then use flipping board to straighten loaf. Repeat with remaining loaf, leaving at least 3 inches between loaves.

13 Holding lame concave side up at 30-degree angle to loaf, make series of three 4-inch-long, ½-inch deep slashes along length of loaf, using swift, fluid motion, overlapping each slash slightly. Repeat with second loaf.

14 Transfer loaves, on parchment, to baking stone, cover with stacked inverted disposable pans, and bake for 5 minutes. Carefully remove pans and bake until loaves are evenly browned, 12 to 15 minutes longer, rotating parchment halfway through baking. Transfer to cooling rack and let cool for at least 20 minutes before serving. Consume within 4 hours.

anatomy of

A GOOD BREAD KNIFE

LONG, TALL BLADE

At least 8.5 inches of usable blade—the part of the blade that has serrations—to span large loaves

RELATIVELY FEW SERRATIONS

Means each serration has more power so you slice cleanly through loaves rather than squish them

CLEARANCE UNDER HANDLE

Keeps your knuckles from dragging on the cutting board

FREQUENTLY ASKED QUESTIONS: BREAD GADGET EDITION

Q: How do I clean a banneton?

A: A layer of flour is considered good "seasoning" for your banneton (or liner, if using), helping dough release more easily. When that seasoning becomes a stiff crust that chips off onto your dough, it's probably time to give your equipment a wash. Because they're made of natural fibers, both rattan and wood pulp bannetons require some care to maintain and clean. Scrub rattan bannetons with a stiff brush under cold water to remove buildup. For wood pulp bannetons, use a damp cloth to remove any thick buildup. Soak cloth liners in warm water and a little dish soap, and then scrub to remove buildup. Dry both bannetons and liners thoroughly after washing.

Q: Are plastic bannetons any good?

A: A plastic banneton is especially easy to clean—it can even be washed in the dishwasher. Unlike natural-fiber bannetons, they dry quickly, so they will never develop mold. But because it's made of slick plastic, dough sticks to it mercilessly. If you choose this style of banneton, you'll need to use a liner.

Q: How do I clean a bread lame?

A: Wipe off any dough that sticks to the blade carefully with a paper towel or dish towel, holding the blade steady with one hand to keep it from slipping as you do so. Don't use water or soap; lame blades can be hard to dry properly and can rust. If you aren't able to remove the gunk easily, either rotate the blade so that you can use a clean edge or exchange the blade for a new one. When in doubt, change the blade. Blades are replaceable; fingers are not.

Q: How often should I replace a lame blade?

A: There are two main signs to look for. First, dulling: When the blade begins dragging at the dough instead of slicing it cleanly, it's time to either rotate the blade or to replace it. Second, messes: If the blade has gotten gunky with dough and you're not able to clean it properly, it won't slice precisely either.

Q: How should I dispose of used lame blades?

A: Dull lame blades can still be sharp enough to slice through a garbage bag. We recommend enclosing used blades securely in cardboard and taping the cardboard shut before you throw them out or buying a dedicated blade disposal container.

Which tools do Lisa and Hannah consider must-haves for beginner bread bakers? Watch this video to find out.

make it
homemade

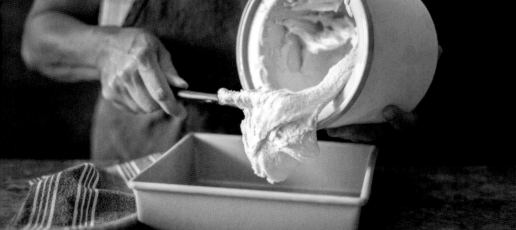

LE RELISH
8/20/15

ST
Jun

Don't Try
This at Home

Sometimes when we test equipment, answering the question "Is this worth it?" gets a little complicated.

Take portable outdoor pizza ovens, for example. We already know that a standard home oven can make great pizza when used right and paired with a baking stone or steel. Pizza ovens promise to reach temperatures much higher than a regular home oven, but they're also highly specialized and expensive. So can they produce pizzas so far superior to those made in a regular oven that the choice is a no-brainer?

To find out, we fired pizza after pizza in a variety of outdoor ovens and compared our results with pizzas baked in regular ovens. We chopped firewood into tiny 6-inch or smaller pieces in order to fit it into the compact chambers of some multifuel pizza ovens, which promised to allow us to cook with wood and/or charcoal in addition to gas. We babysat flames to make sure they didn't burn out before our pizzas

were done. In the end, one thing was clear: Multifuel pizza ovens weren't all they were cracked up to be. Considering that pizzas aren't cooked for long enough to pick up any real wood- or charcoal-fired flavor, the extra effort just wasn't worth it. On the other hand, we found several pizza ovens we loved and could highly recommend.

But did we decisively settle the pizza oven vs. regular oven debate? Uh, well, no. The thing is, while pizza ovens did turn out some terrific pies, the ones we made in our home oven were nearly as good. If you want crackly, spotted-brown Neapolitan-style pizza, a pizza oven would be the way to go. If you want the ability to make most kinds of pizza easily without a specialty appliance, the oven has its advantages. It all comes down to personal preference.

Even after all our tests, sometimes there is no one-size-fits-all choice. And that's OK: What our tests do is lay out the choices clearly, so you can decide what will work best for you.

Pass the Pasta

Making pasta from scratch is a tactile and fun kitchen exercise that forces you to slow down and really feel the process.

Do I Need a Pasta Maker to Make Great Pasta at Home?

No, you don't have to use a pasta maker, but if you choose to forgo this tool it helps to use a dough specifically formulated for rolling out by hand. Pasta doughs developed for machine rolling tend to be relatively stiff; trying to roll these doughs using just a rolling pin and muscle power is no easy feat. You can roll and roll until your forearms are screaming and *still* be left with pasta sheets that are thicker than ideal, which can throw off cooking times and be tough and overly chewy.

The key to a more supple dough and easier hand rolling? Extra egg yolks, plus a little olive oil (a controversial addition, but one that we've found works wonders for this purpose).

What Tools Do I Need, Then?

Certain pasta-specific tools can make your life as a fledgling pasta chef a lot easier, but you can do without any specialized pasta-making equipment if you really want to. You probably have everything on this bare-bones list already: a mixing bowl, measuring cups and spoons, a wooden spoon or rubber spatula, a rolling pin, and a knife. If this is all you're starting out with, you'll also need a good recipe for fresh pasta dough that's easy to roll out by hand (see page 259). If you're serious about making pasta, however, you should consider adding a pasta roller to your collection; it'll expand the number of recipes you can make and also make the process a lot faster and easier.

Are Those Drying Racks for Fresh Pasta Really Necessary?

Pasta drying racks (also called pasta trees) typically feature several thin prongs meant for draping with freshly cut strands or sheets of pasta to allow the pasta to air dry. While it's easy to imagine why you might want one—the last thing you want after going to the effort to roll out fresh pasta is for all those strands to clump together before you can cook them—we actually don't use them in the test kitchen.

Why? Well, because we already have a tool that works just as well for preventing clumping: our trusty rimmed baking sheet. After cutting the pasta into our preferred shape, we lightly dust it with flour before transferring it to a lightly floured baking sheet; the sheet's ample surface area gives us plenty of room to spread the pasta into a single layer. No specialized gadgets necessary!

head to head

PASTA ROLLERS

MANUAL PASTA ROLLERS

Don't require any other equipment to work; crank is turned by hand as sheet of pasta is fed through

Take more practice to comfortably crank roller with one hand and catch pasta with other hand

Slower, but provide more time to make adjustments

Less likely to tear delicate gluten-free pasta sheets

STAND MIXER PASTA ATTACHMENTS

Attach to stand mixer; rollers are powered by mixer's motor

Easier to feed pasta through roller with one hand and catch pasta with other hand

Separate attachments for rolling and cutting pasta

Faster, but require greater attentiveness

Prone to tearing more delicate gluten-free pasta sheets

FRESH PASTA WITHOUT A MACHINE

serves 4 to 6 (Makes 1 pound pasta)

Lots of egg yolks plus a splash of olive oil make a tender, supple dough that's easy to roll thin by hand (although you can use a machine if you have one). If you're using a high-protein all-purpose flour such as King Arthur, increase the number of egg yolks to seven. Serve with a simple sauce of your choice.

2 cups (10 ounces) all-purpose flour, plus extra as needed

2 large eggs plus 6 large yolks

2 tablespoons extra-virgin olive oil

Table salt for cooking pasta

1 Process flour, eggs and yolks, and oil in food processor until mixture forms cohesive dough that feels soft and barely tacky, about 45 seconds. (If dough sticks to your fingers, add up to ¼ cup flour, 1 tablespoon at a time, until barely tacky. If dough doesn't become cohesive, add up to 1 tablespoon water, 1 teaspoon at a time, until it just comes together; process 30 seconds longer.) Turn out dough onto dry counter and knead until smooth, 1 to 2 minutes. Shape dough into 6-inch-long cylinder. Wrap in plastic wrap and let rest at room temperature for at least 1 hour or up to 4 hours.

2 Cut cylinder crosswise into 6 equal pieces. Working with 1 piece of dough at a time (rewrap remaining dough), dust both sides with flour, place cut side down on clean counter, and press into 3-inch square. Using heavy rolling pin, roll into 6-inch square. Dust both sides of dough lightly with flour.

3 Starting at center of square, roll dough away from you in 1 motion. Return rolling pin to center of dough and roll toward you in single motion. Repeat rolling steps until dough sticks to counter and measures roughly 12 inches long. Lightly dust both sides of dough with flour and continue to roll until dough measures roughly 20 inches long and 6 inches wide, frequently lifting dough to release it from counter. (You should be able to easily see outline of your fingers through dough.) If dough firmly sticks to counter and wrinkles, dust dough lightly with flour.

4 Transfer pasta sheet to clean dish towel and let stand, uncovered, until firm around edges, about 15 minutes; meanwhile, roll out remaining dough.

5 Starting with 1 short end, gently fold 1 pasta sheet at 2-inch intervals until sheet has been folded into flat, rectangular roll. Using sharp chef's knife, slice crosswise into ³⁄₁₆-inch-wide noodles. Use your fingers to unfurl noodles and transfer to baking sheet. Repeat folding and cutting with remaining pasta sheets. Cook noodles within 1 hour or freeze for up to 2 weeks.

6 Bring 4 quarts water to boil in large pot. Add pasta and 1 tablespoon salt and cook until tender but still al dente, about 3 minutes. Drain pasta, reserving cooking water as needed to adjust consistency of sauce.

Is It Possible to Make Tubular Pastas at Home?

Pasta rollers can't make tubular shapes such as penne and rigatoni; for that you need an electric pasta extruder. These machines mix the dough for you—you add the dough ingredients directly to the machine—and then extrude the pasta through shaping disks, meaning they can make many more shapes than pasta rollers. You can find stand mixer attachments that claim to do this, but if you really want good tubular pasta, a standalone machine is the way to go.

My New Pasta Extruder Is Constantly Getting Gummed Up With Dough. What Gives?

Electric pasta extruders need a drier dough than you'd use for hand-rolling or a manual roller. Wetter doughs will gum up the machine's inner workings and result in ragged looking pasta. Many pasta extruders come with their own dough recipes, but we've found that even following these recipes doesn't always guarantee good results. Instead, we developed our own recipe for extruder-friendly pasta dough.

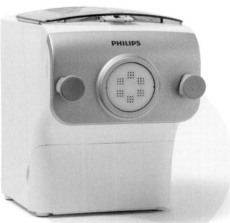

Too wet

Just right

FRESH EGG PASTA FOR AN EXTRUDER

serves 4 to 6 (Makes about 1 pound pasta)

Using a countertop pasta extruder requires a specifically formulated dough that's not too wet, such as this one. Be aware that your extruder may have automatic mixing and extruding settings that will need to be adjusted to match the instructions given in this recipe. If using an extruding attachment for your stand mixer, combine the dough in the mixer bowl on low speed using the paddle attachment and then extrude the dough on low speed using an extruder attachment. Serve with a sauce of your choice.

- 2½ cups (12½ ounces) all-purpose flour, plus extra as needed
- 2 large eggs plus 4 large yolks

  Table salt for cooking pasta

1 Attach desired pasta die to pasta extruder and add flour to mixing chamber. Using fork, beat eggs and yolks and 1 tablespoon warm water together in bowl. Select mixing setting, slowly add egg mixture to flour, and mix until no dry flour remains and mixture begins to form crumbles, about 3 minutes. (Mixture should not form cohesive dough.) Pause extruder and let dough rest for 10 minutes.

2 Lightly dust rimmed baking sheet with flour. Select extruding setting and allow about 3 inches of pasta to extrude through die; pause extruder. Cut off pasta, crumble into small pieces, and return to mixing chamber. Resume extruding, cutting pasta into desired lengths and transferring to prepared sheet. (If extruded pasta does not hold its shape, add up to 2 tablespoons water to mixing , 1 teaspoon at a time, and mix for 30 seconds before extruding further.)

3 Bring 4 quarts water to boil in large pot. Add pasta and 1 tablespoon salt and cook until tender but still al dente, 2 to 3 minutes. Drain pasta, reserving cooking water as needed to adjust consistency of sauce.

Do I Need Specialized Pasta Cutters?

From the simplest strands to more complex shapes, many types of pasta can be formed using a few multipurpose tools. Here are just a few examples of shapes you can make without any specialized shaping tools.

Chef's knife: You can use a chef's knife to cut **lasagna** noodles by simply running it down the sides of the pasta sheets to trim and square off the corners. You can also cut flat strand pasta such as **linguine**, **fettuccine**, **tagliatelle**, and **pappardelle** by using a chef's knife to slice crosswise through rolled sheets.

Fluted pastry wheel: A fluted pastry wheel is instrumental for achieving the signature wavy edges on shapes such as **farfalle** and **agnolotti**, and to add a decorative touch to the edges of **square ravioli**.

Pizza cutter: A pizza cutter makes long, efficient slices through pasta sheets. We use one to cut angled strips for **maltagliati** and to slice between mounds of filling to make **square ravioli**. It's also useful for cutting squares of dough for **cappellacci** and **pansotti**.

Biscuit cutter: A biscuit cutter makes it easy to stamp out the rounds of dough used for many filled pastas, such as **round ravioli** (which can also be cut with a more specialized ravioli stamp if you want ravioli with scalloped edges), **mezzelune**, and **tortellini**.

Help! My Beautiful Ravioli Break Apart When I Try to Remove Them from the Pot. What Should I Do?

Ravioli and other filled pastas require a delicate touch, or they can break open and spill their contents right back into the cooking water. Even vigorous boiling can be enough to blow open their seams, so it's best to cook them at a gentle boil. Once your beautiful filled pasta is cooked, don't try to remove the pieces from the pot with a slotted spoon or pasta fork; these tools are small and can crowd the pasta or accidentally jab them with a pointy prong. Instead, use a spider skimmer (see page 95). These wide wire baskets can gently scoop up lots of pasta in a single motion—helpful for preventing overcooking—and quickly drain them at the same time.

Why Do My Gnocchi Keep Falling Apart?

Lumps can cause gnocchi to break apart during boiling, but luckily there's an easy way to avoid them. Just use a ricer (see page 99) to process the cooked potatoes. The tiny pieces will then easily and evenly incorporate with the flour for gnocchi that's lump-free and tender (because you'll also need to do less mixing).

real talk with lisa

THE BEST TOOLS FOR PLATING PASTA

We tested pasta forks against a basic pair of tongs to see how each tool stacked up. The tongs were fine for stirring long pastas in boiling water and mixing in sauce. But with shorter, smaller pasta the tongs grabbed only tiny amounts, so we had to go back and forth repeatedly to dish out a single portion. A win for the pasta forks. When plating, however, tongs could twirl long strands of pasta into tidy restaurant-worthy nests—a nice touch. When we collaborated with Tiffani Faison on a *Gear Heads* episode about pasta, she told us her favorite pasta utensil is a carving fork—what you use to hold turkey while slicing. She uses the giant fork to separate strands of spaghetti in boiling water, and to plate the perfect *Top Chef*—worthy twirl of pasta.

Tag along with Lisa and Hannah as they learn which tools real pasta pros reach for every day.

Dumplings for Dinner

Dumplings can be formed into a huge variety of shapes and stuffed with any filling you desire—and they're always delicious and rewarding to make at home.

What Makes for a Good Steamer?

First of all, you *can* use a metal steamer basket to steam dumplings. These don't stack, so you'll have to cook fewer dumplings at a time, but they're a solid option if you don't have a bamboo steamer or want to cook up only a serving or two.

But if you steam dumplings regularly, there are several reasons to opt for a bamboo steamer, including higher capacity, the ability to steam foods that might become misshapen in a metal steamer with a curved base, and the fact that the removable layers allow you to steam foods with different cooking times simultaneously. We like steamers with sturdy metal-banded tiers to prevent warping, thick slats, and at least two tiers.

A sturdily-constructed two-tier steamer is capable of handling most steaming tasks.

A three-tier steamer lets you cook greater quantities at once.

Extra-tall tiers accommodate larger foods.

real talk with lisa

MANY HANDS MAKE LIGHT WORK

Making dozens of dumplings alone isn't a lot of fun. But you can turn dumpling-making into a party, as a friend once showed me. Spread all the ingredients on the kitchen counter or dining table and have everyone pull up a chair. After you demonstrate how to fill and pleat the dumplings, turn on music, pour wine, and settle in for the cozy dumpling-making equivalent of a quilting bee. The dumplings practically make themselves. You can freeze some for later, and cook the rest. Transform your work table into a dinner table, start steaming or pan-frying the dumplings, and put out bowls of dipping sauce so you can all enjoy the fruits of your labor.

How Do I Use a Bamboo Steamer?

Using a steamer isn't hard. Here's how to do it.

1 Wash steamer with soapy water before first use, inspecting tiers and lid for any loose fibers and carefully pulling them off so they don't get in your food.

2 Fill wok, skillet, or sauté pan with just enough water so that water level is slightly below slats in bottom tier of steamer. (Water should not touch slats—you don't want to boil food.) Bring water to rolling boil over high heat.

3 Line each steamer tier with cabbage leaves or perforated parchment rounds. Place food on top of cabbage or parchment in single layer, leaving space between each item so that steam can circulate. If you're cooking different types of food, place denser foods (proteins, dumplings, etc.) in lower tier(s) and less dense foods (such as greens) in upper tier(s). Cover tier(s) with steamer lid.

4 Place steamer in vessel with boiling water. Adjust heat level to bring water to simmer. Cook for time specified in recipe. Check on water level periodically and replenish with more water from kettle of boiling water as needed.

Lisa Says . . .

When you're steaming delicate foods such as bao, dumplings, or fish, it's a good idea to line the steamer with perforated parchment paper or cabbage leaves to keep the food from sticking and tearing.

Can I Steam Dumplings Without a Steamer?

If you don't have a steamer, you can mimic one with something you already have in the kitchen: a plate. Just arrange the dumplings on a platter or plate that's about 2 inches shorter in length than the diameter of your cooking vessel. Bring ¾ to 1 inch of water to a boil in your cooking vessel, and then set the plate inside, using an overturned bowl to keep it elevated above the water if necessary. Cover and steam the dumplings for a minute or two beyond the recommended time and then transfer them immediately to a serving platter. (Note that this works best for dumplings that cook in 10 minutes or less; otherwise, too much water will accumulate on the plate and sog out the dumplings.)

How Should I Clean A Bamboo Steamer?

Clean your steamer with warm, soapy water—ideally while it's still warm, so you don't have to scrub too hard to remove dried-on food. Don't put it in the dishwasher; it will absorb too much water and warp. Bamboo is a natural material, after all! After washing, blot excess water from the steamer with a dish towel and then let it air dry. Don't try to stack and store the tiers until they're completely dry, or they'll mold.

STEAMED DUMPLINGS

makes 40 dumplings

Using stackable bamboo steamer baskets allows you to steam 20 dumplings at once, yielding enough dumplings for a crowd in only two batches. Look for freshly ground pork, sold in bulk at the butcher's counter, which has more fat and a coarser texture compared to pre-packaged pork. We prefer to use Chinese light soy sauce here; other styles of soy sauce will also work, but know that they may be more salty. Dumpling wrappers come in egg and wheat varieties; both will work here. You will need a stackable 10-inch bamboo steamer basket for this recipe.

5	cups 1-inch napa cabbage pieces
½	teaspoon table salt, plus salt for salting cabbage
12	ounces ground pork
1½	tablespoons soy sauce, plus extra for serving
1½	tablespoons toasted sesame oil
1	tablespoon vegetable oil
1	tablespoon Shaoxing wine
1	tablespoon hoisin sauce
1	tablespoon grated fresh ginger
¼	teaspoon white pepper
4	scallions, chopped fine
1	(1-pound) package 3½-inch round dumpling wrappers
	Chinese black or red vinegar
	Chili oil

1 Pulse cabbage in food processor until finely chopped, 8 to 10 pulses. Transfer cabbage to medium bowl and stir in ½ teaspoon salt; let sit for 10 minutes. Using your hands, squeeze excess moisture from cabbage. Transfer cabbage to small bowl and set aside.

2 Pulse pork, soy sauce, sesame oil, vegetable oil, Shaoxing wine, hoisin, ginger, salt, and pepper in now-empty food processor until blended and slightly sticky, about 10 pulses. Scatter cabbage over pork mixture. Add scallions and pulse until vegetables are evenly distributed, about 8 pulses. Transfer pork mixture to small bowl and, using rubber spatula, smooth surface. Cover with plastic and refrigerate for at least 30 minutes or up to 3 days.

3 Lightly dust 2 parchment paper–lined rimmed baking sheets with flour. Using rubber spatula, mark filling with cross to divide into 4 equal portions. Transfer 1 portion to separate bowl and refrigerate remaining filling.

4 Working with 1 wrapper at a time (keep remaining wrappers covered), place scant 1 tablespoon filling in center of wrapper. Brush away any flour clinging to surface of wrapper, then fold in half to make half-moon shape. Using forefinger and thumb, pinch dumpling closed, pressing out any air pockets from filling. Transfer to prepared sheet. Repeat with additional 9 wrappers and filling in bowl. Repeat dumpling-making process with remaining wrappers and remaining 3 portions filling. (Dumplings can be refrigerated for up to 24 hours or frozen on sheet until solid, then transferred to zipper-lock bag and stored in freezer for up to 1 month. Do not thaw frozen dumplings before cooking; increase steaming time by 2 minutes.)

5 Bring 4 cups water to boil in 14-inch flat-bottomed wok or 12-inch skillet. Poke about 20 small holes in two 9-inch parchment rounds and lightly coat with cooking spray. Place rounds in two 10-inch bamboo steamer baskets. Arrange 10 dumplings evenly in each prepared basket leaving at least ½-inch space between each dumpling; stack baskets and cover. Reduce heat to maintain vigorous simmer and set steamer in wok. Steam until dumpling wrappers have translucent, glossy sheen, 8 to 10 minutes. Serve immediately, passing extra soy sauce, vinegar, and chili oil separately. (Before cooking second batch of dumplings, replenish water in wok and line steamer baskets with fresh parchment rounds.)

Tortilla Time

Once you've eaten warm, fresh-from-the-pan tortillas, you won't want to go back.

Can I Make Tortillas with a Rolling Pin?

Because flour tortillas contain stretchy, elastic gluten, we like to roll them out by hand; they experience too much snapback to be flattened by a tortilla press alone. So if you're making flour tortillas, then yes, a rolling pin is the way to go. Corn tortillas, on the other hand, lack gluten and are therefore more delicate. While you technically *could* roll them out by hand—people made corn tortillas by hand for millennia before the tortilla press, or tortilladora, was patented in the 20th century—using a tortilla press makes the process much easier, faster, and more consistent.

I'm Not Ready to Invest in a Tortilla Press—Are There Any DIY Alternatives?

We've had success pressing corn tortillas with a pie plate. Here's the setup: Cut open a zipper-lock bag along the side seams, open it up, and place a dough ball in the middle. Fold the other half of the bag back over the dough, and then press it flat using a pie plate—preferably made of glass so you can see the tortilla through it.

real talk with hannah

ALL HAIL THE GREAT TORTILLA WARMER

Tortilla warmers are one of my favorite things I've ever tested, probably because the winner from Imusa works so well. It's shaped like a pita pocket, with triple-layered sides made of two layers of fabric sandwiching a sheet of insulating plastic. It wicks moisture from the tortillas but then holds that moisture close, so they stay soft and pliable. You can put cold tortillas inside and microwave the whole thing, or add freshly-cooked homemade or griddled store-bought tortillas. I once served tacos at a party around 6 p.m., and by the time we were ready for round two at 10 p.m.—four hours later!—the leftover tortillas were still warm and tender.

Pizza Party

Golden-brown, crispy-cheesy homemade pizza doesn't require a ton of equipment—but you can get fancy if you want.

Do Pizza Ovens Make Better Pizza than a Regular Oven?

A good pizza oven can get scorching hot (around 700 degrees Fahrenheit for pizza ovens compared to 550 degrees or so for home ovens). That makes for pretty great pizza: tender and chewy inside, with the sought after leopard-spot char on the outside delivering extra flavor and textural variation. But if you don't feel like investing a lot of money, space, or time into setting up a pizza oven, your home oven is actually a very solid option. We've found that they work well for most kinds of pizzas, and with a few easy hacks (see page 274) they can work even better.

the right pizza oven for you

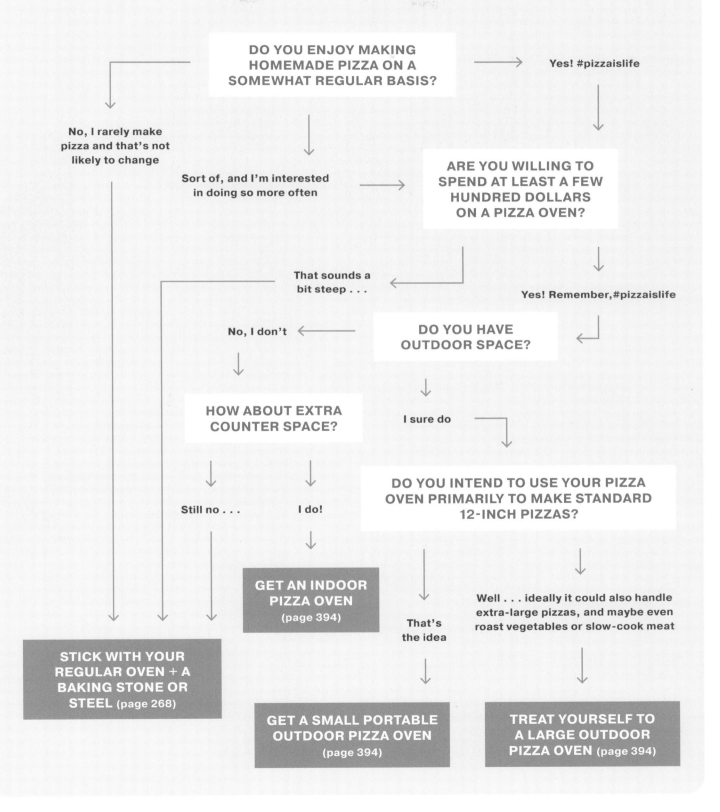

DO YOU ENJOY MAKING HOMEMADE PIZZA ON A SOMEWHAT REGULAR BASIS?

Yes! #pizzaislife

No, I rarely make pizza and that's not likely to change

Sort of, and I'm interested in doing so more often

ARE YOU WILLING TO SPEND AT LEAST A FEW HUNDRED DOLLARS ON A PIZZA OVEN?

That sounds a bit steep . . .

Yes! Remember, #pizzaislife

No, I don't

DO YOU HAVE OUTDOOR SPACE?

HOW ABOUT EXTRA COUNTER SPACE?

I sure do

Still no . . .

I do!

DO YOU INTEND TO USE YOUR PIZZA OVEN PRIMARILY TO MAKE STANDARD 12-INCH PIZZAS?

GET AN INDOOR PIZZA OVEN (page 394)

That's the idea

Well . . . ideally it could also handle extra-large pizzas, and maybe even roast vegetables or slow-cook meat

STICK WITH YOUR REGULAR OVEN + A BAKING STONE OR STEEL (page 268)

GET A SMALL PORTABLE OUTDOOR PIZZA OVEN (page 394)

TREAT YOURSELF TO A LARGE OUTDOOR PIZZA OVEN (page 394)

head to head

BAKING STONES AND STEELS

BAKING STONES

Made of slab of high-temperature ceramic

Can crack or break into pieces if mishandled

Slightly less efficient heat transfer makes stones slower at cooking and browning than steels

Slower browning allows for wider margin of error

Provide slightly less oven spring; pizza crusts are drier and chewier and bread crusts are less crisp

BAKING STEELS

Made of slab of carbon steel

Unbreakable, but can rust if left wet

More efficient heat transfer makes steels faster at cooking and browning than ceramic stones

Prone to overbrowning baked goods if not careful

Provide slightly more oven spring; pizza crusts are airier and more tender, and bread crusts are crisper

Is It OK to Store My Baking Stone or Steel in the Oven?

Short answer: Yes! Baking stones and steels are heavy, so we like to leave them in the oven (almost) all the time. Leaving your baking stone or steel in the oven can even be beneficial to your other oven cooking endeavors because they act as what engineers call "thermal ballast" (see page 27 for more on that). But there are a few things to be aware of:

First, keeping your stone or steel in the oven may add a few minutes to preheating times.

When using the oven, don't place pans directly on the steel or stone unless you want extra heat (and browning) applied to the bottom of your food.

If you're baking delicate items such as cookies or cakes, it's best to take out the steel or stone to avoid disrupting the heat-circulation pattern of your oven and baking the food unevenly.

And finally, don't be tempted to place your stone or steel on the oven floor; many ovens have vents there that for safety reasons must not be blocked.

Lisa Says . . .

It sounds counterintuitive, but don't bother with a round baking stone. Mere inches bigger than a typical pizza, a round stone sets you up for failure: It's a much harder target to hit when you're dropping a pizza onto it to cook. Instead, choose a big rectangular stone or steel, which not only makes it much easier to land your pizza, but also gives you versatility to make large, rectangular pizzas and to bake long loaves of bread.

Hannah Says . . .

If you happen to have a baking steel *and* a baking stone, use them both! If you place your baking steel on top of your baking stone before putting them both in the oven to preheat, the stone will act as a heat sink, keeping the steel hotter for longer and allowing you to bake multiple pizzas in a row, while the steel rapidly transfers that heat to the pizza.

Why Did My Baking Stone Crack?

Baking steels are virtually indestructible, but baking stones are a little more fragile. Obviously dropping the stone can cause it to shatter, but it's also possible for cracks to appear seemingly out of nowhere. If this has ever happened to you, know that there is a reason—and that reason is usually moisture. Pizza stones are made of porous ceramic that absorbs and holds on to moisture. Even if the surface of a stone looks dry, if it recently got wet there's a good chance there's still some water trapped inside. Heating it up causes that water to expand, and boom: cracked stone.

The takeaway: Avoid getting your stone wet. That means never soaking it, or even washing it—seriously. (And don't use soap: Future pizzas will taste soapy!) All you need to do to get your baking stone clean is to scrape off any burnt bits with a spatula or stiff brush and brush off any ash.

Didn't get the memo in time? If your stone has cracked into just a few large pieces, you can just push them together and keep on using it. Assuming the pieces are reasonably close-fitting, nothing bad will happen and your pizzas and breads will continue baking up just fine.

What's a Baking Peel For?

A baking peel, also called a pizza peel, is used for transferring foods such as pizza and bread to and from a hot oven and for rotating them mid-bake. That might not sound like something you need a specialized tool to do, and it's true that in a pinch you can use an overturned baking sheet in place of a peel. Still, a good peel makes transferring pizza and bread a lot easier. For one thing, you need to be quick, since the longer the oven door stays open, the more heat escapes; a sharp jerk once the peel is in position is all it takes to quickly unload the dough. Plus, a good peel will help keep your delicate, carefully formed pizzas and loaves intact by minimizing the risk of sticking.

Should I Buy a Wood Peel or a Metal One?

The prevailing wisdom is that you should have both: a wood peel is good for transferring the uncooked pizza to the oven, as the dough is less likely to stick, and a thinner metal peel is easier to slide under a pizza to rotate it mid-cook or remove it from the oven. But there's room for debate here, especially now that some innovative peels have entered the market.

Lisa Says . . .

A baking stone isn't just for pizza; we also use it to develop a crackly crust on bread and even to make roast turkey. After preheating an empty roasting pan on top of the preheated baking stone, we add the turkey. That extra-hot pan bottom solves the eternal turkey-roasting problem of dark and light meat needing separate cooking temperatures and times. With the pizza stone underneath, the turkey's dark meat cooks faster and finishes at the same time as the white meat.

Metal peel

Wood peel

Super Peel

real talk with lisa & hannah

LM

ONE GOOD PEEL IS ALL YOU NEED

I have a terrible habit of putting all the toppings on my pizza dough right on the counter and then realizing that I have to get that soft, stretchy, laden dough onto a peel if I ever hope to cook it. Enter the Super Peel, which uses a floured conveyor belt to magically lift up the pizza—intact and still perfectly round—and then deposit it just as neatly on the red-hot pizza stone or steel in the oven.

HC

IT TAKES TWO

Some people (like Lisa!) love the Super Peel, the overall winner from our baking peel review, but for me the fabric is too finicky to deal with. I prefer using two peels: a wooden one to launch my pies and a metal one to rotate and remove them. To each their own!

What's With All These Wacky Pizza Cutters?

Classic pizza cutters are basically just sharp wheels with attached handles, but there are many more styles out there. A good pizza cutter should be able to slice cleanly through towering deep-dish pies as easily as thin-crust pizza, without dragging off the toppings or getting all gunked up in the process.

Some models, such as scissor-style cutters, work surprisingly well, although they produce somewhat uneven slices. Cutters shaped like straight blades crush the crust and toppings as they're rocked back and forth, and hand wheels sweep toppings up under their plastic casings where they get stuck. So does the classic cutter still reign supreme? For the most part, we think so—as long as the blade is sharp and large enough to glide through a generous layer of toppings.

Sharp, tall blade cuts cleanly

A real pain to clean

Surprisingly effective, but makes crooked cuts

Too-short wheel

Crushes toppings

Ew! Do All Pizza Cutters Trap This Much Food?

Some pizza cutters come with blade casings that are just perfect for trapping the bits of cheese and toppings that get swept up under there by the blade. Yeah, it's gross—and often hard to clean. That's why we prefer cutters with more streamlined designs with less room for stray food to hide out.

Hannah Says . . .

I tested a pair of dedicated pizza scissors with longer arms that did a really great job of easily and cleanly slicing through thin-crust pizzas. They cut quite unevenly because you're making several cuts instead of continuous longer cuts, so they didn't end up on our winners' podium. But if you're ever in a pinch for a pizza cutter, consider a pair of kitchen scissors.

Lisa Says . . .

Those round black plastic takeout containers with clear plastic lids are the perfect size for letting your dough rise. Oil the interior and add a dough ball. Each holds the dough for one pizza crust. They stack neatly too.

more helpful pizza-making tools

Pizza-specific tools are great, but there are also plenty of multipurpose tools that are especially useful for different parts of the pie-making process.

USE THIS . . .		TO DO THIS!
Food Processor (page 134)		Quickly mix the dough, whip up a quick homemade tomato sauce, and shred blocks of cheese in an instant
Bench Scraper (page 241)		Divide the risen dough into equal pieces without deflating it
Ladle (page 95)		Scoop up sauce and spread it evenly over surface of the pizza
Grater (page 87)		Shred blocks of cheese

THIN-CRUST PIZZA

serves 4 to 6 (Makes two 13-inch pizzas)

This recipe is a great introduction to the techniques involved in homemade pizza. A food processor makes quick work of mixing the dough, and a preheated baking steel or stone gets the bottom nice and brown. A pizza peel helps transfer the pizza to and from the pizza steel or stone, but if you don't have one you can use a rimless or overturned baking sheet. It is important to use ice water in the dough to prevent it from overheating in the food processor. The dough needs to be refrigerated for at least 24 hours before baking. You can shape the second dough round while the first pizza bakes; don't add the toppings until just before baking.

DOUGH

3	cups (16½ ounces) bread flour
2	teaspoons sugar
½	teaspoon instant or rapid-rise yeast
1⅓	cups ice water
1	tablespoon vegetable oil
1½	teaspoons table salt

SAUCE AND TOPPINGS

1	(28-ounce) can whole peeled tomatoes, drained with juice reserved
1	tablespoon extra-virgin olive oil
2	garlic cloves, minced
1	teaspoon red wine vinegar
1	teaspoon dried oregano
½	teaspoon table salt
¼	teaspoon pepper
1	ounce Parmesan cheese, grated fine (½ cup)
8	ounces whole-milk mozzarella cheese, shredded (2 cups)

1 for the dough Pulse flour, sugar, and yeast in food processor until combined, about 5 pulses. With processor running, slowly add ice water; process until dough is just combined and no dry flour remains, about 10 seconds. Let dough rest for 10 minutes.

2 Add oil and salt to dough and process until dough forms satiny, sticky ball that clears sides of bowl, 30 to 60 seconds. Transfer dough to lightly oiled counter and knead by hand to form smooth, round ball, about 30 seconds. Place dough seam side down in lightly greased large bowl or container, cover tightly with plastic wrap, and refrigerate for at least 24 hours or up to 3 days.

3 for the sauce and toppings Process tomatoes, oil, garlic, vinegar, oregano, salt, and pepper in clean, dry workbowl until smooth, about 30 seconds. Transfer mixture to 2-cup liquid measuring cup and add reserved tomato juice until sauce measures 2 cups. Reserve 1 cup sauce; set aside remaining sauce for another use.

4 One hour before baking, adjust oven rack 4 inches from broiler element, set baking steel or stone on rack, and heat oven to 500 degrees. Press down on dough to deflate. Transfer dough to clean counter, divide in half, and cover loosely with greased plastic. Pat 1 piece of dough (keep remaining piece covered) into 4-inch round. Working around circumference of dough, fold edges toward center until ball forms. Flip ball seam side down and, using your cupped hands, drag in small circles on counter until dough feels taut and round and all seams are secured on underside. (If dough sticks to your hands, lightly dust top of dough with flour.) Repeat with remaining piece of dough. Space dough balls 3 inches apart, cover loosely with greased plastic, and let rest for 1 hour.

5 Heat broiler for 10 minutes. Meanwhile, coat 1 dough ball generously with flour and place on well-floured counter. Using your fingertips, gently flatten into 8-inch round, leaving 1 inch of outer edge slightly thicker than center. Using your hands, gently stretch dough into 12-inch round, working along edge and giving disk quarter turns.

6 Transfer dough to well-floured pizza peel and stretch into 13-inch round. Using back of spoon or ladle, spread ½ cup tomato sauce in even layer over surface of dough, leaving ¼-inch border around edge. Sprinkle ¼ cup Parmesan evenly over sauce, followed by 1 cup mozzarella.

7 Slide pizza carefully onto baking steel or stone and return oven to 500 degrees. Bake until crust is well browned and cheese is bubbly and partially browned, 8 to 10 minutes, rotating pizza halfway through baking. Transfer pizza to wire rack and let cool for 5 minutes before slicing and serving. Heat broiler for 10 minutes. Repeat with remaining dough, sauce, Parmesan, and mozzarella, returning oven to 500 degrees when pizza is placed on steel or stone.

CAST-IRON PAN PIZZA

serves 4

This pizza is baked in a 12-inch cast-iron skillet, which means you don't need any specialized tools to get a homemade pizza on the table. Generously oiling the skillet before baking the pizza essentially "fries" the outer crust.

DOUGH

2	cups (11 ounces) bread flour
1	teaspoon table salt
1	teaspoon instant or rapid-rise yeast
1	cup (8 ounces) warm water (105 to 110 degrees)
	Vegetable oil spray

SAUCE

1	(14.5-ounce) can whole peeled tomatoes
1	teaspoon extra-virgin olive oil
1	garlic clove, minced
¼	teaspoon sugar
¼	teaspoon table salt
¼	teaspoon dried oregano
	Pinch red pepper flakes

PIZZA

3	tablespoons extra-virgin olive oil
4	ounces Monterey Jack cheese, shredded (1 cup)
7	ounces whole-milk mozzarella cheese, shredded (1¾ cups)

1 for the dough Using wooden spoon or spatula, stir flour, salt, and yeast together in bowl. Add warm water and mix until most of flour is moistened. Using your hands, knead dough in bowl until dough forms sticky ball, about 1 minute. Spray 9-inch pie plate or cake pan with oil spray. Transfer dough to prepared plate and press into 7- to 8-inch disk. Spray top of dough with oil spray. Cover tightly with plastic wrap and refrigerate for 12 to 24 hours.

2 for the sauce Place tomatoes in fine-mesh strainer and crush with your hands. Drain well, then transfer to food processor. Add oil, garlic, sugar, salt, oregano, and pepper flakes and process until smooth, about 30 seconds. (Sauce can be refrigerated for up to 3 days.)

3 for the pizza Two hours before baking, remove dough from refrigerator and let sit at room temperature for 30 minutes.

4 Coat bottom of 12-inch cast-iron skillet with oil. Transfer dough to prepared skillet and use your fingertips to flatten dough until it is ⅛ inch from edge of skillet. Cover tightly with plastic and let rest until slightly puffy, about 1½ hours.

5 Thirty minutes before baking, adjust oven rack to lowest position and heat oven to 400 degrees. Spread ½ cup sauce evenly over top of dough, leaving ½-inch border (save remaining sauce for another use). Sprinkle Monterey Jack evenly over border. Press Monterey Jack into side of skillet, forming ½- to ¾-inch-tall wall. (Not all cheese will stick to side of skillet.) Evenly sprinkle mozzarella over sauce. Bake until cheese at edge of skillet is well browned, 25 to 30 minutes.

6 Transfer skillet to stovetop and let sit until sizzling stops, about 3 minutes. Run butter knife around rim of skillet to loosen pizza. Using thin metal spatula, gently lift edge of pizza and peek at underside to assess browning. Cook pizza over medium heat until bottom crust is well browned, 2 to 5 minutes (skillet handle will be hot). Using 2 spatulas, transfer pizza to wire rack and let cool for 10 minutes. Slice and serve.

5 Tips for Making Better Pizza at Home

Pizza making can look intimidating, but learning how to do it well isn't as hard as it seems. (But shhh—your admiring friends don't have to know that.)

1

MAKE YOUR OVEN WORK MORE LIKE A PIZZA OVEN

Pizza ovens get hot—really hot, as in 700-plus degrees Fahrenheit for the average outdoor pizza oven or 750 to even 1,000-plus degrees for a commercial pizza oven. By contrast, your home oven probably maxes out around 550 degrees. High heat is an important part of making good pizza. It's responsible for the "oven spring" that makes crusts rise tall and light; for getting nicely crisped, browned bottom crusts; and for melting and browning cheese. While your home oven isn't going to get as hot as a pizza oven, taking the following steps will dramatically improve the quality of the pizzas you make in it.

1 Place baking stone or steel on oven rack and turn oven to 500 degrees Fahrenheit. (Baking stones and steels absorb heat and transfer it directly to the pizza.)

2 Let oven heat for at least 1 hour before baking. (This gives the oven time to come up to temperature, but more importantly, it lets the stone or steel fully absorb and store the heat, so your pizza crust will bake up deeply golden and crisp.)

3 If using baking steel, switch oven to "broil" as soon as pizza goes into oven. (This helps the cheese and toppings cook at the same rate as the bottom crust.)

2

GIVE THE DOUGH A REST

One of the most challenging parts of making pizza is getting the dough to stretch into an even, thin, round crust without it tearing or springing back. Giving the dough a rest can help with that. After forming the dough balls, rest the dough in the refrigerator for at least 4 to 24 hours (choose a longer rest for better flavor). This gives the gluten network time to relax, leading to less of that annoying snapback. Then, before stretching it, let the dough come to room temperature (otherwise it will be stiffer and less flexible). Pro tip: Pull the dough out of the fridge at the same time as you begin preheating your baking stone or steel.

Bottom of pizza baked on stone heated for 30 minutes

Bottom of pizza baked on stone heated for 1 hour

3 STRETCH THE DOUGH THE RIGHT WAY

When it comes to the actual stretching, there's good news: You don't have to toss spinning disks of dough in the air like a professional pizzaiolo to get nicely stretched, beautifully round pizzas. Instead, let gravity do some of the work.

1 First, press dough with your fingertips on well-floured counter, pressing down until your fingertips are about halfway to counter, until dough measures 6 to 8 inches in diameter.

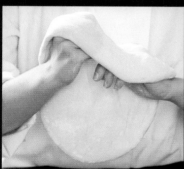

2 Carefully pick up dough round using both hands and drape it over your fists. Let gravity pull dough over your knuckles and gently stretch it out.

3 Rotate dough over your fists until round has reached desired size. If dough begins to stiffen during stretching, let it rest flat on floured counter for 1 to 2 minutes to allow gluten to relax.

4 USE A BAKING PEEL THE RIGHT WAY

Don't let your hard work end in a misshapen mess: Use these tips to ensure that the peel-to-oven transition goes smoothly every time.

1 To prevent sticking, lightly flour peel before adding pizza. Work quickly while saucing and topping; don't leave pizza on peel for longer than necessary.

2 To transfer pizza from peel to oven, position peel just above oven rack and quickly jerk back.

5 TAKE CARE OF YOUR BAKING STONE OR STEEL

First of all, don't wash your baking stone or steel (see page 269), and don't worry about any stains the stone has picked up with use. Here's all the maintenance these tools need.

for a baking stone Scrape off food residue and any excess char. Any leftover bits will be rendered into harmless ash next time stone is heated.

for a baking steel Scrape off food residue and any excess char. If rust forms, scrub it off, oil very lightly, and heat steel to reseason it as you would a carbon-steel skillet (see page 39).

Scream for Ice Cream

With the right equipment, making ice cream at home can be almost as fun as eating it. Plus, you can have as many mix-ins as you like.

How Does an Ice Cream Maker Work?

The key to ice cream's scoopability and creaminess may be surprising: It's air. Without the tiny air pockets distributed throughout that give ice cream (or frozen yogurt or sorbet) its smooth, semisoft consistency, it would be nearly rock hard and impossible to eat when fully frozen—much more on the ice side of the ice-cream spectrum. Ice cream makers work to freeze a liquid base while simultaneously beating air into it through constant but gentle churning.

My Ice Cream Is Icy. Is My Ice Cream Maker to Blame?

It might be. The large ice crystals that are responsible for an icy texture form when ice cream isn't cooled quickly enough, or when it's partly thawed and then refrozen. This can happen if you don't work quickly, if you leave your freshly made container of ice cream out on the counter for too long, or if your freezer has a power outage, but it can also be a sign of a less-than-great ice cream maker. Some ice cream makers require constant starting and stopping to scrape the semi-frozen ice cream or sorbet from the sides where the mixing paddle can't reach it; the more starting and stopping, the more likely it is that ice crystals will form.

What If I Want to Make Lots of Ice Cream at Once?

You have a few options. You could get a self-refrigerating ice cream maker that can churn out batch after batch of ice cream with no downtime except what's required for rinsing and drying the bowl. Alternatively, you can use a canister-style ice cream maker to make multiple batches—as long as you first buy an extra canister (or two if you have a lot of freezer space and *really* want to bulk-produce) and remember to freeze both canisters ahead of time (Hannah has a lot to say about that!). Or you could use your blender to turn out quart after quart of ice cream, limited only by the amount of ingredients you have on hand (see page 279).

One option we can't highly recommend: Using a large bucket-style ice cream maker capable of making a gallon or more in a single batch. While this may seem like the easiest way to make ice cream in bulk, we've found that most of these machines just aren't capable of freezing the ice cream base quickly enough to prevent the formation of the relatively large ice crystals responsible for a grainy, icy texture.

Lisa Says . . .

Before you make ice cream with a canister-style machine, be sure you've frozen the canister for at least a full 24 hours before you try to churn. Otherwise the ice cream will never fully set up.

Hannah Says . . .

Keeping two ice cream canisters on hand can be extremely useful. Having two means you can make back-to-back batches of ice cream in your canister-style ice cream maker, but the frozen canisters come in handy even when you aren't making ice cream. I use mine to chill wine bottles or a small carafe of cream or milk on a brunch table. They take up some freezer space, but I usually store stuff inside them, too, so it's not as much as you'd think.

head to head

ICE CREAM MAKERS

CANISTER-STYLE ICE CREAM MAKERS

Generally less expensive

Have removable coolant-lined canisters that must be frozen for at least 24 hours before use

Have smaller counter footprints, but require freezer space for canisters and finished ice cream

Take less time to churn ice cream (around 20 minutes on average)

Making multiple batches requires purchasing and prefreezing multiple canisters

SELF-REFRIGERATING ICE CREAM MAKERS

Generally more expensive

Have built-in compressors that chill canisters without need for prefreezing

Have larger counter footprints, but require freezer space only for finished ice cream

Take longer to churn ice cream (around 35 minutes on average)

Can make multiple batches back to back

LARGE ICE CREAM MAKERS

Require user to add ice and salt to outer chamber; motor spins inner canister through the salted ice to chill its contents

Can make a gallon or more in a single batch

Most can't chill ice cream quickly enough to prevent iciness

Require more babysitting

Can make multiple batches back to back provided user refills ice and salt

Loud and bulky

STRAWBERRY SORBET

serves 12 (Makes 1½ quarts)

An ice cream maker is good for more than just ice cream; it can also be used to make light, bright sorbet such as this one. Use the freshest strawberries you can find. After hulling the strawberries, you should have 2 pounds of fruit. Weighing the prepped amount is important, as the ratio of fruit to sugar is crucial to the success of the recipe. If using a canister-style ice cream maker, be sure to freeze the empty canister for at least 24 hours and preferably two days before churning the sorbet. For self-refrigerating machines, prechill the canister by running the machine for 5 to 10 minutes before pouring in the sorbet mixture.

2½   pounds strawberries, hulled and quartered

1   cup (7 ounces) sugar

½   cup light corn syrup

1   tablespoon lemon juice

1   teaspoon table salt

1 Process all ingredients in blender until very smooth, about 1 minute. Transfer strawberry mixture to large bowl; cover with plastic wrap; and refrigerate until mixture registers 40 degrees or below, at least 6 hours or up to 24 hours.

2 Place 8½ by 4½-inch loaf pan in freezer. Transfer strawberry mixture to ice cream maker. Churn until mixture has consistency of soft-serve ice cream, 15 to 25 minutes.

3 Using rubber spatula, transfer sorbet to chilled loaf pan, pressing firmly to remove any air pockets. Press plastic flush against surface of sorbet and freeze until firm, at least 6 hours. Serve. (If too firm to scoop, leave on counter for 5 to 10 minutes to soften.) (Sorbet is best eaten within 1 week, but can be frozen for up to 1 month.)

VANILLA ICE CREAM

serves 8 (Makes about 1 quart)

There's nothing quite like the thick, rich, and luxuriously creamy texture of traditional custard-based ice cream made in an ice cream maker. Prefreezing a portion of the custard helps the rest of the base freeze extra quickly once added to the ice cream maker, yielding ice cream with smaller ice crystals and a smoother consistency. If using a canister-style ice cream maker, be sure to freeze the empty canister for at least 24 hours and preferably two days before churning the ice cream. For self-refrigerating machines, prechill the canister by running the machine for 5 to 10 minutes before pouring in the custard.

1	vanilla bean
1¾	cups heavy cream
1¼	cups whole milk
½	cup plus 2 tablespoons (4⅜ ounces) sugar, divided
⅓	cup light corn syrup
¼	teaspoon table salt
6	large egg yolks

1 Place 8- or 9-inch square baking pan in freezer. Cut vanilla bean in half lengthwise. Using tip of paring knife, scrape out seeds. Combine vanilla bean and seeds, cream, milk, 6 table-spoons sugar, corn syrup, and salt in medium saucepan. Heat over medium-high heat, stirring occasionally, until mixture is steaming steadily and registers 175 degrees, 5 to 10 minutes. Remove saucepan from heat.

2 While cream mixture heats, whisk egg yolks and remaining ¼ cup sugar in bowl until smooth, about 30 seconds. Slowly whisk 1 cup heated cream mixture into egg yolk mixture. Return mixture to saucepan and cook over medium-low heat, stirring constantly, until mixture thickens and registers 180 degrees, 7 to 14 minutes. Immediately pour custard into large bowl and let cool until no longer steaming, 10 to 20 minutes. Transfer 1 cup custard to small bowl. Cover both bowls with plastic wrap. Place large bowl in refrigerator and small bowl in freezer and let cool completely, at least 4 hours or up to 24 hours. (Small bowl of custard will freeze solid.)

3 Remove custards from refrigerator and freezer. Scrape frozen custard from small bowl into large bowl of custard. Stir occasionally until frozen custard has fully dissolved. Strain custard through fine-mesh strainer and transfer to ice cream maker. Churn until mixture resembles thick soft-serve ice cream and registers about 21 degrees, 15 to 25 minutes. Transfer ice cream to frozen baking pan and press plastic on surface. Return to freezer until firm around edges, about 1 hour.

4 Transfer ice cream to airtight container, pressing firmly to remove any air pockets, and freeze until firm, at least 2 hours or up to 5 days. Serve.

VARIATION
Coffee Crunch Ice Cream

Look for chocolate-covered cacao nibs (roasted pieces of the cacao bean) in chocolate shops or well-stocked supermarkets. Freeze the cacao nibs for at least 15 minutes before adding them to the churning ice cream.

Substitute ½ cup coarsely ground coffee for vanilla bean. Add ¾ cup chocolate-covered cacao nibs to ice cream during last minute of churning.

Is It Possible to Make Ice Cream Without an Ice Cream Maker?

If you've ever spent a summer's day tossing double-bagged zipper-lock bags of salted ice back and forth or cranking an old-fashioned manual ice cream maker by hand, you know it is indeed possible to make ice cream without a modern electric ice cream maker—just not necessarily easily or with the best-quality results.

But there is, in fact, another way to make silky, creamy ice cream using a multipurpose tool you probably already own: a blender. We've found that we can use a blender to whip air into heavy cream much as an ice cream maker incorporates air into an ice cream base; after mixing the airy whipped cream with a few other ingredients, you're left with an easy no-churn ice cream that just needs to be popped into the freezer to firm up. But hey, don't take our word for it. The easiest ice cream you've ever made is just a blender away.

DARK CHOCOLATE NO-CHURN ICE CREAM

serves 8 (Makes about 1 quart)

The blender's spinning blades mix air into a base of heavy cream and sweetened condensed milk to make ice cream that's rich, smooth, and creamy just like the churned stuff. To melt the chocolate, microwave it in a bowl at 50 percent power for 2 to 3 minutes, stirring it occasionally. The cream mixture freezes more quickly in a loaf pan than in a taller, narrower container. If you don't have a loaf pan, use an 8-inch square baking pan.

2	cups heavy cream, chilled
1	cup sweetened condensed milk
6	ounces bittersweet chocolate, melted
¼	cup whole milk
¼	cup light corn syrup
2	tablespoons sugar
1	teaspoon vanilla extract
½	teaspoon instant espresso powder
¼	teaspoon table salt

1 Process cream in blender until soft peaks form, 20 to 30 seconds. Scrape down sides of blender jar and continue to process until stiff peaks form, about 10 seconds longer. Using rubber spatula, stir in condensed milk, melted chocolate, whole milk, corn syrup, sugar, vanilla, espresso powder, and salt. Process until thoroughly combined, about 20 seconds, scraping down sides of blender jar as needed.

2 Pour cream mixture into 8½ by 4½-inch loaf pan. Press plastic wrap flush against surface of cream mixture. Freeze until firm, at least 6 hours. Serve.

VARIATIONS
Mint-Cookie No-Churn Ice Cream

Omit chocolate and espresso powder. Substitute ¾ teaspoon peppermint extract for vanilla. Add ⅛ teaspoon green food coloring with condensed milk. After transferring cream mixture to loaf pan, gently stir in ½ cup coarsely crushed Oreo cookies before freezing.

Strawberry Buttermilk No-Churn Ice Cream

Omit chocolate and espresso powder. Substitute ½ cup buttermilk for whole milk and lemon juice for vanilla. After transferring cream mixture to loaf pan, dollop ⅓ cup strawberry jam over top. Swirl jam into cream mixture using tines of fork before freezing.

How Should I Store Homemade Ice Cream?

During the initial freeze, you want your ice cream to have as much exposed surface area as possible for faster freezing; that's why we recommend transferring freshly churned (or blended) ice cream from the machine to a container such as a loaf pan for freezing. But once frozen, don't leave it in that loaf pan. Instead, quickly transfer it once more to a sealable, airtight container, pressing out any air pockets as you do. This is to minimize further exposure to air, which alongside the temperature shifts that occur in a home freezer can lead to the formation of those dreaded ice crystals.

Can't I Just Scoop Ice Cream with a Spoon?

Maybe if you have really sturdy spoons—and sturdy hands, for that matter. But we find that spoons dig into our hands uncomfortably when used to scoop hard-frozen, dense ice cream (and sometimes they even bend). With a sturdier construction and a thicker handle, an ice cream scoop gets the job done without the fuss or the pain. Plus, the gentle curve of a good scoop's bowl produces perfect round orbs of ice cream that release easily for picture-perfect cones and bowls.

What About Using a Spring-Loaded Portion Scoop?

We tried using them to scoop ice cream, and we didn't like it. The thin strips of metal meant to swipe the bowl clean and release the ice cream tend to jam on hard ice cream.

worth it

ICE CREAM CONE MAKER

Now that your ice cream is homemade, shouldn't your ice cream cone be too? Freshly made waffle cones have better flavor and a crisper, snappier texture than store-bought ones, and making them is fast and easy with a specially designed cone maker. Sure, it's not exactly an essential kitchen tool, but let's put it this way: If you care enough about good ice cream to invest your money (and counter space) in an ice cream maker, an ice cream cone maker might just be worth it for you too.

Can and Preserve

Home preserving transforms peak-season produce into longer-lasting jams, jellies, pickles, and condiments—and with a few tips and the right equipment, it's easy to do.

How Does Canning Work?

Canning involves heating and cooling fresh foods in jars to kill off harmful microorganisms and deactivate the enzymes that would otherwise cause them to deteriorate over time. There are two methods of home canning approved by the USDA: boiling water canning and pressure canning. Which one you use depends on the acidity, or pH, of the food being preserved.

Boiling water canning is used for processing high-acid foods, including most fruits and pickled vegetables. Hot filled jars are completely immersed in boiling water for a period of time and then allowed to cool. As the jars and their contents cool, the lids vacuum-seal the jars for long-term storage.

Pressure canning is recommended for foods that have very little natural acid, including most nonpickled vegetables, meats, poultry, seafood, and dairy. These must be processed to a temperature hotter than the boiling point of water. A pressure canner is a special pot that heats food to 240 degrees Fahrenheit by way of circulating pressurized steam around the jars instead of boiling water.

worth it
CANNING FUNNEL

If you plan to do much preserving, get a canning funnel. A canning funnel is better suited for this task than a traditional funnel for three reasons: A wide mouth makes it easy to fill, a large opening makes it quicker to fill jars, and it nestles securely into the jar, so the jar is less likely to tip over when full.

anatomy of
A GOOD CANNING POT

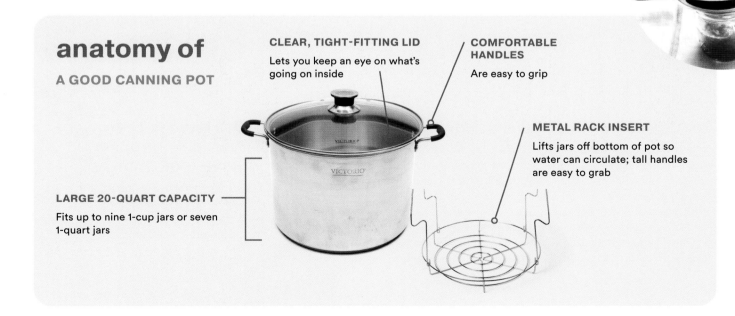

CLEAR, TIGHT-FITTING LID
Lets you keep an eye on what's going on inside

COMFORTABLE HANDLES
Are easy to grip

METAL RACK INSERT
Lifts jars off bottom of pot so water can circulate; tall handles are easy to grab

LARGE 20-QUART CAPACITY
Fits up to nine 1-cup jars or seven 1-quart jars

Can I Use a Regular Stockpot for Canning?

Unless you plan on canning only very small batches, a dedicated canning pot is an essential tool for home canning. Stockpots, while certainly quite large compared to most pots, typically have volumes of only about 12 quarts. In contrast, canning pots have volumes of at least 20 quarts. Plus, canning pots come with metal rack inserts that are important for water circulation and helpful for lifting jars out of the water.

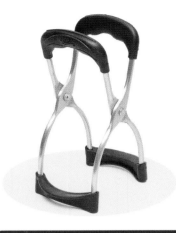

What Kind of Jars Should I Use?

The USDA discourages the use of latch-style jars in boiling water canning because they don't form a consistent seal. We recommend using classic glass canning jars with two-part screw-on lids, since they're widely available and what the USDA has geared their safety protocols toward. Depending on the size of the food and how much of it you're preserving, you might want to use anything from a small 1-cup jar to a larger 1-quart jar; just look for jars with wide mouths to make it easier to access the food inside.

worth it

CANNING JAR LIFTER

A jar lifter: Now that's a single-use gadget for you. But if you want to get serious about canning, it's actually an irreplaceable tool. Jar lifters move glass jars in and out of boiling water during boiling water canning, just as their name implies. Simple enough, but standard kitchen tongs won't work for this: They're too narrow and flat to get a secure grip on the jars' rounded sides, making it all too easy to burn yourself. A jar lifter is safer and faster, which adds up to less time spent leaning over a pot of boiling water—a boon considering that the best time to preserve is typically the warmer summer months.

What's So Bad About Reusing Lids?

It's OK to reuse jars and the ring part of a two-part canning lid, but you should never reuse the flat metal lid itself. The flat metal lid comes with a sealing compound on its underside that helps the lid form a tight seal with the jar once the jar's contents have cooled and formed a vacuum. But this is important: The sealing compound will only form a reliable bond once—and a reliable bond is crucial for keeping bad microorganisms out of your preserves for safe long-term storage. After you break the seal, throw the flat part of the lid away so you're not tempted to reuse it. (You can buy plastic storage caps to use instead after you've opened a jar.)

Do I Need to Leave the Lid Rings on for Long-Term Storage?

No, you don't. In fact, we recommend removing the rings before storing your processed jars. That way you can easily tell if there's a problem with the seal.

real talk with hannah

HOW TO BE A LAZY PRESERVER

I'm the queen of what I call "lazy preserving" (also known as freezing). Now, there's nothing lazy about industriously putting by the fresh bounty of the season, but compared to canning, freezing feels a heck of a lot easier. I bought my vacuum sealer to use with my sous vide machine, but I use it way more often for lazy preserving. Last summer I used it to seal up freshly shucked corn; homemade pesto; strawberry, rhubarb, and lime jam; slow-roasted tomatoes; and whole hot peppers into perfect little packets that I then stacked tidily in bins in my freezer. Pulling out a little packet of summer during the doldrums of winter is like finding a love letter to myself.

DILL PICKLE CHIPS

makes four 1-pint jars

These classic dill pickle chips are an easy way to practice good food preserving habits. The lower temperature used here preserves the pickles' crisp texture. Be sure to use canning and pickling salt, not regular table salt, here. Pickle Crisp is a form of calcium chloride; it keeps the natural pectin in the cucumbers from softening.

2½	pounds pickling cucumbers, ends trimmed, sliced ¼ inch thick
2	tablespoons canning and pickling salt
2	cups chopped dill plus 4 large sprigs
3	cups cider vinegar
3	cups water
¼	cup sugar
1	tablespoon yellow mustard seeds
2	teaspoons dill seeds
½	teaspoon Ball Pickle Crisp
4	garlic cloves, peeled and quartered

1 Toss cucumbers with salt in bowl and refrigerate for 3 hours. Drain cucumbers in colander (do not rinse), then pat dry with paper towels. Bundle chopped dill in cheesecloth and secure with kitchen twine. Bring dill sachet, vinegar, water, sugar, mustard seeds, and dill seeds to boil in large saucepan over medium-high heat. Cover, remove from heat, and let steep for 15 minutes; discard sachet.

2 Meanwhile, set canning rack in canning pot, place four 1-pint jars in rack, and add water to cover by 1 inch. Bring to simmer over medium-high heat, then turn off heat and cover to keep hot. Place dish towel flat on counter. Using jar lifter, remove jars from pot, draining water back into pot. Place jars upside down on towel and let dry for 1 minute. Add ⅛ teaspoon Pickle Crisp to each hot jar, then pack tightly with dill sprigs, garlic, and drained cucumbers.

3 Return brine to brief boil. Using funnel and ladle, pour hot brine over cucumbers to cover, distributing spices evenly and leaving ½ inch headspace. Slide wooden skewer along inside of jar, pressing slightly on vegetables to remove air bubbles, and add extra brine as needed.

4A for short-term storage Let jars cool to room temperature, cover with lids, and refrigerate for 24 hours before serving. (Pickles can be refrigerated for up to 3 months; flavor will continue to mature over time.)

4B for long-term storage While jars are hot, wipe rims clean, add lids, and screw on rings until fingertip-tight; do not overtighten. Before processing jars, heat water in canning pot to temperature between 120 and 140 degrees. Lower jars into water, bring water to 180 to 185 degrees, then cook for 30 minutes, adjusting heat as needed to maintain water between 180 and 185 degrees. Remove jars from pot and let cool for 24 hours. Remove rings, check seal (see FAQ on page 284), and clean rims. (Sealed jars can be stored for up to 1 year.)

VARIATION
Dill Pickle Spears

After trimming both ends from cucumbers, quarter cucumbers lengthwise and cut into 4-inch-long spears. Pack cucumber spears vertically into jars; salting and processing times will remain the same.

CLASSIC STRAWBERRY JAM

makes four 1-cup jars

Make this simple, flavorful jam to practice all the steps of boiling water canning. For safety reasons, use bottled lemon juice, not fresh-squeezed juice, in this recipe. To double this recipe, make two single batches in separate pots. Do not try to make a double batch in a single large pot; it will not work.

3	pounds strawberries, hulled and cut into ½-inch pieces (10 cups)
3	cups sugar
1¼	cups peeled and shredded Granny Smith apple (1 large apple)
2	tablespoons bottled lemon juice

1 Place 2 small plates in freezer to chill. Set canning rack in canning pot, place four 1-cup jars in rack, and add water to cover by 1 inch. Bring to simmer over medium-high heat, then turn off heat and cover to keep hot.

2 In Dutch oven, crush strawberries with potato masher until fruit is mostly broken down. Stir in sugar, apple, and lemon juice and bring to boil over medium-high heat, stirring often. Once sugar is completely dissolved, boil mixture, stirring and adjusting heat as needed, until thickened and registers 217 to 220 degrees, 20 to 25 minutes. (Temperature will be lower at higher elevations) Remove pot from heat.

3 To test consistency, place 1 teaspoon jam on chilled plate and freeze for 2 minutes. Drag your finger through jam on plate; jam has correct consistency when your finger leaves distinct trail. If runny, return pot to heat and simmer for 1 to 3 minutes before retesting. Skim any foam from surface of jam using spoon.

4 Place dish towel flat on counter. Using jar lifter, remove jars from pot, draining water back into pot. Place jars upside down on towel and let dry for 1 minute. Using funnel and ladle, portion hot jam into hot jars, leaving ¼ inch headspace. Slide wooden skewer along inside edge of jar and drag upward to remove air bubbles.

5A for short-term storage Let jam cool to room temperature, cover, and refrigerate until jam is set, 12 to 24 hours. (Jam can be refrigerated for up to 2 months.)

5B for long-term storage While jars are hot, wipe rims clean, add lids, and screw on rings until fingertip-tight; do not overtighten. Return pot of water with canning rack to boil. Lower jars into water, cover, bring water back to boil, then start timer. Cooking time will depend on your altitude: Boil 10 minutes for up to 1,000 feet, 15 minutes for 1,001 to 3,000 feet, 20 minutes for 3,001 to 6,000 feet, or 25 minutes for 6,001 to 8,000 feet. Turn off heat and let jars sit in pot for 5 minutes. Remove jars from pot and let cool for 24 hours. Remove rings, check seal (see FAQ at right), and clean rims. (Sealed jars can be stored for up to 1 year.)

FREQUENTLY ASKED QUESTIONS: PRESERVING EDITION

Q: How do I check the seal?

A: You can tell if the lid is sealed or not by pressing down in the center; a sealed lid won't move, while an unsealed lid will be flexible and make a small popping noise.

Q: Is it bad if there's an air gap in my jar?

A: An ugly but harmless air gap often appears in jars containing larger pieces of fruit or vegetables, such as tomatoes and peaches. This happens when the fruit or vegetables release more water or air than expected. Pieces of fruit or vegetable that poke out of the liquid into the air gap may discolor over time, but they are still safe to eat.

real talk with hannah

WHEN IN DOUBT, THROW IT OUT

It's painful to throw something away that you worked long and hard for. (Also, is it just me or am I always canning on the hottest day of the summer?) Regardless, if you are at all concerned about the integrity of your jar's seal it's best to adhere to the maxim, "When in doubt, throw it out." If you noticed that the seal didn't take right away, you can try to re-can or refrigerate or freeze your goods instead of throwing them away, but please, don't try to eat anything of dubious safety. Botulism is no joke.

more helpful preserving tools

In addition to canning-specific tools, there are several pots, tools, and other equipment you'll use over and over again while preserving.

USE THIS . . .	TO DO THIS!
Digital Scale (page 91)	Measure out precise quantities of ingredients
Chef's Knife and Paring Knife (page 70)	Core, peel, slice, and chop ingredients
Large Saucepan (page 60)	Keep small batches of jam from overevaporating
Instant-Read Thermometer (page 93)	Temp jam and maintain proper water temperature
Potato Masher (page 95)	Mash fruit and crush berries for jam
Whisk (page 95)	Mix ingredients and keep foaming pots under control
Wooden Spoon and Silicone Spatula (page 95)	Stir hot mixtures, scrape out saucepans, and press mixtures through a strainer
Fine-Mesh Strainer (page 375)	Remove particles from pickling brine and turn cooked fruit into smooth puree
Blender (page 132)	Blend liquid-y foods to a smooth texture
Food Processor (page 134)	Quickly prep fruits and vegetables
Colander (page 376)	Rinse fruit and drain salted vegetables
Ladle (page 95)	Transfer ingredients from saucepan to jars
Wooden Skewer	Remove air bubbles from jars

How Can I Make Sure Food Gets Completely Dehydrated?

The most important thing is to slice food thinly and uniformly before dehydrating. Makes sense, right? Dehydrating works by evaporating moisture from the surface of food, so the larger the surface area–to-interior ratio, the faster food will dry out.

Generally, jerky should be dried at temperatures between 135 and 155 degrees Fahrenheit, herbs between 90 and 100 degrees, and most other produce between 135 and 140 degrees.

Do Food Dehydrators Do a Better Job of Drying Food than a Low Oven?

You can dry food in a very low oven or even a microwave, but it's definitely not the most efficient way to go. Drying foods at low temperatures takes hours, so you'll probably have to turn your oven on and off several times to keep it at approximately the right temperature for dehydrating food. Another option is to use an air fryer or air fryer toaster oven, many of which now boast that they can dehydrate food, but the limited space within these appliances means it will take a very long time and several batches to dry a significant amount of food.

Food dehydrators are more convenient and produce better results: They're built to put out steady, low heat; they have fans that circulate air for faster drying; and they have multiple levels of flat rack space for drying large amounts of food at once. Yes, they're a specialty appliance that will take up some counter space, but if you want the option to make lots of your own kale chips, fruit leather, or beef jerky, a dehydrator is a better choice in the long run.

put on a good show

RECIPES

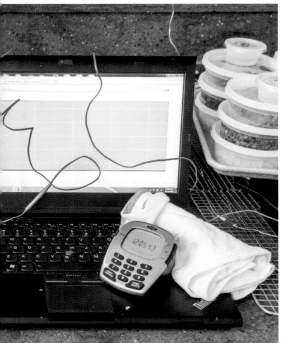

Don't Try This at Home

"High-quality disposable" might seem like an oxymoron, but even for single-use pieces quality matters. That's why we test inexpensive items such as disposable dinnerware and twine as carefully as we do big-ticket equipment like espresso machines: because little things can have a big impact on the success of any gathering. For example, most of us can relate to the woes of using subpar disposable dinnerware at a picnic or potluck: Barbecue sauce drips over the plate's edge and straight onto your neighbor's shoes. Pizza grease soaks through onto your favorite party pants. You accidentally crush your paper cup of soda.

So in our test of disposable plates, we put our chef's whites on the line, loading a variety of plates with a full 2 pounds of picnic favorites including bone-in chicken breast, piping-hot baked beans, coleslaw, and potato salad. Half the plates buckled, sagged, or cracked from the get-go, and after

we let food sit on them for 5 minutes, some plates practically bent in half as we held them, spilling baked beans and coleslaw on us and on the floor. This admittedly messy test quickly clued us in to which plates were the ideal material, size, and thickness to let us enjoy our food with confidence. We gave disposable cups the same scrutiny, repeatedly squeezing both empty and full cups for 10 seconds at a time. Rigid plastic cups cracked immediately, while paper cups—no surprise—were easily crushed, crumpling when empty and sending water over the sides when full. Here, too, the test was worth the cleanup: We found sturdy yet flexible cups that were comfortable to hold and stable when set down.

Sure, testing disposables may not be as exciting as testing the latest food processor or smart oven, but we'll keep doing it because, even for the basics, thoughtful design makes a difference.

Crowd Control

To cook for a large gathering, you don't need a ton of equipment; you just need the right equipment and a bit of organization. We've got you covered on both fronts.

real talk with hannah & lisa

HC

LEARN FROM MY MISTAKES

I love hosting but I make the same mistake every time. I try to plan ahead but end up grocery shopping the same day and get home from the store, exhausted from the effort, with a to-do list as long as my arm. Instead of calmly gliding around before my guests arrive, tweaking floral arrangements and pouring myself a drink, I'm elbow deep in some messy extra cooking project, praying my guests are running late. My advice: Do what you can ahead of time, breaking it into small chunks in the days leading up to your get-together, and serve a mix of homemade and low-to-no prep dishes. Even small, casual events can be made lighter lifts with a little pre-work. And often, the food benefits! Give the flavors in your stew time to meld and deepen. Wash and prep what you can so on the day-of you can coolly and calmly execute the recipe. I know, I know, who am I to give this advice? Someday I'll learn. Here's hoping, at least.

LM

YOU NEED A GAME PLAN

Hannah's advice about advance prep goes for non-food items too. At least a day ahead of time, think about your setup and put everything nonperishable in place. For a buffet, go ahead and lay out plates, napkins, and cutlery. Go find that corkscrew now. Arrange your bar with bottles, glasses, cocktail shaker, blender, ice bucket, and more, depending on what you're serving. Start chilling cold drinks. Buy lots of ice and fill up your biggest cooler before your fridge overflows. Set up your slow cooker (for keeping food hot) near an outlet, along with a big spoon or ladle. Think about what foods you'll serve and dig up serving bowls, platters, and cutting boards, along with serving implements such as big spoons or small knives for cheeses. This way, you'll have more energy to enjoy your own party!

How Can I Ensure the Food Makes It From My Kitchen to the Party in One Piece?

Taking your food on the road—whether for a picnic, a potluck, a bake sale, or any other food-based gathering—can be nerve-wracking. After going to the effort of cooking up an extrabig portion of the most impressive dish in your repertoire, the last thing you want is for it to fall apart in transit.

Cake and pie carriers, insulated casserole totes and shopping totes, coolers, and food storage containers will get your food to its destination in style, keeping hot foods hot and cold foods cold—and all the food safely contained. (See page 178 for more about these pieces of equipment.)

I've Run Out of Burners! What Do I Do?

When you're cooking for a crowd, burner space is often a hot commodity. Portable burners come in handy for dinner parties or during the holidays; they're also great as a backup burner any time in small living spaces. Electric and induction models both work indoors, while gas burners are intended for outdoor use. If you just need to keep food warm, you can use a slow cooker or multicooker (see page 126). Set on low, either one of these appliances will keep soup, chili, mashed potatoes and other side dishes, and fondue at the right temperature for hours. Most warming trays, while designed for the job, are not able to keep food above the safety threshold of 140 degrees, so be cautious about using them. (Temping the food with an instant-read thermometer will tell you if your warming tray is up to the task.)

Can I Use a Portable Burner Indoors?

It depends on the type. Portable electric and induction burners are safe to use indoors. Portable gas burners are designed to be used for camping and outdoor cooking, or by chefs in well-ventilated commercial kitchens and catering establishments. Because they release carbon monoxide, which is odorless, portable gas burners need plenty of fresh airflow to prevent the harmful fumes from being trapped indoors. (Full-size gas stoves are meant to be used in conjunction with ventilation hoods for this reason.)

To see portable burners in action, check out this video.

head to head
PORTABLE BURNERS

PORTABLE GAS BURNERS	**PORTABLE ELECTRIC BURNERS**	**PORTABLE INDUCTION BURNERS**
Powerful cooking, great for woks and deep frying	Hold low temperatures well	Powerful, but not as effective as gas for wok cooking
Dual fuel: use either propane or butane	Not as powerful as gas or induction	Highly adjustable
Can handle pans of any size and weight (if using propane)	Can't be used with pans heavier than 10 pounds	Hold low temperatures well
Should be used outdoors or in well-ventilated areas	Can be used indoors or outdoors	Include temperature probe for precise cooking
No electricity needed (good for power outages)	Compact and lightweight	Require electricity
	Require electricity	Pricey
	Inexpensive	

I Don't Have Enough Baking Pans! Will Disposable Foil Ones Work?

Of course you can cook food in disposable foil baking pans and even reuse them a few times (as long as you wash them by hand between uses). But because they're so thin, disposable pans don't hold heat well, so baked goods won't brown well in them. They're also not as stable as metal, ceramic, or glass options. To a certain extent, you overcome both issues by using a rimmed baking sheet: Preheat the sheet in the oven and place the pan on it. The rimmed baking sheet will transfer more heat to the bottom of the disposable pan and provide a more stable surface for the food.

more tools for cooking for a crowd

You can use these pieces to scale up serving amounts, to help when you're running out of oven or fridge space, and to stay organized when doing lots of cooking.

air fryer
page 122

cooler
page 170

food processor
page 134

food storage containers
page 326

large pot/stockpot
page 364

rimmed baking sheet
page 58

roasting pan with rack
page 62

slow cooker
page 129

timer
page 94

worth it

FAT SEPARATOR

The time-honored way of removing fat from a stock or stew—refrigerating it overnight so the fat will harden—is also time-consuming. A fat separator will help get the job done a lot quicker. The liquid goes into the separator through a built-in strainer at the top. After a short rest to allow the fat to rise to the top, you either pour off the liquid from a spout set in the base (for pitcher-style separators) or pull a lever to release a plug at the bottom (for bottom-draining separators), allowing the liquid to drain into a bowl.

PRESSURE-COOKER PULLED PORK

serves 8

An hour in the multicooker tenderizes pork butt roast effortlessly, streamlining what is normally a labor-intensive dish. Don't shred the meat too fine in step 3; it will break up more as the meat is combined with the sauce. Pork butt roast is often labeled Boston butt in the supermarket.

- 3 tablespoons packed brown sugar, plus extra for seasoning
- 2 tablespoons paprika
- 2 tablespoons chili powder
- 2 teaspoons ground cumin
- 1 teaspoon table salt
- ½ teaspoon pepper
- 1 (4-pound) boneless pork butt roast, trimmed and quartered
- ¾ cup plus 1 tablespoon cider vinegar, divided, plus extra for seasoning
- ½ cup water
- ½ cup ketchup
- ½ teaspoon liquid smoke
- 8 hamburger buns

1 Combine sugar, paprika, chili powder, cumin, salt, and pepper in bowl, then rub mixture evenly over pork. Combine ¾ cup vinegar, water, ketchup, and liquid smoke in pressure cooker, then nestle pork into pot.

2 Lock lid in place and close pressure release valve. Select high pressure cook function and cook for 45 minutes. Turn off pressure cooker and let pressure release naturally for 15 minutes. Quick-release any remaining pressure, then carefully remove lid, allowing steam to escape away from you.

3 Transfer pork to large bowl, let cool slightly, then shred into bite-size pieces, discarding any excess fat.

4 Let braising liquid settle, then skim excess fat from surface using large spoon. Using highest sauté or browning function, cook liquid until reduced to about 2 cups, 15 to 20 minutes. Stir in remaining 1 tablespoon vinegar and season with salt, pepper, extra sugar, and extra vinegar to taste. Stir 1 cup sauce into shredded pork, then add extra sauce to taste. Serve pork on buns, passing remaining sauce separately.

Can I Truss a Bird or Tie a Roast with Any Old Twine?

For any task involving food, stick with kitchen twine; it's made to be food-safe. A typical hardware-store skein isn't intended for use with food; plus, if it's dyed you're likely to wind up with more colorful food than you bargained for (á la Bridget Jones's blue soup). It's worth keeping a ball of kitchen twine (also known as butcher's twine) in your kitchen drawer. You can buy cotton or linen twine. Both work well; they're strong, hold a tight knot, and pull away from cooked meat easily—but we prefer cotton because it's more economical.

By the way, while unwaxed dental floss is commonly touted as an alternative to kitchen twine, that's not a good idea either: It's so thin that it can cut through the meat you are trying to tie, it becomes almost invisible (and thus hard to remove) after cooking, and it's particularly ill-suited to grilling because it easily singes and then breaks.

What's the Point of Tying a Roast?

Most large cuts of meat have an irregular shape, which means thicker and thinner parts that will cook at different rates. Tying a roast helps maintain its shape during cooking so that it cooks evenly. Tying the legs of whole poultry prevents them from splaying open, which could make them cook unevenly.

to tie a roast Use double knots to secure pieces of kitchen twine at 1- to 1½-inch intervals (2 to 3 finger widths apart).

to tie poultry Tie legs together with kitchen twine. Alternatively, if poultry has pocket of skin at tail end, tuck legs in there.

HERB-CRUSTED ROAST BEEF TENDERLOIN

serves 12

We use kitchen twine to tie this pricey cut so it cooks to rosy perfection throughout. Tucking the tapered end under before tying shapes the tenderloin into an even cylinder.

- 1   (6-pound) whole beef tenderloin, trimmed, tail end tucked, and tied at 1½-inch intervals
- 1   tablespoon kosher salt
- 1   tablespoon cracked black peppercorns
- 2   teaspoons sugar
- 2   slices hearty white sandwich bread, torn into pieces
- 2½   ounces Parmesan cheese, grated (1¼ cups), divided
- ½   cup chopped fresh parsley, divided
- 6   tablespoons extra-virgin olive oil, divided
- 2   tablespoons plus 2 teaspoons chopped fresh thyme, divided
- 4   garlic cloves, minced

1 Set wire rack in rimmed baking sheet. Pat roast dry with paper towels. Combine salt, peppercorns, and sugar in small bowl and rub all over roast. Transfer to prepared sheet and let sit at room temperature for 1 hour. (Tenderloin can be trimmed, tied, rubbed with salt mixture, and refrigerated up to 24 hours in advance; allow roast to come to room temperature before putting in oven.)

2 Meanwhile, pulse bread in food processor to fine crumbs, about 15 pulses. Transfer bread crumbs to medium bowl and toss with ½ cup Parmesan, 2 tablespoons parsley, 2 tablespoons oil, and 2 teaspoons thyme until evenly combined. Wipe out food processor with paper towels and process remaining ¾ cup Parmesan, remaining 6 tablespoons parsley, remaining ¼ cup oil, remaining 2 tablespoons thyme, and garlic until smooth paste forms. Transfer herb paste to small bowl.

3 Adjust oven rack to upper-middle position and heat oven to 400 degrees. Roast beef for 20 minutes, then remove from oven. Remove twine. Coat beef with herb paste, then bread-crumb topping. Roast until beef registers 120 to 125 degrees (for medium-rare) and topping is golden brown, 20 to 25 minutes. (If topping browns before beef reaches preferred internal temperature, lightly cover with aluminum foil for remainder of roasting time and remove foil while beef rests.) Transfer to carving board and let rest for 30 minutes. Slice roast ½ inch thick. Serve.

EASY HERB-ROASTED TURKEY WITH GRAVY

serves 10 to 12

Using a fat separator helps you get the gravy finished while the turkey rests. We recommend using a self-basting turkey, such as a Butterball, for this recipe.

TURKEY

2	onions, chopped
1	carrot, peeled and chopped
1	celery rib, chopped
4	cups chicken broth
1	cup dry white wine
5	fresh sage leaves, plus 1 tablespoon minced
1	sprig fresh rosemary, plus 1 tablespoon minced
1	sprig fresh thyme, plus 1 tablespoon minced
8	tablespoons unsalted butter, softened
4	garlic cloves, minced
1	tablespoon grated lemon zest
1	teaspoon table salt
1	teaspoon pepper
1	(12- to 14-pound) prebrined turkey, neck and giblets discarded

GRAVY

4	tablespoons unsalted butter
⅓	cup all-purpose flour
2	tablespoons minced fresh parsley

1 for the turkey Adjust oven rack to lowest position and heat oven to 325 degrees. Scatter onions, carrot, and celery in bottom of large roasting pan; add broth, wine, sage leaves, rosemary sprig, and thyme sprig to pan. Set V-rack over vegetables in roasting pan.

2 Combine butter, garlic, lemon zest, salt, pepper, minced sage, minced rosemary, and minced thyme in bowl and mix until smooth.

3 Pat turkey dry inside and out with paper towels. Using your fingers, gently loosen skin covering breast and legs, being careful not to tear skin. Spoon half of butter mixture under skin, directly onto meat. Using your hands, rub remaining butter mixture over outside of turkey. Tuck wings behind back and tie legs together with kitchen twine.

4 Transfer turkey, breast side up, to V-rack. Roast until breast registers 160 degrees and drumsticks/thighs register 175 degrees, 2½ to 3 hours. Transfer turkey to carving board and let rest for 30 minutes.

5 for the gravy Meanwhile, carefully strain contents of roasting pan through fine-mesh strainer into fat separator; discard solids and let liquid settle for at least 5 minutes.

6 Melt butter in medium saucepan over medium heat. Add flour and whisk constantly until honey-colored, about 2 minutes. Gradually whisk in 4 cups defatted pan juices (if necessary, add enough water to equal 4 cups) and bring to boil. Reduce heat to medium-low and simmer, stirring occasionally, until thickened, about 5 minutes. Off heat, stir in parsley and season with salt and pepper to taste. Carve turkey and serve with gravy.

Feeling Fancy

Serving elegant fare often means spending a bit more on menu items. The right tools help you protect your investment by enabling you to get the most out of pricey ingredients and keep them tasting their best.

What's the Right Way to Shuck an Oyster?

First, you need the right knife. Most oyster knives have a thick, dull blade that acts as a lever to pry oyster shells apart without cutting into them, and a comfortable, non-slip handle that feels secure in your palm—important, since opening oysters requires applying a bit of pressure. (Regular knives are too sharp and too flexible for the task.) For extra security, you'll also need a dish towel. With these two tools and a bit of practice, you can enjoy fresh shucked oysters without waiting for a night out at a restaurant.

1 Fold dish towel several times into thin, tight roll. Grip towel in fist of hand that will be holding oyster, wrapping 1 end over your thumb and tucking it between your thumb and forefinger.

2 Using your protected thumb, hold oyster in place with hinge facing away from thumb. Insert tip of oyster knife into hinge of oyster.

3 Work tip of knife into hinge using twisting motion. When shells begin to separate, twist knife to pop hinge.

4 Run knife along top shell, scraping abductor muscle from shell to release oyster. Slide knife under oyster to scrape abductor muscle from bottom shell.

OYSTERS ON THE HALF SHELL

serves 2 to 3

A sturdy oyster knife makes quick work of opening these briny bivalves, for a super-easy appetizer. A bed of crushed ice not only chills the oysters but also keeps them securely nestled on the platter so that they don't tip. If you're serving the oysters with an accompaniment, embed the serving bowl in the ice before filling it.

3   pounds crushed ice

12   oysters, well scrubbed

Arrange ice in even layer on chilled serving platter. Shuck 1 oyster and discard top shell; place oyster on ice, being careful not to spill much liquid. Repeat with remaining oysters.

RED WINE VINEGAR MIGNONETTE GRANITÉ

serves 8 (Makes about ⅔ cup)

Freezing the tart-sweet mignonette often served with oysters makes it into a topping of flavorful ice flakes. For a traditional mignonette, skip the freezing and scraping steps; simply refrigerate the mixed ingredients for at least 30 minutes or up to two days, and serve chilled.

½   cup red wine vinegar

3   tablespoons water

2   teaspoons finely grated shallot

¾   teaspoon sugar

1   teaspoon coarsely ground pepper

In shallow bowl, stir together vinegar, water, shallot, and sugar. Freeze until fully frozen, at least 1 hour or up to 2 days. One hour before serving, place small serving bowl in freezer. To serve, scrape frozen mixture with fork to create ice crystals. Stir in pepper. Transfer to chilled serving bowl; serve or cover and freeze until ready to use.

What's the Best Way to Crush Ice?

Use this quick, old-fashioned method to produce large amounts of evenly crushed ice:

1 Fill heavy-duty 1-gallon zipper-lock freezer bag about three-quarters full with ice cubes and press out as much air as possible before sealing.

2 Wrap bag tightly with large dish towel. Strike wrapped bag with mallet, skillet, or rolling pin to break ice to desired size. (Don't use a pin made of softwood or one with ball bearings, as it could be damaged by the ice.)

Is a Cheese Plane Better at Slicing Cheese than a Sharp Knife?

If you're serving relatively young semihard to hard cheeses that are fairly uniform in texture, such as young gouda, Manchego, or Comté, there are good reasons to use a cheese plane instead of a knife. The razor-like blade of a cheese plane can make it easier to consistently slice these kinds of cheeses into thin, even pieces that are pleasant to eat. Thin slices come up to optimal serving temperature more quickly than thicker wedges or chunks, allowing you and your guests to better appreciate the cheese's flavor and texture. For firm, crumbly, or harder aged cheeses, however, using a knife allows for the unique texture gradient between the rind and the center of the cheese to be preserved and enjoyed.

How Do I Set up a Cheese Board?

The best cheese boards include a variety of cheeses complemented by sweet and savory accompaniments as well as crackers or bread. Plan on 2 to 3 ounces of cheese per person and provide a range of textures and flavors as well as different types of cheese, such as those made from goat's milk, cow's milk, or sheep's milk. Make sure that each cheese has its own knife; if you've precut some of the cheese you may also want to set out toothpicks. It's a nice touch to label the cheeses so your guests know what they're eating. Cheese is best at room temperature, so remove it from the refrigerator 1 to 2 hours before serving. (To keep it from drying out, don't unwrap it until party time.) To accompany the cheese without upstaging it, opt for mild-tasting bread and crackers. Include embellishments such as chutneys, jams, and honey in small pots or bowls with little spoons for serving.

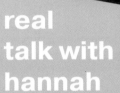

How Can I Keep Cheese Fresh?

It's a conundrum: Wrapping cheese tightly encourages mold, but loosely wrapped cheese dries out and hardens. Cheese paper—wax-coated paper lined with thin, porous polyethylene plastic—allows moisture to wick off the cheese but not escape entirely. In our tests, it kept cheddar, Brie, and goat cheeses free of mold and dryness for three solid weeks. If you don't have cheese paper (also available in bag form), the next best method is to first wrap the cheese tightly in waxed or parchment paper and then loosely in aluminum foil.

real talk with hannah

EASY WAYS TO MAKE A BOARD LOOK FANCY

I learned so much about presentation from my friend Elle's gorgeous book *Boards*. Extra touches that make a cheese board special don't have to involve a lot of work. You can lightly toast thin baguette slices to make a crisp base for creamy cheese. Add nuts, either plain or roasted and spiced; buttery Marcona almonds are a good choice. Include a small bowl of olives and/or cornichons for a savory element (don't forget a little bowl for olive pits!). Dried and fresh fruit such as crisp apple or pear slices, juicy grapes, sweet and chewy dried apricots, or fresh or dried figs all go well with cheese; plus, they add beautiful color to your board.

WHIPPED CASHEW DIP WITH ROASTED RED PEPPERS AND OLIVES

serves 8 (Makes 2 cups)

Serve this creamy, brightly flavored dip in a shallow bowl as part of a cheese or crudité board.

- 1½ cups raw cashews
- ½ cup jarred roasted red peppers, rinsed, patted dry, and chopped
- 3 tablespoons water
- 3 tablespoons extra-virgin olive oil
- 3 tablespoons lemon juice
- 1 garlic clove, minced
- ½ cup minced fresh parsley
- ½ cup pitted kalamata olives, chopped

1 Place cashews in bowl and add cold water to cover by 1 inch. Let sit at room temperature for at least 12 hours or up to 24 hours. Drain and rinse well.

2 Process soaked cashews, red peppers, water, oil, lemon juice, and garlic in food processor until smooth, about 2 minutes, scraping down sides of bowl as needed. Transfer cashew mixture to bowl, stir in parsley and olives, and season with salt and pepper to taste. Cover with plastic wrap and let sit at room temperature until flavors meld, about 30 minutes, before serving. (Dip can be refrigerated for up to 2 days.)

FIG-BALSAMIC JAM

serves 8 to 10 (Makes about 1 cup)

Set out a bowl of this sweet-savory jam on a cheese or charcuterie board, with a small spoon for dolloping.

- 12 ounces fresh figs, stemmed and quartered
- ½ cup sugar
- ¼ cup balsamic vinegar
- ¼ cup water
- 1 tablespoon lemon juice
- 1 teaspoon yellow mustard seeds
- ¾ teaspoon minced fresh rosemary
- Pinch table salt
- Pinch pepper

1 Bring all ingredients to simmer in 10-inch nonstick skillet over medium-high heat. Reduce heat to medium-low and cook, stirring occasionally, until rubber spatula leaves distinct trail when dragged across bottom of skillet, 25 to 30 minutes.

2 Transfer jam to food processor and pulse until uniformly chunky, 4 to 6 pulses. Let jam cool to room temperature, about 1 hour, before serving. (Jam can be refrigerated for up to 2 months.)

Is Fondue Due for a Comeback?

We don't know why this retro party dish ever went away: It's easy to make, customizable, interactive, and fun. While you can make fondue in a saucepan, using a fondue set saves you from having to constantly rewarm the dip, and its color-coded pronged forks let your guests keep track of their utensils; plus, it's just more festive. Fondue sets can be electric or use Sterno; we prefer the former for their adjustability and ability to maintain a consistent temperature.

Lisa Says . . .

Sure, a fondue set is cute, but if you don't have one, and you do have a slow cooker, you can use that instead. You can cook the fondue in the slow cooker or make it on the stove and keep it warm and bubbly in the slow cooker. A portable induction burner also works great—it's nice and safe and table-ready.

CHOCOLATE FONDUE

serves 6 to 8

Serving this glossy ganache in a fondue pot keeps it at the perfect dipping temperature for as long as it lasts. Milk chocolate, bittersweet chocolate, or a combination will work fine here; just use a high-quality chocolate you like straight from the package.

12	ounces chocolate, chopped
1⅓	cups heavy cream
	Pinch table salt
1	tablespoon corn syrup

Place chocolate in bowl. Bring cream and salt just to simmer in small saucepan over medium heat, then pour hot cream over chocolate. Cover bowl and let chocolate soften for 3 minutes. Whisk chocolate mixture until smooth, then add corn syrup and whisk to incorporate. Transfer chocolate mixture to fondue pot, warm pot for 5 minutes, and serve immediately.

VARIATIONS
Five-Spice Chocolate Fondue

Add 2 teaspoons ground cinnamon, 5 whole cloves, 1 teaspoon black peppercorns, 2 star anise pods, and two ½-inch pieces fresh ginger to saucepan with cream. Bring mixture to simmer, then cover, remove from heat, and let steep for 10 minutes. Strain mixture through fine-mesh strainer into bowl; discard spices. Return cream to simmer in now-empty saucepan before pouring over chocolate.

Orange Chocolate Fondue

Add 1 tablespoon grated orange zest to saucepan with cream. Bring mixture to simmer, then cover, remove from heat, and let steep for 10 minutes. Strain mixture through fine-mesh strainer into bowl; discard zest. Return cream to simmer in now-empty saucepan before pouring over chocolate. Add 2 tablespoons orange liqueur, such as Grand Marnier or Cointreau, with corn syrup.

Should I Be Aerating My Wine?

Some exposure to air can alter wine for the better. The interaction of wine and air makes an impact on highly volatile chemicals such as free acetaldehyde, which can translate to flatness in wine, and sulfur compounds, which can produce a harsh taste. (There's no evidence that aeration changes the level of tannins, which give wine its astringency, because tannins are not volatile.)

Simply pouring wine into a glass and swirling it a few times introduces some air to the wine, but for younger red wines, which may taste harsh or flat, aeration can balance flavor and encourage more complex aromas. Some connoisseurs recommend it for certain white wines as well but after testing with several varieties, we've found no benefit to aerating white wine. To aerate wine you can open a bottle and wait 10 to 30 minutes for the wine to "breathe," or you can use a wine aerator. Held above a wine glass or inserted into a bottle, this device exposes the wine to air while you pour, smoothing out harsh notes and bringing forward fruity flavor and aroma.

What's the Best Way to Save Leftover Wine?

While air can improve wine in the short term, prolonged oxidation (exposure to air) degrades its flavor. Wine-saving gadgets protect the wine in an opened and partially empty bottle from oxidation by sucking air out of the wine bottle, by displacing the air by inflating a balloon within the bottle, or by replacing the air with argon (an inert gas). Any of these methods can keep wine drinkable for anywhere from a week to a month. If you don't own, or don't want to buy, one of these gadgets, you can reduce exposure to air by transferring left-over wine to a sealable vessel into which it just fits, with no room for air, such as a smaller bottle or a Mason jar.

What About Leftover Champagne?

Once you've popped open a bottle of champagne (or any sparkling wine), it's just a matter of time before it ceases to sparkle. Sealing the bottle with plastic wrap and a rubber band will keep it reasonably drinkable for a couple of days but the bubbles will be greatly reduced. And contrary to rumor, dropping a raisin into an open bottle of flat champagne can't bring back the bubbles; the raisin's wrinkly surface coaxes the carbon dioxide in the wine to form bubbles, which merely make the champagne look effervescent. But the raisin can't actually add carbon dioxide to the wine, which is necessary to restore fizz.

If you regularly find yourself with leftover champagne, you can buy a specialized cap that creates an airtight seal to preserve the champagne's effervescence for a few days (or longer if you don't open the bottle after fitting it with the cap). Another thought: Use leftover champagne in cooking, such as when deglazing a skillet to make a pan sauce, or in a dressing for fruit salad (see recipe at right).

NECTARINES, BLUEBERRIES, AND RASPBERRIES WITH CHAMPAGNE-CARDAMOM REDUCTION

serves 4 to 6 (Makes 6 cups)

This fresh summer salad is an excellent use for leftover champagne. Dry white wine can be used as an alternative.

1	cup champagne
¼	cup granulated sugar
	Pinch table salt
1	tablespoon grated lemon zest plus 1 tablespoon juice
5	cardamom pods, crushed
3	medium nectarines (about 18 ounces), pitted and cut into ½-inch wedges (about 3 cups)
1	pint fresh blueberries
½	pint fresh raspberries

Simmer champagne, sugar, and salt in small, heavy-bottomed nonreactive saucepan over high heat until syrupy, honey-colored, and reduced to ¼ cup, about 15 minutes. Off heat, add lemon zest and juice and cardamom; steep 1 minute to allow flavors to meld, then strain, discarding solids. Combine nectarines, blueberries, and raspberries in bowl; pour warm dressing over fruit and toss to combine. Serve immediately at room temperature or cover with plastic wrap, refrigerate for up to 4 hours, and serve chilled.

5 Hacks for Party Hosting

Use these simple tips at your next gathering to help things run smoothly so you can focus on the fun.

2 SCHEDULE YOUR OVEN USE

If you're making several recipes that require the oven, it's good to have a strategy and a schedule. Say you've decided to roast a turkey and make roasted squash, which require different cooking temperatures. Unless you have the luxury of two ovens, you'll need to plan when to cook each dish, and how to keep either one hot. The more you can prepare in advance, the more relaxed you'll be when guests arrive. Foods such as dinner rolls and many desserts can be baked ahead of time—even days ahead and frozen.

1 MAKE A LIST AND CHECK IT TWICE

It's one thing to spend a few minutes rummaging around the kitchen for an ingredient, but it's a different story if you have to run out to the store at the last minute. At least a few days before the event, make a checklist of ingredients, including staples you might take for granted such as oil, salt, and pepper. Also note the equipment each recipe requires so you're not short a casserole dish or pie plate. Finally, decide which platters and other serving pieces you'll be using and take the time to locate them so you're sure you have everything you need and know exactly where it is.

3 STOCK UP ON DINNERWARE

Have more plates and silverware on hand than you think you'll need so that you don't get caught short and have to wash items during your get-together. If you don't have matching sets, don't sweat it! Mismatched dinnerware has an eclectic appeal. (Thrift shops are great places to find unique pieces without spending a lot.) That goes for glasses, too, since drinks are prone to being set down and misplaced during a party. (You could also buy a set of charms or markers for wine glasses and cocktail glasses, which is a fun thing to offer guests so they know which glass is theirs.) And if your get-together is casual, it's totally fine to give yourself a break and use disposable dinnerware (see page 308).

4 WARM YOUR DINNER PLATES

Serving a hot meal on a hot plate keeps the food at the right temperature longer and is a nice touch that elevates the dining experience, which is why many restaurants heat their dinner plates. At home you can warm plates in a 200-degree oven or, if the oven is full, stack them at the back of your stove, where the hot air rising from the oven will gently warm them. If your stove is crowded with pots and pans, you can put your plates in your (clean and otherwise empty) dishwasher and run the drying cycle.

5 CHILL YOUR DINNER PLATES

Just as hot food should go on a hot plate, cold food should go on a cold plate. When serving cold dishes such as crudo, sushi; and especially salad, which stay fresh and cool longer on a cold plate, store the plates in the fridge for 30 minutes to an hour before serving. Alternatively, rinse the plates under cold water and dry them off.

You've Been Served

Preparing great food is half of the equation when it comes to gatherings—serving it is the other half. Proper utensils ensure that your presentation is as polished as your meal.

real talk with lisa

SERVE RIGHT IN THE COOKING VESSEL

From a few memorably bad experiences, I've learned lots of ways to make entertaining easy and not get too tired to enjoy the occasion. If you're happy and relaxed, your guests will be too. Pro tip: I love when the cooking pot is pretty enough to go right onto the table for serving, like when you've cooked in a cast-iron braiser, skillet, or Dutch oven; broiler-proof baking dish; or paella pan. Last Thanksgiving, I made my stuffing from start to finish—from sautéing onions to topping the bread stuffing with chicken wings for poultry flavor, to baking it and finally running it under the broiler to crisp up the top—in our winning paella pan. Then I put the pan of stuffing right on the table. We had a big crowd for dinner and it was a hit.

Hannah Says . . .

Electric knives have a retro vibe but they work impressively well. Just playing around with our winner I was able to slice through roast turkey breast like Martha-Freakin'-Stewart, leaving a perfect sliver of golden brown skin atop each slice. They are motorized, so they make noise, and a sharp chef's knife works well, but if you want effortless, perfect slicing, a good electric knife delivers.

Lisa Says . . .

Unlike Hannah, I don't actually love electric knives; I prefer to carve chickens and big roasts such as turkey and other bone-in meats with my trusty, sharp, agile chef's knife. It can get into tight corners to maneuver around bones and joints, and also makes lovely slices.

Should I Buy a Carving Set?

A matching carving knife and fork look impressive when you're standing tableside behind a large roast, but you likely already own the right knife: A good, sharp chef's knife is more than up to the task of cutting meat away from the bones of a whole turkey or a ham and then slicing it neatly. For large plain roasts without bones, the long, straight blade of a slicing knife makes perfect, presentation-worthy slices, so if you serve a lot of brisket, for example, a slicing knife is a worthwhile buy. As for the fork, holding a roast firmly in place while you carve takes something with more presence than a dinner fork. A carving fork is a sturdy, oversize utensil with two tines; we prefer curved tines, which provide a better sight line and keep your fork-holding arm at a closer, more comfortable angle.

Are Electric Knives Actually Any Good?

Electric knives may seem like relics of the past, but they're still shimmying away in 21st-century kitchens. Their two identical serrated blades are riveted together and move in opposite directions—one forward, one backward—which creates a sawing motion that cuts food with minimal downward pressure. In theory this makes them ideal for cutting delicate items that you don't want to squish, such as breads and other baked goods, as well as for carving skin-on poultry without ripping or pulling the skin. When we tested electric knives, we found that they struggled somewhat with bread; however, many users found them easier to carve a turkey with than our favorite chef's knife. They also worked well on double-crust pies, cutting slices without smashing the top crust.

Yuck! My Salad Bowl is Covered in a Slimy Film. How Do I Get It Off?

Years of exposure to oily salad dressings can leave a wooden salad bowl with tacky, rancid residue. Here's how to make it look and feel new again—and keep it that way.

To remove sticky buildup: Adjust an oven rack to the middle position and heat the oven to 275 degrees. Line a rimmed baking sheet with aluminum foil or parchment paper and set a wire rack in the sheet. Place the bowl upside down on the rack, turn off the oven (don't forget this step!), and place the sheet in the oven. Within minutes, oils will start to bead on the surface of the bowl. After 1 to 2 hours, oils will run off the bowl and onto the sheet. Once the bowl appears dry, remove the sheet from the oven and wipe down the bowl with paper towels to remove any residue. (If the bowl is still sticky, repeat the process.)

To reseason: Whenever the bowl becomes dry or dull-looking, use a paper towel to liberally apply food-safe mineral oil (which, unlike cooking oils, won't turn rancid) to all its surfaces. Let stand for 15 minutes, then wipe away any residue with a clean paper towel.

To clean and maintain: Use mild dish soap and warm water to clean a well-seasoned wooden bowl. Always dry the bowl thoroughly after cleaning. Never put the bowl in the dishwasher or let it soak in water, as it will warp and crack.

How Do I Use Chopsticks?

For a secure, comfortable grip, follow these tips from our colleague, and author of *A Very Chinese Cookbook*, Kevin Pang.

1 Let bottom chopstick rest against your ring finger. Let top chopstick rest between your index and middle finger, using your thumb to hold it in place.

2 To make sure both chopsticks are even, gently rest ends on table.

3 To use chopsticks, keep bottom chopstick still and move top chopstick to pinch mouthful of food. To pick up noodles, dig in and then turn chopsticks as you lift.

Why Are There So Many Kinds of Chopsticks?

Chopsticks were first used in China more than 4,000 years ago and were adopted by many other countries in Asia, including Japan and Korea, which adapted them to suit their own cuisines and customs. Although shapes and materials can vary, there are some distinctions that are characteristic of chopsticks in each country.

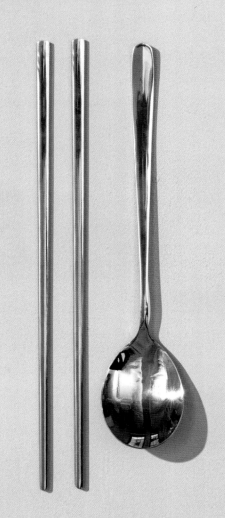

JAPANESE

- Medium length (usually around 9 inches)
- Sharply tapered, with rounded or squared handles and pointed tips designed to make it easier to pick up delicate foods and pick bones from fish
- Usually made of wood (often lacquered), bamboo, or melamine
- Tips are often scored to help chopsticks grip food

KOREAN

- Medium length (usually around 9 inches) makes it easier to eat when holding a bowl close to the face
- Sharply tapered, with flat handles
- Usually made of stainless steel
- Tips are often scored to help chopsticks grip food
- Often come in a set with a spoon

CHINESE

- Relatively long length (around 10 inches) makes it easier to reach into communal dishes
- Subtly tapered, with squared handles (to prevent rolling) and blunt tips
- Usually made of wood, bamboo, or melamine

anatomy of

A GOOD BASIC FLATWARE SET

STAINLESS STEEL CONSTRUCTION

Makes flatware durable and dishwasher-safe

KNIVES WITH SERRATIONS

Help cut food

ROUNDED, TEARDROP-SHAPED HANDLE

Is comfortable to hold and ensures a secure grip

WELL BALANCED

Utensils don't tip when in use

MODERATE WEIGHT

Pieces feel substantial but not too heavy

Lisa Says . . .

I was truly pleasantly surprised when I first picked up the reusable plastic cups that my teammate Carolyn tested for our review. My mental image of "plastic cups" was of something cheap and basic, and these looked and felt anything but. In fact it took a second to realize that they were not glassware, and the designs were attractive. It's great to know they're also inexpensive and unbreakable, so you can take them outdoors or use them at a lively party without a second thought.

FREQUENTLY ASKED QUESTIONS: FLATWARE EDITION

Q: What's the difference between silverware and flatware?

A: The terms "silverware" and "flatware" are often used interchangeably, but they have slightly different meanings. Silverware is made from sterling silver or silver-plated metal, and it's expensive. A single sterling silver place setting can easily run $400 or more. Real silverware also requires special care; you have to wash it by hand, dry it by hand (instead of letting it air-dry), and polish it regularly. "Flatware" describes utensils that are made from other materials. Most of what you'll find in restaurants, cafeterias, and home kitchens is made from stainless steel. Compared with sterling silverware, stainless steel is much more durable and—as the name implies—doesn't become tarnished and is unlikely to stain or rust.

Q: What's the difference between 18/10 and 18/0 stainless steel?

A: Most of the stainless steel used to make flatware contains nickel—which makes the steel glossier, stronger, and resistant to rust and corrosion. It's called 18/10 stainless steel because it's 18 percent chromium and 10 percent nickel. Manufacturers can also use 18/0 stainless steel, which is less expensive and contains no nickel. While flatware sets of both types performed equally well in our tests, those made with 18/10 stainless steel should hold up better over time.

Which Glasses Should I Use?

Using the right shape glasses for wine, beer, and other drinks serves a practical purpose, whether it's keeping drinks at the right temperature, preserving bubbles, or even improving flavor. It also makes any gathering more festive. (See page 205 for more about basic glass shapes as well as some fun specialty glassware.) Disposable cups are great for parties, large dinners, outdoor meals, and holiday gatherings where you don't have enough regular glasses to go around or you just don't want to risk breaking any. They also make for easy cleanup. If you have the right disposal facilities in your area, clear plastic recyclable or compostable glasses make the best choice: They're somewhat environmentally friendly, plus they look nice and hold up well.

Disposable Dinnerware Is Made to Be Thrown Out. Why Care About Its Quality?

Equipment doesn't get much more simple or basic than a disposable plate, bowl, or cup, but there are still variations among types and brands—and those differences matter. Load up a flimsy plate with heavy or wet foods and dinner could wind up on the floor. Because eating from disposable dinnerware often means eating standing up or with a plate or bowl in your lap, it's important that the item in question be thick and sturdy enough to avoid buckling, even when you stab it with a fork or slice it with a knife. Thicker walls also help prevent grease and liquid from soaking through onto your clothes. Material matters too; plates and bowls made of polystyrene are thick, but you can't use them to reheat food in the microwave because they melt and warp. Dinnerware made from thick traditional paper or bagasse (paper made from sugarcane pulp), on the other hand, is strong, durable, and microwave-safe. And finally, shape is a factor: Steep rims and high sides help contain food, but rims that are too large give you less surface area to work with.

Is Compostable Dinnerware Really Better for the Environment?

As long as you compost it correctly, the answer is a definite yes. But composting isn't always as simple as throwing it in your backyard bin, as our colleague Carolyn Grillo found out.

Compostable dinnerware can be made from a variety of materials, not all of which will break down in a backyard composting system. Bamboo utensils and dinnerware made from bamboo, bagasse (sugar cane), palm leaves, and uncoated paper can be composted at home. But utensils, plates, and cups made from polylactic acid (PLA), and crystallized polylactic acid (CPLA), both of which are vegetable starch–based plastics, require the higher, more consistent temperatures of a commercial facility to help them break down. (Some commercial composting facilities also introduce microorganisms to the mix to speed up the process.) If you put them in your compost, they won't biodegrade. So ideally you should dispose of these items either by using your city's composting program or through a subscription composting service.

What happens if you simply throw your compostable dinnerware in the trash? In a landfill, compostable utensils will break down faster than plastic utensils only if there's oxygen available—a rare occurrence. In landfills where there's little to no oxygen available, compostable utensils can take hundreds of years to break down. However, some argue that there are benefits to using utensils made from renewable resources instead of petroleum, which is often used to make plastic.

Bottom line: If you're trying to minimize the impact of your disposable dinnerware, first check if you have access to a commercial composting facility. If you don't have access to commercial composting, check to see if your town or city recycles any paper or plastic dinnerware.

Hannah Says . . .

Like many, I strive to make small changes in my life to minimize my environmental impact. For me, a negative side effect of this is quite a lot of guilt when I'm not 100 percent perfect. Now, this could be attributed to my Irish Catholic heritage (*makes note to bring up with therapist*) but intellectually I know all we can do is the best we can, allowing ourselves grace along the way. For me, this means not beating myself up about using paper goods occasionally. Hosting brings me joy, and I hope through my hosting I bring joy to others, and lightening my load makes me want to do it more often.

is compostable dinnerware a good option for you?

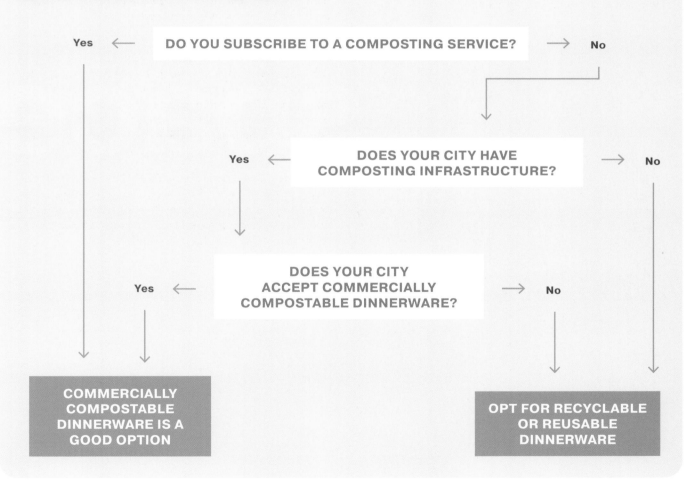

Yes ← DO YOU SUBSCRIBE TO A COMPOSTING SERVICE? → No

Yes ← DOES YOUR CITY HAVE COMPOSTING INFRASTRUCTURE? → No

Yes ← DOES YOUR CITY ACCEPT COMMERCIALLY COMPOSTABLE DINNERWARE? → No

COMMERCIALLY COMPOSTABLE DINNERWARE IS A GOOD OPTION

OPT FOR RECYCLABLE OR REUSABLE DINNERWARE

optimize your space

RECIPES

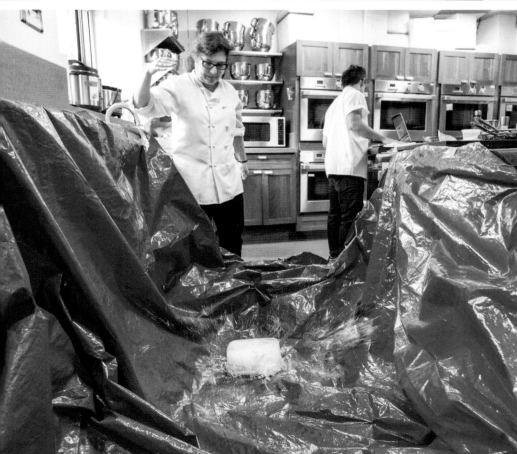

Don't Try This at Home

Cooking in a disorganized kitchen is a nonstarter. Turning every spice jar until you find the cardamom, trepidatiously digging through a drawer for a sharp boning knife, fussing with dusty paper bags of sugar and flour—these are annoyances that waste time and make cooking feel laborious. To find out which organizational tools were up to the task of making your life easier, we threw all sorts of sloppy situations at them.

Your knives need safekeeping. Magnet distribution and coverage determined the usable space for knife placement on our favorite solution, a magnetic universal knife block—the more the better. To evaluate the coverage, we made a mess that required protective goggles. We wrapped each knife block in parchment paper and sprinkled large amounts of iron filings onto it to reveal the size and placement of magnets.

We tested reusable food wraps as an alternative to rolls of plastic wrap. To test whether the wraps would stain, we crushed blackberries in them and let them sit overnight. Purposefully bruising berries was a little crushing but it gave us good insight into which wraps to recommend. When we tried to wash off the blackberry residue, we found that the less waxy wraps were easier to clean but were also more likely to stain.

Our messiest (and wildest and stinkiest) testing applied to the most essential organizational items in your kitchen: glass and plastic storage containers. We filled containers with dyed water and shook them vigorously to test how tight their supposed leakproof seals were. And we put our noses to the test (which wasn't for sensitive schnozzes). We filled the containers with oil-packed tuna and anchovies, refrigerated them overnight, washed them carefully, and conducted a "sniff test." And we can tell you, that's all we could smell for the rest of the day because nearly every container retained odors.

Sort It Out

Collecting kitchen gear is undoubtedly fun if you're into cooking (ahem, have you seen *our* kitchen?). But identifying what you most need in your kitchen is key for staying organized; a reasonable amount of functional gear makes it easy to access what you need when you need it. And, maybe even more important are the systems you use to organize that gear.

What's the Safest Way to Store Knives?

Good, sharp knives should be kept close at hand when cooking. There are three main ways to store these important tools: in or on a knife block, on a magnetic strip, or in a drawer. All three are acceptable (see page 316 to follow your preference).

For the third, you'll need to purchase or make your own guards for your knives. Reaching into a drawer full of knives is, of course, dangerous. But in addition to looking out for your safety, you need to look out for the safety of your knives. Whenever knives are jostled around among other utensils, they can get dull and nicked. These fitted sheaths keep your knives—and you—safe.

Lisa Says . . .

Julia Child installed her knife strips vertically—and you might want to do so as well. Most people hang magnetic knife strips horizontally, but Julia Child was a renegade: Check out her kitchen in the Smithsonian and you'll see vertical knife strips between the windows over the sink. It's a great space-saving solution for a kitchen that was absolutely packed with cooking gear.

How Can I Make My Own Knife Guards?

If you don't want to buy a knife guard, you can make a DIY knife protector to keep any knife safe for short stints. All you need is a manila folder (color of your choice for those with coordinated kitchens).

1 Place your knife's blade along the crease of a manila folder and mark a line about ½ inch from the tip of the blade and another about ½ inch from the spine.

2 Using these marks as guides, cut the folder into a rectangle.

3 Staple the top half and side of the rectangle at ½-inch intervals, leaving the back end open to slide in the knife.

4 If the handle of the knife prevents the guard from fully covering the blade, snip the opening at an angle to accommodate it.

What's a "Universal" Knife Block?

Conventional knife blocks hold only knives of specific sizes (the small slot for the paring knife, the deep slot for the bread knife, etc.). Universal blocks are designed to accommodate knives of any size and any brand, in any configuration.

There are two types of universal knife blocks: those that use magnets to secure the knives and those that use a mass of bristles or folds or an open grid to hold them. While they're more expensive, we prefer magnetic models. They hold the knives more securely—usually in a side-by-side configuration that makes it less likely that the knives would scrape against the block or each other and dull. And since you don't need to drag them in and out of slots, you get to skip the usual frustrating game of pulling up each blade to see which knife you're getting (Wait, is this the chef's knife? Nope. How about this one? Nope.)

Hannah Says . . .

We're not fans of classic knife blocks, designed to hold the exact knives in a given set. We don't believe knife sets in general are the best deal. They often include random filler knives that you could skip (but are certainly paying for), and no manufacturer makes the best version of every type of knife. We prefer to assemble our own "à la carte" set of the best-performing knives across multiple brands, and therefore we prefer universal knife blocks that can hold a broader array of knives.

Are Knife Blocks Sanitary? How Do I Get Mine Clean?

A magnetic universal knife block is easy to clean, but the style with slots for all your kitchen knives (the type that commonly comes with a set of knives) is among "the germiest kitchen items" according to the National Sanitation Foundation. All those narrow, deep, dark slots can harbor dirt and dampness, and encourage bacterial growth. The block itself sits on the kitchen counter right beside your food prep, and it's all too easy to put knives away before they're fully dry and perfectly clean.

So what's the best way to clean your knife block if it has slots? Not dishwashing. Wood is organic material, so it will absorb water, swell, and likely crack. Meanwhile, dishwasher detergents will damage or strip finish off the block. Plus, dishwasher jets can't really reach into the knife slots to deep-clean them.

A better way: Using a skinny but firm bottle brush and hot, soapy water (use liquid dish soap), scrub each slot and then rinse under the tap. Also wash the exterior of the block with a sponge and hot, soapy water—top, bottom and sides—and rinse well. Make sure to let the block dry completely before reloading your knives so they don't rust.

the right knife storage system for you

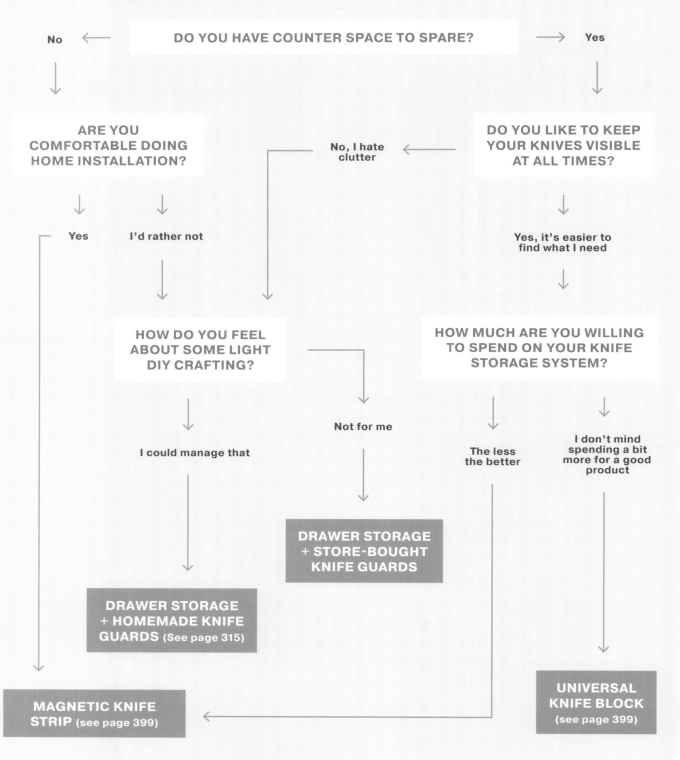

DO YOU HAVE COUNTER SPACE TO SPARE?

No

Yes

ARE YOU COMFORTABLE DOING HOME INSTALLATION?

DO YOU LIKE TO KEEP YOUR KNIVES VISIBLE AT ALL TIMES?

No, I hate clutter

Yes

I'd rather not

Yes, it's easier to find what I need

HOW DO YOU FEEL ABOUT SOME LIGHT DIY CRAFTING?

HOW MUCH ARE YOU WILLING TO SPEND ON YOUR KNIFE STORAGE SYSTEM?

I could manage that

Not for me

The less the better

I don't mind spending a bit more for a good product

DRAWER STORAGE + STORE-BOUGHT KNIFE GUARDS

DRAWER STORAGE + HOMEMADE KNIFE GUARDS (See page 315)

MAGNETIC KNIFE STRIP (see page 399)

UNIVERSAL KNIFE BLOCK (see page 399)

How Should I Organize My Utensils?

You can keep some utensils you don't use often in a drawer, but it's a pain to hunt for a wooden spoon in a too-full drawer that will inevitably get jammed. The best way to keep your most-used tools accessible is in a utensil crock. That's a generous amount of tools—we look for crocks that fit 17 or more utensils comfortably. If the tools get tangled (spatulas cutting through whisk tines, pastry brush bristles getting caught in a spider skimmer), however, storing them in the crock isn't much better than a drawer, so we like tall (but not so tall that small items get lost) models and those with removable dividers. (To learn what tools we think you should keep in your crock, see page 95.)

Is There Anything I Shouldn't Keep In My Crock?

You want to be able to reach for a tool in your crock quickly and without paying much attention. That means you don't want to pack the crock too tightly (ever pull one tool and have four fall out?). It also means you don't want to store knives or other sharp objects such as a Microplane (unless it has a guard on it). Finally, shorter tools—measuring spoons, vegetable peelers, bowl scrapers, tomato corers, and mini whisks—get lost in a crock and are difficult to remove.

I Can Never Find the Spices I Want When I Need Them. Is There a Better Way?

Rummaging through cupboards or on top of counters for the one spice you need is such a pain. (Why is it that the one you want is never one of the first several you turn over?) Organizing your spices will help you find them—and it may also help you get rid of expired or excess spices, freeing up space. No matter where you'd like to store your spices, we suggest you purchase an organizational device. Look for something sturdy and solid that can fit a lot of spices and that positions containers so it's easy to find what you're looking for. There are options for cabinets (tiered shelves and lazy Susans) and drawers (expandable inserts), which are our preferences as spices are best stored in a cool, dark place; skip the counter-top storage options unless you have no other space. Or, if you're a seasoning maximalist, try an over-the-door approach that holds far more than just spice jars.

Hannah Says . . .

Transferring your spices to matching jars may make your cabinets look pretty but there are practical benefits too. Matching jars will fit more compactly to save space, and consistent heights and shapes provide better visibility so you can more easily find what you're looking for. Opt for wider-mouthed jars that fit measuring spoons for easier measuring. Just remember to label everything! A sharpie and masking tape works, or go full-on Khloe Kardashian and use a label maker.

Is It True That Light Can Degrade Some Spices?

Yes, in addition to being stored in an airtight container, spices should be kept away from excessive light and direct sunlight, especially highly pigmented spices and leafy dried herbs, as they are photosensitive. That's why we recommend spice organizers that live in cabinets or drawers if possible for your space.

Is It True That Some Spices Can Melt Plastic Containers?

It's always best to store spices in glass jars (the original containers or your own) because glass doesn't absorb flavors or odors. And some spices can indeed actually degrade plastic. Cloves and star anise contain high concentrations of two chemically similar oils called eugenol and anethole. The chemical structures of these oils are similar to that of the plastic called polystyrene (stamped PS or plastic #6 on the bottom of containers) and are therefore able to soften or dissolve the plastic.

Some spices chemically interact with certain plastics

What's the Best Way to Store Salt?

We like to place salt containers near the stove or our workstation to season a pot of boiling water or a steak on the fly.

There are two basic kinds: Salt pigs are open-mouthed cylindrical vessels, while salt boxes have lids and tend to be slightly smaller. We prefer boxes, especially those with a hinged lid that can be propped open and re-closed with a single hand. Boxes shield the salt from errant splatters, better protect the salt from humidity, and are easier to fill.

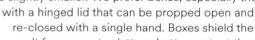

Lisa Says . . .

I love my salt box, which I fill with my beloved Maldon salt, a flaky sea salt that's perfect for finishing foods and dressing salads. The salt box has made using the salt so much simpler, since I can flick the lid open with one hand, grab just what I need, and pop the lid back down. I think a salt box makes a perfect housewarming gift, too, along with a box of (you guessed it) Maldon salt.

FIVE-SPICE POWDER

makes about ¼ cup

In traditional Chinese cooking, the five elements of the cosmos—earth, fire, metal, water, and wood—are represented by five-spice powder. Homemade spice blends have amazing fresh flavor; to maintain that, store your spices in glass jars after mixing them and use them within a month. Label the date on the jar so you know when it's time to make a new batch.

5	teaspoons fennel seeds
4	teaspoons white peppercorns or 8 teaspoons Sichuan peppercorns
1	tablespoon whole cloves
8	star anise pods
1	cinnamon stick, broken into pieces

Process fennel seeds, peppercorns, and cloves in spice grinder until finely ground, about 30 seconds; transfer to small bowl. Process star anise and cinnamon in now-empty spice grinder until finely ground, about 30 seconds; transfer to bowl with other spices and stir to combine. (Five-spice powder can be stored in airtight container for up to 1 month.)

RAS EL HANOUT

makes about ½ cup

This North African blend delivers complex flavor from a mix of warm spices. Homemade spice blends have amazing fresh flavor; to maintain that, store your spices in glass jars after mixing them and use them within a month. Label the date on the jar so you know when it's time to make a new batch.

16	cardamom pods
4	teaspoons coriander seeds
4	teaspoons cumin seeds
2	teaspoons anise seeds
2	teaspoons ground dried Aleppo pepper
½	teaspoon allspice berries
¼	teaspoon black peppercorns
4	teaspoons ground ginger
2	teaspoons ground nutmeg
2	teaspoons ground cinnamon

Process cardamom pods, coriander seeds, cumin seeds, anise seeds, Aleppo, allspice, and peppercorns in spice grinder until finely ground, about 30 seconds. Stir in ginger, nutmeg, and cinnamon. (Ras el hanout can be stored in airtight container for up to 1 month.)

ZA'ATAR

makes about ½ cup

Za'atar is an aromatic eastern Mediterranean spice blend that is used as both a seasoning and a condiment. Homemade spice blends have amazing fresh flavor; to maintain that, store your spices in glass jars after mixing them and use them within a few months. Label the date on the jar so you know when it's time to make a new batch.

½	cup dried thyme
2	tablespoons sesame seeds, toasted
1½	tablespoons ground sumac

Working in batches, process thyme in spice grinder until finely ground, about 30 seconds; transfer to small bowl. Stir in sesame seeds and sumac. (Za'atar can be stored in airtight container for up to 3 months.)

5 **Strategies** for Better Kitchen Organization

No matter if your kitchen is big or small, it will be easier to work in if you keep stock of what's old and new, and count on clever storage solutions for items you use often. Clear the clutter and see clearly in the kitchen.

1 PARE DOWN YOUR GEAR COLLECTION

Over the years, kitchens can become pretty packed with extraneous items—you might always forget you have a cake pan when you need one so now you have three, or one of your gadgets wasn't as innovative as advertised. Don't keep anything you don't need. Negotiate multiples with housemates if you have them or part with models you've since upgraded. Store away, give away, or add to the yard sale items you haven't used in a year.

2 USE A ROLLING CART

A rolling cart is a good companion in any kitchen, but it's especially useful in smaller spaces or those without a lot of cabinets. Use it to stack pots, pans, and equipment items without taking up a lot of real estate or improvise a pantry with your oft-used items. You can roll it where you need it when you're cooking and roll it out of the way at other times.

Another use for a rolling cart? You can keep an empty one by you while you're cooking if you need to extend your counter space or to deposit gear you might be done using or dirty dishes as you go. Roll everything to the sink at once when you're done.

3 ORGANIZE YOUR DRAWERS

Not only is a messy drawer frustrating, if there are utensils involved, it can also be dangerous. Keep what you can in a utensil crock (see page 95). Purchase or make guards (see pages 314–315) for your knives if you keep them in drawers, and invest in drawer organizers to keep things in line.

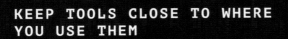

4 KEEP TOOLS CLOSE TO WHERE YOU USE THEM

There are usually a few zones in a kitchen, such as where you chop and prep, where you wash, and where you cook with the stove or oven. The tools you need for those tasks should live within their corresponding zones. That prevents you from misplacing items (especially if you've got a lot of gear), allows you to grab items quickly, and helps eliminate general franticness (see page 323). For example, keep your knives near your prep zone, a crock with utensils such as spatulas and a wooden spoon next to your cooking zone, and kitchen towels near your dishwashing zone. What you store away will depend on what kind of a cook you are: For example, if you bake only once a month, it makes sense to store your stand mixer out of the way in a cabinet or on a bottom shelf. On the other hand, if you bake multiple times a week, it probably makes more sense to keep your mixer at the ready near your prep zone.

5 LABEL EVERYTHING

Whether it's with a label maker, a piece of painter's tape, or an easy-to-remove rubber band, you should label anything you want to know the contents of. Never confuse flour for confectioners' sugar again, and prevent waste by identifying leftovers. Dates are particularly useful on labels—you'll know just how long you've had those grits you rarely use, or when it's time to throw out the half-can's worth of tomato paste. If you're writing out your labels, be sure to use a permanent marker. (Sharpies are our best friends in the test kitchen and at home!)

5 Space-Saving Storage Hacks

A little ingenuity can go a long way for making the most of your space, especially in smaller kitchens. Living in city apartments and homes has upped our own ingenuity. Learn from us.

1 USE NESTING BOWLS

Whether they're glass or metal, mixing size or prep size, we make sure to buy nesting bowl sets. That way the space they take up is only as large as the largest bowl.

2 SAFELY STACK YOUR SKILLETS (IF YOU MUST)

Few have the space to give each skillet a spot on the shelf, but be careful when stacking skillets so you don't scratch or damage them. We put a piece of paper towel or a paper plate inside each skillet before placing another on top.

3 HANG YOUR POTS AND PANS

You don't have to worry about shelving your pans at all if you hang them. Use hooks on the walls or use a peg board (have you seen the one from Julia Child's famous home kitchen?). Note: If you like your kitchen to look like a showroom, don't do this. Well-loved pans are rarely perfectly pristine.

4 STORE FLAT TOOLS ON THEIR EDGES

Kitchen items with thin profiles such as cutting boards, skillet lids, and sheet pans can rest on their side edges to take up remarkably less space. You can order special shelving for your cabinets to hold these items upright.

5 ADD EXTRA SHELVING TO LARGE CABINETS

Sometimes those large, tall cabinets waste so much airspace. Consider installing a dividing shelf to fit more equipment behind closed doors.

Set Up for Success

How you prepare for cooking might be more important than how you actually cook because the latter depends on the former. Organizing your workspace, preparing your ingredients, and gathering your equipment ensure things go smoothly. And there are some great tools to help you keep things straight.

How Can I Make Cooking in My Kitchen Feel Less Frantic(!)?

No matter if a recipe is five or 20 ingredients long, it's a roadmap to a destination: a delicious dish. To start, cooking is similar to preparing for a trip: To get to your destination in time and without worry, you need to familiarize yourself with the directions ahead to avoid making unnecessary pit stops or getting lost. Read through the whole recipe to grasp the major motions. Then gather and measure your ingredients and arrange them in the order you'll need them—which is called mise en place—so they're ready at go time. You can do this prep work right before you begin a recipe, or in some cases you can do it further in advance (the morning of, the day before), which is particularly helpful when preparing something complicated or for a crowd. You'll want to store these ingredients in tight-locking food storage containers (which will also come in handy for storing leftovers or small-yield dry goods). You can keep your area clear while you're prepping by using a mixing bowl as a "garbage" bowl for herb stems, onion peels, and the like. Use a bench scraper to clear your surface.

Some recipes move particularly fast. Having your ingredients prepped helps. When timing is important, however—as it often is—we recommend using a dedicated timer for cooking. It comes in handy for longer cooking times such as when you're roasting meat or baking a cake, and it also takes the stress out of step-by-step times in recipes like stir-fries.

worth it

MINI PREP BOWLS

You already have mixing bowls (see page 89); maybe you even have them in both glass and in metal. So why would you need more bowls to wash, and why so small? Using mini prep bowls is a professional-chef trick that translates perfectly to the home kitchen. They allow you to measure out, separate, and organize ingredients so they're at the ready for more efficient cooking. No second-guessing how much paprika you dropped in your soup. No forgetting whether you salted your sauce. This is especially helpful for divided ingredients—ones that are used at two different points in a recipe—so you don't add something all at once when you shouldn't.

real talk with lisa

THE IMPORTANCE OF MISE EN PLACE

I've learned the hard way how important it is to do mise en place, which means "put in place" or basically: Get Everything Ready Before You Start to Cook. My basic system: 1) Read the whole recipe. 2) Measure and/or prep each ingredient in order and put it in its own bowl. 3) Put away the spice jar or package you just measured from before proceeding to the next ingredient (my favorite part). 4) Arrange the ingredients in the order called for in the recipe, right by the stove. Voilà! You are ready to cook and feel like a pro.

STIR-FRIED SHRIMP AND LONG BEANS

serves 4

You should always complete your mise en place before cooking but if there's one type of recipe it's mandatory for, it's the stir-fry. Prepping ahead makes it easy to add the ingredients to the wok and prevent overcooking during the fast-paced stir-frying. We recommend placing all your prepped ingredients in bowls and corralling them near the stove in a rimmed baking sheet. Long beans may also be labeled as yard-long beans, snake beans, or asparagus beans. A 12-inch nonstick or carbon-steel skillet can be used instead of a wok.

¾ cup chicken broth	¼ cup vegetable oil, divided
3 tablespoons oyster sauce	1½ tablespoons grated fresh ginger
2 tablespoons Shaoxing wine or dry sherry	2 garlic cloves, minced
1 tablespoon toasted sesame oil	1½ pounds long beans, trimmed and cut into 1½-inch pieces
1 tablespoon unseasoned rice vinegar	1 pound large shrimp (26 to 30 per pound), peeled, deveined, and tails removed
1½ teaspoons cornstarch	
¼ teaspoon white pepper	

1 Whisk broth, oyster sauce, Shaoxing wine, sesame oil, vinegar, cornstarch, and white pepper together in bowl. Combine 1 tablespoon vegetable oil, ginger, and garlic in small bowl; set aside.

2 Combine long beans and ¼ cup water in large bowl. Cover and microwave until beans are pliable, 7 to 9 minutes, stirring halfway through microwaving. Drain beans, transfer to paper towel–lined plate, and pat dry.

3 Heat 1 tablespoon vegetable oil in 14-inch wok over high heat until just smoking. Add half of long beans in single layer and cook, without stirring, until beans begin to blister and char, about 3 minutes. Stir and continue to cook, stirring occasionally, until beans are just softened and well charred, about 3 minutes longer. Transfer beans to serving platter and cover loosely with aluminum foil to keep warm. Repeat with 1 tablespoon vegetable oil and remaining beans; transfer to platter.

4 Heat remaining 1 tablespoon vegetable oil in now-empty wok over high heat until just smoking. Add shrimp in single layer and cook, without stirring, until shrimp turn opaque and brown around edges, about 1 minute. Push shrimp to sides of wok. Add ginger mixture to center and cook, mashing mixture into wok, until fragrant, about 30 seconds. Stir mixture into shrimp; transfer to platter with beans.

5 Whisk broth mixture to recombine, then add to now-empty wok. Cook over high heat, stirring occasionally, until sauce is thickened and reduced slightly, about 1 minute. Return beans and shrimp to wok and toss gently to coat with sauce. Serve.

How Can I Keep My Cookbooks Open While I'm Cooking?

Cooking from an open cookbook can present real challenges: The book may not lie flat so pages flip over, splatters soil the pages, and pages can be difficult to turn with slippery hands. Short of photocopying the recipe or rewriting it on a separate sheet of paper, the solution is to use a cookbook holder. Arguably, any book holder can act as a cookbook holder, but for the kitchen we like one with a shield that protects pages from splatters.

Most of My Recipes are Digital. Is It Worth It to Buy a Tablet Stand?

Bringing slim, portable tablets into the kitchen puts online recipes at your fingertips—but also places the pricey gadgets within range of splatters and sticky hands. A tablet stand can be worth it to prop up the flat computers for easy reference, although there are a lot of shaky ones out there so be careful what you buy. Make sure to buy one that doesn't hog most of your counter. Some cookbook stands are marketed also as tablet stands, but we recommend avoiding these; if they have a splatter shield, they'll render the touchscreen useless. Note that, generally, tablet stands' screen protection is lacking, and those that do fully protect screens from grime often turn the touch pad unresponsive.

How Do I Protect My Tablet Screen From Splatters?

Well, there are plastic sheaths tailored to specific tablets, which are nice as they don't leave baggy spots, but they're not worth the cost when regular zipper-lock bags offer just as much protection for much less money (up to 20 times less!) and let you use the touch screen right through the bag. Zipper-lock bags can be taped back for a snug fit and they're watertight.

Put It Away

Putting your food—groceries, leftovers, snacks—away properly today means an easy-to-navigate kitchen tomorrow, not to mention less food waste, a common problem in a disorganized kitchen. Learn how to pack and store with purpose.

How Can I Keep My Pantry Staples Fresh and Organized?

Simple dry storage containers are designed to ensure that staples such as flour and sugar stay fresh, dry, and safe from bugs or dust. The ideal containers are spacious, durable, and easy-to-clean, with wide enough openings to let us dip a measuring cup into their contents and sweep a knife across the rim of the cup to level it off without spills, and a lid that seals tightly and simply. Clear materials are important for viewing contents (even better if there are measurements on the sides). These containers' stacking capabilities optimize pantry space and keep things straight.

We're going to highlight one here: Restaurant people call them Cambros (see page 400) after the company that makes them and they're basically containers on steroids. They're big as you want them, sturdy, and easy to use and clean. You might find most use for the 6-quart size (which holds a 5-pound bag of flour). They go up to 22 quarts in size, and as a bonus, they're our favorite containers for brining (even turkeys), sous-viding, and proofing dough.

Is It Safe to Store Food in Plastic Containers?

Plastic containers are fine for food; we like them as a lightweight choice for stacking leftovers, taking food to the office, and for the clumsy among us. Concerns about plastic usually surround BPA, or bisphenol A. This is an industrial chemical used in some plastics and epoxy linings of metal food cans. Some studies have linked it to cancer and thyroid dysfunction. These days, however, you'll find it hard to purchase plastic containers that aren't labeled BPA-free—none of the containers we tested contained BPA (according to the manufacturers).

Why Did My Plastic Containers Stain?

Staining is the plague of plastic containers. They might still function, but they look terrible. We've found that containers made of a clear plastic called Tritan are extra durable and don't stain; containers made from polypropylene (that's a lot of them), will always stain.

Lisa Says . . .

I tested many brands of both plastic and glass food storage containers, and one feature that proved exceptionally useful is when the containers had stable, flat bottoms and lids so you can stack them securely in the refrigerator or freezer. If space is tight, choose square or rectangular containers, which pack close together more easily than round ones. For freezing, pick flatter, shallower containers because food can freeze faster and more uniformly than it will in taller, deeper containers.

Hannah Says . . .

I am downright evangelical about rimmed baking sheet lids, such as the one Nordic Ware makes to go with our winning baking sheet. It snaps on top of the pan so you can transport or store things easily in it. It turns it into a giant container with plenty of room to say, transport your prettily frosted mini bunny cakes to Easter (me last year) or store your breaded raw chicken in the fridge to dry it out over night for an extra crispy crust (me this weekend). The lid is sturdy so you can stack things on top of it, making it easier to fit in a busy fridge than you'd think.

Can Glass Storage Containers Go in the Oven?

Yes! We think tempered glass containers' oven-safe quality is one of the best things about them—transferring them from storage to oven for heating or even cooking makes them incredibly convenient. (Look for an ovensafe claim just to be sure and don't place plastic lids in the oven.) One thing to note, however: Products almost always list extensive warnings about thermal shock, which is when rapid, extreme temperature changes cause glass to shatter. We recommend that you read these instructions carefully before using your container in the oven. In every case, you should put glass vessels into only a fully preheated oven, since ovens preheat unevenly, with much hotter and cooler zones forming until the oven reaches its target temperature (see page 23 for more information). Also, never use glass containers under the broiler.

MAKE-AHEAD GARLIC-POTATO SOUP

serves 6

This soup recipe is designed to be stored. Make the soup and, once cooled, freeze it in reusable storage containers and then reheat as desired within a month.

SOUP BASE
3	tablespoons unsalted butter
1	leek, white and light green parts only, halved lengthwise, chopped, and washed thoroughly (about 1 cup)
3	garlic cloves, minced, plus 1 whole head garlic, outer papery skins removed and top third of head cut off and discarded
6	cups chicken broth
2	bay leaves
¾	teaspoon table salt
1½	pounds russet potatoes, peeled and cut into ½-inch cubes
1	pound Red Bliss potatoes, unpeeled, cut into ½-inch cubes

REHEATING SOUP
1	cup chicken broth
½	cup heavy cream
1½	teaspoons minced fresh thyme leaves
	Ground black pepper
¼	cup minced fresh chives

GARLIC CHIPS
3	tablespoons extra-virgin olive oil
6	garlic cloves, sliced thin
	Table salt

1 for the soup base Melt butter in Dutch oven over medium heat. Add leek and cook until softened, 5 to 8 minutes. Stir in minced garlic and cook until fragrant, about 1 minute. Add garlic head, broth, bay leaves, and salt and bring to simmer. Partially cover pot, reduce heat to medium-low, and cook until garlic is very tender when pierced with tip of knife, 30 to 40 minutes. Stir in potatoes, partially cover pot, and bring mixture to simmer over medium-high heat. Take pot off heat and let cool completely. Divide soup between 2 storage containers and freeze for up to 1 month.

2 to reheat and serve Run hot water over surface of storage containers to help release frozen blocks of soup. Add soup and broth to Dutch oven. Cover and cook over medium-high heat, stirring occasionally, until soup is hot and potatoes are tender, about 20 minutes. Discard bay leaves. Remove garlic head and squeeze cooked garlic from skins into bowl. Mash garlic to smooth paste with fork. Stir cream, thyme, and half of mashed garlic into soup; heat soup until hot, about 2 minutes. Taste soup; add remaining garlic paste if desired. Transfer 1½ cups potatoes and 1 cup broth to blender and process until smooth. (Process more potatoes for thicker consistency.) Return puree to pot and stir to combine.

3 for the garlic chips Meanwhile, heat oil and garlic in 10-inch nonstick skillet over medium-low heat. Cook, stirring occasionally, until garlic is golden brown, about 15 minutes. Using slotted spoon, transfer garlic to paper towel–lined plate and season with salt to taste; set aside for serving. Discard garlic oil or save for another use.

4 Season soup with salt and pepper to taste. Serve, sprinkling individual portions with chives and garlic chips.

Is It OK to Reuse Regular Plastic Food Storage Bags?

Plastic zipper-lock bags are technically single use, but we've found that you can reuse them (unless they were holding raw meat or spoiled food) if you gently wash them between uses. Don't turn them inside out before washing them—it's not only unnecessary, but it also damages their seams and seals. Just add warm, soapy water to the bag; seal it and slosh the water around to clean its inside; rinse it; and give the bag a good shake to remove any excess water. After washing, storage bags must dry open, or they will stay wet forever and breed bacteria. Luckily, there's a gadget for that.

Bag drying racks allow you to dry storage bags without draping them all over your dish rack and counters. This applies to disposable plastic bags and reusable food storage bags. Look for sturdy models with at least four long arms. And if you don't want a rack, you can simply use a dry cloth to help dry bags faster.

Are Reusable Alternatives to Single-Use Plastics Actually Any Good?

There are more and more replacements for single-use plastics on the market. We love the idea of reducing how much plastic goes to the landfill—and reducing how much we deal with it. (Plastic wrap, for example, can be so frustrating to use when it's tangled on the roll or stuck to itself.) Many products work really well, but not all existing replacements are created equal. The ones in the chart are our favorites.

USE THIS . . .		TO DO THIS!
Reusable Food Wraps		• Wrap directly around food, creating an airtight seal that keeps the food fresh • Seal bowls and other containers by folding and overlapping the material and pressing firmly to adhere
Silicone Food Covers		• Seal bowls to keep the food stored inside fresh • Cover containers and contain splatters while microwaving
Reusable Food Storage Bags		• Store dry goods (or liquids, as long as you don't drop the bags!) • Bring sandwiches and snacks with you on-the-go
Food Storage Containers		• Store leftovers and/or prepped ingredients to keep fresh

Check out our video to see just how well our favorite alternatives to single-use plastics perform.

Do Reusable Food Wraps Actually Work?

Wax-coated reusable food wraps (made of cotton or hemp) work with the heat of your hands to seal food and containers, and we've found that good versions are as effective as traditional plastic wrap at keeping food fresh.

Reusable food wraps can be wrapped directly around food or used to seal bowls and other containers. To use them, you fold and overlap the material and press firmly to adhere the wrap. While the wraps gradually lose their clinging ability over time, they're reusable for up to a year if cleaned and stored properly. Once they've worn out, the wraps can be cut into strips and composted or even used as simple fire starters.

Sticky reusable wraps create good seals capable of keeping avocados fresh for three days.

head to head

FOOD WRAPS AND COVERS

PLASTIC WRAPS

Sheets of polyvinyl chloride or polyethylene

Single use

Cling to glass, metal, and ceramic

Directly wrap around food or seal bowls

Dispensed and cut to any length

Can get tangled

Can be used with any food

REUSABLE FOOD WRAPS

Sheets of cotton or hemp dipped in a layer of beeswax or soy wax

Multiple uses up to a year when washed with cool, soapy water

Cling to glass, metal, and ceramic

Directly wrap around food or seal bowls

Can be trimmed

Cannot be used with meat; not a good choice for baked goods

Can leave residue and retain odors

SILICONE FOOD COVERS

Silicone with a strong suction seal

Infinite uses and dishwasher-safe

Cling to glass, metal, plastic, ceramic, and wood

Cover and seal bowls

Come in different sizes

Lie flat

Can be used with any food

How Should I Clean My Reusable Food Wraps?

Manufacturers call for washing wraps with a sponge. We lay the wraps flat in the bottom of a clean sink and scrub them with the soft side of a sponge and a bit of soap and cool water (hot water can melt wax, degrading its use). For wraps used for stinky items such as onions, you can apply a paste of baking soda and water and then let the wraps sit for 15 minutes before rinsing them. This method won't completely remove the odor, but it should fade in three to five days. If you're worried about your wraps retaining odors for a short period of time, however, we recommend not using them with smellier foods.

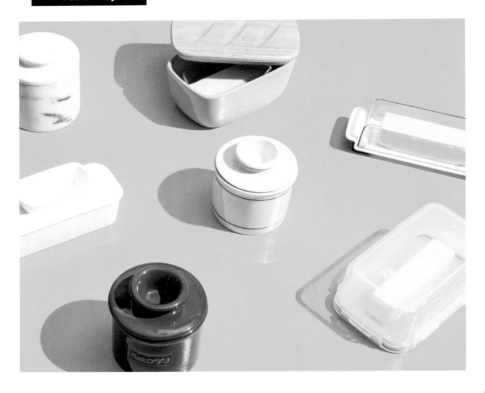

real talk with hannah

HOW TO STORE BUTTER

When testing butter keepers, I tasted a dozen butters stored in different containers over the course of a month. Because it's so high in fat, butter is prone to absorbing flavors and odors, so each day I'd take a tiny taste of all the butters to test how effectively each container sealed out these off flavors. The key takeaway from my month of butter tasting: A container's ability to form a strong, airtight seal is essential to keeping butter fresh. Our winning keeper kept butter fresh-tasting for an entire month. While our winner has unique benefits, such as a wide "lid" that includes measurement markings and can double as a butter dish, other airtight containers can work nicely for butter storage too.

Can I Store Butter in a Regular Plastic or Glass Container?

You can. We like storing butter in good airtight containers. A tight-sealing container keeps butter fresh, and if turned upside-down the bottom "lid" doubles as a tray with a flat cutting surface. There are some factors to consider, however, such as the container's shape and size. You may not be able to use the same product line as your favorite large containers. The smaller versions of our favorite food storage containers are not always right for sticks of butter; some are too short and squish butter. Also, some containers have lid flaps that swing up rather than out so the lid can't be used as a tray.

Are Butter Bells Safe?

Butter bells are safe when used correctly. These butter storage containers originated in France and are intended for use only at room temperature, keeping butter soft and ready for spreading. You pack softened butter into the bell-shaped dish before inserting it upside down into a crock filled with a small amount of water, forming an airtight seal. The "used correctly" part comes down to changing this water regularly. To keep the butter fresh and prevent mold growth, you should replace the water in the crock every two to three days.

CHIPOTLE-CILANTRO COMPOUND BUTTER

serves 8 to 10 (Makes ½ cup)

You'll want the butter you use here to be free of off-flavors, so be sure to store it properly in an airtight container until you're ready to make the compound butter.

8	tablespoons butter, softened
2	teaspoons minced canned chipotle chile in adobo sauce, plus 2 teaspoons adobo sauce
4	teaspoons minced fresh cilantro
2	garlic cloves, minced
2	teaspoons honey
2	teaspoons grated lime zest

Whip butter in bowl with fork until light and fluffy. Mix in chipotle and adobo sauce, cilantro, garlic, honey, and lime zest. Season with salt and pepper to taste. Cover with plastic wrap and let rest so flavors meld, about 10 minutes, or roll into log and refrigerate. (Butter can be refrigerated in airtight container for up to 4 days or frozen, wrapped tightly in plastic wrap, for up to 2 months.)

VARIATIONS
Chive-Lemon-Miso Compound Butter

Substitute ¼ cup white miso, ¼ cup minced fresh chives, 2 tablespoons grated lemon zest plus 4 tablespoons juice (2 lemons), and ¼ teaspoon pepper for chipotle and adobo sauce, cilantro, garlic, honey, and lime zest.

Tarragon-Lime Compound Butter

Substitute ¼ cup minced scallions, 2 tablespoons minced fresh tarragon, and 4 teaspoons lime juice for chipotle and adobo sauce, cilantro, garlic, honey, and lime zest.

clean up
your act

Don't Try This at Home

There are times when just using a product to make sure it works as promised is too messy or too risky, even for us. Take cut-resistant gloves: Each pair has a "cut score" that represents how resistant it is to a blade being pressed and dragged across the fabric. We weren't about to take the manufacturers' word that their gloves met the standard, but we also weren't about to test them using our own fingers (we're rather attached to them and wanted to stay that way). Hot dogs proved too wide and floppy to double for our digits, but Slim Jim Beef Jerky Sticks worked great. We stuffed Slim Jims in the fingers of each glove and used fresh razor blades to cut across them with increasing levels of force. We were happy to note that no Slim Jims were harmed; each glove held up to the cut score it claimed.

For people whose pets sometimes make messes around the house, having a robot vacuum dutifully spread poo through every room is a nightmare. While testing these vacuums, we noted that two robots in our lineup promised to spot and swerve away from solid pet "accidents" on the floor. We needed to test this claim, but even for our dedicated team, using real pet poo was a bridge too far. So instead we ordered several all-too-realistic-looking assorted pieces of soft plastic pet poo online (an experience we never expected would be part of our jobs), scattered them around hallways and rooms, and set each robot to work vacuuming the areas. One robot failed outright, dragging poo around the floor at every encounter, while the other neatly avoided large piles but plowed right into ones a smaller dog or a cat might make.

We'll hazard a guess that there aren't many culinary career paths that involve working with beef jerky sticks and imitation pet excrement, but for us, it's all in a day's work.

Safety First

Cooking comes with risks; it's important to keep a cool head and be prepared. Extinguishers, alarms, and protective gear help you cook worry-free.

safety guides

Lots of kitchen tools and appliances require a little know-how so you can use them safely. That's why we've included best-practice tips throughout this book for the equipment listed below.

Help! My Pan Caught on Fire! What Do I Do?

Stovetop fires can happen when oil or another fat heats up way beyond its smoke point. If smoke turns into flames when you're cooking, quickly turn off the stove and cover the pan with a lid; depriving the fire of oxygen will extinguish it. To be sure the fire is out, leave the lid in place until the pan has cooled—no peeking! Don't add water or try to carry the pan to the sink; both actions could result in you being splashed with burning oil. And while it's true baking soda can put out a grease fire, odds are, you can clamp a lid on the pan faster than you can locate your baking soda, open the container, and dump out enough to do the job (it takes a *lot* of baking soda to extinguish flames).

I'm Careful in the Kitchen. Do I Really Need a Fire Extinguisher?

Absolutely. Even if you never have to actually use it, safe is definitely better than sorry here. Home cooking fires are responsible for more than $1 billion in property damages each year. Neglecting a pan of hot oil or leaving a dish towel too close to a burner are all-too-easy ways to find yourself suddenly facing flames. And fire spreads fast—experts say you have less than 2 minutes before a fire will be out of control. That's why it's wise to always keep a fire extinguisher within easy reach. And don't walk away from the stove while you're cooking!

What Does the "ABC" on My Extinguisher Mean?

Fire extinguishers with an "ABC" rating are known as "multipurpose" extinguishers, meaning they can tackle (A) cloth, wood, and paper; (B) flammable liquids and gases, such as grease and gasoline; and (C) electrical fires. "BC"-rated extinguishers cover only the latter two categories.

Because dish towels and potholders can potentially catch on fire, you'll want the ABC designation on an extinguisher that's meant to be used in the kitchen.

OK, So I Have a Fire Extinguisher. Now How Do I Use It?

Traditional fire extinguishers typically have a pressure gauge, a locking pin, a spray nozzle, and a handle, and they're designed to be used in a similar way. If a fire breaks out, stand 4 to 6 feet back and take these four steps, with the acronym PASS:

PULL: Pull the pin

AIM: Aim low, pointing the extinguisher nozzle (or its horn or hose) at the base of the fire

SQUEEZE: Squeeze the handle to release the extinguishing agent

SWEEP: Sweep the spray from side to side to cover the fire until it is out

Using a fire extinguisher isn't hard if you follow some key advice:

Keep it handy: Store your extinguisher in an easily accessible, visible place and make sure everyone in your household knows where it is.

Be prepared: Periodically check the gauge on top to make sure the extinguisher has enough pressure to spray. If it points to green, you're good to go; if it's red, you need a new extinguisher.

Practice: If the thought of using a fire extinguisher is intimidating, buy an extra one (they're fairly inexpensive) and practice using it outdoors to get the feel for it.

Don't be a hero: If there's a fire, stand next to the exit and use the extinguisher, and then get out and call the fire department—even if you think the fire is out. Leave it to the experts to make sure the fire won't flare back up.

Replace it: Finally, remember that once you use your extinguisher (even for practice!), you'll need a new one.

There Goes My Smoke Alarm Again! How Can I Stop Tripping It During Normal Cooking?

There are few interruptions more unpleasant than the blare of a smoke alarm when you're trying to get dinner ready. Here's what to do—and not do—to cut down on the likelihood of false alarms.

DO	DON'T
Install your kitchen smoke alarm at least 10 feet from your stove.	Start heating your oil long before you plan to start cooking.
Use your hood vent when cooking potentially smoky foods.	Let spilled food (such as fruit pie juices or chicken grease) build up on your stovetop or in your oven.
Run your air purifier if you have one, or use a window fan.	Disconnect your alarm. It may be annoying, but it's doing a very important job!
Preheat pans over medium heat.	
Use less fat (unless otherwise directed by the recipe).	
Temporarily override your smart alarm, if you must.	

PAN-SEARED STRIP STEAKS

serves 4

To achieve sizzle without smoke, we start the steaks in a "cold" (not preheated) nonstick skillet, turning the heat first to high and then lowering it to medium, and flipping the steaks every 2 minutes. If you have time, salt the steaks for 45 minutes or up to 24 hours before cooking: Sprinkle each of the steaks with 1 teaspoon of kosher salt, refrigerate them, and pat them dry with paper towels before cooking. This recipe also works with boneless rib-eye steaks of a similar thickness.

- 2 (12- to 16-ounce) boneless strip steaks, 1½ inches thick, trimmed
- 1 teaspoon pepper

1 Pat steaks dry with paper towels and sprinkle both sides with pepper. Place steaks 1 inch apart in cold 12-inch nonstick skillet. Place skillet over high heat and cook steaks for 2 minutes. Flip steaks and cook on second side for 2 minutes. (Neither side of steaks will be browned at this point.)

2 Flip steaks, reduce heat to medium, and continue to cook, flipping steaks every 2 minutes, until browned and meat registers 120 to 125 degrees (for medium-rare), 4 to 10 minutes longer. (Steaks should be sizzling gently; if not, increase heat slightly. Reduce heat if skillet starts to smoke.)

3 Transfer steaks to cutting board and let rest for 5 minutes. Slice steaks against grain, season with flake sea salt to taste, and serve.

GLAZED SALMON

serves 4

When fatty salmon and sugary glaze meet high heat, it's often a recipe for a smoky kitchen and a blaring smoke alarm. Rather than run the glazed fish under the broiler, we bake it in a moderate oven to create a shiny, not burnt, coating. When sautéing the salmon fillets, be sure to turn on your hood vent, and add the fish to the pan as soon as you see wisps of smoke rising from the oil. To ensure uniform pieces of fish that cook at the same rate, buy a whole center-cut fillet and cut it into four pieces. If your nonstick skillet isn't ovensafe, sear the salmon as directed in step 4, then transfer it to a rimmed baking sheet, glaze it, and bake as directed in step 5. You will need a 12-inch ovensafe nonstick skillet for this recipe.

HOISIN-GINGER GLAZE

2	tablespoons ketchup
2	tablespoons hoisin sauce
2	tablespoons rice vinegar
2	tablespoons packed light brown sugar
1	tablespoon soy sauce
1	tablespoon toasted sesame oil
2	teaspoons chili-garlic sauce
1	teaspoon grated fresh ginger

SALMON

1	teaspoon packed light brown sugar
½	teaspoon kosher salt
¼	teaspoon cornstarch
4	(6- to 8-ounce) skin-on salmon fillets
	Ground black pepper
1	teaspoon vegetable oil

1 Adjust oven rack to the middle position and heat oven to 300 degrees.

2 for the hoisin-ginger glaze Whisk ingredients together in small saucepan. Bring to boil over medium-high heat; simmer until thickened, about 3 minutes. Remove from heat and cover to keep warm.

3 for the salmon Combine brown sugar, salt, and cornstarch in small bowl. Pat salmon dry with paper towels and season with pepper. Sprinkle brown sugar mixture evenly over top of flesh side of salmon, rubbing to distribute.

4 Heat oil in a 12-inch ovensafe nonstick skillet over medium-high heat until just smoking. Place salmon, flesh side down, in skillet and cook until well browned, about 1 minute. Using tongs, carefully flip salmon and cook on skin side for 1 minute.

5 Remove skillet from heat and spoon glaze evenly over salmon fillets. Transfer skillet to oven and cook until centers of fillets are still translucent when checked with tip of paring knife and register 125 degrees (for medium-rare), 7 to 10 minutes. Serve.

Will Cut-Resistant Gloves Get in My Way?

Not if they're the right size; proper fit is key. Cut-resistant gloves protect your hands when you're using a mandoline or a sharp grater or cutting slippery or unstable foods, but to be truly useful, they should feel comfortable and unobtrusive so you'll actually wear them. Gloves that are too baggy or thick are not only less pleasant to use, they can also limit your dexterity and make it harder to get a secure grip on smaller or more slippery objects, such as carrots or avocados. When testing, we found thin gloves—1 millimeter or less thick—to be just as protective as thicker gloves. As for size, almost all manufacturers provide guides to help you find the size that is most likely to fit your hands, usually by providing palm and/or finger measurements. Ultimately, the best glove is the one that fits your hand the most closely.

Lisa Says . . .

Cut-resistant gloves are fairly tough and protective, but you can still hurt yourself when you are using a sharp object. A glove can't protect against stabs from knife tips and pointed objects. If you're using a knife or mandoline, exercise reasonable caution even when wearing a glove. A direct slice may still penetrate the glove's material.

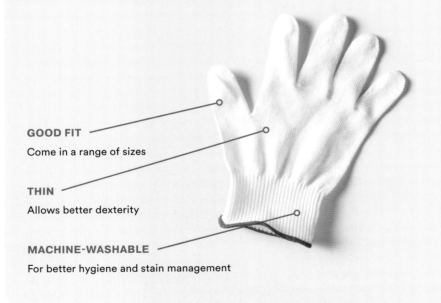

anatomy of
GOOD CUT-RESISTANT GLOVES

GOOD FIT
Come in a range of sizes

THIN
Allows better dexterity

MACHINE-WASHABLE
For better hygiene and stain management

Will a Skillet Handle Cover Make It Safer to Maneuver A Hot Cast-Iron Skillet?

A skillet handle cover can help you avoid burns, but it's important to be aware of its limitations. As long as the cover is in contact with a hot handle, it will absorb the handle's heat, eventually becoming too hot to hold. The safe time interval can range from several minutes on the stovetop to less than a minute for a pan coming out of a hot oven. So handle covers are more effective when used like potholders, put on the handles only when needed and then taken off. And because a cast-iron skillet itself is so heavy, especially when full, you'll still need another potholder or mitt to grab the other side of the skillet when you're removing food (such as a roast chicken) from the oven.

WEEKNIGHT ROAST CHICKEN

serves 4

Draping a dish towel over the preheated skillet's hot-from-the-oven handle is a great way to avoid accidentally burning yourself. We prefer to use a 3½- to 4-pound chicken for this recipe. If roasting a larger bird, increase the time when the oven is on in step 2 to 35 to 40 minutes. Cooking the chicken in a preheated skillet will ensure that the breast and thigh meat finish cooking at the same time.

CHICKEN

1	tablespoon kosher salt
½	teaspoon pepper
1	(3½- to 4-pound) whole chicken, giblets discarded
1	tablespoon extra-virgin olive oil

PAN SAUCE

1	shallot, minced
1	cup chicken broth
2	teaspoons Dijon mustard
2	tablespoons unsalted butter
2	teaspoons minced fresh tarragon
2	teaspoons lemon juice

1 for the chicken Adjust oven rack to middle position, place 12-inch ovensafe skillet on rack, and heat oven to 450 degrees. Combine salt and pepper in bowl. Pat chicken dry with paper towels. Rub entire surface with oil. Sprinkle evenly all over with salt mixture and rub in mixture with hands to coat evenly. Tie legs together with twine and tuck wingtips behind back.

2 Transfer chicken, breast side up, to preheated skillet in oven. Roast chicken until breast registers 120 degrees and thighs register 135 degrees, 25 to 35 minutes. Turn off oven and leave chicken in oven until breast registers 160 degrees and thighs register 175 degrees, 25 to 35 minutes. Transfer chicken to carving board and let rest, uncovered, for 20 minutes.

3 for the pan sauce While chicken rests, remove all but 1 tablespoon of fat from now-empty skillet (handle will be very hot) using large spoon, leaving any fond and jus in skillet. Place skillet over medium-high heat, add shallot, and cook until softened, about 2 minutes. Stir in broth and mustard, scraping up any browned bits. Simmer until reduced to ¾ cup, about 3 minutes. Off heat, whisk in butter, tarragon, and lemon juice. Season with pepper to taste; cover and keep warm.

4 Carve chicken and serve with pan sauce.

Hannah Says . . .

I love our recipe for Weeknight Roast Chicken where you jump-start cooking by preheating a skillet in the oven. But I must have burned my hand about 70 times on the pan's handle before I developed a system of remembering that it's hot, hot, hot. Now I drape a kitchen towel over the preheated handle right when it comes out of the oven, before I load my bird in, to remind myself. I do this now for any hot pan on my stove, to protect myself and my family members from accidental burns.

head to head

HEAT PROTECTORS

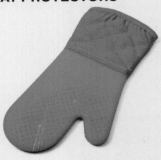

OVEN MITTS	POT HOLDERS	DISH TOWELS
Protect your entire hand and wrist	May have a pocket to put your hand in or may be flat	Must be folded into a square to use like a potholder
Silicone models are water-resistant	Pocket style is more protective	Microfiber towels may melt and should not be used as potholders
Can be bulky, which makes it hard to grab small handles	Flat style is quicker and simpler to grab and use	Don't protect against heat when wet

Are Silicone Oven Mitts Better than Fabric Ones?

Silicone doesn't need to be as thick as fabric to be protective, which gives it a clear advantage as oven mitt material. While the main job of an oven mitt is to prevent burns, it also needs to let you grasp hot pans securely and let you pull pans out of the oven without sticking your thumb in the food. Fabric mitts that are thick enough to be effective can also be pretty unwieldy. And if a fabric mitt gets wet, it's no good at all—heat will go right through. (This goes for pot holders and towels too.) Mitts with silicone on the outside and a fabric lining provide the best combination of protection, dexterity, comfort, and water-resistance.

Lisa Says . . .

I love the big, tall collar of our favorite silicone splatter guard for containing messy splatters, and it's also great for cooking down big heaps of greens in a skillet. You can really pile them on, and simply remove the collar once they've wilted.

Why Doesn't My Splatter Screen Contain 100% of the Splatters?

It's a catch-22: A splatter screen needs to contain oil but also let steam escape safely, all while allowing you to monitor the food you're cooking. Mesh splatter screens allow both visibility and moisture evaporation while reducing mess—particularly larger blobs of oil that can be painful if they hit you—but those tiny holes let some oil mist through. A different kind of splatter guard, essentially a large silicone collar that you set inside a skillet, has high walls that do a good job of creating a barrier to prevent oil splatters. But even with this type, some amount of oil is still going to escape.

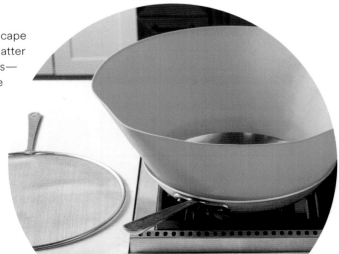

Dress the Part

What you wear in the kitchen goes beyond fashion; the comfort and peace of mind you get from a protective apron and a pair of clogs can help you up your cooking game.

Does It Matter If My Apron is Bib, Crossback, or Smock-Style?

Each style of apron provides good coverage to protect your clothes from spills; what you choose comes down to personal preference and comfort. All three styles come in crisp cotton, soft linen, or blends; whatever you choose, the fabric should be thick and sturdy enough so that food doesn't soak right through and stain your clothes. To keep your apron clean and fresh, make sure it's machine washable.

Bib aprons are probably what comes to mind when you think about aprons. This style has a neck loop and ties either behind your back or in front of you. We recommend this style for most folks—chefs and those new to aprons alike—and think that a bib apron is an essential you'll find yourself reaching for time and time again.

Crossback aprons are like bib aprons, but they take the pressure off your neck. Instead of the neck loop resting on your neck, a crossback apron goes over your head and rests on your shoulders, with straps that cross behind your back. This style is a good choice if you're cooking for long periods of time or even all day.

A smock apron has a looser fit and no ties. It goes over your head and crosses in the back and often has pockets at the sides. We recommend this style if you're looking for a stylish apron that almost feels like an extension of your outfit, you want something super-comfortable, and you'd rather not bother with having to tie an apron.

Should I Invest in a Leather Apron?

You can if you want to look trendy, but it's not a must-have. Leather aprons provide a barrier against burns and punctures (useful when welding or woodworking). For cooks, these hazards might take the form of a splash of hot grease or a slipping blade. On the downside, while leather aprons are made in different weights, they're heavier, stiffer, and potentially hotter and less comfortable to wear than cloth. They're also not washable, which might be considered a plus or a minus (you simply wipe them down). For the average cook who practices common sense in the kitchen, a leather apron is probably overkill. If you routinely do heavy-duty, messy, or dangerous cooking (think barbecue pit master), a lighter alternative to leather is waxed canvas—it's sturdier and provides more of a barrier than cotton or linen.

anatomy of
A GOOD BIB APRON

NECK STRAP
Adjustable and approximately 1 inch wide for comfort

LONG TIES
Can be tied in back or front

POCKETS
Handy for holding a thermometer or pair of tongs

PROTECTIVE, WASHABLE FABRIC
Comfortable and lightweight, yet thick enough to protect you from stains

GENEROUS WIDTH
Covers your torso and fully wraps around your hips for good coverage

Why Do So Many Professional Cooks Swear by Thick-Soled Clogs?

Any one of our test cooks can tell you that a good pair of shoes is as important as any piece of kitchen equipment. Not only do they protect our feet in case a knife accidentally falls onto the ground or hot pasta water splashes over the side of a pot and onto unsuspecting toes, but they also offer support—many of us are on our feet for eight hours a day. Even if you don't normally cook for hours at a time, wearing the right shoes can help prevent back, leg, and foot pain. The gold standard is closed-toe professional clogs because they're easy to slip on, have a great sturdy sole with excellent arch and heel support, and have built-in cushioning that conforms to your foot for a perfect, custom fit. They're also slip-proof, making them safer on wet or greasy floors. We all have our favorite brand and style but we would never be without them.

Lisa Says . . .
Even if you don't require an anti-fatigue mat for health reasons, spending some money on a good pair of professional clogs such as those worn by chefs may be a good step. (Sorry, couldn't resist the pun!) Your feet and back will thank you. Unlike a stationary mat, clogs stay with you wherever you go in the kitchen.

real talk with hannah

ANTI-FATIGUE MATS CAN HELP EASE PAIN

Supportive closed-toed shoes are your first defense against knee and foot pain in the kitchen, but if they're not doing the trick an anti-fatigue mat might be a worthwhile investment. These mats work not just by providing a supportive layer under your feet but also by encouraging the muscles in your legs and feet to make tiny adjustments that stimulate blood flow and prevent blood from pooling in your lower body. There are a range of options to choose from: Stay away from thin, soft mats and stiff ones, which can curl at the edges and become a tripping hazard. In the test kitchen we prefer heavy, smooth, firm, medium-thick mats with gently beveled edges. They stay in place, are easy to clean, and are supportive.

Do the Dishes

We've heard there are people who actually like washing dishes by hand. With the proper gear and the right techniques, you could become one of them.

What Kind of Sponge Is Best?

A truly all-purpose sponge should be thick enough to put distance between your hand and a knife yet small and compressible enough to reach into a wine glass; a 1-inch-thick sponge that's about 4½ by 2½ inches works well. To be effective at scrubbing, the sponge should have at least one surface that's textured, with ridges, bumps, woven fibers, or loops to lift up cooked-on, gummy, and sticky foods from an assortment of kitchen equipment. As for material, both cellulose and foam work well—we found sponges of each type that were sturdy and absorbent.

Is Leaving a Wet Sponge in the Sink Actually That Big a Deal?

Given that a kitchen sponge and a kitchen sink are the two germiest things in the average house, letting your sponge hang out in the sink is a very big deal. Bacteria love to grow in a moist environment such as a wet sponge, especially one with food scraps on it, and it doesn't take long for them to multiply out of control. Our colleague Kate Shannon had an independent lab measure the total bacteria count in sponges that we used and left wet versus sponges that we carefully wrung out and let air-dry for two weeks, and the difference was staggering. The sponges that had been left wet averaged more than half a million colony-forming units per milliliter (CFU/mL), while the wrung-out sponges came in at just 20 CFU/mL. The lab didn't differentiate species of bacteria, so we don't know if any of this bacteria was potentially harmful. But the conditions for growing good bacteria and bad bacteria are the same, and the results were clear: Wet sponges really do harbor more bacteria.

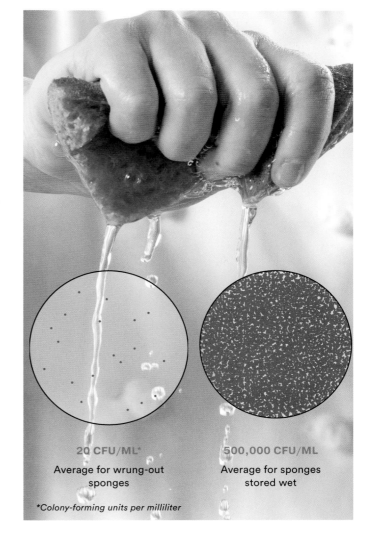

20 CFU/ML*
Average for wrung-out sponges

500,000 CFU/ML
Average for sponges stored wet

*Colony-forming units per milliliter

test it yourself

HOW ABSORBENT IS YOUR SPONGE?

To clean up spills we often reach for a sponge, but if it's not absorbent enough it just winds up pushing the liquid around. We found that for a sponge to be effective it needs to absorb at least 45 grams of water. See how your sponges stack up to this standard by performing a simple test.

1 Using kitchen scale, weigh new, dry sponge; record its weight in grams. Place empty bowl on scale, then press tare button.

2 Fill second bowl with enough room-temperature water to completely submerge your hand. Submerge sponge in water and squeeze it (so sponge compresses), then release your grip (so it fills with water).

3 Transfer sponge to empty bowl on tared scale and record its weight. To calculate amount of water absorbed, subtract weight of dry sponge from weight of soaked sponge.

worth it

SPONGE HOLDER

A kitchen sponge holder gives you an easy way to break the bad habit of leaving your sponge at the bottom of your kitchen sink. A sponge holder goes right in your sink, either attaching to the side with suction cups or hanging from the faucet. It keeps your sponge handy but out of contact with the sink's surface. And it allows the sponge to drain and dry between uses, cutting down on bacteria growth and keeping your sponge cleaner.

How Often Should I Replace My Sponge?

More often than you might think. When we checked with microbiologist Lisa Yakas, a home product certification expert at the public health and safety organization NSF International, she told us that a good rule of thumb is to replace your sponge every one to two weeks. (Do we replace ours that often? We plead the fifth!)

But What If I Clean It?

Even thorough cleaning can't remove every bit of bacteria or make your sponge last forever. That said, regularly cleaning a sponge is considered essential by home safety experts. Here are two cleaning methods from Lisa Yakas at NSF International.

Method 1: Run your sponge through your dishwasher on a setting that reaches at least 155 degrees and has a heated dry cycle (sometimes called sani-rinse, sani-wash, or sanitation cycle), preferably every time you run your dishwasher.

Method 2: Submerge your sponge in a bleach solution (¾ cup of bleach for every gallon of water) for at least 5 minutes and then rinse it thoroughly.

After cleaning, allow the sponge to dry completely before using it again, ideally in a dish rack or a container that allows air to circulate around all surfaces of the sponge. If, despite your best efforts, the sponge starts smelling funky or it starts breaking down, break out a new one for dishes and demote your old sponge to grubbier cleaning jobs.

Method 1

Method 2

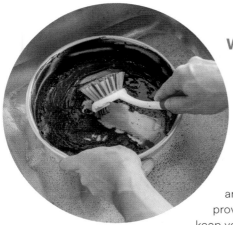

What's the Best Tool for Scrubbing Away Really Tough Messes?

Even if your sponge has a textured side for scrubbing, there are some messes that require a bit more muscle. When we're confronted with food that seems glued to the pan, we reach for a scrub brush. Scrub brushes offer a few advantages to sponges: Their stiff, flared bristles are better at cutting through tough messes and are less likely to cling to food, their handles help provide good leverage, and as a bonus they tend to keep your hands out of the mess.

anatomy of

A GOOD SCRUB BRUSH

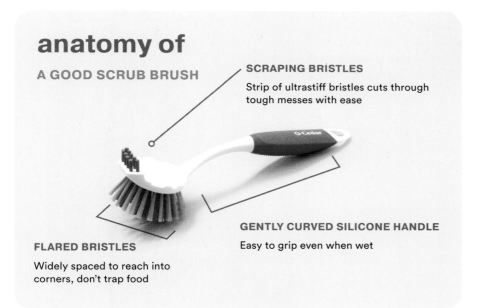

SCRAPING BRISTLES

Strip of ultrastiff bristles cuts through tough messes with ease

GENTLY CURVED SILICONE HANDLE

Easy to grip even when wet

FLARED BRISTLES

Widely spaced to reach into corners, don't trap food

Hannah Says . . .

We've tested chain mail scrubbers and found them useful for cleaning gunk off of cast-iron skillets without ruining the seasoning. But scrub brushes also do a great job of this and they're more versatile. You can use them on a wider range of messes and on stainless steel and enamel without fear of damage—not so with chain mail scrubbers, which can scratch those surfaces. My scrub brush gets a daily workout and lives next to my sink. My chain mail scrubber hasn't seen the outside of my kitchen tools drawer in months.

real talk with hannah

HOW TO REDUCE YOUR PAPER TOWEL CONSUMPTION

I've been trying to cut back my paper towel usage as part of an overall mission to reduce my single-use product consumption. Along the way, I've learned a few tricks. First—and this may sound counterintuitive—I buy the right paper towels. In testing, we found that using thinner, less effective paper towels translates to a lot of wasted paper. Going with tough, absorbent ones, such as our winner from Bounty, means I can use fewer towels for the job. Second, in addition to my pretty dish towels, I keep a stock of dish towels that I don't feel precious about, so I don't hesitate to use them for any yucky messes. I've got them in a range of sizes and thicknesses, so I can choose the best towel for the task at hand. And instead of reaching for paper towels when I season my cast-iron and carbon-steel pans with oil after use, I now keep an old dish towel that I *really* don't care about on a magnetic hook on the side of my oven. I use it to layer on the oil, rotating and refolding it to get an unused swath of fabric for each application. After about six or seven uses, I toss it in the wash and get a new one.

Any Old Towel Will Work to Dry My Dishes . . . Right?

All dish towels are not created equal. Whether you're using it to dry a dish or soak up a spill, first and foremost, a dish towel must be absorbent. Microfiber towels excel at soaking up water, while cotton towels run the gamut. The best towels have thinner areas that quickly transport water and thicker sponge-like zones that hold on to it; these midweight cotton towels with combination weaves seem to grow thicker and sturdier with repeated use. The best size is generous enough to last for an entire dishrack's worth of wet dishes, but not gigantic: Towels that are overly large and thick can be awkward to fit into tight spots, such as the inside of a champagne flute.

How Dirty Is My Dish Towel?

As our colleagues Sawyer and Paul found, if you use the same towel for drying your hands and your dishes, it's probably pretty dirty. Even after you wash your hands (which honestly can sometimes be more of a quick rinse when you're busy cooking) some lingering germs will wind up on the dish towel and, eventually, on your clean dishes. The risk increases when you use a damp dish towel. Bacteria such as salmonella, staph, and E. coli thrive and multiply in wet conditions, and can lead to upset stomachs and other foodborne illnesses.

The first step to cleaner, safer dish drying is to use separate towels for dishes and hands, choosing colors or designs that let you easily distinguish one from the other. Every few days, replace your towels and wash them separately from other items. And after using your dish towel, hang it up so it completely dries (or toss it in the dryer) instead of leaving it in a heap on the counter.

Hannah Says . . .

Carrie Bradshaw famously used her oven to store her shoe collection on Sex and the City because she never cooked. I have the opposite problem: I cook so much I often run out of places to put my clean dishes as they dry. Sometimes they simply sprawl across the stovetop, but if I want to be able to cook and speed up drying I press other tools into service. Wire cooling racks, oven racks, and colanders all encourage air flow to dry your dishes more quickly and contain everything in an out-of-the-way place.

Lisa Says . . .

All new cloth typically has "sizing" on it, which is a protective treatment that keeps the fabric from absorbing too much water. Washing your towels helps remove this treatment and improves their absorbency. Pro tip: Never, ever use fabric softener on your dish towels. It will make them repel water rather than absorb it!

worth it

REUSABLE BAG DRYING RACK

Washing your food-storage bags (see page 328) for reuse is thrifty, eco-friendly, and easy: Use warm, soapy water on the outside; add some to the bag and then seal it and slosh the water around to clean its inside; rinse it; and give the bag a good shake. But drying them can be tricky, as they need to be propped open and held aloft so that air can circulate inside. A good bag drying rack provides the perfect setup for drying: Its long arms hold bags up off the counter, and its stable base keeps it from tipping over. As a bonus, you can also use it to dry inverted water bottles and baby bottles. When it's not in use, it folds up for compact storage, so in addition to saving you money, it saves your counters from clutter.

Deep Clean

A sparkling-fresh kitchen is a pleasure to work in. Understanding how cleaning agents and tools work will help you achieve that goal with (relative) ease.

How Do Soaps and Other Household Cleaning Products Work?

Cleaning products such as soap, detergents, and spray cleaners contain surfactants, which are chemicals that emulsify grease and dirt, making them easy to rinse away. Surfactants (short for surface-active agents) have a part that likes oil and a part that likes water on the same molecule. The two parts form a film between the oil and the water that makes it easy for the oil to get carried away by the water you're cleaning with. Cleaners also contain solvents, which dissolve soils, and buffering agents, which raise or lower the product's acidity to let it bond with (and fight) different types of soils.

In tandem, some soap molecules disrupt the chemical bonds that allow bacteria, viruses, and grime to stick to surfaces, lifting them off your skin, dishes, cookware, or kitchen surfaces. They can also form around particles of dirt and fragments of viruses and bacteria, suspending them in floating cages. A good rinse will then wash away all the microorganisms that have been damaged, trapped, and killed by soap molecules.

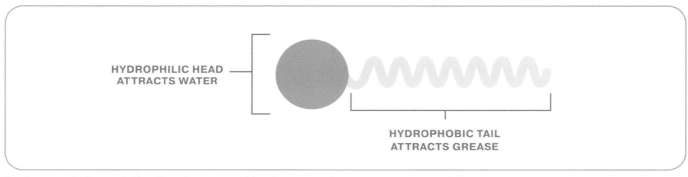

HYDROPHILIC HEAD
ATTRACTS WATER

HYDROPHOBIC TAIL
ATTRACTS GREASE

Surfactants help emulsify oil and water, making it easy to rinse away grease and dirt.

What's the Difference Between Cleaning, Sanitizing, and Disinfecting?

According to the Environmental Protection Agency (EPA), cleaning is mainly a physical process of removing dirt, soil, and stains from surfaces. Sanitizing is the process of chemically neutralizing (killing) bacteria on surfaces. Disinfecting is similar to sanitizing, but it also kills viruses.

Since Disinfecting Kills Bacteria and Viruses, Do I Really Need to Clean Something Before I Disinfect It?

Yes; when you're trying to kill germs on a surface, you still need to physically remove any messes or soils first. For example, if you've spilled marinade from raw chicken on your counter, first clear away the sticky liquid using soap and water or a multipurpose spray cleaner (for this step it doesn't matter whether the spray is antimicrobial). Now you're ready to disinfect, using either an antimicrobial spray cleaner or solution of bleach and water.

How Quickly Do Disinfectants Work?

Antimicrobials don't kill on contact. They take time, usually about 10 minutes, to fully neutralize bacteria and viruses. If you don't wait long enough, the antimicrobials (or bleach) may not fully neutralize the germs you're trying to get rid of—and who wants to go through all that cleaning and disinfecting and still have germs lurking around? To make sure you're doing a thorough job, check the label of the spray you're using to see how long it should sit before wiping it off.

Well-designed bottles disperse a lot of cleaning solution over a wide area with each spray, making the cleaning process more efficient.

common kitchen cleaners and what they're best for

CLEANER	WHAT MAKES IT EFFECTIVE	WHAT IT'S USED FOR
Abrasive Cleaner	Mineral abrasives in these cleaners help remove dirt from surfaces with scrubbing. They also contain agents such as oxalic acid (found in Bar Keeper's Friend), sodium carbonate (in Bon Ami), or bleach (in Comet and Ajax), which remove difficult stains, including rust.	Gets rid of sticky, stubborn messes such as baked-on grease, milk, or sugar on surfaces such as stainless steel and porcelain.
Chlorine Bleach	Bleach works via oxidation, breaking the chemical bonds of stains and soils into soluble particles that can be removed with detergents and rinsed away with water. Sodium hypochlorite is a component of bleach that deactivates bacteria, fungi, and viruses by denaturing their proteins.	Sanitizes surfaces, cutting boards, and cookware that have been in contact with potential pathogens such as those found on raw chicken or cold or flu viruses. Removes food stains such as turmeric, annatto, pesto, and mustard from cookware, surfaces, and fabrics. Note: Always dilute according to manufacturer's instructions and never combine with other cleaners.
Non-Chlorine Bleach	These products use hydrogen peroxide to create an oxidizing reaction that helps to lift dirt from fabrics.	Removes stains from laundry and is safe on most fabrics. Mixed with hot water, it can pretreat stains such as mustard, adobo sauce, and fruit and vegetable stains such as tomato or carrot juice.
Non-Bleach Disinfectant	These cleansers contain antimicrobial ingredients such as benzalkonium chloride or citric acid as well as multiple surfactants that help to remove soils.	Cleans and sanitizes counters, cabinets, faucets, and stovetops.
Glass Cleaner	The active ingredient in glass cleaner is ammonia or vinegar. Ammonia chemically converts grease and grime in a way that leaves no residue behind. It also evaporates rapidly, which helps to avoid streaking. The acetic acid in vinegar breaks up grease, grime, and streaky films on glass.	Lightly cleans glass and the exterior of countertop appliances, stoves, and microwaves, leaving behind a pleasant shine.
Washing Soda	Sodium carbonate (or soda ash) is a fairly strong alkaline salt that raises pH. A high pH gives fabrics a negative charge, which helps push dirt away from fabrics so that they stay whiter and brighter. Washing soda also acts as a water softener, which helps the detergent to lift soil from fabrics.	Removes greasy, sticky buildup from walls, appliances, or grills. In the laundry, it cleans grimy kitchen towels and aprons; helps to brighten whites.
Liquid Dish Soap	Surfactants in dish soap emulsify grease and dirt, making them easy to rinse away.	Removes grease, starch, and proteins from dishes, utensils, and cookware.

Can Vinegar Get My Kitchen Clean?

Our colleague Sarah found that there are plenty of ways vinegar—plain, inexpensive distilled white vinegar—can spruce up your kitchen. Vinegar is about 5 percent acetic acid, which helps it break down the structure of some dirt, oils, films, stains, and bacteria. A spray of vinegar diluted with water (one part vinegar to four parts water) cleans surfaces such as your stovetop, fridge and freezer shelves, counters, mirrors, and windows. Microwaving a mixture of equal parts vinegar and water helps loosen stuck-on food and grease in the microwave. Diluted vinegar can be used to wash fruits and vegetables as an alternative to store-bought produce sprays. And spraying plastic cutting boards with vinegar helps get rid of garlic odors.

Note that while vinegar does clean, when diluted it doesn't thoroughly disinfect—for that, you should stick to antibacterial cleaning products. Vinegar alone will disinfect, but it's less user-friendly, as you'll have to wash the surface again to remove the vinegary smell. And a word of caution: You should never mix vinegar with hydrogen peroxide or bleach. This can produce toxic vapors.

Is There Anything I Shouldn't Clean with Vinegar?

The acid in vinegar can dull natural stone such as limestone and marble and can also dissolve the finish that protects hardwood floors. For this reason, it should be avoided when cleaning stone floors, wood floors, and certain countertops. And although some coffee maker manuals suggest running a solution of distilled vinegar and water through your machine to descale, we found that vinegar can be corrosive and may not effectively remove all the scale. A better solution is to use a dedicated descaling product (either powder or liquid).

Can I Kill Germs Without Using Heavy-Duty Cleaners?

Yes; the surfactants in standard cleaners are effective at washing away most harmful germs. So for most day-to-day cleaning, doing a thorough job with hot, soapy water is sufficient and should always be your first line of defense. But if you have a sick family member and want to disinfect high-contact surfaces such as light switches, or if you want to disinfect your counters and sink after handling raw meat, you'll need a cleaner formulated to kill "99.99 percent of bacteria and viruses." These products contain antimicrobials, a class of chemicals that neutralize germs by disrupting their cell membranes or proteins. Traditional anti-microbials, called quarternary ammonium compounds or "quats" for short, work well but are potentially harmful to inhale or touch. (Common complaints from quat exposure include worsening asthma and skin irritation.) Newer disinfecting products contain milder antimicrobials such as citric acid. We worked with an independent, ISO-accredited lab to test both styles of antimicrobials and found they were equally effective at eliminating salmonella when used according to manufacturer instructions. We think the gentler products are the wiser choice.

GOO REMOVER

makes ¾ cup

This simple DIY formula removes sticky adhesive residue without potentially toxic solvents. The oil dissolves fat-soluble adhesives and holds the paste together, alkaline baking soda helps break down the adhesive and acts as a mild abrasive, and the compound limonene in orange essential oil (a common additive in industrial cleaners) is a powerful solvent that helps lift off the goo while also bringing a pleasant fragrance to the mixture. You can stir this mixture together right in the container you use to store it.

½   cup baking soda

¼   cup vegetable oil

6   drops orange essential oil

Stir baking soda, vegetable oil, and essential oil together to make a paste. (Stored in airtight container, mixture will keep indefinitely.)

to use Apply ½ teaspoon paste to residue on glass, plastic, or metal surfaces; let sit for 10 minutes; and then rub with damp towel for 1 minute before rinsing with warm water.

What's the Best Way to Clean and Maintain My Wooden Tools and Utensils?

Because wood swells as it absorbs water and then shrinks (and potentially cracks) as it dries, we don't recommend using the dishwasher to clean wooden utensils or leaving them to soak. Just like wooden cutting boards (see page 81), wooden tools should be washed by hand with hot, soapy water and dried with a dish towel after each use to prolong their useful life. If soap and water don't get rid of strong smells such as onion, you can scrub wooden tools with a mixture of 1 tablespoon of baking soda and 1 teaspoon of water. And to keep your wooden tools—and boards—looking their best, treat them occasionally with mineral oil or, better yet, spoon butter.

Lisa Says . . .

We've seen advice about boiling wooden spoons and spatulas to get them extra clean, and while this might seem appealing, it's actually a terrible idea. Wood is a natural material and does not need to be boiled to get clean; in fact, boiling will shorten the lifespan of the kitchen tool by drying out the wood's natural oils and encouraging it to crack.

SPOON BUTTER

makes about 1½ cups

This simple mixture of mineral oil and beeswax gives wooden utensils and cutting boards a smooth, durable, and water-repellent finish. It takes a bit more effort than using straight mineral oil but we think the results are superior. Beeswax can be ordered online in bars or pellets; if you buy pellets, use the same weight and skip the chopping. This recipe can be scaled up or down using a 3:1 ratio of oil to beeswax by weight.

1   cup plus 2 tablespoons (9 ounces) food-grade mineral oil

3   ounces food-grade or cosmetic-grade beeswax, chopped fine

Combine oil and beeswax in 1-pint Mason jar. Set jar in small saucepan filled with 2 inches water and heat over low heat until beeswax has melted, stirring occasionally to combine. Let cool to room temperature.

to use Rub small amount into wooden utensils or cutting boards with clean cloth. Let sit for 24 hours, then buff off excess coating.

It's About Time I Upgraded My Kitchen Trash Can. What Should I Look For?

Because you often approach a trash can with your hands full, a can with a foot pedal can be more convenient as well as more sanitary than one where you have to lift the lid by hand. Motion-sensor trash cans promise the same hands-free benefits but we find them unreliable. The lid of a good foot-operated trash can opens quickly and fully to allow easy access and then seals tight to trap odors. Our favorite model also has a switch that keeps the lid up if needed—but all this convenience comes at a cost: over $100. If paying top dollar for a trash can isn't your thing (although trust us, you won't regret it), opt for a simple plastic can with a hinged lid that can be left open while you're filling it and then covers the can securely.

What's the Best Way to Dispose of Kitchen Scraps?

Letting scraps of food decompose in the trash isn't great for the ambiance of your kitchen—or for the environment. (Food in landfills produces greenhouse gases such as methane.) There are better ways to deal with kitchen scraps that won't cramp your style. If you have a backyard composting system, you might find that a simple mixing bowl on your counter works fine to collect the day's coffee grounds, grapefruit rinds, and such. If it usually takes you a couple of days between visits, use a countertop compost bin, which keeps scraps covered and out of sight until you empty it. Compost bins can be used unlined or with liners. Some come with filters, but as long as the cover fits tightly it will contain odors. Plastic models are lightweight and can go in the dishwasher; a handle makes for easy carrying.

Hannah Says . . .

I love fried food. Dealing with the frying oil afterwards? Not so much. One of my favorite tips is to save the container the oil came in and pour the cool used oil back into it. Then just seal it up and toss the whole thing in the trash. We also like a product called Waste Cooking Oil Powder. When you stir a sachet of these small white flakes into a pot of warm frying oil, the contents transform as they cool into a solid disk that is easy to remove from the pan and dispose of directly in the trash, no container needed.

FREQUENTLY ASKED QUESTIONS: COMPOST EDITION

Q: Is it OK if the food in my compost bin gets moldy?

A: Moldy food is fine in the compost bin. However, if you're regularly noticing an overgrowth of mold, it may be an indication that you need to empty the bin more frequently.

Q: Do I need to do anything to prepare food scraps before adding them to the bin?

A: Remove plastic stickers from fruit and veggies. For backyard composting, cut larger foods (such as watermelon rind and corn on the cob) into smaller pieces for faster processing. If not backyard composting, always follow the instructions provided by the company taking your compost.

Q: Can I store my bin in the refrigerator or freezer?

A: Yes, but this depends on the size of both your bin and your refrigerator or freezer. Storing your bin in the freezer slows down or stops the decomposition process and is perfect if you're going away and don't have time to dump your bin or if you want to eliminate the possibility of fruit flies.

What Kinds of Kitchen Scraps Can I Compost in My Backyard?

Backyard composting is a great way to dispose of kitchen scraps but not all food makes good compost. Here's the breakdown:

You can compost coffee grounds, tea leaves (only include bags if biodegradable), fruit and vegetable scraps (remove produce stickers), eggshells, bread, pasta, grains, nuts, and nut shells.

You should not compost meat, fish, bones, oils and other fats, dairy products, or eggs.

You should limit cooked food and leftovers, which may be oily or fatty (such as pastries or dressed pasta).

In addition to kitchen scraps, which are nitrogen-rich, your compost pile needs carbon-rich materials such as dry leaves, plant stalks, and shredded brown paper bags. If you participate in a municipal or commercial composting program, you can compost a wider variety of foods, including animal products; check with your program for specifics. (Note that backyard composting systems can't handle compostable dinnerware; for more, see page 308.)

How Can I Clean All Those Hard-to-Reach Places?

There are plenty of kitchen spaces where a full-size broom or vacuum just won't fit. That's where a good dustpan and brush set comes in handy. Not only is this duo quicker to use for small spills than pulling out a broom, but the brush can reach into corners around cabinets and pull out stray coffee grounds or dust bunnies. Then there are spots where you might not even be able to see the dirt or debris but you know it's there (like those frozen peas that rolled under your fridge). For those, an under-appliance duster comes in handy. Basically a slender microfiber mop on a long stick, it lets you reach into really narrow spaces and sweep out whatever's hiding there. For jobs where you'd rather vacuum than sweep, a handheld vacuum with a pivoting or rotating nozzle easily navigates tight corners and makes cleanup superquick.

anatomy of
A GOOD DUSTPAN AND BRUSH

HORIZONTAL HANDLE
Comfortable to grip

RUBBER BUMPER
Provides smoother transition to floor for complete cleanup

LONG BRUSH HEAD
Covers plenty of ground in one pass

PLASTIC BRISTLES
Durable, yet flexible enough to sweep easily

What's Wrong with a Vertical Brush Handle?

When you use a dust brush with a vertical handle, your hand always has to be directly over whatever you're cleaning, which is an awkward, tiring position, and one that makes it hard to get into corners. Brushes with horizontal handles act like extensions of your hand, allowing you to reach into tight spaces (corners, the backs of cabinets, etc.) more easily.

What About Silicone Brush Bristles?

The grippy quality of silicone may seem like a plus when it comes to picking up dirt, but silicone bristles tend to stick to the floor as you sweep, making the task feel laborious. And debris sticks to the bristles just as tenaciously, so it's there to stay until you wash the brush. We prefer plastic bristles, which are flexible enough to sweep up flour and dust, sturdy enough to corral chickpeas or broken glass, and tough enough to scrape up bits of stuck-on food.

head to head

MOPS

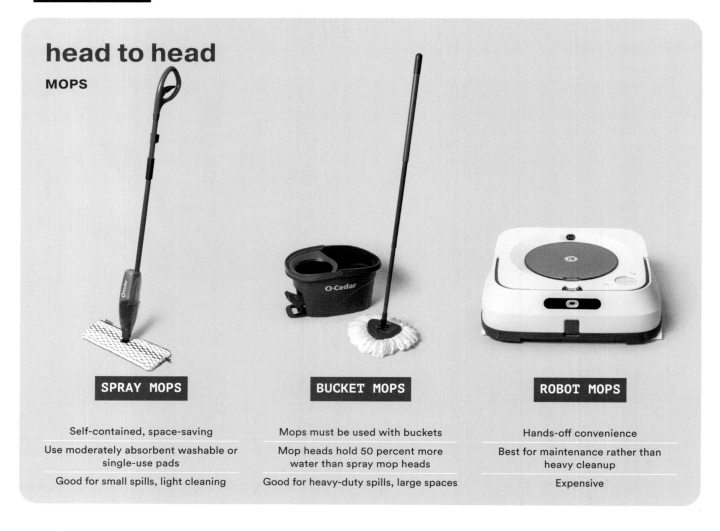

SPRAY MOPS	BUCKET MOPS	ROBOT MOPS
Self-contained, space-saving	Mops must be used with buckets	Hands-off convenience
Use moderately absorbent washable or single-use pads	Mop heads hold 50 percent more water than spray mop heads	Best for maintenance rather than heavy cleanup
Good for small spills, light cleaning	Good for heavy-duty spills, large spaces	Expensive

Do I Really Need a Mop?

To find your answer, take this simple quiz from our resident cleaning expert and self-confessed "spillomatic" Chase Brightwell.

1 Do you have a pet, a child, a messy partner, a messy roommate, or are you yourself a fellow spillomatic? (Yes/No)

2 Are you a normal sentient human who enjoys keeping your space clean, fresh-smelling, and free of stains? (Yes/No)

3 Are your hands and knees sore/filthy from toweling away large spills? (Yes/No)

4 Do you draw circles on the floor with your foot in a futile attempt to wipe up spills, aka "footing it"? (Yes/No)

5 Do your relatives, roommates, friends, or in-laws like to comment judgmentally on your grubby floors? (Rude, but OK.) (Yes/No)

6 Do you have one single square foot of storage space in a closet, basement, or cupboard in order to store a new, life-changing cleaning tool? (Yes/No)

If you answered "Yes" to any of these questions, Chase says it's time for a mop—and we agree!

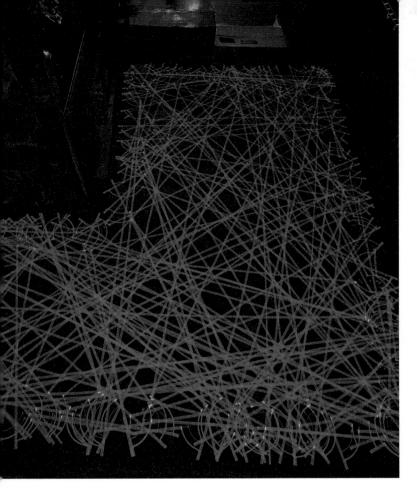

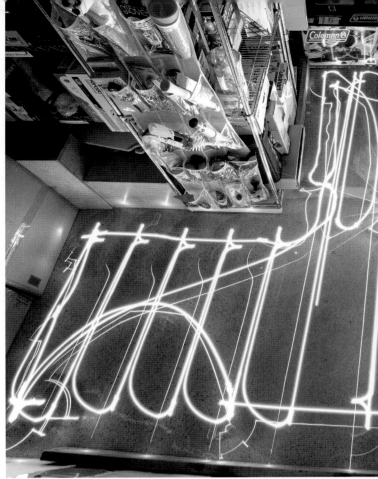

How Do Robot Mops and Vacuums Navigate?

Robot vacuums, robot mops, and hybrid mop/vacuums use a wide range of navigation systems. At the most basic level, these cleaning robots rely on sensors to help them reverse course when they hit obstacles, keep from falling down stairs, find their way around or along things such as walls, and sense areas that are extra dirty. Most "no-frills" robots traverse the floor randomly until they eventually cover the whole room (as in the time-lapse photo above left), while others travel in a grid pattern or in rows (above right).

In addition to sensors, high-end robot cleaners have the technology to build a virtual map of the room. Some use a mapping system called visual simultaneous localization and mapping (vSLAM), which employs a camera to help the robot "see" the shape and size of objects in the room. Others use a smart mapping technology called light detection and ranging

(LiDAR) that relies on lasers. Our winning high-end vacuum robot also uses waypoints high on the walls and ceiling to navigate; these are things that don't typically change in a room, even if you move the furniture.

The most sophisticated robots pair these navigational technologies with an app to create a map of your home. After a few uses, you can use this map to name specific rooms and designate certain "no-go" areas. The result is a more customized experience; you can tell the robot to clean a specific room or to avoid cleaning a specific area (for instance, staying away from the cat's water bowl). You can also schedule cleanings.

Can a Robot Clean Floors Better Than a Broom and Mop?

Robot mops aren't a replacement for a good scrubbing—think of them as hands-free daily maintenance, not deep cleaning. The results from most mops are similar to what you'd expect by using a wet sweeper such as a Swiffer.

So while robot mops can lengthen the time between deep cleans, you're still eventually going to need to break out a broom, mop, and bucket if you want truly sparkling floors.

Is There a Reason So Many Cleaning Robots Are Round?

One word: maneuverability. You might think a square machine would work better getting into corners, but that shape actually makes it more prone to getting stuck. When a round machine gets into tight spaces, it can simply rotate 180 degrees and leave the way it went in. (On round robots, spinning brushes typically extend a few inches beyond the body of the robot to sweep, so corners do get cleaned.)

How Long Does a Handheld Vacuum Battery Last?

Handheld vacuums aren't made for deep-cleaning large areas; the models we tested have rechargeable batteries that last for about 9 to 20 minutes of continuous use. That's not a long time, but it should be enough for cleaning the interior of your car, under your kitchen cabinets, or several pieces of furniture in your living room. If you want a vacuum that does more in one go, a different style may be for you.

Is It OK to Leave My Cordless Vacuum Plugged in All the Time?

Some manufacturers recommend unplugging your vacuum 24 hours after a full charge to reduce energy consumption; others make no recommendation. Regardless of what brands say, leaving batteries plugged in full time can reduce their capacity and lifespan, so we think it's best to unplug a vacuum once it's fully charged. (That can take from an hour and a half to eight hours.)

What Can I Do to Make My Handheld Vacuum Last?

If we've learned anything as equipment testers, it's that people often neglect to clean their cleaning tools. To keep your handheld vacuum going strong, empty the collection bin after every cleaning session, and clean the filter often, after every five or six uses. A filter that doesn't receive routine TLC is a filter that will prevent your machine from performing optimally. And after six months of regular cleaning or when you start to notice filter damage or wear and tear, buy and install a certified replacement filter from your unit's manufacturer. They usually cost about $10 to $15 apiece and often are sold in packs of two or four.

Check out this video to learn which cleaning tools and tips Lisa and Hannah think are the real deal.

cleaning gadgets

Anything that claims to make cleaning easier is a tempting purchase. Here are five such gadgets and our verdict on whether they live up to the hype.

MORE USEFUL

GARLIC ODOR REMOVER BAR
Rubbing this stainless-steel soap bar–shaped tool under cold water easily eliminates garlic odors from your hands. While any stainless-steel item does the same trick (the metal bonds with sulfur compounds in garlic, which can then be easily washed away), this low-priced gadget is convenient and comfortable to use.

RUST ERASER
This slim eraser removes rust quickly and easily from the blades of carbon steel knives. You can also remove rust spots by using Bar Keepers Friend, but you may not like having your fingers close to the blade's edge.

ANGRY MAMA MICROWAVE CLEANER
This gadget, which holds a combination of vinegar and water to create steam in the microwave, cleans like a charm and is cute too. But a bowl of vinegar and water works just as well; see page 117 for gadget-free cleaning instructions.

CHAIN MAIL SCRUBBER
These scrubbers work very well for big messes on cast-iron or Pyrex pans. But they'll scratch and damage enameled and stainless-steel pans, which limits their usefulness. Scrub brushes work on a wider range of materials.

GRILLBOT
This expensive grill-cleaning robot can't finish any job that couldn't be done with a grill brush in a fraction of the time. It's a pain to clean as well.

LESS USEFUL

5 Things
You Should Be Cleaning
(That You Probably Aren't)

We get it: Compared to cooking, cleaning the kitchen is not a ton of fun. But believe us, your kitchen will be much better off if you give these five often-neglected items a good cleaning—and so will you.

1

YOUR TRASH CAN

Clean at least once a month using these three steps to guard against mold and mildew and discourage insects.

1 Spray inside of can with 1:4 vinegar to water solution. Let it sit for a few minutes, then wipe away any stuck-on material with paper towel or rag.

2 Wash with water and dish soap. Let can sit for a few minutes, then pour out soapy water and dry can with paper towel or rag.

3 Spray exterior with disinfectant spray or bleach solution made of 4 teaspoons of bleach per quart of room temperature water. Leave spray or solution on can for at least 1 minute before wiping it away.

2

YOUR DISH RACK

Clean once a week to discourage mold and bacteria.

Take the rack apart if possible. Run any dishwasher-safe parts through the dishwasher, using the top shelf for plastic parts. Wash all the parts that aren't dishwasher safe using warm, soapy water, then rinse with hot water and set them aside. (If you don't have a dishwasher, just wash all the parts by hand.) Finally, use a clean, absorbent dish towel to dry all the parts thoroughly before reassembling.

3 YOUR SINK

Clean at least once a week to cut down on the thousands of bacteria a typical kitchen sink harbors.

Using a scrub brush, cloth, or sponge (just not the same one you use for dishes!), scrub the sink thoroughly with hot, soapy water or a product such as Bar Keepers Friend. Make sure you get in all the corners, up where the sink meets the countertop, and into the grooves around your drain. Then spray the faucet and handles with all-purpose cleaner and wipe them dry.

4 YOUR OVEN MITTS

Whenever they become stained, wash your oven mitts to rid them of germs and to preserve their ability to insulate.

Look for a tag or check online for the manufacturer's instructions and launder or wash the mitts accordingly. Then gently squeeze or wring out the mitts to get rid of excess water and lay them flat to dry.

5 YOUR SPONGE HOLDER

Clean at least once a month to get rid of soap residue and traces of food.

Detach the sponge holder; scrub it thoroughly with hot, soapy water; and rinse it well before reattaching it to your sink.

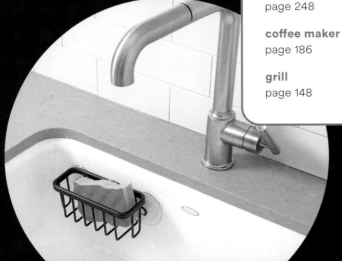

more cleaning guides

There are even more helpful cleaning guides scattered throughout this book. Flip to the pages below to read more.

ATK Recommended Equipment

Over the years, we've evaluated thousands of pieces of equipment. Each product in this chart has gone through multiple rounds of tests aimed at identifying its most important attributes and has been awarded the ATK Recommended seal of approval, meaning it meets our highest standards. Because America's Test Kitchen accepts no free products or support from product manufacturers, you can trust our ratings. Prices in this chart are based on shopping at online retailers and will vary. In cases where an item has multiple winners, the first model listed is the one pictured. For complete and up-to-date information for all our reviews, see AmericasTestKitchen.com/KitchenGearRecommended.

TURN UP THE HEAT	ITEM	WHAT TO LOOK FOR	ATK RECOMMENDED
	STAINLESS-STEEL SKILLET	• Fully clad stainless-steel and aluminum construction for even heat distribution • Broad cooking surface and low, flared sides encourage browning • Secure, ovensafe handle • Tight-fitting lid	**Best 12-Inch:** All-Clad D3 Stainless Steel 12" Fry Pan with Lid $119.95 **Best 10-Inch:** All-Clad D3 Stainless 10" Fry Pan with Lid $99.95 **Best 8-Inch:** All-Clad Stainless 8" Fry Pan $98.49
	COPPER SKILLET	• Broad cooking surface • Open, flared sides with rounded corners • Responsive, even heating	**Best 12-Inch Steel-Lined:** Mauviel M'Heritage M'200Ci Round Frying Pan, 11.9 In $435.00 **Best 12-Inch Copper-Core:** All-Clad Copper Core 5-ply Bonded Fry Pan, 12 inch $264.95
	CARBON-STEEL SKILLET	• Thick, solid construction • Broad cooking surface • Ergonomically angled handle • Flared, moderately high sides allow for easy access while containing splashes	**Best 12-Inch:** Matfer Bourgeat Black Steel Round Frying Pan, 11⅞" $74.83 **Best 10-Inch:** Matfer Bourgeat Black Steel Round Frying Pan, 10¼" $62.60 **Best 8-Inch:** Matfer Bourgeat Black Steel Round Frying Pan, 8⅝" $55.00

| --- | --- | --- | --- |

CAST-IRON SKILLET
Traditional

What to look for:
- Thick bottom and straight sides
- Broad cooking surface
- Helper handle
- Preseasoned

ATK Recommended:

Winner, 12-Inch: **Lodge 12-Inch Cast Iron Skillet**
$33.31

Upgrade Pick, 12-Inch: **Smithey Ironware No. 12 Cast Iron Skillet**
$200.00

Winner, 10-Inch: **Smithey Ironware No. 10 Cast Iron Skillet**
$160.00

Best Buy, 10-Inch: **Lodge 10.25-Inch Cast Iron Skillet**
$14.88

Winner, 8-Inch: **Lodge 8-Inch Cast Iron Skillet**
$9.88

Enameled

What to look for:
- Long handle and/or large helper handle
- Enameled surface requires no seasoning
- Balanced weight

ATK Recommended:

Best 12-Inch: **Le Creuset Signature 11¾" Iron Handle Skillet**
$237.49

Best 10-Inch: **Le Creuset Signature 10¼ Inch Iron Handle Skillet**
$220.00

Best 9-Inch: **Le Creuset Signature 9-Inch Iron Handle Skillet**
$149.95

NONSTICK SKILLET
Traditional

What to look for:
- Durable nonstick coating
- Comfortable, ovensafe handle
- Cooking surface diameter of at least 9 inches

ATK Recommended:

Best 12-Inch: **OXO Good Grips Non-Stick Pro 12" Open Frypan**
$59.95

Best 10-Inch: **OXO Good Grips Non-Stick Pro 10-inch Open Fry Pan**
$39.95

Best 8-Inch: **OXO Good Grips Hard Anodized Pro Nonstick 8-Inch Fry Pan**
$29.95

Ceramic

What to look for:
- Slick PTFE-free nonstick surface
- Gently sloped walls
- Cooking surface diameter of at least 9 inches

ATK Recommended:

Winner, 12-Inch: **GreenPan Valencia Pro Hard Anodized Nonstick Frypan**
$89.99

Best Buy, 12-Inch: **Kyocera Ceramic-Coated 12" Nonstick Frypan**
$64.95

Winner, 10-Inch: **GreenPan Valencia Pro Hard Anodized Nonstick Frypan, 10-Inch**
$69.99

Winner, 8-Inch: **GreenPan Valencia Pro Hard Anodized Nonstick Frypan, 8-Inch**
$49.99

TURN UP THE HEAT	ITEM	WHAT TO LOOK FOR	ATK RECOMMENDED
	DUTCH OVEN Traditional	• Enameled cast iron construction • Capacity of at least 6 quarts • Broad cooking surface; light interior; and straight, relatively low sides • Tight-fitting lid • Large, easy-to-grip, sturdy handles	Winner: **Le Creuset 7¼ Quart Round Dutch Oven** $409.95 Best Buy: **Cuisinart Chef's Enameled Cast Iron Casserole** $119.02
	Lightweight	• Large capacity • Fully clad stainless steel construction • Cooking surface diameter of at least 9 inches • Straight sides • Large, easy-to-grip, sturdy handles	Winner: **All-Clad D3 Stainless Stockpot with Lid, 6 Quart** $294.99 Best Buy: **Tramontina 6 Qt Tri-Ply Clad Stainless Steel Pot** $119.95
	BRAISER	• Thick cast iron construction retains heat • Wide cooking surface • Light interior • Easy-to-grip handles and knob	Winner: **Le Creuset Enameled Cast-Iron 3.5-Qt. Braiser** $367.95 Best Buy: **Tramontina Enameled Cast Iron Covered Braiser** $82.64
	WOK	• Carbon steel construction • Measures 14 inches from rim to rim • Flat bottom with a diameter of at least 7 inches • Straight, stay-cool wooden handle • Large helper handle	Co-winner: **Taylor and Ng Natural Nonstick Wok Set** $49.17 Co-winner: **Joyce Chen Classic Series 14-Inch Carbon Steel Wok with Birch Handles** $36.81 Co-winner: **IMUSA 14" Non-Coated Wok with Wood Handle, Silver** $29.41
	RIMMED BAKING SHEET Traditional	• Thick, sturdy aluminum construction browns food evenly and resists warping • Straight, low sides contain food • Standard half-sheet pan measures 18 by 13 inches	Best Half-Sheet: **Nordic Ware Baker's Half Sheet** $14.97 Best Quarter-Sheet: **Nordic Ware Naturals Quarter Sheet** $8.99 Best Eighth-Sheet: **Nordic Ware Naturals Eighth Sheet Pan** $9.75
	Nonstick	• Slick nonstick coating releases food easily • Roomy cooking surface equal to that of a standard-size half-sheet pan • Textured cooking surface browns food evenly	Co-winner: **USA Pan Half Sheet Baking Pan** $19.99 Co-winner: **OXO Good Grips Non-Stick Pro Half Sheet Pan** $24.99 Co-winner: **Williams Sonoma Goldtouch Nonstick Half Sheet Pan** $29.95

TURN UP THE HEAT	ITEM	WHAT TO LOOK FOR	ATK RECOMMENDED
	RIMMED BAKING SHEET LID	• Easy to attach to and remove from a rimmed baking sheet • Sturdy enough to support 10 pounds without bending, cracking, or touching food stored underneath it • Easy to clean and doesn't retain odors	Best Half-Sheet: **Nordic Ware Half Sheet Cover** $16.98 Best Quarter-Sheet: **Nordic Ware Storage Lid for Quarter Sheet** $8.32
	WIRE COOLING RACK	• Bars are arranged in a tight grid pattern • Six feet on three bars provide extra stability • Fits snugly inside a standard 18 by 13-inch rimmed baking sheet • Broiler-safe and dishwasher-safe	**Checkered Chef Cooling Rack** $12.95
	COOKIE SHEET	• Raised edges on two sides for superior maneuverability without sacrificing airflow • Thick aluminum construction browns food evenly and resists warping	**Vollrath Wear-Ever Cookie Sheet (Natural Finish)** $47.81
	SAUCEPAN Large	• Fully clad steel and aluminum construction heats evenly and reasonably quickly • Tall, straight sides make it easy to monitor browning • Stay-cool, easy-to-grip main handle and large helper handle • Tight-fitting lid	Winner: **All-Clad Stainless 4-Qt Sauce Pan** $211.13 Best Buy: **Tramontina Tri-Ply Clad 4 Qt. Sauce Pan** $89.95
	Small Nonstick	• Sturdy, solid construction • Durable nonstick coating • Shallow shape and generous cooking surface diameter	**Calphalon Contemporary Nonstick 2½ Quart Saucepan** $99.00
	SAUCIER	• Relatively broad cooking surface • Smooth, curvy, gently flared walls • Lightweight frame and straight-angled handle for easy lifting	**Le Creuset 3½ Quart Stainless Steel Saucier Pan** $250.00
	SAUTÉ PAN	• Broad cooking surface diameter of at least 9½ inches • Moderately high, straight sides • Long, straight, comfortable handle • Large helper handle	**Made In Stainless Clad Saute Pan** $149.00

ITEM	WHAT TO LOOK FOR	ATK RECOMMENDED
ROASTING PAN WITH RACK	• Measures at least 15 by 11 inches • Fully clad steel and aluminum construction distributes heat evenly • Upright handles for easy gripping • Light interior makes it easy to monitor browning • Rack fits snugly inside pan	**Cuisinart MultiClad 16" Roasting Pan with Rack** $129.95
GRIDDLE Stovetop	• Heats quickly and evenly • Large usable cooking surface • Walls at least 1 inch high contain grease • Upright, sturdy, easy-to-grab handles • Relatively lightweight	**Cuisinart Chef's Classic Nonstick Double Burner Griddle** $68.47
Electric	• Thick cooking surface heats evenly • Large usable cooking surface • Easy-to-clean nonstick coating • Intuitive temperature controls • Detachable power supply allows griddle to be washed in the sink	Winner: **BroilKing Professional Griddle with Backsplash** $151.56 Best Buy: **Presto 19-Inch Electric Tilt-n-Fold Griddle** $58.96
GRILL PAN	• Cast iron construction retains heat • Well-defined ridges at least 4 to 5.5 millimeters high keep food perched above rendered fat • Generous cooking surface	Co-winner: **Lodge Chef Collection Cast Iron Square Grill Pan** $35.99 Co-winner: **Borough Furnace Grill Pan/ Braising Lid** $180.00
PAELLA PAN	• Shallow, wide shape maximizes cooking surface area • Thick, heavy carbon steel distributes heat evenly • Easy-to-grab vertical handles	**Matfer Bourgeat Black Steel Paella Pan** $81.99

	COOKWARE SET	• Fully clad stainless steel pieces with aluminum cores for responsiveness and even heat distribution • Lids are included • Set includes a 10-inch frypan, 8-inch frypan, 3-quart saucepan, 2-quart saucepan, 3-quart sauté pan, and 8-quart stockpot	Winner: **All-Clad D3 Tri-Ply Bonded Cookware Set, 10 piece** $699.95 Best Buy: **Goldilocks Cookware Set** $175.00
	13 BY 9-INCH BAKING PAN/DISH Broiler-Safe	• Large looped handles • 14¼- to 16¼-cup capacity • Broiler-safe • Easy to clean	**Mrs. Anderson's Baking Lasagna Pan with Handle** $36.96
	Glass	• Large handles • Relatively lightweight • Easy to grip and maneuver	**Pyrex Easy Grab 3-Quart Oblong Baking Dish** $7.29
	Metal	• Straight sides with crisp corners produce professional-looking baked goods • Durable nonstick coating releases baked goods easily • Gold color promotes moderate browning	**Williams Sonoma Goldtouch Nonstick Cake Pan** $32.95

DO YOUR PREP WORK	ITEM	WHAT TO LOOK FOR	ATK RECOMMENDED
	CHEF'S KNIFE	• High-carbon stainless-steel blade • 8-inch blade with a narrow edge angle • Lightweight • Nonslip handle provides a comfortable grip	Best 8-Inch: **Victorinox Swiss Army Pro 8"** **Fibrox Chef's Knife** $39.95 Best 6-Inch: **Victorinox Swiss Army Fibrox** **Pro 6" Chef's Knife** $33.95
	SANTOKU KNIFE	• Sharp cutting edge • Narrow spine (top edge of blade) that measures less than 2 millimeters • Slim tip for precision work • Moderate-length handle with neutral shape is comfortable to grip	Winner: **Misono UX10 Santoku 7.0"** $179.50 Best Buy: **MAC Superior Santoku 6½"** $74.95
	GYUTOU KNIFE	• Slim, sharp tip • Tapered blade is light and slightly flexible • Curved blade assists rocking cutting motion	**Masamoto VG-10 Gyutou, 8.2"** $187.80
	PARING KNIFE	• Blade measures 3 to 3½ inches • Thin, flexible blade with pointed tip • Comfortable grip	**Victorinox Swiss Army Spear Point** **Paring Knife** $7.51
	BIRD'S BEAK PARING KNIFE	• Moderately long, razor-sharp blade that is narrow from tip to heel • Grippy, moderately long, medium-thick handle • Lightweight	**MAC Paring Knife, Bird's Beak, 2½"** $29.95
	SERRATED PARING KNIFE	• Thin, deft blade • Razor-sharp serrations easily pierce thin tomato skin and citrus peels for safe, precise slicing	Winner: **Wüsthof Classic 3.5-Inch Fully** **Serrated Paring Knife** $95.00 Best Buy: **Victorinox Swiss Army 4"** **Serrated Paring Knife** $5.95
	SERRATED KNIFE	• 10-inch blade is capable of slicing wide loaves of bread • Relatively broad, deep, pointed serrations • Narrow edge angle • Comfortable, grippy handle	**Mercer Culinary Millennia 10-Inch** **Bread Knife** $22.10
	CLEAVER	• Medium weight of 14 to 15 ounces • Good balance • Long, tall, subtly curved blade • Relatively thin, sharp blade	**Masui AUS8 Stainless Meat Cleaver 180mm** $90.00

	ITEM	WHAT TO LOOK FOR	ATK RECOMMENDED
	NAKIRI	• Razor-sharp, moderately long and tall blade is capable of both coarser work and fine, precise cuts • Textured handle is comfortable to grip • Lightweight	Best Stainless-Steel: **Masamoto Sohonten Wa-Nakiri** $245.00 Best Carbon-Steel: **Sakai Kikumori 165mm Nakiri - Aogami 2 - Nashiji** $255.00 Best Buy: **Masutani VG1 Nakiri 165mm** $69.99
	SLICING KNIFE	• 12-inch blade is capable of slicing large cuts of meat • Oval scallops (called a Granton edge) in the side of the blade make it lighter, for better maneuverability • Fairly rigid blade with rounded tip	**Victorinox Swiss Army 12" Granton Slicing Knife** $54.65
	BONING KNIFE	• Sharp, moderately flexible, 5½-inch blade that maintains its edge • Slender handle and slim profile for agility and maneuverability	Winner: **Zwilling Pro 5.5" Flexible Boning Knife** $99.95 Best Buy: **Victorinox Swiss Army Fibrox Pro Boning Knife** $26.95
	PETTY/UTILITY KNIFE	• Sharp, thin blade measures 6 inches in length or less • Handle measures at least 4¼ inches in length, with at least 0.6 inch in clearance underneath for fingers	Winner: **Tojiro 150mm Petty R-2 Powder Steel** $117.00 Best Buy: **MAC PKF-60 Pro Utility 6"** $71.99
	SERRATED UTILITY KNIFE	• Stiff, ultrasharp blade • Long, flexible, tapered blade design • Textured, comfortable grip	Winner: **Zwilling Pro 5.5" Serrated Prep Knife** $115.00 Best Buy: **Cangshan TS Series 5-Inch Serrated Utility Knife and Wood Sheath Set** $55.97
	STEAK KNIVES	• Supersharp, straight-edged blade that holds its edge well • Less than ¾-inch difference between length of the blade and handle for good balance • Comfortable, lightweight handle	Winner: **Victorinox Swiss Army 6-Piec Rosewood Steak Set** $219.99 for set of 6 ($36.67 per knif Best Buy: **Chicago Cutlery Walr Steak Knife Set** $31.79 for set of 4 ($7.95 per '
	HONING ROD	• Rod made of steel or ceramic, without a diamond coating • Alternating lightly ridged and smooth textures on rod • Rod is consistently thick from base of handle to tip	Winner: **Bob Kramer Douł Sharpening Steel** $69.95 Best Buy: **Idahone F Rod, 12"** $34.99

	ITEM	WHAT TO LOOK FOR	ATK RECOMMENDED
	KNIFE SHARPENER Manual	• Sharpens to a 15-degree edge angle • Diamond abrasive • Spring-loaded guide supports blade • Grippy, comfortable handle	**Chef'sChoice Pronto Diamond Hone Knife Sharpener** $49.99
	Electric	• Sharpens to a 15-degree edge angle • Diamond abrasive • Multiple slots from coarser to finer grits • Spring-loaded chambers precisely guide blades • Can convert a 20-degree edge to a narrower 15 degrees	Winner: **Chef'sChoice Trizor 15XV Knife Sharpener** $139.99 Best Buy: **Chef'sChoice 315XV Knife Sharpener** $109.99
	CUTTING BOARD Heavy-Duty	• Roomy work surface that measures at least 20 by 15 inches • Teak wood for minimal maintenance • Durable edge-grain construction (wood grain runs parallel to surface of board) • Two flat surfaces (no feet) so board is reversible • Finger grips on short sides	**Teakhaus Edge Grain Cutting Board (XL)** $104.95
	Large Plastic	• Moderate weight contributes to stability without sacrificing portability • Rubber grips for optimal stability • Moderately thick to resist warping • Dishwasher-safe	Winner: **Winco Statik Board Cutting Board 15" x 20" x ½"** $45.00 Best Lightweight: **OXO Good Grips Carving and Cutting Board** $27.99
	Small	• Moderately thin, lightweight plastic • Rubber grips for optimal stability • Does not warp, crack, stain, or retain odors • Dishwasher-safe	**OXO Good Grips Utility Cutting Board** $17.95
	Bar Board	• Moderate weight and/or silicone grips for stability • Measures about 10 by 7 inches	Best Wood: **Teakhaus Square Marine Board with Juice Canal** $21.94 Best Plastic: **OXO Good Grips Prep Cutting Board** $11.99
	CARVING BOARD	• Large and stable enough to hold large roasts • Trenches are large enough to contain ½ cup of liquid • Reversible • Medium weight for easy carrying, carving, and cleaning	**J.K. Adams Maple Reversible Carving Board** $98.50

	ITEM	WHAT TO LOOK FOR	ATK RECOMMENDED
	FLEXIBLE CUTTING MATS	• Thick and sturdy but still flexible • Textured sides keep mat and food in place • Textured surface conceals nicks	Co-winner: **Dexas Heavy Duty Grippmats** $19.99 for set of 4 ($5.00 per mat) Co-winner: **Prepworks by Progressive Flexible Color-Coded Chopping Mats - Set of 4** $10.39 for set of 4 ($2.60 per mat)
	CUTTING BOARD STABILIZER	• Securely stabilizes different kinds of cutting boards on different types of counters • Relatively easy to clean • Thin and flexible enough to be rolled up for storage • Durable	**Architec SmartMat** $15.95
	CAN OPENER Manual	• Long driving handle • Grippy arms • Blades that cut into the can rim, leaving no sharp edges (for safety openers)	Best Traditional: **OXO Good Grips Soft-Handled Can Opener** $16.95 Best Safety: **Fissler Magic Can Opener** $43.95
	Electric	• Straightforward latching mechanism • Responsive, easy-to-use controls • Cutting blade leaves smooth, safe edges on cans and lids • Sturdy construction accommodates cans of all sizes	Winner: **Hamilton Beach Smooth Touch Electric Can Opener** $29.85 Best Battery-Powered: **Kitchen Mama Electric Can Opener** $24.20
	VEGETABLE/FRUIT PEELER	• Razor-sharp carbon-steel blade • 1 inch of space between blade and peeler body to prevent jamming • Lightweight and comfortable	Best Y Peeler: **Kuhn Rikon Original Swiss Peeler** $3.50 Best Straight Peeler: **OXO Good Grips Swivel Peeler** $11.99
	KITCHEN SHEARS	• Supersharp blades can be taken apart for easy cleaning • Sturdy construction • Work for both right- and left-handed users	Winner: **Shun Multi-Purpose Shear** $49.95 Best Buy: **J.A. Henckels Intern Take-Apart Kitchen Shears** $14.94
	SEAFOOD SCISSORS	• Comfortable handles • Sharp blades that are slim, gently arched, and slightly serrated • Durable design is capable of standing up to thick shells	**RSVP International F Scissors** $14.99

ATK Reco

DO YOUR PREP WORK	ITEM	WHAT TO LOOK FOR	ATK RECOMMENDED
	GRATER	• Wide, long grating surface • Stamped holes • Grippy plastic bumper or feet for stability • Large, comfortable handle	Best Paddle-Style: **Rösle Coarse Grater** $35.93 Best Box-Style: **Cuisinart Box Grater** $11.95
	RASP-STYLE GRATER	• Medium-size, U-shaped grating teeth arranged in staggered lines • Sharp teeth require little pressure to grate • Comfortable rounded, grippy handle	**Microplane Premium Classic Zester/Grater** $14.95
	MANDOLINE	• Razor-sharp blades capable of handling tough produce • Broad, customizable range of thickness settings • Slices and juliennes	Winner: **Super Benriner Mandoline Slicer** $69.00 Easiest to Use: **OXO Good Grips Chef's Mandoline Slicer 2.0** $84.99 Best Compact: **Kyocera Soft Grip Adjustable Mandoline Ceramic Slicer** $24.95
	MIXING BOWLS Stainless-Steel	• Lightweight and easy to handle • Durable • Conducts heat well for improvised use as a double boiler	**Vollrath Economy Stainless Steel Mixing Bowls** $2.90 for 1.5-quart bowl; $4.50 for 3-quart bowl; $6.90 for 5-quart bowl
	Glass	• Tempered to increase impact and thermal resistance • Microwave-safe • Durable	**Pyrex Smart Essentials Mixing Bowl Set** $19.88 for 4-bowl set
	MEASURING CUPS Dry	• Accurate measurements with easy-to-read measurement markings that don't fade or rub off • Handles flush with cups for easy leveling • Stack and store neatly • Stable when empty and filled	**OXO Good Grips Stainless Steel Measuring Cups** $19.99
	Liquid	• Crisp, unambiguous markings that include ¼- and ⅓-cup measurements • Heatproof, sturdy cup with handle	Best Glass: **Pyrex 1-Cup Liquid Measuring Cup** $9.99 Best Plastic: **OXO Good Grips 1 Cup Angled Measuring Cup** $6.99
	Adjustable	• Plunger-like bottom with tight seal • 1- or 2-cup capacity • Dishwasher-safe	**KitchenArt Pro 2 Cup Adjust-A-Cup, Satin** $23.81

	MEASURING SPOONS	• Long, comfortable handles • Rim of bowl flush with handle for easy leveling • Slim design fits in most jar mouths	**Cuisipro Stainless Steel 5-Piece Measuring Spoons** $12.33
	KITCHEN SCALE	• Easy-to-read display not blocked by weighing platform • Roomy weighing platform • 11-pound capacity • Simple, intuitive, accessible buttons • Gram-to-ounce conversion feature	Winner: **OXO Good Grips 11 lb Food Scale with Pull Out Display** $49.99 Best Buy: **Ozeri Pronto Digital Multifunction Kitchen and Food Scale** $11.79
	THERMOMETER Instant-Read	• Digital model with automatic shut-off • Produces readings in 1 second • Wide temperature measurement range • Long stem that can reach interior of large cuts of meat • Water-resistant	Winner: **ThermoWorks Thermapen ONE** $105.00 Best Mid-Priced: **Lavatools Javelin PRO Duo** $49.99 Best Buy: **ThermoWorks ThermoPop** $29.00
	Clip-On Probe	• Digital model • Easy-to-read console • Intuitive design and ovensafe probe	Winner: **ThermoWorks ChefAlarm** $59.00 Best Buy: **Polder Classic Digital Thermometer/Timer** $24.99
	Remote Probe	• Easy to set up • Large, bright display • Loud, easy-to-set alarm • Magnetic base and kickstand	Winner: **ThermoWorks Smoke 2-Channel Alarm** $99.00 Upgrade Pick: **FireBoard 2** $189.00 Best Buy: **NutriChef Bluetooth Wireless BBQ Grill Thermometer** $43.99
	Infrared	• Accurate • Big distance-to-spot ratio • Large, highly visible laser guide • Easy-to-use interface • Comfortable, medium-length handle	**ThermoWorks Industrial IR with Circle Laser** $89.00
	Refrigerator/Freezer	• Accurate and customizable • Sends alerts when temperatures remain outside safe zone for more than 30 minutes	**ThermoWorks Fridge/Freezer Alarm** $22.00
	Oven	• Clearly marked numbers for easy readability • Large, sturdy base • Measures temperatures up to 600 degrees	Winner: **CDN Pro Accurate Oven Thermometer** $8.70 Best Alternative: **ThermoWorks ChefAlarm** with **ThermoWorks Pro-Series High Temp Air Probe and Stainless Steel Grate Clip** $76.00 ($56.00 for thermometer and $17.00 for air probe accessory)

DO YOUR PREP WORK	ITEM	WHAT TO LOOK FOR	ATK RECOMMENDED
	DIGITAL TIMER	• Accurate and easy to use • Clearly labeled buttons • Large readable digits	Best Single-Event: **ThermoWorks Extra Big & Loud Timer** $33.00 Best Multiple-Event: **Oxo Good Grips Triple Timer** $25.00
	WHISK All-Purpose	• At least 10 wires • Wires of moderate thickness • Comfortable rubber handle • Balanced, lightweight feel	**OXO Good Grips 11" Balloon Whisk** $9.99
	Mini	• Five sturdy wire loops • Relatively broad head • Thick, medium-length handle that is easy to grip and clean	**Tovolo Stainless Steel 6" Mini Whisk** $7.00
	Nonstick	• Moderately flexible silicone-coated wires • Loops of widely varying lengths • Comfortable, grippy handle	**OXO Good Grips 11" Silicone Balloon Whisk** $12.99
	Flat	• Comfortable to use for longer periods • Grippy handle • Well-spaced, rigid wires	**OXO Good Grips Flat Whisk** $6.95
	Dough	• Thick, stainless-steel coil capable of mixing thick, sticky dough and batter • Coiled wire resists batter clumps and is easy to clean • Long, sturdy wooden handle provides excellent leverage	**King Arthur Baking Dough Whisk** $14.95
	SPATULA Silicone	• Firm enough to handle both scraping and scooping • Fits neatly into tight corners • Straight sides and wide, flat blade ensure that no food is left unmixed	Winner: **Di Oro Living Seamless Silicone Spatula—Large** $10.97 Best Large: **Rubbermaid 13.5" High-Heat Scraper** $14.50
	Metal	• Thin, flexible, gently upward-curving head that measures about 3 inches wide and 5 inches long • Long, vertical slots • Comfortable handle provides good leverage	Winner: **Wüsthof Gourmet 7" Slotted Spatula** $49.95 Best Nonstick-Safe: **Matfer Bourgeat Exoglass Pelton Spatula** $13.25 Best Buy: **MIU France Flexible Fish Turner—Slotted** $16.57
	Jar	• Slim, sturdy, flexible head can maneuver around tight corners and edges • Flat surface can be wiped clean in a single swipe • Long, comfortable handle	Winner: **GIR Skinny Spatula** $12.95 Best Buy: **OXO Good Grips Silicone Jar Spatula** $5.95

	ITEM	WHAT TO LOOK FOR	ATK RECOMMENDED
	KITCHEN TONGS	• Scalloped edges • Moderate tension for comfortable gripping • Open wide to grab large foods securely • Precise, slightly concave pincers • Long enough to keep hands safely away from heat	**Best 12-Inch: OXO Good Grips 12-Inch Tongs** $12.95 **Best 9-Inch: OXO Good Grips 9" Tongs** $11.99
	WOODEN SPOON	• Moderate weight • Head has scooped bowl and thin front edge for scooping and scraping • At least 12 inches in length to keep hands safely away from heat • Rounded, tapered handle for comfortable grip, good leverage, and control • Durable and easy to clean and maintain	**Winner: Jonathan's Spoons Spootle** $28.00 **Best Buy: FAAY 13.5" Teak Cooking Spoon** $10.99
	SLOTTED SPOON	• Lightweight • Wide, shallow, thin-edged bowl • Long, comfortable handle	**Cuisinart Stainless Steel Slotted Spoon** $9.12
	LADLE	• Durable stainless steel construction • Hooked, 9- to 10-inch-long handle • Pouring rim prevents dripping	**Winner: Rösle Hook Ladle with Pouring Rim** $38.50 **Best Buy: Cuisinart Stainless Steel Ladle** $19.67
	PASTA FORK	• Long handle • Small drainage holes • Gently angled head, making it comfortable and easy to maneuver	**OXO Nylon Spaghetti Server** $7.00
	SPIDER SKIMMER	• Long handle protects hands from hot water and oil • Well-balanced and easy to maneuver	**Rösle Wire Skimmer** $41.68
	POTATO MASHER	• Round metal mashing plate with lots of small holes • Moderately sized footprint that maneuvers easily in small and large pots • Sturdy construction • Long, comfortable handle	**Zyliss Stainless Steel Potato Masher** $12.99
	FINE-MESH STRAINER	• Roomy, medium-depth basket with fine, stiff mesh • Long, wide hook • Rounded steel handle	**Rösle Fine Mesh Strainer, 7.9 inches** $45.00

	ITEM	WHAT TO LOOK FOR	ATK RECOMMENDED
	GARLIC PRESS	• Sturdy stainless-steel construction • Large hopper capable of holding multiple garlic cloves at once • Long handle and short distance between pivot point and plunger provide leverage • Hopper opens completely for easy cleaning	**Kuhn Rikon Epicurean Garlic Press** $44.95
	TOMATO CORER	• Comfortable handle • Lightweight • Sharp serrated head	**Norpro Tomato Core It** $2.99
	APPLE CORER Crank-Style	• Peels, cores, and slices quickly and efficiently, and can be set to peel or slice only • Accommodates oddly shaped fruit (and potatoes) • Suction base holds corer firmly in place • Adjustable blades	**VKP Brands Johnny Apple Peeler, Suction Base, Stainless Steel Blades, Red** $23.38
	Push-Style	• Cores and slices • Plastic base that aids in finalizing cuts • Easy to clean by hand or in dishwasher	**Norpro Grip EZ Fruit Wedger, 16 Slices with Base** $9.00
	CHERRY PITTER	• Thick, straight dowels • Easy to load, pit, and retrieve cherries • Contains messes	**Leifheit Cherry Pitter "Cherrymat"** $44.99
	COLANDER Traditional	• 4- to 7-quart capacity • Metal ring attached to the bottom for stability • Many holes for quick draining • Small holes so pasta doesn't slip through	**RSVP International Endurance Precision Pierced 5 Qt. Colander** $25.60
	Mini	• Capacity of at least 3 cups • Fairly wide, broad bowl that allows food to settle into a thin layer • Sturdy collapsible walls pop open and closed with ease and require minimal storage space • Snap-on base catches drips and allows colander to be filled with water for deeper cleaning	**Progressive Prepworks Collapsible Mini Colander** $18.98

	ITEM	WHAT TO LOOK FOR	ATK RECOMMENDED
	FOOD MILL	• Legs (not hooks) for stability • Comfortable, grippy handle • Lightweight • Medium spring force on blade	**Cuisipro Deluxe Food Mill** $84.00
	RICER	• Comfortable, easy-to-squeeze handles • Interchangeable disks neatly produce a range of fine to coarse textures • Sturdy hook rests securely on pot rim	**RSVP International Potato Ricer** $26.67
	SALAD SPINNER	• Large capacity • Large gap between bottom of basket and outer bowl keeps water away from clean greens • Easy-to-operate central pump and brake • Wide base for stability • Flat lid for easy cleaning and storage	**OXO Good Grips Salad Spinner** $29.99

PLUG IT IN	ITEM	WHAT TO LOOK FOR	ATK RECOMMENDED
	COUNTERTOP ICE MAKER	• Lightweight, quiet, and compact • Simple controls • Makes ice in under 10 minutes • Self-cleaning	**IGLOO Premium Self-Cleaning Countertop Ice Maker** $153.00
	COUNTERTOP DISHWASHER	• Holds two to four place settings • Quiet • Simple to use • Cleans and dries effectively	Best Small: **Comfee' Countertop Portable Dishwasher with 6L Built-In Water Tank** $369.99 Best Large: **Black and Decker Compact Countertop Dishwasher (6 Place Setting)** $360.00
	MICROWAVE OVEN	• Moderate wattage of 900 to 1,000 watts • Simple, intuitive controls • Moderate capacity of 0.9 to 1.0 cubic foot • Fingerprint-free matte silver or white finish • Light, bright interior	**Breville The Compact Wave Soft Close Microwave** $243.33

PLUG IT IN	ITEM	WHAT TO LOOK FOR	ATK RECOMMENDED
	SILICONE MICROWAVE LID	• Silicone stays cool • "Nostrils" vent steam • Washes clean easily	**Piggy Steamer** $18.00
	LONG-SLOT TOASTER	• Slots long enough to fit large rustic bread slices or two slices of sandwich bread side by side • Intuitive, simple controls • Ability to monitor toasting progress without interrupting toasting cycle	**Russell Hobbs Glass Accent Long Slot 2-Slice Toaster** $47.36
	TOASTER OVEN	• Quartz heating elements for steady, controlled heat • Compact design with roomy interior • Simple, intuitive controls	**Breville Smart Oven** $269.95
	AIR FRYER Traditional	• Drawer-style model with extra-large capacity • Quick 2-minute preheat • Sturdy handle • Intuitive digital controls	Winner: **Instant Vortex Plus 6-Quart Air Fryer** $119.95 Upgrade Pick: **Instant Vortex Plus ClearCook + OdorErase 6-Quart** $149.99
	Air Fryer Toaster Oven	• Clearly displayed settings • Versatile; works as both a toaster oven and an air fryer • Large capacity	Winner: **Breville Smart Oven Air Fryer Pro** $399.95 Best Buy: **Instant Oven 18L Air Fryer Toaster Oven** $199.95
	AIR FRYER LINERS	• Low sides allow air to circulate • Thin material allows heat to reach food quickly • Solid (no holes) to catch grease and crumbs better • Surface area should match that of your air fryer	Best Paper: **Loveuing 9.1 inch Disposable Paper Liners** $21.83 for 100 ($0.22 per liner) Best Silicone: **Infraovens Air Fryer Silicone Mat & Reusable Liners** $13.99 for 3 ($4.66 per liner)
	SMART OVEN	• Easy to use with responsive control panel • Well-designed app that does not lose connectivity with oven • Capable of operating as a traditional countertop oven • Accurate food-temperature probe that ensures food doesn't under- or overcook	Winner: **June Smart Oven (3rd Generation)** $899.00 Best Buy: **Tovala Smart Oven** $299.00

PLUG IT IN	ITEM	WHAT TO LOOK FOR	ATK RECOMMENDED
	COUNTERTOP STEAM OVEN	• Precision control to adjust steam in 5-percent increments • Big, clear window • Sturdy racks	**Anova Precision Oven** $699.00
	MULTICOOKER	• Programmable and easy to use • Large flat-bottomed pot for sautéing • Stay-cool handles • Safe pressure release switch	Winner: **Instant Pot Pro 8QT** $169.95 Best Buy: **Crock-Pot 8-Quart Express Crock XL Pressure Cooker** $102.00
	STOVETOP PRESSURE COOKER	• Solidly built • Stovetop model with low sides and wide base for easy access and better browning and heat retention • Easy-to-read pressure indicator	Winner: **Fissler Vitaquick 8½-Quart Pressure Cooker** $289.95 Best Buy: **Zavor Duo 8.4 Quart Pressure Cooker** $119.95
	SLOW COOKER	• At least 6-quart capacity • Dishwasher-safe insert with handles • Clear lid makes it easy to monitor food • Intuitive control panel with programmable timer and warming mode	Co-winner: **KitchenAid 6-Quart Slow Cooker with Solid Glass Lid** $129.99 Co-winner: **Hamilton Beach Temp Tracker 6 Quart Slow Cooker** $74.99 Best with Searing Capabilities: **Cuisinart 6-Quart 3-in-1 Cook Central** $156.95
	SOUS VIDE IMMERSION CIRCULATOR	• Slim, lightweight, and small enough to store in drawer • Heats water quickly and accurately • Magnetic bottom allows circulator to stand stably in center of metal pots • Comes with user-friendly app that's compatible with iOS and Android	Winner: **Breville Joule Sous Vide-White Polycarbonate** $249.95 Best Buy: **Yedi Houseware Infinity Sous Vide** $99.95
	SOUS VIDE LID	• Fits a variety of vessels • Slim, flexible design that's easy to store	**Everie BPA-Free Plastic Lids** $9.99
	VACUUM SEALER	• Compact, sturdy frame • Clearly labeled buttons and screen • Pulse button • Automatic mode and manual option • Easily closed lid	Winner: **Nesco Deluxe Vacuum Sealer** $118.00 Best Chamber: **Anova Precision Chamber Vacuum Sealer** $349.00

| --- | --- | --- | --- |
	BLENDER Traditional	• Combination of straight and serrated blades set at different angles • Jar with curved base • At least 44-ounce capacity • Heavy base for stability	Best High-End: **Vitamix 5200** $498.93 Best Mid-Priced: **Breville Fresh & Furious** $199.95 Best Inexpensive: **NutriBullet Full Size Blender** $99.99
	Personal	• Quick and effective blending • Sharp, six-pronged blades angled both up and down • Well-designed travel lid with drinking spout and hinged arm that seals tight	**Ninja Nutri Ninja Pro** $105.00
	Immersion	• Grippy rubber handle • Easy to change speeds • Lightweight	**Braun Multiquick 5 Hand Blender** $64.95
	FOOD PROCESSOR Large	• 14-cup capacity • Sharp and sturdy blades • Wide feed tube makes it possible to add food while processor is running • Comes with steel blade, dough blade, and shredding/slicing disk	**Cuisinart Custom 14 Cup Food Processor** $249.00
	Small	• Capacity of 3½ to 4 cups • Powerful, responsive controls • Feed tube makes it possible to add food while processor is running • Very small 3- to 4-millimeter gap between blade and processor bowl bottom allows processor to engage with very small amounts of food	**Cuisinart Elite Collection 4-Cup Chopper/ Grinder** $59.95

PLUG IT IN	ITEM	WHAT TO LOOK FOR	ATK RECOMMENDED
	STAND MIXER	• Powerful enough to mix dense doughs • Heavy, for better stability • Multiple distinct speeds • Simple, intuitive controls	Winner: **Ankarsrum Original 6230 Creme and Stainless Steel 7 Liter Stand Mixer** $749.95 Best Mid-Priced: **KitchenAid Classic Series 4.5 Quart Tilt-Head Stand Mixer** $329.99 Best Small: **KitchenAid Artisan Mini 3.5 Quart Tilt-Head Stand Mixer** $379.95 Best Buy: **Farberware 6 Speed 4.7-Quart Professional Stand Mixer** $107.00
	HAND MIXER	• Silicone-tipped, wide beater heads • Well-positioned display screen • Powerful motor, with a variety of speeds	Winner: **Breville Handy Mix Scraper** $149.95 Best Buy: **Cuisinart Power Advantage Plus 9 Speed Hand Mixer** $79.95
	WAFFLE MAKER	• Indicator lights and audible alert • Makes two waffles at a time • Six-point dial for customizing waffle doneness	**Presto Flipside Belgian Waffle Maker** $59.99
	RICE COOKER	• Clearly labeled water measurement markings • Intuitive and clearly labeled displays • Digital countdown timers and audible alerts • Removable inner lid for easy cleaning • Handy "Keep Warm" setting	**Zojirushi 5.5-Cup Neuro Fuzzy Rice Cooker & Warmer** $185.90

	ITEM	WHAT TO LOOK FOR	ATK RECOMMENDED
	GRILL Charcoal	• Sturdy construction, with well-designed cooking grate, handles, lid, and wheels • Generous cooking and charcoal capacity • Well-positioned vents control air flow • Gas ignition instantly and easily lights coals • Ash catcher for easy cleanup	*Winner:* **Weber Original Kettle Premium Charcoal Grill, 22-Inch** $219.00 *Upgrade Pick:* **Weber Performer Deluxe Charcoal Grill** $549.00
	Gas	• At least two, and preferably three, burners for varying heat levels • Made of thick, heat-retaining materials such as cast aluminum and enameled steel • Low, narrow vent retains heat	**Weber Spirit II E-310 Gas Grill** $569.00
	Portable Gas	• Compact and light with big, sturdy handles • Powerful heat output • Steel grate • Low, narrow vent retains heat • Thick, heat-retaining grill lid and body	*Winner:* **Char-Broil X200 TRU Infrared Portable Gas Grill** $168.29 *Best Buy:* **Weber Go-Anywhere Gas Grill** $89.00
	Flat-Top	• Carbon-steel cooktop with a cooking surface that measures at least 35 by 20 inches • High back and side walls • Two side tables • Four wheels • Large opening and drip cup for easy cleanup	**Nexgrill 4-Burner Propane Gas Grill with Griddle Top** $299.00
	CHIMNEY STARTER	• 6-quart capacity • Holes in canister so air can circulate around coals • Sturdy construction • Heat-resistant handle • Dual handle for superior control	*Winner:* **Weber Rapidfire Chimney Starter** $14.99 *Best Compact:* **Weber Rapidfire Compact Chimney Starter** $14.99
	CHARCOAL FIRE STARTER	• Relatively water-resistant • Ignites easily without impacting food flavor	**Weber Lighter Cubes** $3.29 for 24 cubes ($0.14 per cube)
	GRILL BRUSH	• Short metal bristles • Triangular head without a scraper reaches to the very ends of the grates and can be wedged between the bars • Short handle provides leverage without putting hands uncomfortably close to heat	**Weber 12" Grill Brush** $7.99

TAKE IT OUTSIDE	ITEM	WHAT TO LOOK FOR	ATK RECOMMENDED
	GRILL TONGS	• 16 inches in length to keep hands away from heat • Precise pincers with scalloped edges • Lightweight • Moderate amount of springy tension • Handy loop on end for storage	**OXO Good Grips Grilling Tongs** $16.99
	GRILL GLOVES	• Pliant leather protects hands from heat without sacrificing control • Long, wide cuffs protect forearms	**Steven Raichlen Ultimate Suede Grilling Gloves** $29.99 per pair
	GRILL ROTISSERIE	• Powerful motor • Two-pronged forks • Grooved spit; weight rests on collar, not motor	**Weber 2290 22-inch Charcoal Kettle Rotisserie** $234.99
	SMOKER	• Burns charcoal for superior flavor • Large cooking area • Water pan • Multiple vents for precise temperature control • Generously sized charcoal basket	**Weber Smokey Mountain Cooker Smoker 22"** $549.00
	PORTABLE SMOKE INFUSER	• Medium length tube • Adjustable fan speed • Easy to clean • Heavy weight for stability	**Breville/PolyScience Smoking Gun Pro** $149.95
	TURKEY FRYER	• Sturdy, durable stainless-steel pot • Simple to use, powerful propane burner • Comes with a steamer basket and perforated turkey rack	**Bayou Classic Stainless Steel 32-Quart Turkey Fryer and Gas One High Pressure Burner** $176.80
	COOLER Large Hard	• Insulated lid • At least 2 inches of not-too-dense insulation all around body to trap pockets of insulating air • Sturdy, easy-to-close latches • Durable handles	Winner: **Yeti Tundra 45** $325.00 Best Buy: **Coleman 50 QT Xtreme Wheeled Cooler** $64.99
	Soft	• Thick, closed-cell foam insulation • Smooth-pull zipper • Roomy, boxy shape	Winner: **Engel HD20 22-qt Heavy Duty Soft Sided Cooler Tote Bag** $199.99 Best Buy: **Arctic Zone Titan Guide Series 36-can Cooler** $80.00

TAKE IT OUTSIDE	ITEM	WHAT TO LOOK FOR	ATK RECOMMENDED
	BACKPACKING STOVE	• Extremely compact and lightweight • Built-in igniter • Refined heat control • Four pot supports	Best for Wind: **Soto WindMaster Stove with 4Flex** $64.95 Best for Heat Control: **JetBoil MightyMo** $59.95
	CAR CAMPING STOVE	• Automatic igniter • Powerful 20,000 BTU output for fast cooking • Two roomy burners with windscreen • Compact and portable	**Camp Chef Mountain Series Everest High Pressure Two-Burner Stove** $171.99
	WATER BOTTLE	• Wide mouth • Lid is easy to remove and replace • Few parts to disassemble and clean	**Lifefactory 22 oz Glass Bottle with Classic Cap** $22.99
	TRAVEL MUG	• Double-wall insulation maintains temperature well • Enclosed drinking spout stays clean • Lid locks to prevent spills • Narrow, lightweight bottle is easy to hold and drink from	**Zojirushi Stainless Steel Mug SM-SE (16 ounce)** $29.97
	PICNIC BASKET/ BACKPACK	• Spacious storage compartments • Easy access to food storage • Dinnerware set includes large plates for greater versatility	Winner: **Sunflora Picnic Backpack for 4** $99.99 Easiest to Store: **Picnic at Ascot Collapsible Picnic Basket for 4** $74.00
	PIE CARRIER	• Plastic tote expands to accommodate tall pies or two standard pies • Large, nonstick base • Collapses for easy storage	**Prepworks Collapsible Party Carrier** $39.00
	CAKE CARRIER	• Fits cupcakes and both round and square cakes • Snap locks • Nonskid base • Collapses for easy storage	**Progressive Collapsible Cupcake and Cake Carrier** $41.99
	INSULATED FOOD CARRIER	• Capable of carrying two 13 by 9-inch baking dishes • Sturdy, expandable frame • Insulation keeps food above 140 degrees Fahrenheit for more than 3 hours	**Rachael Ray Expandable Lasagna Lugger** $34.99

TAKE IT OUTSIDE	ITEM	WHAT TO LOOK FOR	ATK RECOMMENDED
	INSULATED SHOPPING TOTE	• Capable of holding 25 pounds of grocery items • Keeps food cold for more than 2 hours	**Rachael Ray ChillOut Thermal Tote** $24.99
	WINE TUMBLER	• Thick, grippy silicone base • Slim, stainless-steel body • Leakproof lid with slider cover	**Swig Stemless Wine Cup (12 oz)** $24.95

RAISE A GLASS	ITEM	WHAT TO LOOK FOR	ATK RECOMMENDED
	COFFEE MAKER Automatic Drip	• Heats to ideal coffee brewing temperature range and brews at correct speed • Simple controls and instructions • Brewing basket is large enough to hold sufficient amount of grounds • Thermal carafe pours neatly	Winner: **Technivorm Moccamaster KBT** $329.00 Best Buy: **Zojirushi ZUTTO Coffee Maker** $69.99
	Pour-Over	• Ribs or accordion-style pleats • Broad, round openings • Well designed drainage holes • Round base about 2⅜ inches in diameter • Wide semicircular handle	Best for Dark-Roast Coffee: **Kalita Wave Dripper 185 S** $42.48 Best for Light-Roast Coffee: **Hario V60 Ceramic Coffee Dripper 02** $23.45 Best for Professional-Quality Results: **Origami Pour Over Coffee Dripper Medium** $39.95
	French Press	• Insulated pot keeps coffee hot • Shatterproof stainless-steel construction • Dishwasher-safe, with few pieces to disassemble	Winner: **Bodum Columbia French Press Coffee Maker** $79.95 Best Buy: **Bodum Chambord French Press, 8-Cup** $39.95
	Single-Serve Manual	• Durable, easy-to-clean brewing mechanism • Adjustable; capable of brewing 1 to 6 ounces of coffee concentrate at a time • Collapsible components allow for maximum portability	**AeroPress Go Travel Coffee Press** $31.95
	Cold Brew	• Easy-to-seal lid • Relatively large capacity • Few parts to disassemble and clean	**Toddy Cold Brew System** $49.00
	Moka Pot	• Large openings on the center tube • Easy-to-find valve • Comfortable handle • Broad base maximizes contact with heat	Winner: **Bialetti Moka Express** $32.66 Best Electric: **Bodum Chambord 12 oz Electric Espresso Maker** $49.99

RAISE A GLASS	ITEM	WHAT TO LOOK FOR	ATK RECOMMENDED
	ESPRESSO MACHINE	• Can make both high-quality espresso and frothed milk • Clear, intuitive display and controls • Easy to clean and maintain	Best Fully Automatic: **Gaggia Anima Automatic Coffee Machine** $690.06 Best for DIY-ers: **Breville Barista Express** $749.95
	COFFEE GRINDER Blade-Style	• Relatively even grinding • Clear lid makes it easy to monitor grinding • Roomy grinding chamber	**Krups Coffee and Spice Grinder** $17.99
	Burr-Style	• Simple design • Clear and intuitive controls • No-fuss, even grinding • Easy-to-clean grounds container	Winner: **Baratza Encore** $139.00 Best Buy: **Capresso Infinity Conical Burr Grinder, Black** $99.99
	PRECISION COFFEE SCALE	• Sensitive and accurate to within 0.5 gram • User-friendly controls • Short boot-up time	**Timemore Black Mirror Basic Plus Scale** $59.00
	MILK FROTHER	• Simple, one-button operation • Clear settings for various foam textures and/or temperatures • Easy to clean and maintain • Durable mechanism that holds up to consistent use	Best Handheld: **Zulay Kitchen Milk Boss Electric Milk Frother** $12.49 Best Countertop: **Breville Milk Cafe** $129.00 Countertop Best Buy: **Instant Milk Frother** $39.00
	KETTLE Stovetop	• Large capacity without excess weight • Wide opening for easy filling • Comfortable, secure handle that stays cool • Loud whistle that can be shut off if desired • Smooth, precise pouring	**Chantal Anniversary Teakettle Collection** $44.95
	Electric	• Wide, easy-to-fill opening • Clear water-level indications • Bright, visible light-up power indicator • Pours neatly and precisely	Winner: **OXO Brew Cordless Glass Electric Kettle** $79.95 Best Buy: **Cosori Original Electric Glass Kettle** $35.38
	Gooseneck	• Sharply curved spout that dispenses slowly, ideal for pour-over coffee • Weighs less than about 1½ pounds when empty • Easily visible capacity line • Easily interpretable controls	Best Adjustable: **OXO Brew Adjustable Temperature Pour-Over Kettle** $99.95 Best Boil-Only: **Bodum Bistro Gooseneck Electric Water Kettle** $60.00

	ITEM	WHAT TO LOOK FOR	ATK RECOMMENDED
	TEA INFUSER	• Ultrafine-mesh basket • Roomy, long basket that sits low in mug and allows leaves to expand fully • Stay-cool plastic- or silicone-lined handles	**Finum Stainless Steel Mesh Brewing Basket, Large** $11.20
	TEA MACHINE	• Perforated tea basket for thorough infusion • Programmable temperature and steeping times • Fully automated brewing • Dishwasher-safe accessories	**Breville Tea Maker** $279.95
	ELECTRIC JUICER Masticating	• Straightforward assembly, with parts that fit together well • Relatively fast and efficient, producing smooth juice • Relatively easy to clean	**Omega VSJ843QS Vertical Square Low-Speed Juicer** $399.95
	Centrifugal	• Straightforward assembly, with parts that fit together well • Relatively heavy, so juicer is stable while in use • Keeps debris contained	**Breville Juice Fountain Cold** $199.95
	CITRUS JUICER Electric	• Comes with small ridged reamer for smaller citrus and large ridged reamer for larger citrus • Quiet, smooth, and fast	Winner: **Breville Stainless Steel Juicer** $229.95 Best Buy: **Dash Go Dual Citrus Juicer** $19.99
	Manual	• Large draining slots direct juice in steady stream with no splattering • Large, rounded, easy-to-squeeze handles • Roomy bowl can accommodate up to medium-size oranges	**Chef'n FreshForce Citrus Juicer** $23.04
	SODA MAKER	• Sturdy and fairly compact • Conveniently sized dishwasher-safe bottles • Can add carbonation along a spectrum from mildly fizzy to very bubbly • Uses SodaStream "quick-connect" CO_2 canisters	Winner: **SodaStream Terra** $79.00 Easiest to Use: **SodaStream One Touch** $126.90

	ITEM	WHAT TO LOOK FOR	ATK RECOMMENDED
	COCKTAIL SHAKER Boston-Style	• Consistently forms tight, leakproof seal • Wide mouth allows for effortless filling, muddling, and cleaning • Medium-height mixing cup facilitates stirring	**The Boston Shaker Professional Boston Shaker, Weighted** $14.50
	Cobbler-Style	• Wide mouth allows for effortless filling, muddling, and cleaning • Carafe-like shape is comfortable for users of all hand sizes to grip	**Tovolo Stainless Steel 4-in-1 Cocktail Shaker** $24.50
	BARSPOON	• Moderately tall, twisted handle is easy to grip without sacrificing control • Medium-size bowl corrals ice and helps with building layered cocktails	**Cocktail Kingdom Teardrop Barspoon** $17.99
	COCKTAIL ICE MOLD	• Hard plastic frame ensures safe transport and shapely ice formation • Relatively small footprint • Includes a lid to reduce odor absorption	Best Cube Mold: **OXO Good Grips Silicone Ice Cube Tray - Large** $9.99 Best Clear Ice Mold: **True Cubes** $39.87 Best Sphere Mold: **Zoku Ice Ball Molds** $16.99 for two molds
	CITRUS ZESTER/ CHANNEL KNIFE	• Capable of zesting all types of citrus • Sharp channel knife set at least ¾ inch from top of handle • Capable of producing long, wide, pith-free ribbons of zest • Comfortable, grippy handle	**Norpro 113 Grip-EZ Zester and Stripper** $6.74
	JIGGER	• Single mouth at least 2 inches wide • Tiny spout for clean pouring • Clearly labeled volume lines and numbers • Measurement lines on the interior	**OXO Good Grips Angled Measuring Cup, Clear** $4.99
	HAWTHORNE STRAINER	• Well-balanced with lightweight handle measuring 3½ inches or shorter • Long wings or prongs and finger tab on head • Fine, adjustable straining coil	**Cocktail Kingdom Koriko Hawthorne Strainer** $15.99
	CORKSCREW Waiter's	• Ergonomically curved body and hinged fulcrum • Notched ledge rests on bottle lip • Sturdy construction	Winner: **Pulltap's Classic Evolution Corkscrew by Pulltex** $39.95 Best Buy: **Trudeau Double Lever Corkscrew** $12.99
	Twist	• Nonstick-coated worm measuring at least 1¾ inches • Comfortable, easy-to-grip wings or handle	**Le Creuset Table Model Corkpull** $19.95

ITEM	WHAT TO LOOK FOR	ATK RECOMMENDED
ROLLING PIN	• Slightly textured surface holds dusting of flour to reduce sticking • Long, straight shape makes it easy to roll dough to even thickness	Best Straight: **J.K. Adams Maple Wood Rolling Dowel** $22.00 Best Tapered: **J.K. Adams Tapered French Rolling Pin** $19.99
PARCHMENT PAPER	• Paper fits in standard-size rimmed baking sheet with minimal trimming • Paper is flat or requires little effort to smooth out • Food releases easily	**King Arthur Flour Parchment Paper 100 Half-Sheets** $19.95 per package ($0.20 per sheet)
SILICONE BAKING MAT	• Fits in standard half-sheet pan • Relatively heavy weight prevents shifting • Dishwasher-safe	**DeMarle Silpat Non-Stick Silicone Baking Mat** $22.35
KITCHEN RULER	• Straight edged and accurate • Easy-to-read markings • Inches divided into 32nds on one side and 16ths on other side	**Empire 18-inch Stainless Steel Ruler** $8.49
PORTION SCOOP	• Comfortable, grippy handles • Easy to squeeze • Neat, controlled dispensing	**OXO Good Grips Large Cookie Scoop** $14.97
CAKE PAN Round	• Light gold-colored pan produces tall, well risen, golden-brown, evenly cooked baked goods • Slick, durable nonstick surface	Winner, 8-Inch: **Nordic Ware Naturals Nonstick 8" Round Layer Cake Pan** $13.97 Best for Browning, 8-Inch: **Chicago Metallic Professional Non-Stick Round Cake Pan, 8-Inch** $12.25 Winner, 9-Inch: **Williams Sonoma Goldtouch Pro Nonstick Round Cake Pan** $29.95 Best Buy, 9-Inch: **Nordic Ware Naturals Nonstick 9" Round Cake Pan** $14.32
Square 8-Inch	• Handles make pan easy to hold and maneuver • Smooth, seamless interior for professional-looking baked goods and easy cleaning • Slick, durable nonstick surface	Winner: **All-Clad Pro-Release NonStick Bakeware 8 inch Square Cake Pan** $31.64 Best Buy: **Wilton Perfect Results Premium Non-Stick Bakeware Square Cake Pan** $13.11 Best Straight-Sided: **Williams Sonoma Goldtouch Nonstick Square Cake Pan, 8"** $26.95

ITEM	WHAT TO LOOK FOR	ATK RECOMMENDED
BAKER'S EDGE PAN	• Heavy-gauge cast aluminum construction distributes heat evenly • Six more baking surfaces than regular pans create baked goods with more chewy edges	**Baker's Edge Brownie Pan** $54.99
BUNDT PAN	• Deep, well-defined ridges • Nonstick surface releases cakes cleanly • Handles make pan easy to hold and maneuver	**Nordic Ware Anniversary Bundt Pan** $30.99
TUBE PAN	• Dark-colored finish produces better browning • Removable bottom for easier release • Feet for inverted cooling	**Chicago Metallic 2-Piece Angel Food Cake Pan with Feet** $17.99
LOAF PAN	• Measures 8½ by 4½ inches along top inside edges, so baked goods are narrow and tall • Folded metal construction gives pan sharp edges that produce straight-sided baked goods • Capacity of at least 1.4 liters so baked goods don't overflow	Best for Professional-Quality Results: **USA Pan Loaf Pan, 1 lb Volume** $14.95 Best for Cleanup: **OXO Good Grips Non-Stick Pro 1 Lb Loaf Pan** $16.95
SPRINGFORM PAN	• Light-colored finish allows for controlled, even browning • Tall sides make it easy to maneuver pan using potholders • Base trough catches leaks to help prevent messes • Raised base makes cutting and removing slices easy	Co-winner: **Williams Sonoma Goldtouch Leakproof Springform Pan** $49.95 Co-winner: **Nordic Ware 9" Leakproof Springform Pan** $16.22
PIE PLATE	• Gold-colored finish for better browning • Nonfluted lip for maximum crust-crimping flexibility • Measures at least 9 inches wide and 0.4 millimeter thick • Dishwasher-safe	**Williams-Sonoma Goldtouch Nonstick Pie Dish** $18.95
TART PAN	• Dark-colored finish produces better browning • Sharp fluted edges that make tarts look crisp and professional • Nonstick coating promotes flawless release • Removable bottom	**Matfer Steel Nonstick Tart Mold with Removable Bottom** $27.00

ITEM	WHAT TO LOOK FOR	ATK RECOMMENDED
MUFFIN TIN Full-Size	• Gold-colored finish promotes better browning • Nonstick coating • Wide rim on all four sides for easy gripping	**OXO Good Grips Non-Stick Pro 12-Cup Muffin Pan** $24.99
Mini	• Steel pans with gold-colored finish for better browning • Nonstick coating • Moderately sized, narrow cups for perfectly proportioned mini muffins • Wide rim on at least two sides for easy gripping	Winner: **Williams Sonoma Goldtouch Pro Mini Muffin Pan** $34.95 Best Buy: **Wilton Perfect Results Premium Non-Stick Mini Muffin and Cupcake Pan, 24-Cup** $12.00
6-Cup	• Gold-colored finish promotes better browning • Nonstick coating • At least 1 inch of space between each cup • Cup capacity of about 6½ tablespoons	Co-winner: **Williams Sonoma Goldtouch Pro Muffin Pan, 6-Well** $25.95 Co-winner: **USA Pan 6 Cup Muffin Pan** $20.95 Best Buy: **Wilton Recipe Right Non-Stick/ MD 6 Cup Muffin Pan** $11.03
BENCH SCRAPER	• Ridged handle allows for secure grip • Moderate-size blade • Thin, moderately sharp edge • Dishwasher-safe	**Dexter-Russell Sani-Safe 6" x 3" Dough Cutter/Scraper** $13.80
OFFSET SPATULA	• Comfortable rubber-coated handle • Blade is offset to approximately 30-degree angle • Blade has at least 6½ inches of flat, usable surface area • Thin and easy to slide beneath cake layers	**OXO Good Grips Bent Icing Knife** $9.99
BISCUIT CUTTER	• Sharp edges cut dough evenly • Strong, durable stainless-steel construction • Resistant to warping and rusting	**Ateco 5357 11-Piece Plain Round Cutter Set** $14.95
CAKE STRIP	• Easily slips around cake pan, with no need to presoak • Dishwasher-safe	**Rose's Heavenly Cake Strip by Rose Levy Beranbaum** $9.99 for 1 band (must buy additional band for 2-pan layer cakes)
CAKE STAND	• 4½ to 6 inches tall for better visibility and comfort when in use • Spins smoothly • Guides etched into surface make it easy to center cake	**Winco Revolving Cake Decorating Stand** $55.87
PIE SERVER	• Relatively short, wide blade for maneuvering under and holding slices • Comfortable offset handle • Serrated edges effortlessly cut crust	**OXO SteeL Pie Server** $9.99

ITEM	WHAT TO LOOK FOR	ATK RECOMMENDED
PIE WEIGHTS	• Weights completely fill pie shell • Heavy enough to prevent crusts from puffing up, baking unevenly, and slumping	**Mrs. Anderson's Baking Ceramic Pie Weights** $5.99 each or $23.96 for set of four (our recommended amount)
PIPING SET	• Sturdy disposable pastry bags hold a generous amount and can be reused • Plastic couplers allow you to change tips in the midst of use • Basic but versatile collection of tips in round, star, leaf, and petal shapes	Best Self-Assembled: **Test Kitchen Self-Assembled à La Carte Decorating Set** $15.23 for twelve 16-inch disposable bags, four plastic couplers, and six Wilton tips: #4 round, #12 round, #70 leaf, #103 petal, #2D large closed star, and #1M open star. Best Preassembled: **Wilton 20-Piece Beginning Buttercream Decorating Set** $12.20
PASTRY BRUSH	• 1½-inch-wide head • Flexible bristles that pick up and distribute liquid well • Comfortable handle	Best with Natural Bristles: **Winco Flat Pastry and Basting Brush, 1½ Inch** $6.93 Best with Silicone Bristles: **OXO Good Grips Silicone Pastry Brush** $7.99
CAST-IRON BREAD OVEN	• Sturdy cast-iron construction • Large oval base • Two sets of large, easy-to-grip handles	Winner: **Challenger Bread Pan** $299.00 Best Buy: **Lodge 3.2 Quart Cast Iron Combo Cooker** $49.88
BREAD MACHINE	• Easy-to-use interface • "Homemade" option lets you customize the kneading, rising, and baking times • Two kneading paddles • Produces traditional, rectangular-shaped loaves	Winner: **Zojirushi Home Bakery Supreme Breadmaker** $319.99 Best Buy: **Hamilton Beach HomeBaker 2 Lb. Breadmaker** $139.95
COUCHE	• Fine weave • Easy to handle; not too floppy or too stiff • 18-inch width matches well with dimensions of standard baking sheets	**San Francisco Baking Institute 18" Linen Canvas (Couche)** $8.00
BREAD LAME	• Long handle allows for varied grips • Two cutting edges so either side can be used • Easy-to-attach, adjustable blade capable of making straight or curved cuts	Winner: **Baker of Seville Artisan Bread Lame** $15.55 Best for Intricate Scoring: **Wire Monkey UFO Bread Journey** $27.95

BAKE IT TILL YOU MAKE IT	ITEM	WHAT TO LOOK FOR	ATK RECOMMENDED
	BANNETON	• Made of natural fibers that absorb moisture such as rattan or wood pulp • For rattan models: Removable linen or cotton liner is helpful for high-hydration doughs and for creating a smooth loaf surface for decorating	Best Round: **Breadtopia Round Bread Proofing Basket and Round Proofing Basket Liner** $19.00 ($16.00 for banneton, $3.00 for liner) Best Oval: **Breadtopia Oval Bread Proofing Basket and Oval Proofing Basket Liner** $19.00 ($16.00 for banneton, $3.00 for liner) Easiest to Use: **The Flourside Wood Pulp Banneton,** Round with Weave (LG) $32.00 or Oval with Spiral (LG) $32.00

MAKE IT HOMEMADE	ITEM	WHAT TO LOOK FOR	ATK RECOMMENDED
	PASTA MACHINE Manual	• Wide range of thickness settings • Sharp noodle-cutting attachment • Knob that can be turned with one hand	**Marcato Atlas 150 Wellness Pasta Machine** $69.25
	Electric	• Simple, intuitive control panel • Mixes and dispenses the dough • Extrudes pasta frontward, making it easy to see • Comes with tool for cutting extruded pasta	**Philips Pasta Maker** $289.10
	STEAMER Bamboo	• Solid construction with few loose fibers and tiers that fit together securely • Tiers with metal bands • Thick, glued bamboo slats	Co-winner: **Juvale 10 Inch Bamboo Steamer with Steel Rings for Cooking** $23.99 Co-winner: **Zest of Moringa Bamboo Steamer Basket Set** $36.99
	Collapsible Steamer Basket	• At least 60 square inches of usable surface area • Telescoping handle for easy insertion and removal	**OXO Good Grips Stainless Steel Steamer with Handle** $17.95
	TORTILLA PRESS	• Heavy metal or wood construction • Pressing plates at least 8 inches wide • Handles at least 10 inches long for greater leverage	Winner: **Doña Rosa x Masienda Tortilla Press** $95.00 Best Buy: **Victoria 8" Tortilla Press** $19.59

	ITEM	WHAT TO LOOK FOR	ATK RECOMMENDED
	TORTILLA WARMER	• Large enough to fit 10-inch tortillas, with a capacity of up to 30 tortillas • Keeps tortillas warm for almost 1½ hours • Machine-washable	**IMUSA 12" Cloth Tortilla Warmer** $19.99
	PORTABLE OUTDOOR PIZZA OVEN	• Compact design • Propane powered with easy to ignite flame • Easily adjustable heat	Best Small Gas: **Ooni Koda 12 Gas-Powered Pizza Oven** $399.00 Best Large Gas: **Ooni Koda 16 Gas-Powered Pizza Oven** $599.00 Best Small Multifuel: **Ooni Karu 12 Multi-Fuel Pizza Oven** $498.99 ($399.00 for oven, $99.99 for gas burner) Best Large Multifuel: **Ooni Pro 16 Multi-Fuel Pizza Oven** $698.99 ($599.00 for oven, $99.99 for gas burner)
	INDOOR PIZZA OVEN	• Oven gets very hot, very quickly • Can be adjusted to cook different styles of pizza • Deck slides out and down when door opens, making pizza easy to reach • Easy to set time and temperature	**Breville Smart Oven Pizzaiolo** $999.95
	BAKING STONE/ STEEL	• Heavy steel or stone quickly transfers heat to pizza • Durable • Easy to clean	Co-winner: **The Original Baking Steel** $119.00 Co-winner: **Nerd Chef Steel Stone, Standard ¼"** $109.95 Best Buy: **Outset Pizza Grill Stone Tiles, Set of 4** $29.99
	BAKING PEEL	• Cloth "conveyor belt" easily loads and unloads raw pizza and bread doughs onto baking stone • Blade width of 14 inches • Handle length of about 8 inches	Winner: **EXO Non-Stick Super Peel Pro Composite** $68.00 Best Wood Peel: **New Star Foodservice 50295 Restaurant-Grade Wooden Pizza Peel, 16" L x 14" W** $21.97 Best Metal Peel: **American Metalcraft Pizza Peel 2814** $26.89

MAKE IT HOMEMADE	ITEM	WHAT TO LOOK FOR	ATK RECOMMENDED
	PIZZA CUTTER	• Comfortable handle allows for firm grip • Streamlined design that doesn't trap food • Sharp, tall blade for neat, precise cutting	**OXO Good Grips 4" Pizza Wheel** $12.99
	ICE CREAM MAKER	• Paddles with open tops and low blades that submerge fully in mixer to allow for monitoring temperature • Easy to assemble and clean, with few crevices and simple parts • Churns and freezes quickly	Best Canister-Style: **Cuisinart Frozen Yogurt, Ice Cream & Sorbet Maker** $53.99 Best Self-Refrigerating: **Whynter 2.1 Quart Capacity Upright Automatic Compressor Ice Cream Maker** $319.37
	ICE CREAM SCOOP	• Gently curved oval bowl for perfectly shaped scoops • Wide, comfortable handle • Heat-conductive fluid in handle helps soften ice cream for easier scooping	**Zeroll Original Ice Cream Scoop** $18.44
	ICE CREAM CONE MAKER	• Color-control knob allows you to set preferred browning level • Nonstick plates release cones smoothly • Overflow channel contains messes	**Chef'sChoice 838 Waffle Cone Express** $49.95
	CANNING POT	• Pot is broad and deep enough to submerge a rack full of canning jars • Clear lid for easy monitoring • Comfortable handles • Comes with wide, level rack • Durable stainless steel resists rust	**Roots and Branches Stainless Steel Multi-Use Canner** $75.19
	CANNING JAR LIFTER	• Comfortable grip and secure hold on jars of all sizes • Durable and rust-resistant • Spring-loaded hinge pops grabbers open when handles are released	**Ball Secure-Grip Jar Lifter** $10.99
	FOOD DEHYDRATOR	• Tray measures at least 11 inches across • At least 1 inch of vertical space between trays facilitates airflow around bulky foods • Built-in timer and automatic shut-off • Lids or doors that lift off easily for checking doneness • Dishwasher-safe parts	Winner: **Excalibur Food Dehydrator** $241.50 Best Buy: **Presto Dehydro Electric Food Dehydrator** $74.47

	ITEM	WHAT TO LOOK FOR	ATK RECOMMENDED
	PORTABLE BURNER Induction	• Powerful, responsive, even heating • Precise temperature control • Intuitive controls that are easy to understand and clearly labeled • Easy-to-clean surface with no nooks, crannies, or grooves that trap grease • Stable on countertop	Winner: **Breville/PolyScience Control Freak** $1,500.00 Best Buy: **Duxtop Portable Induction Cooktop 9600 LS/BT-200DZ** $116.96
	Gas	• Powerful dual-fuel burner capable of running on either propane or butane • Responsive to heat adjustments and stays lit even at lowest settings • Cooking surface lifts off for easy cleaning	**Grill Boss 90057 Dual Fuel Camp Stove** $54.90
	Electric	• Simple to operate • Responsive to heat adjustments • Easy-to-clean surface with no nooks, crannies, or grooves that trap grease	**IMUSA USA GAU-80305 Electric Single Burner 1100 Watts** $12.20
	WARMING TRAY	• Able to keep food above 140 degrees Fahrenheit for food safety • Stay-cool handles • Wipes clean easily	**BroilKing Professional Stainless Warming Tray** $126.06
	FAT SEPARATOR	• True 4-cup capacity • Strainer with lots of small holes drains quickly while holding back solids • Tall sides contain splashes • Large, comfortable handle • Accurate volume measurements	Winner: **OXO Good Grips Good Gravy Fat Separator–4 Cup** $29.95 Best Buy: **Trudeau Gravy Separator** $16.99
	KITCHEN TWINE/TIES	• Made of food-safe 100 percent cotton or linen • Strong; resists burning, fraying, splitting, or breaking • Twine releases from center of ball	**Librett Cotton Butcher's Twine** $8.29 ($0.02 per foot)
	OYSTER KNIFE	• Comfortable, grippy wooden handle • Slightly upturned tip slices oyster muscle without damaging meat	**R. Murphy New Haven Oyster Knife** $16.65

PUT ON A GOOD SHOW	ITEM	WHAT TO LOOK FOR	ATK RECOMMENDED
	CHEESE PLANE	• Straight, sharp blade measuring about 2¼ inches long • Angled blade produces cheese slices about the thickness of a nickel • Thin, flexible head is easy to maneuver • Relatively long handle	**Wüsthof Gourmet 4¾-inch Cheese Plane** $35.00
	FONDUE POT	• Electric (not fuel-powered) pot maintains consistent temperature • Wide crock opening • Scratch-resistant nonstick interior • Clearly labeled temperature controls	**Oster Titanium Infused DuraCeramic 3-Qt Fondue Pot** $59.95
	WINE AERATOR	• Small holes draw air into wine as you pour • Slides into neck of bottle for neat, hands-free aerating	**Nuance Wine Finer** $37.65
	WINE SAVER	• Easy-to-use, reliable sealing mechanism • Keeps wine drinkable for at least one month	**Air Cork The Wine Preserver** $24.95
	CHAMPAGNE SAVER	• Attaches to bottle with an easy one-handed motion • Compact design allows capped bottles to fit easily in the refrigerator	**Cilio Champagne Bottle Sealer** $7.50
	CARVING FORK	• Sturdy, sharp, and slightly curved prongs • Comfortable rubberized handle	**Mercer Culinary 6-Inch High-Carbon Carving Fork** $22.20
	ELECTRIC KNIFE	• Sharp multipurpose blade • Comfortable rounded handle stays cool during use • Easily accessible start button and safety lock feature • Comfortable noise level (80 decibels)	**Black + Decker ComfortGrip 9" Electric Knife** $19.92

PUT ON A GOOD SHOW	ITEM	WHAT TO LOOK FOR	ATK RECOMMENDED
	FLATWARE SET	• Moderately heavy, well-balanced utensils • Knives with serrations • Curved, teardrop-shaped handles for a comfortable grip • Durable, dishwasher-safe stainless steel	Winner: **Crate and Barrel Caesna Mirror 20-Piece Flatware Place Setting** $7.49 per utensil ($149.95 for 20-piece set) Best Buy: **Oneida Voss 45-Piece Flatware Set** $2.78 per utensil ($124.99 for 45-piece set)
	DISPOSABLE PLATES	• Large, roomy eating surface with steeply angled sides to contain food • Thick bottom prevents sogging and flopping • Stays intact when food is cut on surface • Microwavable	**Hefty ECOSAVE Compostable 10⅛ inch Plates** $2.99 for 16 plates ($0.19 per plate)
	DISPOSABLE BOWLS	• Wide base and short walls for ease of holding and eating from • Wide rim to facilitate lifting • Withstands punctures and cuts from utensils and resists becoming soggy • Microwave-safe	Best Large: **Dixie Ultra Heavy Duty 20oz Disposable Paper Bowls** $3.39 for 26 bowls ($0.13 per bowl) Best Small: **Dixie Everyday 10oz Disposable Paper Bowls, 36 Count** $2.99 for 36 bowls ($0.08 per bowl) Best Compostable: **Stack Man 100% Compostable 12 oz. Paper Bowls** $12.69 for 125 bowls ($0.10 per bowl)
	DISPOSABLE CUPS	• Easy to grasp tapered shape • Moderately thick rim is comfortable to drink from • Does not crack or crumple when squeezed • Sturdy base keeps cup from easily tipping over	Best Recyclable: **Hefty Party Perfect Clear Plastic Cups-9 Ounce** $4.99 for 40 cups ($0.12 per cup) Best Compostable: **Greenware Squat Clear Premium Cold Drink Cup 9 oz** $8.63 for 50 cups ($0.17 per cup)
	DISPOSABLE UTENSIL SET	• Sturdy, rigid, and made from smooth plastic or crystallized polylactic acid • Fork tines are pointy and sharp • Knife blades are thin and have sharp serrations • Spoon bowls are moderately deep • Handles are flat, smooth, and comfortable to hold	Winner: **Ecovita 100% Compostable Cutlery Combo 380 Set** $54.56 for 380 utensils ($0.14 per utensil) Best Set Under 100 Pieces: **The Diamond Entertaining 96 Combo** $16.95 for 96 utensils ($0.18 per utensil)

OPTIMIZE YOUR SPACE	ITEM	WHAT TO LOOK FOR	ATK RECOMMENDED
	MAGNETIC KNIFE STRIP	• Thick strip stands out from wall • Evenly distributed medium-strength magnets • Easy to install	Winner: **Brooklyn Butcher Blocks Knife Rack, 20" Walnut** $120.00 Best Buy: **Schmidt Brothers Acacia 18" Magnetic Wall Bar** $49.99
	UNIVERSAL KNIFE BLOCK	• Large capacity • Neatly and safely contains most or all of the knife blades • Good magnetic coverage and strength • Sturdy, nonslip base • Easy to clean	Winner: **Design Trifecta 360 Knife Block** $350.00 Best Buy: **Schmidt Brothers Midtown Block** $67.99
	UTENSIL CROCK	• Fits 17 or more utensils comfortably • Round, with at least 6-inch-diameter opening and height between 6½ and 7 inches • Has removable dividers • Sturdy and durable • Easy to wipe down; dishwasher-safe	**Le Creuset Stoneware Utensil Crock** $49.95
	SPICE STORAGE SOLUTION	• Large capacity • Sturdy construction • Provides good visibility • Easy to clean	Best Overall Cabinet Option: **Spicy Shelf Deluxe** $24.97 Best Tiered Cabinet Option: **mDesign 3 Tier Expandable Spice Rack Organizer** $24.99 Best Drawer Option: **Lynk Professional 4 Tier Steel Spice Drawer Organizer** $44.63 Best Over-the-Door Option: **Home-Complete Over the Door Storage Rack** $59.31
	MINI PREP BOWLS	• Wide, shallow, and smooth for easy accessibility • Small lip makes bowls comfortable to grip	**Anchor Hocking Custard Cups** $13.15 for set of 4 ($3.29 per cup)
	COOKBOOK HOLDER	• Clear shield protects pages from spills • Holds a wide range of book sizes • Easy to use	**Clear Solutions Deluxe Cookbook Holder** $62.50
	TABLET STAND	• Folds up small and expands to hold a range of sizes • Stable enough that tablet won't easily tip over	**Arkon Portable Fold-Up Stand for Tablets** $10.16

OPTIMIZE YOUR SPACE	ITEM	WHAT TO LOOK FOR	ATK RECOMMENDED
	DRY STORAGE CONTAINER	• Roomy enough to hold 5 pounds of flour • Sturdy, with tight-fitting lid • Wide opening for easy access	**Cambro 6-Quart Square Storage Container** $23.74 total ($16.67 for container, $7.07 for lid)
	FOOD STORAGE CONTAINER	• Leakproof seal • Stackable, shallow rectangular shape • Resists odors and stains • Dishwasher-, freezer-, and microwave-safe • For glass containers: oven-safe up to 450 degrees Fahrenheit	Best Glass: **OXO Good Grips 8 Cup Smart Seal Rectangle Container** $14.99 Best Plastic: **Rubbermaid Brilliance Storage Container, Large** $12.99
	SILICONE FOOD COVER	• Strong suction seal and sturdy handle • Useful sizes from 4 inches to 12.5 inches in diameter • Microwave-safe	**GIR Suction Lids** $7.95 for 6"; $9.95 for 8"; $15.95 for 12.5"
	FOOD STORAGE BAGS Traditional	• Made of thick plastic • Forms tight seal • Protects food from freezer burn and ice crystals for at least two months	Winner: **LK Plastics Ziplock Heavy Weight Freezer Bag** $9.69 for 100 bags ($0.10 per bag) Best Supermarket Option: **Ziploc Brand Freezer Bags with Easy Open Tabs** $5.37 for 28 bags ($0.19 per bag)
	Reusable	• Made of vinyl material • Large capacity with wide opening of at least 6¾ inches • Gussets and flat bottom • Leak-resistant and protects food from freezer burn	**BlueAvocado (re)Zip Stand-Up 4 Cup/32 oz** $8.99
	REUSABLE FOOD WRAP	• Clingy, malleable material creates strong seals • Leaves minimal residue on bowls and hands • Washes clean and holds up to repeated washing	**Abeego Food Wrap** $18.00 for set of three ($6.00 per wrap)
	BUTTER STORAGE CONTAINER Classic	• Tight-fitting lid creates airtight seal to prevent off-flavors • Wide enough to fit butter of all shapes and sizes • Easy-to-grab handle or knob • Includes tablespoon measurement markings	**LocknLock Rectangular Food Container with Tray** $9.00
	Butter Bell	• Ceramic crock holds water that creates airtight seal • Easy-to-grab handle or knob • Spacious capacity	**The Original Butter Bell Crock** $26.95

CLEAN UP YOUR ACT	ITEM	WHAT TO LOOK FOR	ATK RECOMMENDED
	FIRE EXTINGUISHER	• Fast and effective • Powerful spray • Simple design, with basic trigger and easy-to-read gauge	**Kidde ABC Multipurpose Home Fire Extinguisher** $19.99
	SMART SMOKE ALARM	• Easy to install • Linked app is easy to navigate and silence • Detects smoke well and differentiates between low and high levels of smoke	**Google Nest Protect** $119.00
	CUT RESISTANT GLOVE	• Comes in a range of sizes • Fits most hands closely, with little or no excess fabric • Thin for better dexterity • Machine-washable	**Mercer Culinary MercerGuard Cut Glove** $19.39 for one glove
	CAST-IRON SKILLET HANDLE COVER	• Fits snugly over skillet handles • Easy to put on and remove • Resists heat well	**Nokona Leather Handle Mitt** $24.90
	OVEN MITT	• Flexible material that moves with your hand • Offers enough heat protection to hold a hot cast-iron skillet handle for at least 13 seconds • Machine washable	**OXO Silicone Oven Mitt** $14.99 each ($29.98 for 2)
	POT HOLDER	• At least 4.4 millimeters thick • Offers enough heat protection to hold a hot cast-iron skillet handle for at least 15 seconds • Flexible material for better control • Has snug pockets or is made from naturally grippy neoprene • Resists stains and odors	**OXO Good Grips Silicone Pot Holder** $13.96 each ($27.92 for 2)
	DISH TOWELS	• Generous size of about 3 square feet • Midweight fabric with thick and thin areas absorbs well without excessive bulk • Becomes more absorbent with use and repeated washings	**Williams-Sonoma Striped Towels, Set of 4** $19.95 ($4.99 per towel)

	ITEM	WHAT TO LOOK FOR	ATK RECOMMENDED
	SPLATTER SCREEN	• High sides prevent oil droplets from hitting you or the stovetop • Fits a wide range of pans	**Frywall Stovetop Splatter Guard** $28.95
	ANTI-FATIGUE MAT	• Heavy, moderately thick material with no-slip backing • Dark color and smooth surface for easy cleaning • Firm foam provides good support	Winner: **Williams-Sonoma WellnessMat** $149.95 Best Buy: **ComfiLife Anti Fatigue Floor Mat** $45.95
	SPONGES	• Moderate size and thickness • Textured scrubbing side • Can absorb at least 45 grams of water • Easily rinses clean and resists stains and odors	**O-Cedar Scrunge Multi-Use Scrubber Sponge** $9.99 for pack of 6 ($1.67 per sponge)
	SPONGE HOLDER	• Large opening • Open, cage-like construction • Large, widely spaced suction cups • Slim profile	**SunnyPoint NeverRust Kitchen Sink Suction Holder** $9.99
	BOTTLE BRUSH	• Medium-sized brush head • Moderate-length bristles for better scrubbing • Strong, rigid handle with rubber grip	**Quickie Bottle Brush** $5.80
	SCRUB BRUSH	• Stiff, flared plastic bristles arranged in clusters with wide spaces between them • Extra strip of ultrastiff bristles on back of head for scraping • Gently curved, angled handle coated with grippy silicone • Dishwasher-safe	**O-Cedar Rinse Fresh Pot & Pan Brush** $7.99
	DISH DRYING RACK	• Holds a large amount of dishes and utensils securely • Allows water to drain away easily	Best Large: **simplehuman Steel Frame Dishrack** $99.99 Best Small: **Progressive Prepworks Over-The-Sink Dish Drainer** $24.99 Best Buy: **Rubbermaid Antimicrobial Sink Drainer, Large** $45.05 ($27.06 for basket, $17.99 for mat)

CLEAN UP YOUR ACT	ITEM	WHAT TO LOOK FOR	ATK RECOMMENDED
	REUSABLE BAG DRYING RACK	• Sturdy, with a heavy base so it resists tipping over • Long arms hold large bags as well as bottles • Folds for compact storage	Co-winner: **FloWorks Design Plastic Bag and Bottle Dryer** $23.95 Co-winner: **Yamazaki Home Tower Kitchen Eco Stand** $17.00
	PAPER TOWELS Traditional	• Soft, plush sturdy two-ply sheets about 0.4 millimeter thick • Available in full-sheet and variable-sheet styles	**Bounty Paper Towels** $2.49 for 1 roll (full sheet, regular and Select-A-Size, regular)
	Reusable	• Sheets absorb at least three times their weight in liquid • Pliable and soft yet capable of scrubbing tough messes without tearing • Measure at least 11½ by 10 inches, comparable in size to traditional paper towels	Best Bamboo: **Full Circle Tough Sheet Reusable Plant Towels** $9.99 for 30 sheets ($0.33 per sheet) Best Cotton: **Marley's Monsters UNpaper Towels** $38.00 for 12 sheets ($3.20 per sheet)
	PAPER TOWEL HOLDER	• Sturdy, secure, and easy to carry • Allows you to pull paper towels off roll with one hand	**Simplehuman Tension Arm Paper Towel Holder** $55.00
	ALL-PURPOSE SPRAY CLEANER	• Cleans thoroughly and effectively with a minimum number of squirts • Pleasant, not overpowering scent • Uses surfactants derived from natural sources	**Method All-Purpose Cleaner, French Lavender** $3.79 for 28 oz ($0.14 per oz)
	LIQUID DISH SOAP	• Cuts through grime quickly and effortlessly • Derived mostly from natural sources • Pleasant, not overpowering scent	**Mrs. Meyer's Clean Day Liquid Dish Soap, Lavender** $3.99 for 16 oz ($0.25 per oz)

CLEAN UP YOUR ACT	ITEM	WHAT TO LOOK FOR	ATK RECOMMENDED
	TRASH CAN	• Foot pedal for hands-free operation • Switch that enables lid to stay open • Spacious interior with removable plastic liner • Fingerprint-proof stainless-steel exterior	Winner: **Simplehuman 50L Rectangular Step Can** $180.00 Best Buy: **Sterilite Lift-Top Wastebasket** $17.99
	COUNTERTOP COMPOST BIN	• Lightweight bin with secure handle • Wide opening and flip-top lid • Designed without nooks and crannies, which trap dirt	Winner: **OXO Good Grips Easy-Clean Compost Bin - 1.75 Gal** $32.95 Best for Larger Households: **Exaco Eco 2000 Kitchen Compost Pail** $21.99
	DUST PAN AND BRUSH	• Long brush head with angled plastic bristles • Horizontal brush handle • Large dustpan edged with rubber bumper	**Rubbermaid Dustpan and Brush Set with Comfortable Grip** $9.65
	UNDER-APPLIANCE DUSTER	• Head that is at least 21 inches long and less than 1 inch thick • Microfiber pad	**OXO Good Grips Under Appliance Duster** $15.51
	VACUUM Handheld	• Powerful suction • Spacious, easy-to-empty collection bin • Customizable nozzle length and mounted attachments	**Black + Decker 20V MAX Cordless Pivot Vac** $76.99
	Robot	• Powerful suction • Fast, accurate mapping for thorough coverage • Easy to operate • Simple, sturdy charging dock	Winner: **iRobot Roomba j7+ Robot Vacuum** $776.00 Best Buy: **Shark ION Robot Vacuum** $199.00

| --- | --- | --- | --- |
	MOP Traditional	• Microfiber head • Easy and efficient wringing mechanism • Long handle helps cover more ground	Best Mop-and-Bucket Set: **O-Cedar EasyWring Spin Mop & Bucket System** $58.79 Best Self-Wringing: **Rubbermaid Microfiber Twist Mop** $12.59
	Spray	• Large, absorbent, machine-washable microfiber pads • Long handle helps cover more ground • Powerful spraying mechanism • Comfortable grip with large spray trigger	**O-Cedar ProMist MAX Microfiber Spray Mop** $31.24
	Robot	• Intelligent navigation system plots the most efficient route through the room • Functions well with or without app, and has smart assistant compatibility • Mops well and does light sweeping • Easy-to-fill water tank and simple-to-attach mopping pads • Automatic docking and recharging	Winner: **iRobot Braava jet m6 Robot Mop** $499.00 Best Buy: **iRobot Braava jet 240 Robot Mop** $179.99
	GARLIC ODOR REMOVER BAR	• Stainless steel material eliminates garlic odor from hands • Comfortable to hold	**Amco Rub-A-Way Bar** $6.95
	RUST ERASER	• Slim eraser fits against tight edges of knife blade • Firm, abrasive exterior • Fits comfortably and securely in hand	**Sabitoru Medium Grit Rust Eraser** $7.29

Conversions and Equivalents

Some say cooking is a science and an art. We would say that geography has a hand in it too. Flours and sugars manufactured in the United Kingdom and elsewhere will feel and taste different from those manufactured in the United States. So we cannot promise that the loaf of bread you bake in Canada or England will taste the same as a loaf baked in the States, but we can offer guidelines for converting weights and measures. We also recommend that you rely on your instincts when making our recipes. Refer to the visual cues provided. If the dough hasn't "come together in a ball" as described, you may need to add more flour—even if the recipe doesn't tell you to. You be the judge.

The recipes in this book were developed using standard U.S. measures following U.S. government guidelines. The charts below offer equivalents for U.S. and metric measures. All conversions are approximate and have been rounded up or down to the nearest whole number.

EXAMPLE:

1 teaspoon = 4.9292 milliliters, rounded up to 5 milliliters
1 ounce = 28.3495 grams, rounded down to 28 grams

VOLUME CONVERSIONS

U.S.	METRIC
1 teaspoon	5 milliliters
2 teaspoons	10 milliliters
1 tablespoon	15 milliliters
2 tablespoons	30 milliliters
¼ cup	59 milliliters
⅓ cup	79 milliliters
½ cup	118 milliliters
¾ cup	177 milliliters
1 cup	237 milliliters
1¼ cups	296 milliliters
1½ cups	355 milliliters
2 cups (1 pint)	473 milliliters
2½ cups	591 milliliters
3 cups	710 milliliters
4 cups (1 quart)	0.946 liter
1.06 quarts	1 liter
4 quarts (1 gallon)	3.8 liters

WEIGHT CONVERSIONS

OUNCES	GRAMS
½	14
¾	21
1	28
1½	43
2	57
2½	71
3	85
3½	99
4	113
4½	128
5	142
6	170
7	198
8	227
9	255
10	283
12	340
16 (1 pound)	454

CONVERSIONS FOR COMMON BAKING INGREDIENTS

Baking is an exacting science. Because measuring by weight is far more accurate than measuring by volume, and thus more likely to produce reliable results, in our recipes we provide ounce measures in addition to cup measures for many ingredients. Refer to the chart below to convert these measures into grams.

INGREDIENT	OUNCES	GRAMS
FLOUR		
1 cup all-purpose flour*	5	142
1 cup cake flour	4	113
1 cup whole-wheat flour	5½	156
SUGAR		
1 cup granulated (white) sugar	7	198
1 cup packed brown sugar (light or dark)	7	198
1 cup confectioners' sugar	4	113
COCOA POWDER		
1 cup cocoa powder	3	85
BUTTER†		
4 tablespoons (½ stick or ¼ cup)	2	57
8 tablespoons (1 stick or ½ cup)	4	113
16 tablespoons (2 sticks or 1 cup)	8	227

* U.S. all-purpose flour, the most frequently used flour in this book, does not contain leaveners, as some European flours do. These leavened flours are called self-rising or self-raising. If you are using self-rising flour, take this into consideration before adding leaveners to a recipe.

† In the United States, butter is sold both salted and unsalted. We generally recommend unsalted butter. If you are using salted butter, take this into consideration before adding salt to a recipe.

OVEN TEMPERATURES

FAHRENHEIT	CELSIUS	GAS MARK
225	105	¼
250	120	½
275	135	1
300	150	2
325	165	3
350	180	4
375	190	5
400	200	6
425	220	7
450	230	8
475	245	9

CONVERTING TEMPERATURES FROM AN INSTANT-READ THERMOMETER

We include doneness temperatures in many of the recipes in this book. We recommend an instant-read thermometer for the job. Refer to the table above to convert Fahrenheit degrees to Celsius. Or, for temperatures not represented in the chart, use this simple formula:

Subtract 32 degrees from the Fahrenheit reading, then divide the result by 1.8 to find the Celsius reading.

EXAMPLE:

"Roast chicken until thighs register 175 degrees."

To convert:

175°F − 32 = 143°

143° ÷ 1.8 = 79.44°C, rounded down to 79°C

Index

Note: Page references in *italics* indicate photographs of completed recipes.